P9-BEE-441

FIRST BOOK

Latin

FOR AMERICANS

FIRST BOOK

Latin FOR AMERICANS

Eighth Edition

B. L. Ullman

Charles Henderson, Jr.

Norman E. Henry

GLENCOE

McGraw-Hill

New York, New York   Columbus, Ohio   Mission Hills, California   Peoria, Illinois

About the Authors

B. L. Ullman enjoyed a distinguished career of teaching and scholarship at the Universities of Pittsburgh, Iowa, Chicago, and North Carolina. An authority on all aspects of the Roman world, ancient, medieval, and Renaissance, he was also a pioneer in modern methods of teaching elementary Latin.

Charles Henderson, Jr. collaborated with Professor Ullman in the previous revisions of this book. He has taught at New York University, the University of North Carolina, and at Smith College.

Norman E. Henry, collaborator with Professor Ullman in earlier editions of the *Latin for Americans* series, taught for many years at the Peabody High School, Pittsburgh, and contributed material that has been tested in high school classrooms.

Glencoe/McGraw-Hill

A Division of The **McGraw-Hill** *Companies*

Send all inquiries to:
Glencoe/McGraw-Hill
15319 Chatsworth Street
P.O. Box 9609
Mission Hills, CA 91346-9609

ISBN 0-02-640912-7 (Student Text)

Printed in the United States of America

2 3 4 5 6 7 8 9 10 RRDW 01 00 99 98 97 96

Acknowledgements

The editors would like to thank the following individuals for their assistance in this revision of Latin for Americans:

Sally Davis
Wakefield High School
Arlington, Virginia

Dr. Malcolm Donaldson
The Alabama School of Mathematics and Science
Mobile, Alabama

Kay Ruhle
Lakeland Senior High School
Lakeland, Florida

Marcia Stille
Lakeland, Florida

Ron Tetrick
Kokomo High School
Kokomo, Indiana

Carolyn Beach White
Columbus School for Girls
Columbus, Ohio

Front cover:
Louis-Joseph Duc, *The Colosseum,* 1830-1831, École Nationale Supérieure des Beaux-Arts, Paris, France

This painting of a detail of the Roman Colosseum exterior is a 19th century reconstruction of what the building might have looked like when it was built in the first century A.D.

Started by the Emperor Vespasian in 72 A.D., it was formally called the Flavian Amphitheater in honor of the emperor's family. Its popular name—Colosseum—may have caught on because of its great size in relation to the buildings around it (see the aerial photo on page 10-11).

Built for large-scale gladiatorial combats, naval battles, and fights with wild beasts, the building was well organized. It could hold 50,000 people, who could enter and leave rapidly through 160 doors. Three stories of arches—Doric (first story), Ionic (second story), and Corinthian (third story), with a top story consisting of a wall interrupted by windows—have influenced many architects down through the ages in the building of public structures. Whether the arches on its second and third stories actually held statuary is very doubtful.

Inside the Colosseum, there were three tiers of seats: the first for knights **(equites)** and distinguished citizens, the second for other citizens, and the third for the general public. At the very top were members of the lowest class, who had to stand. Below the first tier was a podium for the highest dignitaries. On this podium was a section reserved for the emperor and his party.

The Colosseum is a tribute to the genius of Roman architecture and engineering—important aspects of the Roman heritage from which we still draw knowledge and inspiration.

Title page:
Erich Lessing/PhotoEdit

The Appian Way was known as the **Regina Viarum** (Queen of Roads). It was the triumphal road of the victorious Roman armies and an important artery for trade. It extended some 540 miles from Rome to southern Italy. The paving was made of slabs of basalt.

Contents

Our Roman Heritage 1
The Alphabet; Pronunciation

Unit I The Romans' World

Lesson I: Rōma et Italia 13
Understanding Latin; Nouns; Predicate Nominative; The First Declension; Word Studies

Lesson II: Sicilia 19
Adjectives; Accusative Case; Word Order; Roman Numerals in English

Lesson III: Anna et Rāna 24
Verbs; Infinitive; First Conjugation Present Tense; Word Studies

Lesson IV: Viae 30
The Second Declension; Gender and Agreement; Word Studies

Glimpses of Roman Life: Roman Roads and Travel 34

Unit I Review 36

Unit II Rome and Her Empire

Lesson V: Rōma 40
The Genitive Case; The Ablative of *Place Where*; Word Studies

Lesson VI: Eurōpa 46
The Future Tense; Prepositions; Word Studies

Lesson VII: Sunt Saturnalia 52
The Dative Case; Word Studies

Lesson VIII: Gallia 58
Ablative of Means; Adjectives as Substantives; Word Studies

Lesson IX: Cornēlia Nautam Servat 62
Second Declension Nouns in *–r;* Present Imperative; Word Studies

Glimpses of Roman Life: The Eternal City 68

Unit II Review 71

Unit III Latin and the Romans

Lesson X: Lingua Latīna 76
Second Conjugation: Present and Future Tenses; Word Studies

Lesson XI: Britannia 81
Neuters of the Second Declension; Sentence Analysis; Word Studies

Lesson XII: Puerī Rōmānī 87
The Perfect Tense; Word Studies

Lesson XIII: Servī 92
The Vocative Case; Ablative of *Place From Which*; Word Studies

Lesson XIV: Aristotelēs et Alexander 97
The Second Declension: Adjectives in *–r;* The Present Tense of *Sum*; Word Studies

Glimpses of Roman Life: Slavery 104

Unit III Review 107

Unit IV Roman Social Life

Lesson XV: Rōmulus, Numa, et Tullus 112
The Future and Perfect of *Sum*; Uses of the Infinitive; The Ablative of Accompaniment; Word Studies

Lesson XVI: Spartacus 118
Asking Questions; Conjunctions; Apposition; Word Studies

Lesson XVII: Patrōnus et Clientēs 124
The Third Conjugation; Word Studies

Lesson XVIII: Rōmānī 129
Third *(–io)* and Fourth Conjugation Verbs; Word Sense and Idiomatic Expressions; Word Studies

Lesson XIX: Lupercalia 134
Formation of Adverbs; Word Order; Numbers; Word Studies

Glimpses of Roman Life: Signs of the Times 140

Unit IV Review 142

Unit V Roman Myths and Legends

Lesson XX: Cerēs et Prōserpina 148

Third Conjugation: Future; Word Studies

Lesson XXI: Plāgōsus Orbilius 153

Future of Third *(–io)* and Fourth Conjugation Verbs; Word Studies

Lesson XXII: Poēta Clārus 157

The Imperfect Tense; Word Studies

Lesson XXIII: Aenēās 162

The Perfect Passive Participle as Adjective; Word Studies

Lesson XXIV: Ulixēs 167

The Third Declension: Masculine and Feminine Nouns; Word Studies

Lesson XXV: Ad Italiam 172

The Active and Passive Voice; Word Studies

Glimpses of Roman Life: Dress and Appearance 178

Unit V Review 180

Unit VI The Founding of Rome

Lesson XXVI: In Āfricā Aenēās Auxilium Accipit 186

Transitive and Intransitive Verbs; Ablative of Agent; Present Passive Infinitive; Word Studies

Lesson XXVII: Aenēās et Dīdō 192

Personal Pronouns; Conversation; Word Studies

Lesson XXVIII: Aenēās et Īnferōs 197

The Pluperfect and Future Perfect Tenses; Word Studies

Lesson XXIX: In Italiā Aenēās Auxilius Accipit 202

Possessive Adjectives; Infinitive Object With Certain Verbs; Word Studies

Lesson XXX: Aenēās et Turnus 207

The Perfect Passive Tenses; Word Studies

Glimpses of Roman Life: Education 212

Unit VI Review 214

Unit VII Gods, Goddesses, and Games

Lesson XXXI: Templa Deōrum 220
Relative Pronouns; Word Studies

Lesson XXXII: Colossēum 225
Ablative of Manner; Ablative of *Time When*; Ablative of *Time Within Which*; Accusative of *Time How Long*; Accusative of Extent of Space; Word Studies

Lesson XXXIII: Niobē 231
Interrogative Pronouns; Interrogative Adjectives; Word Studies

Lesson XXXIV: Pūblius Mārcō Sal. 236
Third Declension Neuter Nouns; Ablative of Respect; Word Studies

Glimpses of Roman Life: Food and Meals 242

Unit VII Review 245

Unit VIII Ancient Travel and Adventure

Lesson XXXV: Mārcus Pūbliō Sal. 250
Perfect Passive Participles Used as Clauses; The Latin Influence upon English

Lesson XXXVI: Circē 255
Ablative Absolute

Lesson XXXVII: Sīrēnēs et Phaeācia 261
The Conjugation of *Possum*; Irregular First and Second Declension Adjectives; Word Studies

Lesson XXXVIII: Pēnelopē 267
Third Declension: I–Stem Nouns; Word Studies

Lesson XXXIX: Fīnis Labōrum 272
Third Declension Adjectives; Word Studies

Glimpses of Roman Life: Amusements and Sports 278

Unit VIII Review 281

Unit IX Gods, Goddesses, and History

Lesson XL: Deī 286
The Fourth Declension; Word Studies

Lesson XLI: Sāturnus et Iuppiter 290
The Demonstratives *Hic* and *Ille*; Word Studies

Lesson XLII: Cīvitās Rōmāna 295
The Demonstrative *Is*; The Declension and Use of *Mille*; Word Studies

Lesson XLIII: Midās 301
The Demonstrative *Idem*; Word Studies

Lesson XLIV: Horātius 306
The Intensive Adjective/Pronoun *Ipse*; Words Often Confused

Glimpses of Roman Life: Religion 310

Unit IX Review 313

Unit X Famous Romans

Lesson XLV: Cicerō et Tīrō 318
The Fifth Declension; The Third Person Reflexive Adjectives; Word Studies

Lesson XLVI: Quīntus Cicerō et Pompōnia 323
The Present Participle; The Future Active Participle; Word Studies

Lesson XLVII: Cincinnātus 328
The Perfect Active Infinitive; Word Studies

Lesson XLVIII: Bella 333
The Perfect Passive and Future Active Infinitives; Direct and Indirect Statement; Word Studies

Lesson XLIX: Coriolānus 339
How Indicative and Infinitive Differ in Tense; Word Studies

Glimpses of Roman Life: Agriculture and Commerce 344

Unit X Review 346

Unit XI Greeks Myths and Roman History

Lesson L: Quattuor Aetātēs 352
Comparison of Adjectives; Word Studies

Lesson LI: Baucis et Philēmōn 357
Formation and Comparison of Adverbs; Word Studies

Lesson LII: Daedalus et Īcarus 362
Comparison of *–er* Adjectives and Their Adverbs; Adjectives with Superlative in *–limus*; Dative with Adjectives; Word Studies

Lesson LIII: Pyrrhus et Eius Victōria 367
The Comparison of Irregular Adjectives; Word Studies

Lesson LIV: Pyrrhus et Fabricius 372
Reflexive Pronouns; Use of Reflexive Pronouns; Word Studies

Glimpses of Roman Life: The Emperors 378

Unit XI Review 381

Grammar Appendix 386

Vocabulary

Latin-English 407
English-Latin 419

Subject Index 425

Grammar/Vocabulary Index 431

Credits 436

Maps

Imperium Romanum (Second Century A.D.) 12
Italia 57
Imperium Romanum (264 B.C.—Second Century A.D.) 102-103
Sicilia 164

Scala/Art Resource, NY

The Arch of Titus was begun by the emperor Vespasian to honor his son Titus's victory over Jerusalem in A.D. *70. It was completed in* A.D. *81. It is located on the Sacred Way in Rome and is one of the best examples of a distinctively Roman style of architecture, the triumphal arch.*

Our Roman Heritage 

The Romans used great arches as monuments to celebrate military victories or famous heroes. All over the world other people have built triumphal arches in imitation of this Roman custom.

Arches are also gateways, and the Latin language is the arch through which countless generations of Western people have been able to enter into their past and discover the ideas and traditions that have shaped their lives. All over the world, for centuries, people have studied Latin because of their curiosity about the ancient world. Now you too stand before the arch. Step right ahead! Just through that arch is the rich inheritance the Romans have left to all of us.

The first thing you will notice as you begin the study of Latin is the close resemblance between many Latin and English words, since the English language owes a great debt of vocabulary to Latin. But the Roman heritage is not just one of vocabulary; more important are the ways in which the ancient Romans have influenced our forms of government, our social institutions, our habits of thinking, and have provided inspiration to statesmen, writers, artists, architects, engineers, and almost all educated people.

But your own greatest reward beyond the arch will be the broadened vision you will find in yourself. Some things in the ancient world will be strikingly familiar to you, others totally new; some things will seem primitive, others remarkably modern. How did an ancient Roman live? What was life like in his or her family? What were their ideas about government and religion? How could they believe in both freedom and slavery? What were the moral qualities and the skills that made the Romans, once simple farmers, the masters of the world? To all these questions you will discover the answers; and the comparisons between the Roman experience and yours will help to make another person of you. As so many others have learned before you, you will see that "to learn another language is to gain another soul."

But why study Latin and Rome rather than a modern language and a modern city? Because no other language and no other city have had so much influence—and for so long a time—upon our own culture. More than twenty-seven hundred years ago Rome was an insignificant settlement on the Tiber River in a central district of Italy called Latium. From small beginnings, the military, political, and cultural power of Rome spread, first throughout Latium, then through Italy and over the Mediterranean. By the second century after the birth of Christ, the Romans dominated almost the entire civilized world; Rome itself was at the same time **urbs et orbis**—*city and world.*

The Romans' language, Latin (which gets its name from Latium), came to be used everywhere, largely displacing the languages of the conquered

Scala/Art Resource, NY

The Emperor Justinian (sixth century) was responsible for establishing the Justinian Code, a collection of Roman laws, edicts, and decisions of the previous 1000 years. It is still the basic law of many nations. In this mosaic, we see the Emperor Justinian with his court.

peoples. Only Greek, a language much older than Latin, successfully resisted the invasion, mainly because it was the vehicle of great literature and culture that the Romans admired and imitated. Just as we today study Latin, so did the Romans then study Greek, and for similar reasons.

From the map on pages 102-103 you can see the stages of growth of the Roman Empire, and from it you can see why the languages of Spain, Portugal, France, Italy, and Romania are called *Romance* languages: they are the living descendants of the Latin spoken by the Romans who conquered and colonized these lands. And although English is basically a Germanic language, Latin has influenced it so much throughout the centuries that it would be almost fair to call it a Romance language also. More than sixty percent of our English vocabulary has been derived or taken intact from Latin!

Thus the Latin language and the ideas it conveys have actually survived the Roman Empire itself. As the centuries passed, and as the empire was gradually transformed into the beginnings of modern Europe, Latin continued to be the international language of all educated men and women, living a sort of parallel existence with the different national languages that were growing up from and alongside it. When the Middle Ages ended, interest in the classical Latin of Cicero, Caesar, and Vergil gained great impetus from the discovery of more works of the ancient authors in the monasteries and libraries of Europe. This rebirth of interest in the ancient world was one of the major causes for the amazing period of transition to the modern world that we call the Renaissance. From their deeper knowledge of the past, the people of the Renaissance found a new confidence in themselves and new horizons to explore. Since the colonization of the New World was the work of Europeans who were the heirs of the Roman tradition, Latin was transplanted by them to the western hemisphere. Even today, the people of Mexico, Central America, and South America are called Latins, and the region they live in is called Latin America.

Our own country was settled under the same influences. The Revolutionary War was led and the Constitution drafted by men who cherished the classical ideals of liberty and the dignity of the individual. The two names by which we refer to our country, America and the United States, are both derived from Latin. Our motto *e pluribus unum* is Latin. In one sense, there could have been no Declaration of Independence without Latin, and its first sentence would have looked like this: "We hold these truths to be self-________, that all men are _________ ______, that they are _______ by their ______ with ________ _______ rights; that among these are life, _______, and the _______ of happiness." The Romans not only gave us the omitted words, but the ideas themselves, which they in turn had borrowed from the Greeks. Hardly a page of this book does not show you some specific example of the way in which classical literature, mythology, art, history, or social custom is still part of our lives in the twentieth century.

To be sure, Latin itself is seldom written or spoken today, outside of ecclesiastical circles. But its immense influence upon English and other languages makes its study a very practical one. Most of the difficult words in English come from Latin (or Greek)—in a short time you will see how even an elementary knowledge of Latin makes it easy to figure out the meaning and spelling of such words as *impecunious, equanimity, collaborate, obdurate,* and many others. Latin abbreviations, words, mottoes, and phrases in common English use will no longer be a mystery. Latin will help build the technical vocabulary you will need if you are to become a doctor, lawyer, teacher, or scientist—someday it may be you who uses Latin to coin a new word like *astronaut* or *urbiculture!* Practice in translating Latin will give polish and precision to your English style, and will help do away with the narrow prejudice that *our* way of saying something is always the easiest or best.

Nevertheless, the best reason for passing through the arch is that you will enter a new and different world that will tell you much about your own, and will help educate you, for understanding what you owe to the past is a major part of being "educated." As the famous Roman orator Cicero said, "Not to know what happened before you were born is to be forever a child."

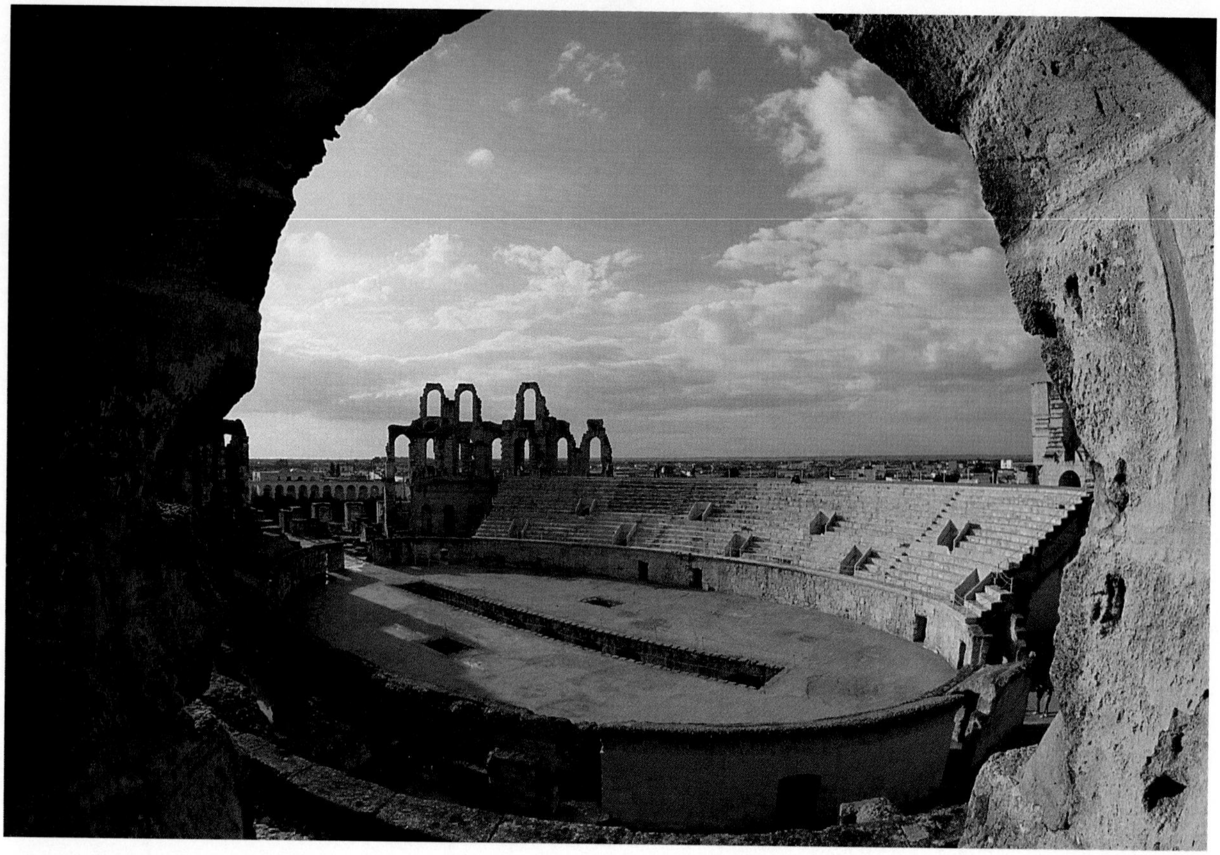

J.D. Dallet/SuperStock

Roman influence was far flung. Still standing today is the well-preserved Roman amphitheater at El jem, Tunisia. Equipment, wild animals, and gladiators were kept in the vast area under the amphitheater floor until needed for the show.

QUESTIONS

1. How many events of Roman history can you list?
2. Which famous Romans can you name?
3. What Roman gods and goddesses can you recall?
4. What do you know about the city of Rome as it is today?
5. Make a list of the Latin words, phrases, legal terms, scientific terms, mottoes, proverbs, and abbreviations you already know.

The Alphabet

Without writing, the continuity of civilization would be impossible. People can pass on hard-won experience and ideas by word of mouth, but only to a few individuals, in a limited area, and only for a brief time. And what is only heard can easily be misunderstood. But whatever is written down can be read by people far and wide, can be preserved for long periods of time, and can, if it is proved wrong, be changed with later experience. Since writing gives permanence and wide distribution to knowledge and ideas, it is a more effective way to move people's minds than such violent means as war, slavery, and torture. This is what we mean when we say that the "pen is mightier than the sword."

There are many forms of writing, some better than others. The earliest, used long ago by prehistoric humans, was *pictographic*, in which stories were told using pictures. The ancient Egyptians and Chinese, and even modern Native Americans, have used pictographic writing. But although the pictures are often quite beautiful, they are difficult to draw, they leave a lot out of the story, and, as they become more numerous and complicated, they are too much for any one person to remember. *Ideographic* writing is similar to pictographic: the pictures have gradually been standardized into simpler characters that convey an idea. But they too are often difficult for the untrained reader to understand: for example, a foreign visitor driving along a highway might think that the signpost on the right + stood for a gravestone instead of a crossroad (and in his case indeed it might!). In *logographic* writing the characters are associated with the sounds of the words of which they were originally pictures: if a wavy line represents the "sea" and the figure of a small boy represents a "son," then  becomes "season." When, in this way, a limited number of characters become firmly fixed as the standard signs for the sounds of the syllables of a language, *syllabic* writing is the result. Many ancient people used syllabic writing, often together with the other types; this is the form the Japanese use today.

The simplest and clearest system of writing is the *alphabetic*, which developed from the syllabic, and in which there is a single character for almost every vowel or consonant sound. This system helps people "hear" more easily the sounds they see, and thus simplifies learning to read and write. Furthermore, in the alphabetic system the sounds of one language can be represented fairly exactly in the writing of another language, and this makes learning the new language that much simpler. But not even the alphabetic system is perfect; in English we still have difficulty learning to spell because custom often requires us to use a different set of characters for the same sound: compare *debt* and *let*, or *there* and *their*.

Scala/Art Resource, NY

A wax-covered tablet, called an abecedarium. The ABCs were scratched on the wooden rim as a model to imitate. The letters run from right to left, as in the earlier Semitic alphabets.

Nevertheless, the Roman alphabet that we use and share with so many other countries is the best yet invented, and is one of the Romans' greatest contributions to our culture. Its history is an excellent example of the way in which valuable inventions are passed from one civilization to another. Sometime before 1500 B.C. the Semites, a people of western Asia, developed a syllabic script from Egyptian pictographic characters, and gave these characters names from their own language. The first letter was *aleph* ("ox," because the character looked like the head of an ox, although upside-down); the second was *beth* ("house"), and so forth. The Phoenicians, a sea-faring Semitic people related to the Jews and Arabs, passed this set of characters to the Greeks, who adapted it to their own language, and made the signs for the vowels (*a, e, i, o, u*) separate and distinct (the Semitic alphabet had not done this). *Aleph* became *alpha*, and *beth* became *beta*, and thus the alphabet was born, because *alpha* and *beta* no longer had anything to do with "ox" and "house," but were simply signs for the sounds *A* and *B*. From the Greeks the alphabet was passed to the Etruscans, northern neighbors of the Romans in Italy. When the Romans in turn borrowed it from the Etruscans, they made some changes in the values and forms of the letters, and passed it on to the modern world, where it is used almost universally today. All of Europe, except Greece and Russia (which uses a modified Greek alphabet), writes in Latin letters. In the latter half of the twentieth century, almost as a symbol of its emergence into the modern world, Turkey abandoned the Arabic alphabet (a descendant of the ancient Semitic one) in favor of the simpler Latin alphabet. In Japan today, particularly in the business community, "our" Roman alphabet is gaining rapid acceptance. This is, in fact, a trend throughout Asia.

Roman	A B C D E F G H I K L M N O P Q R S T V X Y Z
English	A B C D E F G H I J K L M N O P Q R S T U V W X Y Z

You can see that the alphabet has changed little since Roman days. The Romans used *i* for both *i* and *j*. Three centuries ago it became the custom in English to use a long form of *i* for *j*, and thus our *j* was formed. Similarly, the Romans used only one character for *u* and *v*, but we have introduced the useful distinction between them, even in Latin, and in this book *u* is printed for the vowel, *v* for the consonant. The original identity of the two is shown by another modern letter, *w*, which is a double *u* in name and a double *v* in form. (The letters *j* and *w* are not found in Latin words in this textbook.)

The Romans made no distinction between capitals and small letters. Our small letters gradually developed out of capitals in late antiquity.

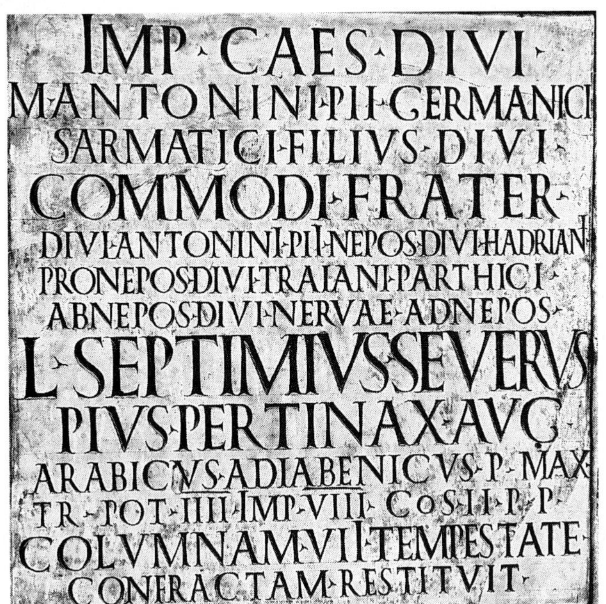

The Bettmann Archive

This inscription is a decree issued by the emperor Septimius Severus, who was emperor 193-211. He expanded the empire in a war against the Parthians but died in an attempt to take Scotland. Do you recognize any words?

Pronunciation

The pronunciation of Latin has naturally changed in the course of centuries. During the Middle Ages it was variously pronounced in different countries in accordance with the rules for pronouncing the everyday languages of those countries, and this practice has continued in some places even to the present time. A century ago scholars discovered in various ways how Latin was pronounced in the days of Caesar and Cicero. This "new" ancient pronunciation first came into general use in the United States. It is now fairly general everywhere except in Italy and Vatican City. According to the ancient pronunciation, Cicero pronounced his name *Ki´kero*, and so you are taught in this book—but once it was pronounced *Si´sero* in England and the United States, *See´sero* in France, *Tsi´tsero* in Germany and Austria, *Chee´chero* in Italy, *Thi´thero* in Spain. But we know that *Kikero* is most nearly correct because, for example, Greek writers spell his name Κικερων (*Kikeron*), and the *k* sound in Greek cannot be confused with the *s* sound, for which there is an entirely different letter. Caesar pronounced his own name *Kysar*. We used to pronounce it in Latin as in English (*Seezer*), and each of the other languages had its own way of saying the word.

The system of pronunciation that you are taught in this textbook is thus ancient, "modern," and standard. Pronouncing Latin is not difficult: the rules are few and simple, and unlike English, each consonant (except *b*) has only one sound, and each vowel at most only two sounds. The best way to get started is by imitating your teacher carefully and by listening to the audio cassettes which accompany this book. Pay particular attention to the length (*quantity*) and sound (*quality*) of the vowels, and to the position of the stress (´). You will find that Latin is a sonorous and almost musical language.

PRONUNCIATION EXERCISES

1. Each of the first five columns drills a different vowel, either long or short; the sixth column is devoted to the different diphthongs.

   Pronounce:

ā	ē	quī	nōn	iūs	aes
Mārs	mē	hīc	prō	cūr	quae
pār	pēs	vīs	mōns	lūx	Aet´nae
ab	ex	in	nox	nunc	aut
iam	sed	quid	post	cum	cau´sa
dat	per	fit	mors	dux	clau´sae
nār´rat	cer´tē	di´gitī	cō´gor	iūs´tus	poe´nae
ma´lā	lē´ge	mī´litis	ro´gō	cur´rū	moe´nia

2. Read the verse. Can you tell from the rhythm and arrangement of words what it is?

   Mi´cā, mi´cā, par´va stēl´la!
   Mī´ror quae´nam sīs, tam bel´la,
   Splen´dēns ē´minus in il´lō,
   Al´ba ve´lut gem´ma, cae´lō.

3. This is a translation by George D. Kellogg of the first two stanzas of "America":

   Tē ca´nō, Pa´tria,
   Can´dida, lībera;
   Tē re´feret
   Por´tus et ex´ulum
   Et tu´mulus se´num;
   Lī´bera mon´tium
   Vōx re´sonet.

   Tē ca´nō, Pa´tria,
   Sem´per et ā´tria
   Inge´nuum;
   Lau´dō viren´tia
   Cul´mina, flū´mina;
   Sen´tiō gau´dia
   Caeli´colum.

Messages were scratched into wax that covered wooden writing tablets. Often, two tablets were placed with their right sides together, tied, and sealed with sealing wax to preserve the integrity of the message.

4. Here is part of a translation of Lincoln's Gettysburg Address made for the Vatican Library:

   Octōgin´tā et sep´tem ab´hinc iam an´nōs rem pū´blicam no´vam, lībertā´te incep´tam at´que homi´nibus nātū´rā pa´ribus dēdicā´tam, maiō´rēs hīs in regiō´nibus ēdidē´runt.... Sēn´sū ta´men altiō´re hanc ter´ram dēdicā´re, cōnsecrā´re, sānctificā´re, nō´bīs nōn com´petit.... Quō fī´et ut cī´vitās haec De´ō adiuvan´te lībertā´tī renāscē´tur; et di´ciō in po´pulō fundā´ta, ā po´pulō ges´ta, ad po´pulī salū´tem dīrēc´ta, nēquā´quam dē mun´dō tābēs´cēns interī´bit.

5. These are ancient Latin quotations, some of which you probably have seen:

   a) **Vē´nī vī´dī, vī´cī,** *I came, I saw, I conquered* (Caesar's famous dispatch to the senate after a victory).

   b) **In hōc sig´nō vin´cēs,** *In this sign* (the cross) *you will conquer* (motto of Constantine, the first Christian emperor).

   c) **Pos´sunt qui´a pos´se viden´tur,** *They can because they think they can.*

   d) **Aman´tium ī´rae amō´ris integrā´tiō est,** *The quarrels of lovers are the renewal of love* (Terence; quoted by Winston Churchill in a message to Franklin D. Roosevelt).

6. The two verses that follow were used by Roman children in some of their games:

   a) **Ha´beat sca´biem quis´quis ad mē vē´nerit novis´simus,** *May he have the itch who comes to me last.*

   b) **Rēx e´rit quī rēc´tē fa´ciet; quī nōn fa´ciet nōn e´rit,** *He will be king who does right; he who does not will not be king.*

7. Here is the most famous sentence of President John F. Kennedy's Inaugural Address, translated into Latin:

   I´taque concī´vēs me´ī Americā´nī, nē rogē´tis quid pa´tria ves´tra prō vō´bis fa´cere pos´sit, im´mo quid vōs prō pa´triā fa´cere possī´tis, id rogā´te.

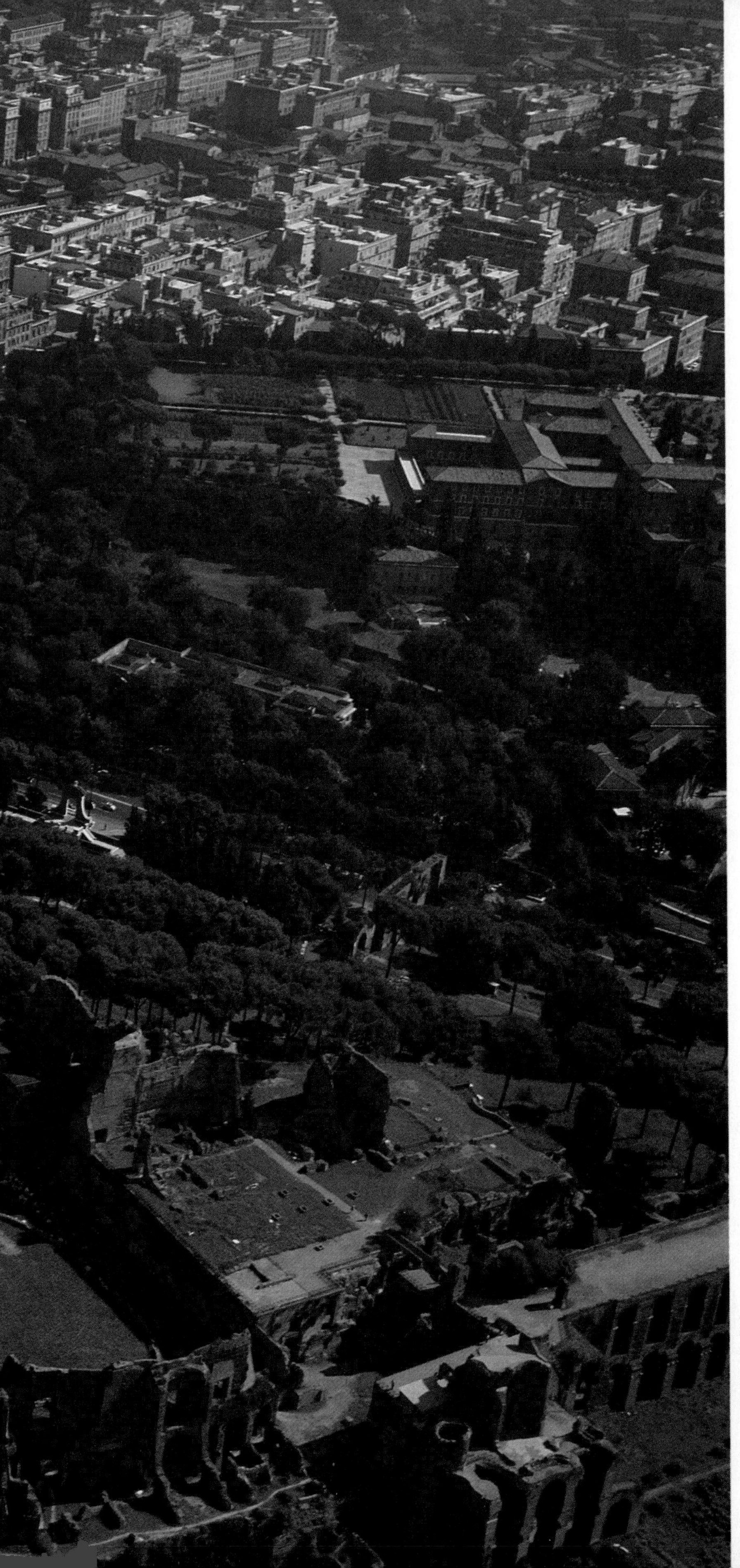

Unit I

The Romans' World

Archivio e Studio Folco Quilici

An aerial view of part of ancient Rome. Prominent are the Flavian Amphitheater, popularly called the Colosseum (dedicated 80 A.D.), and the Arch of Constantine (erected 313 A.D.) near it.

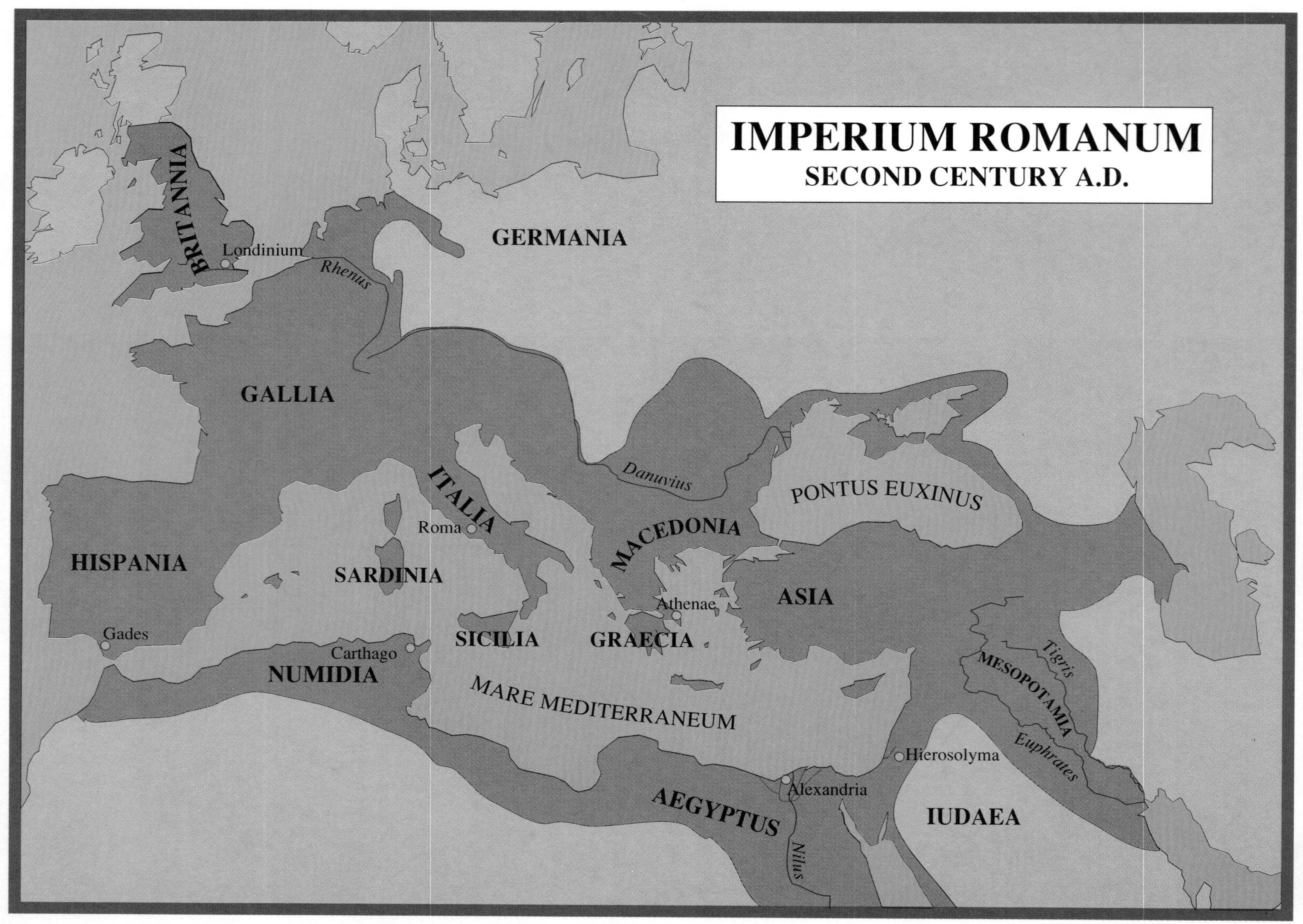
IMPERIUM ROMANUM
SECOND CENTURY A.D.
BRITANNIA
Londinium
GERMANIA
Rhenus
GALLIA
Danuvius
PONTUS EUXINUS
ITALIA
Roma
MACEDONIA
HISPANIA
SARDINIA
Athenae
ASIA
Gades
Carthago
SICILIA
GRAECIA
Tigris
NUMIDIA
MESOPOTAMIA
MARE MEDITERRANEUM
Hierosolyma
Euphrates
Alexandria
AEGYPTUS
IUDAEA
Nilus

Rōma est in Italiā. Italia est in Eurōpā. Britannia est in Eurōpā. Britannia est īnsula. Italia nōn est īnsula. Italia paene[1] est īnsula. Italia paenīnsula est. Sicilia et Sardinia sunt īnsulae. Īnsulae in aquā sunt. Austrālia īnsula est, sed Asia nōn est īnsula.

Sunt viae et silvae in paenīnsulā Italiā. Viae et silvae et paenīnsulae in Eurōpā sunt. Italia et Graecia et Hispānia paenīnsulae sunt. Rōma nōn in Graeciā sed in Italiā est. Est Graecia in Eurōpa?

Est aqua in Antarcticā, sed nōn sunt silvae in Antarcticā. Silvae in Āfricā sunt. Est America īnsula?

[1] *almost*

QUESTIONS

1. Can you use other islands, countries, states, and cities whose names end in *–a*, such as Bermuda, India, Virginia, Philadelphia, to make up additional Latin sentences?
2. What do we call an "almost-island" in English?
3. Which of the words in the reading seem related to English?

Getting Started

Understanding Latin

Here is the easiest method to get the sense and make a good translation of a Latin sentence:

- Read through the complete sentence aloud in Latin, trying to grasp the meaning of each word as you come to it. At the same time, try to get the general idea of the whole sentence as you go along.
- Be careful with your pronunciation, remember that there are no silent syllables, and pay particular attention to the endings of the words. Make your ears help your eyes, and vice versa.

- Often the meaning of the sentence will become clear from a single reading aloud. But if a word stumps you, try to find a clue to its meaning from some English word that has been formed from the Latin one such as *insular* from **īnsula.** Use the vocabulary only as a last resort.
- Since Latin has no words for *a, an,* and *the*, you must supply them with the nouns that need them in order to make your English translation smoother. **Est** means not only *is*, but also *he, she,* or *it is*, and even *there is.*
- Be patient with the Latin word order. English is much more strict about making the sense of the sentence depend upon the word order. Compare *Dog bites man* with *Man bites dog*. The word order in Latin is more flexible because a word's *ending*, not its *position*, indicates its role in a sentence.

  This principle of the change of word endings, called *inflection*, is the most important concept to master. Unfamiliar vocabulary can often be worked out (or, as a last resort, looked up) and the now strange word order will soon seem natural. There is no short cut to learning the various endings, which are the signposts of the sentence.
- When you have read the whole sentence through and understand it, convert it into the English that is natural to you. Try to be as exact as possible, but do not stick blindly to the English meanings given in the vocabulary. Latin has fewer words in its vocabulary than English does, so it is common for a Latin word to have more than one English equivalent. Use *synonyms* whenever they make better sense.
- Keep in mind that your goal is to understand Latin as Latin, the way the Romans did. Eventually **Britannia īnsula est** and *Britain is an island* will have exactly the same meaning to you without the need for translation.

Grammar

Nouns

Nouns are used to name persons, places, or things. In Latin, it is very important to know three things about every noun, in addition to its meaning. These three things, called *attributes,* are its *gender, number,* and *case.*

Gender refers to whether the noun is *masculine, feminine,* or *neuter* in Latin. In English, you are used to calling female people and animals "she," and male people and animals "he." You normally refer to everything else using the neuter word "it." In Latin, every noun has a gender that must be learned as you learn the meaning of the noun. You cannot rely on guessing that something "seems female," so it must be feminine.

īnsula	island	*feminine*
equus	horse	*masculine*
bellum	war	*neuter*

Number simply means whether the noun is *singular* or *plural.* A noun is singular in number when it names one person, place, or thing. It is plural when it names more than one. The ending of the noun changes to show whether it is singular or plural.

īnsula	island	**īnsulae**	islands
equus	horse	**equī**	horses
bellum	war	**bella**	wars

The *case* of a noun is determined by its use in a sentence. In Latin, the subject of the sentence is in the *nominative* case. The subject of the sentence will always have a nominative ending. The direct object in a sentence is in the *accusative* case. It will always have an accusative ending.

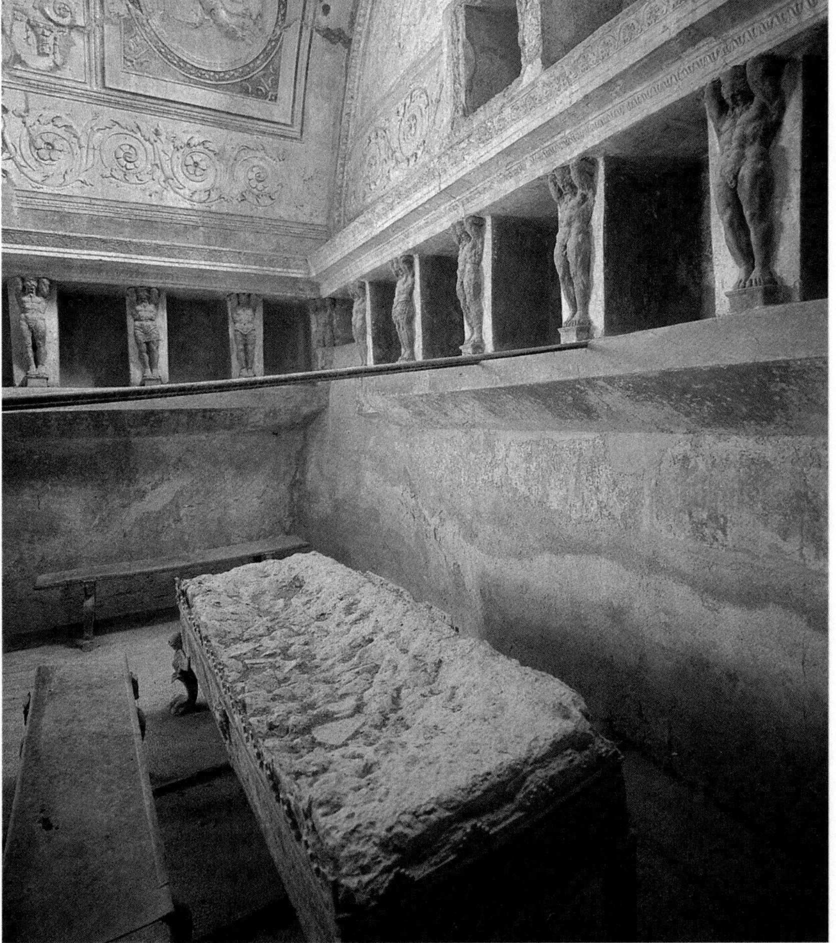
Erich Lessing/PhotoEdit

Public baths were popular throughout the Roman world. There were warm and hot rooms (heated by hot air ducts), massage rooms, open areas for exercise, lecture halls, and public libraries. Many baths were magnificently decorated with marble and statues. There were usually separate baths for men and women, although coed bathing was allowed at one time.

Because each noun has a special ending to indicate its function, the word order in Latin is much more flexible. There are five main cases in Latin. Their names are nominative, genitive, dative, accusative, and ablative. You will learn about each one, one at a time, as you continue your Latin studies.

Puella equum amat.	*The girl loves the horse.*
Equus puellam amat.	*The horse loves the girl.*

A *declension* is a group of nouns that shares the same general pattern of endings. There are five declensions in Latin. Nouns in the first declension all end in **–a** in the nominative singular. But you cannot always tell a noun's declension by its nominative singular form. You also need to know the noun's genitive singular form. All nouns in your lesson vocabulary lists have the nominative singular, genitive singular, gender, and meaning. It is important to learn all of these pieces when you are studying your vocabulary.

īnsula, īnsulae, *f. island*

Latin for American Students

*Did you know that the Romans often gave names to their racing horses? Sometimes a horse was named after a legendary figure like **Ajax, Daedalus,** or **Phaedrus.** Sometimes the name described its appearance or character like **Maculosus** (Spotty), **Candidus** (Snowy), or **Hilarus** (Good-tempered). Often it represented the hopes of the owner like **Advolans** (Flier), **Calidromus** (Gorgeous Runner), or **Sagitta** (Arrow).*

Predicate Nominative

The word *sentence* comes from the Latin word **sententia,** which means "thought." In both Latin and English, sentences are words grouped together to express thoughts.

Every sentence has two parts: the *subject,* about which something is said, and the *predicate,* which includes the verb and everything that follows the verb.

After a linking verb (*is, are, seem,* etc.) a noun in the predicate is in the nominative case. This is called the *predicate nominative.* A linking verb is really nothing more than an equals sign (=).

ISOLATION = INSULATION

A = B	A = B
Britannia est īnsula.	*Britain is an island.*

The First Declension

All first declension nouns are declined like **silva,** *forest.* To decline a noun, you must find its stem, and then add the endings. To find the stem, drop the **–ae** from the genitive form. Learn the case endings by practicing them aloud.

	SINGULAR	PLURAL
NOMINATIVE	sil´va	sil´vae
GENITIVE	sil´vae	sil´vārum
DATIVE	sil´vae	sil´vīs
ACCUSATIVE	sil´vam	sil´vās
ABLATIVE	sil´vā	sil´vīs

Vocabulary

Nouns

a´qua, a´quae, *f. water* (aqueduct, aqueous)
īn´sula, īn´sulae, *f. island* (insulate, isolate)
sil´va, sil´vae, *f. forest, woods* (Pennsylvania, sylvan)
vi´a, vi´ae, *f. road, way, street* (viaduct, viator)

Verbs

est, *is*
sunt, *are*

Adverb

nōn, *not* (nonentity, nonsense)

Conjunctions

et, *and*
sed, *but*

Word Studies

English has borrowed many words from Latin. Sometimes these words are spelled and used exactly as they were in Latin; other times the spelling changes a little, and so does the meaning. The words in parentheses that follow the vocabulary words are derivatives of the Latin words. Becoming familiar with these and other derivatives will help increase your English vocabulary and help you learn other Romance languages like Spanish and French.

Let's look at a few examples of first declension nouns that have been borrowed by English. The Latin noun *larva,* for example, which meant "ghost" to the Romans, now means the just-hatched egg of some insects because, in a pale and formless way like a ghost, the *larva* "masks" the form of the future insect. The *larva* then grows into a *pupa*, the Latin word for "doll," which looks somewhat like a small version of the adult form. The plural of both these words in English is the same as in Latin: *larvae, pupae.*

Other words of this sort are *alumna, antenna, minutiae* (singular rare). But others have adopted the English plural in *–s*: *area, arena, camera, formula, scintilla.* In a dictionary, look up the present and the former meanings of each of the italicized words.

LESSON II
Sicilia

Sicilia est īnsula magna in Eurōpā. Magna est fāma Siciliae,[1] sed fortūna Siciliae nōn bona est. In Siciliā vīta est dūra. Terra et aqua sunt bonae, sed familiae sunt magnae. Magnae silvae in Siciliā nōn sunt. Viae nōn bonae sed parvae sunt. Vīta est dūra in Siciliā, et fortūna nōn bona est.

In Siciliā sunt parvae et magnae puellae. Parvae puellae pūpās[2] amant. Magnae puellae aquam portant. Familiae puellās amant. Familiae Siciliam et fāmam Siciliae amant, sed fortūnam dūram nōn amant.

[1] *of Sicily*
[2] *dolls*

QUESTIONS

1. Why is life hard in Sicily?
2. What is wrong with Sicilian roads?
3. How do Sicilians feel about their daughters?

Australian Picture Library/Westlight

Sicily was an important stepping-stone for the Romans as they expanded; in fact, it was the first Roman province. The remains of the Temple of the Dioscuri (Castor and Pollux) still stands in the Valley of the Temples in Agrigento, Sicily. The Romans valued very highly the friendship and loyalty of the Sicilians.

Grammar

Adjectives

An *adjective* is a word used to describe a noun. We say that an adjective *modifies* its noun. Pick out the adjectives in the second paragraph of the reading on Sicily.

In English, an adjective does not change. For example, we say *good dog* and *good dogs*, but not *goods dogs*.

In Latin an adjective changes its ending to agree with the noun it modifies in gender, number, and case. The adjective most often follows the noun, but because an adjective must agree with its noun in gender, number, and case, its position is less important than in English.

magna silva	*a large forest*
magnae silvae	*large forests*
aquam bonam	*good water*

An adjective may be used directly with a noun, as in the examples above, or in the predicate, as follows:

Magna familia est bona.	*A large family is good.*
Magnae silvae sunt bonae.	*Large forests are good.*

Just as it is important for you to learn the nominative, genitive, and gender when you study nouns, it is just as important to learn the three nominative forms of adjectives. In your chapter vocabulary lists, you will find each adjective presented with three forms: the masculine, feminine, and neuter nominative singular forms.

bonus, bona, bonum	*good*
dūrus, dūra, dūrum	*hard*

Latin for American Students

Did you know that the Roman ***familia*** *does not correspond exactly with our concept of family? It consisted of all individuals under the authority of the* ***pater familias*** *(male head of the household): his wife, unmarried daughters, sons, clients, slaves, and all real estate and personal property belonging to the household head to include property acquired and used by those under his authority.*

The Accusative Case

The *accusative case* is used to indicate the *direct object* of the sentence. The direct object is the noun that receives the action of the verb. Remember that the accusative endings of first declension nouns are **–am** in the singular and **–ās** in the plural.

Aqu*am* mult*am* portant.	*They carry much water.*
Puellae silv*ās* amant.	*The girls like the forests.*

NOTĀ • BENE

Remember that after a linking verb, the predicate nominative is used.

Aqua *est* bona.
The water **is** *good.*

Silvae *sunt* magnae.
The forests **are** *great.*

Word Order

The greatest difference between Latin and English is the concept of word order. In English, the word order shows the connection between the words in a sentence; in Latin, that connection is shown by using endings. Compare the following sentences.

Anna Clāram occīdit.	*Anna killed Clara.*
Clāram occīdit Anna.	*Anna killed Clara.*
Occīdit Anna Clāram.	*Anna killed Clara.*

Because **Anna** has a nominative ending, we know it is the subject no matter where it is positioned in the sentence. We know that **Clāram** is the direct object because it has an accusative ending. Normally, the verb stands last in a Latin sentence.

EXERCISES

A. Translate the following sentences into good English.

1. Via est bona.
2. Silva est parva.
3. Īnsula est magna.
4. Familiae sunt magnae.
5. Fāmam et vītam amant.
6. Familiae īnsulam amant.
7. Puellae Siciliam amant.
8. Parvae puellae sunt bonae.
9. Puellae aquam bonam portant.
10. Crēta et Sicilia sunt magnae īnsulae.

B. Add the correct endings to the following nouns and adjectives.

1. Vi__ sunt bon__.
2. Vit__ est magn__.
3. Puell__ est parv__.
4. Puell__ sunt parv__.
5. Terr__ nōn bon__ est.
6. Puellae aqu__ portant.
7. Via et silva sunt magn__.
8. Familiae vīt__ bon__ amant.
9. Familiae fortūn__ bon__ amant.
10. Puell__ terr__ dūr__ nōn amant.

C. For the English words supply Latin words with the correct endings. Then translate the sentences into English.

1. Puellae (*the land*) amant.
2. Familiae (*water*) portant.
3. Puellae (*the good roads*) amant.
4. (*Large*) familiae (*small lands*) nōn amant.

Vocabulary

Nouns

fā´ma, fā´mae, *f. report, fame*	(defamation, famous)
fami´lia, fami´liae, *f. family*	(familial, familiar)
fortū´na, fortū´nae, *f. fortune, luck*	(fortunate, misfortune)
puel´la, puel´lae, *f. girl*	
ter´ra, ter´rae, *f. earth, land*	(terrain, territory)
vī´ta, vī´tae, *f. life*	(vital, vitamin)

Adjectives

bo´nus, bo´na, bo´num, *good*	(bonbon, bonus)
dū´rus, dū´ra, dū´rum, *hard*	(durable, duress)
mag´nus, mag´na, mag´num, *great*	(magnify, magnitude)
par´vus, par´va, par´vum, *small*	(parvovirus)

Verbs

amant, *(they) love, like*	(amateur, amatory)
portant, *(they) carry*	(portable, porter)

Roman Numerals in English

Roman numerals are used often in English. Dates on inscriptions, on the title screens of movies, and (in lower case) on the first few pages of any textbook are just a few places. There are seven symbols used to indicate numbers:

I = 1	L = 50	D = 500
V = 5	C = 100	M = 1000
X = 10		

The other numbers are formed by combining these seven numerals as follows: by placing one or more numerals of equal or lesser value after a numeral to *add:*

III = 3	VII = 7	CCLVI = 256

or by placing a smaller numeral before a larger one to *subtract:*

IV = 4	IX = 9	XCV = 95

A smaller numeral placed between two larger numerals subtracts from the following numeral:

CCCXLV = 345

Try writing your birthdate as well as these numbers using Roman numerals: 53, 178, 29, 543, 2010.

BALL III, STRIKE II

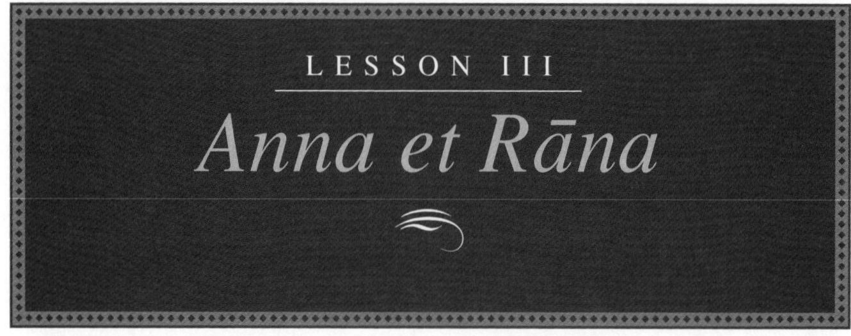

LESSON III

Anna et Rāna

Agricolae in[1] Sardiniā labōrant. Feminae[2] etiam[3] labōrant. Sardinia īnsula magna est et terra ibi[4] dūra est. Agricolae terram exarant et irrigant.[5] Puellae parvae agricolās spectant et temptant[6] adiuvāre.[7] Puella nōmine[8] Anna magnam urnam[9] portat.

FĒMINA NŌMINE CLAUDIA: Salvē, Anna. Quid[10] portās?

ANNA: Salvē, Claudia. Urnam portō.

FĒMINA NŌMINE SOPHIA: Quid in urnā est, Anna?

ANNA: Aquam in urnā portō.

AGRICOLA NŌMINE SYLVESTER: Mactē![11] Aquam bonam amāmus. In terrā dūrā labōrāmus.

(*Agricolae et fēminae aquam spectant. Exclāmant.*[12])

AGRICOLA NŌMINE LABŌRIŌ: Quid in aquā est, puella?

ANNA: Rāna[13] parva in aquā est.

CLAUDIA: Rānās amās, Anna?

ANNA: Sīc![14] Rānās amō. In silvā multa aqua est. In aquā multae rānae sunt. Rānās amātis?

SOPHIA: Minimē![15]

(*Rāna subsultat*[16] *et Sophia exclāmat. Sylvester rīsitat.*[17])

LABŌRIŌ: Rānās in silvā amāmus, Anna, sed nōn in urnā.

(*Anna etiam rīsitat.*)

CLAUDIA: Valē, Anna.

ANNA: Valēte, Claudia et Sophia.

(*Urnam novam parat.*)

[1] *on*
[2] *women; wives*
[3] *also*
[4] *there*
[5] *plow and irrigate*
[6] *try*
[7] *to help*
[8] *by the name of*
[9] *water jar*
[10] *what*
[11] *Well done!*
[12] *shout*
[13] *frog*
[14] *Yes*
[15] *No*
[16] *jumps up*
[17] *laughs*

QUESTIONS

1. Why is work difficult for farm families?
2. What is wrong with the water in Anna's jar?
3. Why does Sophia shout?

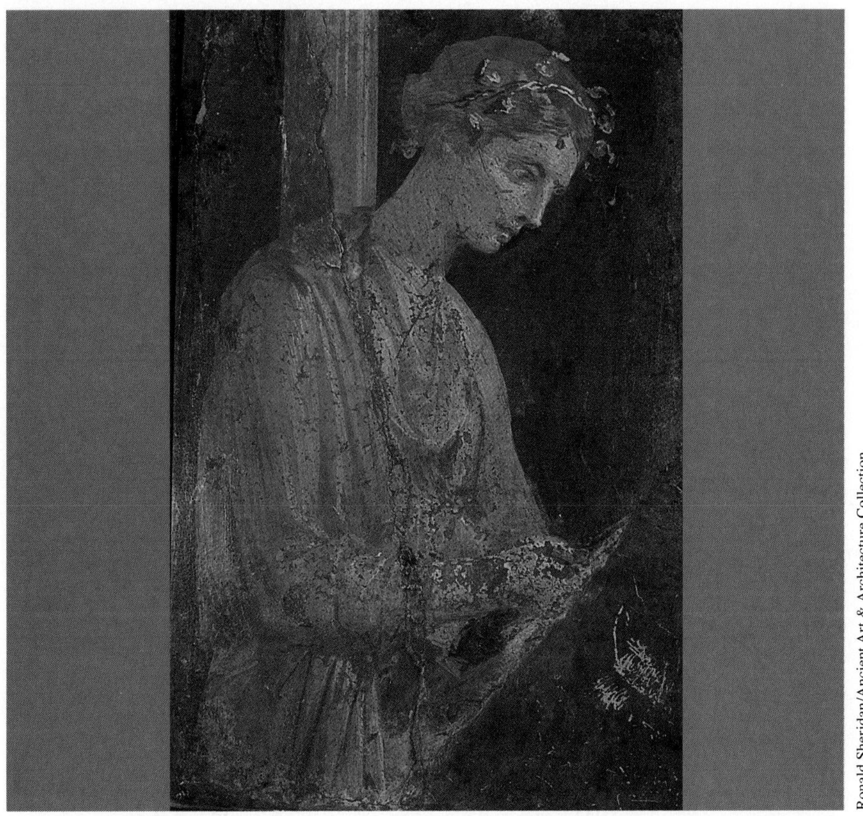

Ronald Sheridan/Ancient Art & Architecture Collection

A young Roman girl gets ready to spin. In the early days, mothers taught their daughters such skills as cooking and spinning. Later, wealthy women handed over the care of their children to nurses and slaves.

Grammar

Verbs

Verbs tell what a subject *is* or *does*. The verb is either the whole predicate or part of it.

Puella parva *est.*	*The girl* **is** *small.*
Puellae *labōrant.*	*The girls* **work.**

Verbs also indicate the time or *tense* of an action, that is, whether the action is past, present, or future. In English the verb is usually changed to show the tense. Latin verbs regularly change.

Verbs have three *persons,* in both the singular and the plural. English indicates the persons by the use of *personal pronouns:*

	SINGULAR	PLURAL
1st (the person speaking)	*I*	*we*
2nd (the person spoken to)	*you*	*you*
3rd (the person or thing spoken about)	*he, she, it*	*they*

Latin, however, usually omits personal pronouns, and uses *personal endings* to show the person and number of the subject. These, in a sense, are the equivalent of personal pronouns. The most common personal endings are:

	SINGULAR	PLURAL
1st person	–ō (or –m) *I*	–mus = *we*
2nd person	–s = *you*	–tis = *you*
3rd person	–t = *he, she, it*	–nt = *they*

These endings must become as familiar to you as the personal pronouns in English.

Infinitive and Present Stem

In English, the infinitive is the verb form that is introduced by *to: to go, to be, to prepare*. It does not show person or number.

In Latin, there is no separate word corresponding to the English *to*. The present infinitive of the regular Latin verbs ends in **–re:**

parā*re* = *to get* **amā*re*** = *to love* **portā*re*** = *to carry*

Drop the infinitive ending **–re** and you have the *present stem:*

parā– **amā–** **portā–**

First Conjugation Present Tense

The hundreds of verbs in Latin are divided into four groups according to their present stem. These groups are called *conjugations*. Verbs with a present stem ending in **–ā** belong to the *first* conjugation.

The present tense of a first-conjugation verb like **portō** (stem **portā–**) is *conjugated* by adding the personal endings to the present stem:

SINGULAR	PLURAL
por´tō, *I carry, am carrying, do carry*	portā´mus, *we carry, are carrying, do carry*
por´tās, *you carry, are carrying, do carry*	portā´tis, *you carry, are carrying, do carry*
por´tat, *he, she, it carries, is carrying, does carry*	por´tant, *they carry, are carrying, do carry*

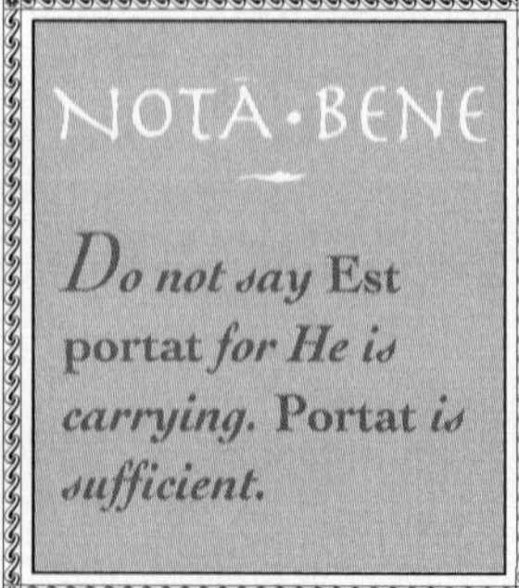
NOTĀ·BENE

Do not say Est portat *for He is carrying.* Portat *is sufficient.*

Note that there are three ways to translate each Latin verb form—*common, progressive,* and *emphatic*. Unlike English, Latin does not use *do* and *am* as auxiliary verbs. For example, English says, *Do you carry? Are you carrying?* Latin says simply **Portās?**

Two singular subjects connected by **et** require a plural verb, just as in English when *and* joins two singular subjects.

Puella et agricola labōrant.	*The girl and the farmer are working.*

Note that all stem vowels are shortened before **–nt** and final **–m** and **–t.** In the first person singular, the stem vowel **–ā–** disappears entirely before the personal ending **–ō.**

NOTĀ·BENE

Also remember that when a noun is used as the subject, the personal pronoun should not be expressed. **Puella portat,** *The girl carries, not The girl she carries.*

EXERCISES

A. Read aloud in Latin and get the meaning; then translate the following into good English.

1. Amo, parās, spectat
2. Spectās, parō, labōrat
3. Portāmus, amātis, parant
4. Portant, amāmus, parātis
5. Labōrāmus, parat, est, sunt

B. Read the following sentences aloud, then translate. Pay attention to the endings.

1. Puella terram spectat.
2. Multam aquam portant.
3. Puella bona viam dūram spectat.
4. Puellae et agricolae aquam parant.
5. Agricola et puella silvam spectant.

C. Supply Latin words with the correct endings for the English words.

1. Puella (*is working*).
2. Agricolae (*carry*) aquam.
3. Multās īnsulās (*I am looking at*).
4. (*You (sing.) like*) parvam puellam.
5. Terram bonam (*we like*).
6. Parat (*to carry*) aquam.
7. (*Are they watching*) agricolam?
8. (*We do love*) puellās; bonae (*they are*).

D. Copy the following sentences and add the correct endings to the verbs.

1. Vit_ dūr_ est.
2. Vi__ nov__ sunt bon__.
3. Puellae silv__ (*forest*) amant.
4. Agricol__ aquam bonam spectant.
5. Long__ īnsul__ agricolae amant.

C. M. Dixon

Town water systems, such as this one in Pompeii, were common. Very often, children and slaves were sent to fetch water from the public fountains, which then had to be carried home.

Vocabulary

Noun

agri´cola, *m. farmer* (agriculture, agribusiness)

Verbs

a´mō, amā´re, (amateur, amatory)
[amā´vī, amā´tus],[1] *love, like*

labō´rō, labōrā´re, (labor, laborious)
[labōrā´vī, labōrā´tus], *work*

pa´rō, parā´re, (preparation)
[parā´vī, parā´tus], *get, get ready, prepare*

por´tō, portā´re, (import, portable)
[portā´vī, portā´tus], *carry*

spec´tō, spectā´re, (inspect, spectacle)
[spectā´vī, spectā´tus], *look (at), watch*

Adjectives

lon´ga, *long* (elongated, longitude)
mul´ta, *much;* (pl.), *many* (multitude, multiply)
no´va, *new, strange* (novel, novelty)

Interjections

minimē, *no*
salvē, salvēte (pl.), *hello*
sīc, *yes*
valē, valēte (pl.), *good-bye*

ELONGATED

[1] The first person singular, present tense, of the verb is given first, then the present infinitive. The two forms in brackets complete the four *principal parts* of the verb. You will not need them for a while, but their regularity and rhythm make them easy to learn now.

C. M. Dixon

Wall paintings, or frescoes, were often used to create the effect of a garden indoors. Many Roman houses had pictures or murals painted on the walls. Wallpaper, of course, was unknown.

Latin for American Students

Did you know that the early Romans had three forms of marriage? The first, **coemptio**, *was a fictitious bride-purchase during which the bridegroom paid a penny to the father or guardian in exchange for his bride. The second form,* **usus**, *involved the cohabitation of a man and woman for at least one year. The third form,* **confarreatio**, *was the most elaborate wedding ceremony during which priests officiated and animal sacrifices were made.*

Word Studies

1. An *amiable* person is basically "lovable." What is a *portable* computer? A *respectable* job? Why do we use *insulation?* What does a *porter* do? An *elaborate* carving is one that required a lot of *work*. An *amateur* pursues his interest for the *love* of it.
2. As we have already seen, many scientific terms in English are borrowed directly from the Latin first declension. Here are a few more: *amoeba, amoebae* (or *amoebas*); *nebula, nebulae* (or *nebulas*); *nova, novae* (or *novas*); *scapula, scapulae* (or *scapulas*); *vertebra, vertebrae* (or *vertebras*). Look up the meanings of these words. Remember to pronounce *–ae* as English *eye*.

Multae viae in Italiā erant et sunt. Multae viae Rōmānae erant bonae. Via Appia in Italiā erat et est. Ōlim Via Appia erat via Rōmāna. Nōn nova est sed fāma eius[1] est magna, quod longa et bona via est. Multae viae Americānae ōlim erant malae, sed nunc bonae sunt. In Italiā et in Americā bonās viās laudāmus. Viās malās nōn amāmus. Viās dūrās amātis?

Multī carrī et equī erant in viīs[2] Rōmānīs. Agricolae in Viā Appiā erant. Servī magnī et parvī in viīs erant. Ubi nunc equī sunt? Ubi carrī sunt? Nunc servī nōn sunt.

Agricola carrum bonum parat. Agricola carrum laudat, quod novus et magnus est. Puellae carrōs nōn amant, quod dūrī sunt. Puellae equōs amant, quod bonī sunt. Agricola equōs amat, quod in terrā labōrant. Servum malum nōn laudat, quod nōn labōrat.

[1] *of it = its*
[2] *on the roads*

QUESTIONS

1. Why is the Appian Way famous?
2. What two great cities did the Appian Way connect?

Grammar

The Second Declension

Most nouns of the second declension are declined like **servus,** *slave.* Remember to add the endings to the stem, which you can find by dropping the genitive singular ending.

	SINGULAR	PLURAL
NOMINATIVE	ser´vus	ser´vī
GENITIVE	ser´vī	servō´rum
DATIVE	ser´vō	ser´vīs
ACCUSATIVE	ser´vum	ser´vōs
ABLATIVE	ser´vō	ser´vīs

Gender and Agreement

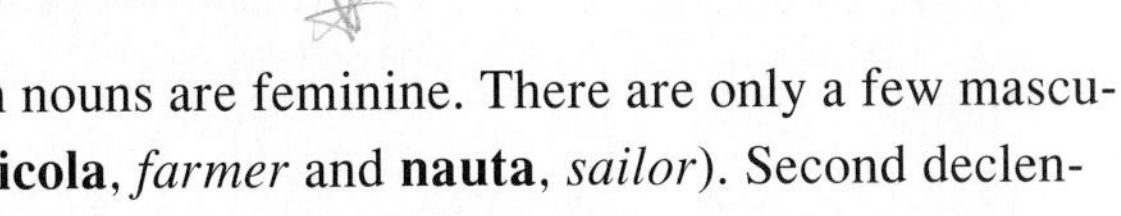

Most first declension nouns are feminine. There are only a few masculine nouns (such as **agricola**, *farmer* and **nauta**, *sailor*). Second declension nouns are either masculine or neuter. We will discuss the neuter nouns in a later lesson.

Remember that adjectives must agree with the noun they modify in gender, number, and case. Sometimes this means that they have the exact same ending. Adjectives whose masculine nominative singular form ends in **–us** are declined just like **servus**. Adjectives whose feminine nominative singular ends in **–a** are declined just like **silva.**

	servōs magnōs	masculine accusative plural
	aquam multam	feminine accusative singular
BUT	**agricola bonus**	masculine nominative singular

ORAL PRACTICE

1. Give the nominative plural of **īnsula, equus, fortūna, carrus.**
2. Give the accusative plural of **aqua, servus, fāma, carrus, via.**
3. Give the Latin for *you* (sing.) *get, they are carrying, we do praise, she is working.*

SEF/Art Resource, NY

The Romans built a highly efficient road system throughout the empire. This one, still in use in Vetulonia, Italy, shows how well the top layer of stones fitted together. The various layers of sand, stone, and pebbles provided a very stable foundation.

A mail coach was often used to deliver messages and parcels throughout Rome and her empire. The excellent road system built by the Romans helped mail move fairly efficiently.

Erich Lessing/Art Resource, NY

EXERCISES 

A. Translate the following sentences into good English.

1. Viae sunt malae.
2. Servus erat parvus.
3. Servus nōn est malus.
4. Magnī equī sunt et bonī.
5. Carrī magnī sunt sed equī sunt parvī.
6. Servī aquam laudant.
7. Servus malus in terrā labōrat.
8. Agricola magnōs carrōs spectat.
9. Ubi servī multōs carrōs parant?
10. Puella et agricola longam vītam laudant.

B. Supply the Latin words for the English.

1. (*Wagons*) nunc nōn sunt.
2. Nunc fortūna (*bad*) est.
3. (*The farmer*) equōs bonōs parat.
4. Agricolae (*the good slaves*) laudant.
5. Ubi est (*the large island*)?
6. Amāmus (*the girl*) quod bona est.
7. Aquam (*the large slaves*) portant.
8. (*Large wagons*) agricolae spectant.

C. Copy the following sentences, adding the correct endings.

1. Bon__ est equus.
2. Carrī long__ sunt.
3. Serv__ aqu__ portant.
4. Ubi sunt vi__ long__?
5. Puella est parv__ et bon__.
6. Puellae īnsulam ama__.
7. Serv__ agricola specta__.
8. Servus equum mal__ nōn ama__.
9. In īnsulā terr__ dūr__ erat.
10. Bon__ serv__ puellam bon__ laudat.

Latin for American Students

Did you know that slaves in Roman times were sometimes slaveowners themselves? A cashier named Musicus Scurranus, who was employed in one of the provincial treasuries of Emperor Tiberius, was very wealthy and had at least sixteen household slaves of his own. Scurranus was evidently admired by his slaves because they dedicated a funeral monument in his honor which exists today.

Vocabulary

Nouns

car´rus, car´rī, *m. cart, wagon*	(car, carriage)
e´quus, e´quī, *m. horse*	(equestrian, equine)
ser´vus, ser´vī, *m. slave, servant*	(servile, servitude)

Adjective

ma´lus, ma´la, ma´lum, *bad* (malice, malign)

Verbs

e´rat, *he, she, it was*
e´rant, *they were*
laudō, laudāre, [laudāvī, laudātus], *praise* (applaud, laudatory)

Adverbs

nunc, *now*
ōlim, *once, formerly, sometime*
u´bi, *where* (ubiquitous)

Conjunction

quod, *because*

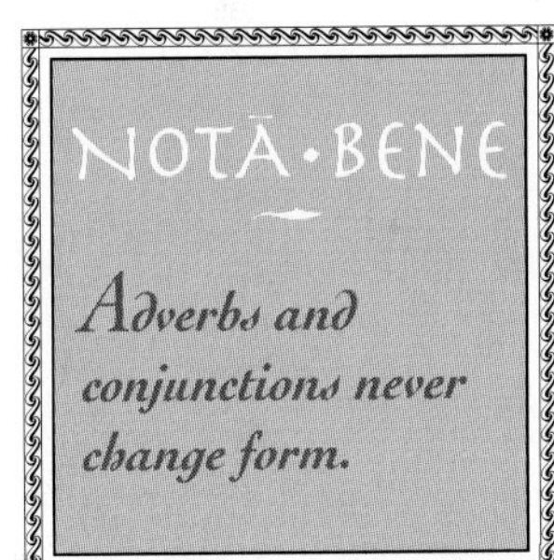

NOTĀ·BENE
Adverbs and conjunctions never change form.

Word Studies

Like first declension nouns, second declension nouns have also contributed several words to our English language and heritage. It does not take a *genius* to see that a *bonus* is something good. Use a dictionary to look up the meanings and plurals of the following words. Which ones retain the Latin (**–i**) plural and which have adopted the English plural form?

alumnus	*stimulus*	*locus*
bacillus	*campus*	*focus*
circus	*fungus*	*humus*

Work with a partner (and a map of the U. S., if necessary) to make a list of the states, cities, and towns that show how Latin influenced the building of this country. Here are a few to get you started: Alma, Augusta, Cincinnati, Columbus, Paramus, and Urbana. Compare your list with other classroom partners.

Glimpses of Roman Life

ROMAN ROADS AND TRAVEL

Perhaps nothing better demonstrates the industry, thoroughness, and engineering skill of the Romans than the system of roads with which they linked their empire. Built like walls as much as three feet deep into the ground, and running in straight lines across all but the most difficult terrain, many of these roads are still in use today, an example to the modern world. They are more than monuments to Roman building skills; they are testimony to the practical vision of a people who quickly saw that their military conquests would be made permanent, and commerce and colonization would flourish, only with extensive and efficient means of communication. The Roman army, under the supervision of engineers, built much of the nearly 50,000 miles of hard-surface highways—enough to circle the globe twice—radiating out from Rome through Italy and beyond. For a faster means of travel, the world had to wait until the eighteenth century, when the invention of the steam engine made railroads and steamships possible.

The construction of our railroads is a better parallel to the Romans' efforts than our present system of superhighways, for westward expansion was supported initially by the railway system. Even now, well over 2000 years after the Romans built many of their roads, America's system of interstate highways is still being completed.

The queen of Roman highways (**rēgīna viārum,** as the Roman poet Statius said) was the Appian Way, built in 312 B.C., just after the Romans had subdued Latium. Like most Roman roads, it took its name from its builder, the censor Appius Claudius. The **Via Appia** stretched about 130 miles from Rome to Capua, the most important city in southern Italy, and brought all Campania close to the capital. Later it was extended more than 200 miles across Italy to Brundisium, the important seaport gateway to Greece and the Orient. The first part of its course, just outside the boundaries of ancient Rome, was lined by family tombs. Much of the **Via Appia** is still in use today.

It is not difficult to imagine the bustle and confusion of these great arteries of commerce, crowded with all sorts of travelers and vehicles. Horses, mules, carriages, and litters were used by those who did not wish to journey on foot. All along the roads there were milestones to indicate distances from the **milliarium aureum,** the golden milestone erected by Augustus in Rome. Footpaths often were constructed along the roadside. There were benches and fountains where the weary might refresh themselves, and watering troughs for the animals. Still, travel was slow and difficult (the word *travel* basically means "torture"; compare the related word *travail*). Fifty to sixty miles a day was a fast rate for people in a great hurry. Half that speed was average.

If the roads were good, the hotel accommodations were often poor. Those who could afford it avoided the cramped, dirty, and uncomfortable inns where horses were sheltered under the same roof, and stayed overnight at country villas belonging to themselves or to their friends. A wealthy Roman might have half a dozen or more villas scattered throughout Italy and was always prepared to extend hospitality to friends.

Travel by water was avoided if possible, but there were fortunes to be made in overseas trade, and merchants swallowed their fear of the unpredictable sea and weather and took their cargoes to sea in small vessels propelled by sails and oars. Sailing was often dangerous, and without a compass for guidance the ships skirted the coast as much as possible. Sailors almost never put to sea during the winter months.

All these roads, by land or sea, led back to Rome as well. Along them came not just people and goods, but ideas too: Greek art and literature, Eastern religions, and eventually Christianity.

QUESTIONS

1. Why were the Romans great road builders?
2. What effect has rapid transportation had on the development of the United States, Canada, and Europe?
3. For many centuries, humans could travel no faster than the horses they rode. What discoveries have enabled us to move faster?

Larry Mulvehill/Photo Researchers

The Appian Way was known as the "Regina Viarum" (Queen of the Roads). It was the triumphal road of the victorious Roman armies and an important route for trade. Built in 312 B.C. between Rome and Capua, it eventually stretched for over 500 miles, uniting Rome with southern Italy. The paving stones are slabs of basalt.

Unit I Review
LESSONS I-IV

Vocabulary

Nouns

Pronounce the following nouns, and provide the gender and meaning of each.

agricola	fāma	puella	terra
aqua	familia	servus	via
carrus	fortūna	silva	vīta
equus	īnsula		

Adjectives

Pronounce the following adjectives, and provide the feminine nominative form and meaning.

bonus	longus	malus	novus
dūrus	magnus	multus	parvus

Verbs

Pronounce the following verbs and provide the rest of the principal parts and meanings (for *erat, erant, est,* and *sunt,* just provide the meanings).

erat, erant	amō	laudō	portō
est, sunt	labōrō	parō	spectō

Adverbs

Pronounce the following adverbs and provide their meanings.

minimē	nunc	sīc	ubi
nōn			

Conjunctions

Pronounce the following conjunctions and provide their meanings.

et quod sed

Interjections

salvē, salvēte valē, valēte

Grammar Summary

Nouns

In Latin, nouns

- show number by their endings.

Agricola equum spectat.	**Agricolae equōs spectant.**
Equus agricolam spectat.	**Equī agricolās spectant.**

Adjectives

In Latin, adjectives

- change form to agree with the noun they modify in number, gender, and case.
- generally follow the noun.

Servus bonus aquam multam portat.

Verbs

In Latin, verb

- endings show person and number.
- pronoun subjects are usually omitted.

Longam īnsulam spectat. **Equum amō.**

Unit I Review
LESSONS I-IV

Endings and Stems

1. What are the endings of the nominative case, singular and plural, in the first declension? In the second declension?
2. What are the endings of the accusative case, singular and plural, in the first declension? In the second declension?
3. How do you find the present stem of a Latin verb? With what letter does the stem of a first-conjugation verb end? What are the six personal endings?

Unit Practice

A. In the following sentences, identify the subject, the verb, and the object (when there is one). Translate each sentence into English.

1. Equus est parvus.
2. Longam viam nunc parātis.
3. Carrī parvī equōs nōn portant.
4. Agricola fortūnam bonam laudat.
5. Servus et puella multam aquam portant.
6. Anna puellās spectat.
7. In Siciliā viae sunt parvae.
8. Virginia et Anna equōs amant.
9. Silvae erant magnae et longae.
10. In silvā aquam bonam parātis?

B. Give the Latin for the italicized words.

1. Anna loves *horses.*
2. It is *a long road.*
3. My slaves are *small.*
4. Anna is *a good girl.*
5. I see the *large wagons.*
6. These horses are *small.*
7. He sees *a small island.*
8. We praise *good water.*

C. Identify the number and case of the following: **fortūna, īnsulam, equī, servōs, via.** Give the correct form of **magnus** with each of the above words.

D. Working with a partner, create a short dialogue using as many words as possible from page 36. Then act out your dialogue in class.

Word Studies

Judging from the meaning of their Latin roots, what do you think the following italicized words mean?

a *laudable* success, *conservation* of energy, to live in *amity*, a *multitude* of errors, *aquatic* sports

Unit II

Rome and Her Empire

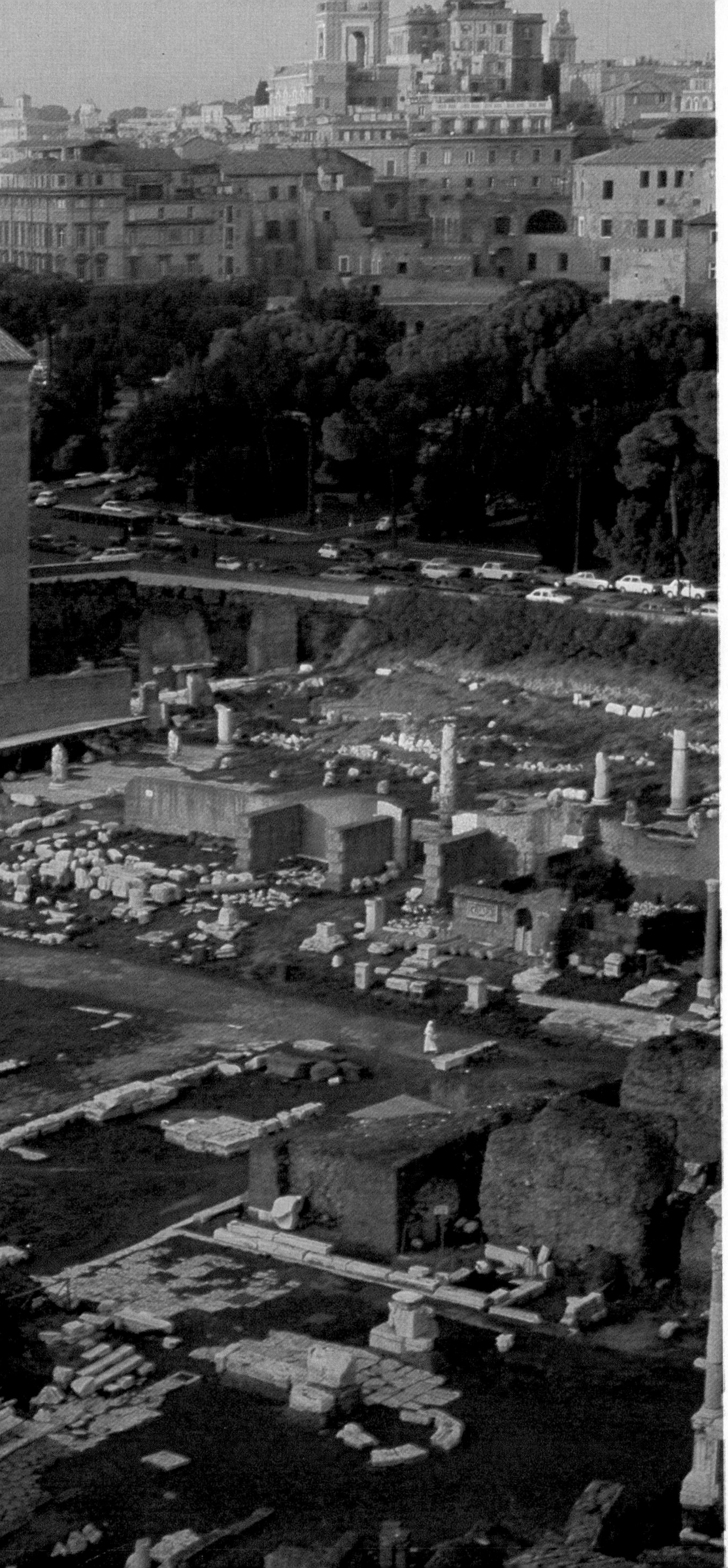

C. M. Dixon

*The square building known as the Senate House, or **Curia** in the Roman Forum, is where the Roman lawmakers assembled. This building was the scene of all the major decisions that made Rome a great power. Modern public buildings often recall ideas that were important in ancient Rome.*

Rōma prīmō[1] parva erat et Rōmānī nōn multī erant. Propter septem montēs,[2] urbs[3] nōn plāna erat, sed fōrma Rōmae quadrāta[4] erat. Postea urbs magna et clāra erat; regīna terrārum erat. Fortūna Rōmae et Rōmānōrum bona erat.

Viae Romanae multae et longae erant. Regīna viārum erat Via Appia. Olim erat magnus numerus carrōrum et equōrum in Viā Appiā. Nunc in viīs Italiae nōn multī carrī et equī sunt. Olim multī servī erant in viīs Rōmānīs, sed nōn iam.[5]

Quod aqua bona erat magna cura Rōmānōrum, erant multī et longī aquaeductūs[6] in Latiō[7] antīquō. Etiam nunc copia aquae clārae est cūra multōrum Italiānōrum et multōrum Americānōrum.

Fāma Rōmae magna est. Fāma Americae etiam magna est. Americānī viās bonās et aquaeductionēs et architecturam Rōmānōrum amant.

Multī Americānī Rōmam laudant; ruīnās antīquās Rōmae spectant et laudant. Fōrmam Rōmae antīquae et novae spectant. Pictūrās ruīnārum Rōmānārum amātis?

[1] *at first*
[2] *on account of its seven hills*
[3] *city*
[4] *square*
[5] *not now = no longer*
[6] *aqueducts*
[7] *Latium*

QUESTIONS

1. What was Rome's original size and shape?
2. What did Rome's water supply have to do with its growth?
3. What attraction now does Rome have for tourists?
4. How do people today show their appreciation for Roman art and architecture?

Grammar

The Genitive Case

In Latin, the *genitive case* is used to show possession. There is no need to use an apostrophe or the word "of." You simply place the genitive ending on the person or thing that is doing the possessing. A genitive will usually follow its noun.

Scala/Art Resource, NY

A model of ancient Rome as seen from the Aventine hill. The Circus Maximus is the long oval near the center and the Colosseum is to the right; beyond the Circus Maximus is the Palatine hill and then the Roman Forum. The Tiber River is in the foreground.

aqua Annae	*the water of Anna OR Anna's water*
equus agricolae	*the horse of the farmer OR the farmer's horse*
carrus servī	*the wagon of the servant OR the servant's wagon*

Of course, you sometimes need to use the plural.

aqua puellārum	*the water of the girls OR the girls' water*
terra agricolārum	*the land of the farmers OR the farmers' land*
viae Rōmānōrum	*the roads of the Romans OR the Romans' roads*

However, sometimes when there is no possession shown, the preposition *of* is used in English. In Latin, the genitive case is also used to show this relationship.

copia cibī	*a supply of food*
multī Rōmānōrum	*many of the Romans*

PRACTICE

1. Give the genitive of the following nouns: **servus, silva, puella, equus.**
2. Give the Latin for the following phrases: *of the queen, of Rome, of the wagons.*

The Ablative of *Place Where*

The ablative case is used in several ways in Latin. You have already seen, and probably used, one of them a few times. The ablative is used to show *where* something or someone is. To do this, you use the preposition **in** + the ablative.

in silvā	*in the forest*
in Siciliā	*in Sicily*

PRACTICE

1. Translate the following phrases into Latin: *in the forest, on the island, in the water.*
2. Translate the following phrases into good English: **in Britanniā, in viā.**

EXERCISES

A. Translate the following sentences into good English. Pay careful attention to the endings.

1. Equōs amāmus.
2. Est cōpia aquae bonae.
3. Fōrma terrae in Siciliā plāna nōn est.
4. Cūrae puellārum parvae sunt.
5. Numerus servōrum in īnsulā erat magnus.
6. Silvās clārās īnsulae magnae spectātis.

B. Translate the words in parentheses into Latin.

1. Cōpiam (*of good water*) portāmus.
2. Terram novam (*we are looking at*).
3. (*There is not*) rēgīna Americae.
4. Parvus est numerus (*of the girls*) (*in Italy*).
5. Cibus (*of the slaves*) parvus erat.

C. Working with a partner, ask and answer questions following the model.

cibus / equus / via — *–Ubi est cibus equī?* *–Cibus equī est in viā.*

1. aqua / servī / carrus
2. carrī / agricola / terra
3. equī / puellae / silva
4. terrae / regina / Britannia
5. rana / servus / aqua

Latin for American Students

Did you know that the early Romans were strict vegetarians and often ate their food cold? There was very little difference between the meals of the wealthy and the poor. However, these frugal eating habits contrasted sharply with those of wealthy Romans of the later Republic who relished such delicacies as sow's udder in tuna sauce, raw sea urchins, peacock brains, flamingo tongues, and jellyfish.

Even today, tourists admire the ruins of the Colosseum in Rome, built over two thousand years ago. Gladiators sometimes fought against each other to the death, other times against wild animals. One of the most incredible spectacles that took place here was a re-enactment of a naval battle using real ships. The whole arena basin was flooded.

N. Yoshida/SuperStock

Vocabulary

Nouns

ci´bus, ci´bī, *m. food*

cō´pia, cō´piae, *f. supply, abundance* (copious, cornucopia)

cū´ra, cū´rae, *f. care, concern* (curator, curious)

fōr´ma, fōr´mae, *f. shape* (formal, reformatory)

nu´merus, nu´merī, *m. number* (enumerate, numerical)

rēgī´na, rēgī´nae, *f. queen* (regina)

Adjectives

anti´quus, anti´qua, anti´quum, *old, ancient* (antiquary, antiquated)

clā´rus, clā´ra, clā´rum, *clear, famous* (clarinet, clarion)

plā´nus, plā´na, plā´num, *level* (aquaplane, plain)

Rōmā´nus, Rōmā´na, Rōmā´num, *Roman* (romaine, romance)

Adverbs

etiam, *even, also*

pos´teā, *afterwards*

Preposition

in (+ abl.), *in, on*

Word Studies

Many Latin phrases and abbreviations are used regularly in English. Which of the following have you heard or used when speaking?

i.e. (id est), *that is*

e.g. (exemplī grātiā), *for example*

etc. (et cetera), *and the rest, and so forth*

nōn sequitur, *it doesn't follow*

magnā cum laude, *with great praise, honor*

in locō parentis, *in place of a parent*

carpe diem, *seize the day*

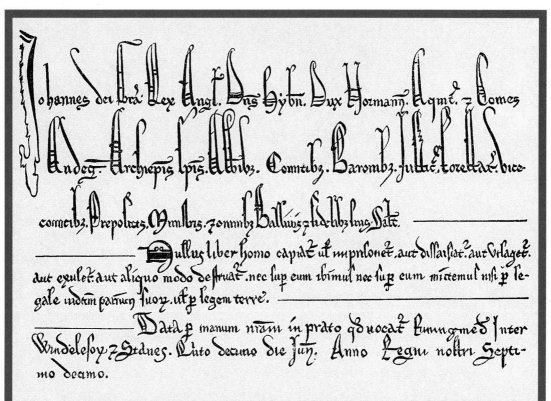

Stock Montage

A detail of the Magna Charta, the charter of English political and civil liberties, written in 1215. Which of these Latin words are familiar to you?

Perhaps you have heard of the **Magna Charta** (the *Great Paper*), a document signed in 1215 that is one of the cornerstones of English liberties.

Work with another student or in small groups to figure out what the following phrases mean.

an *ad hoc* committee	a professor *emeritus*
a *per diem* allowance	a *de facto* decision
a *quid pro quo* arrangement	a *post mortem* examination
a story that is told *ad nauseam*	a *status quo* situation

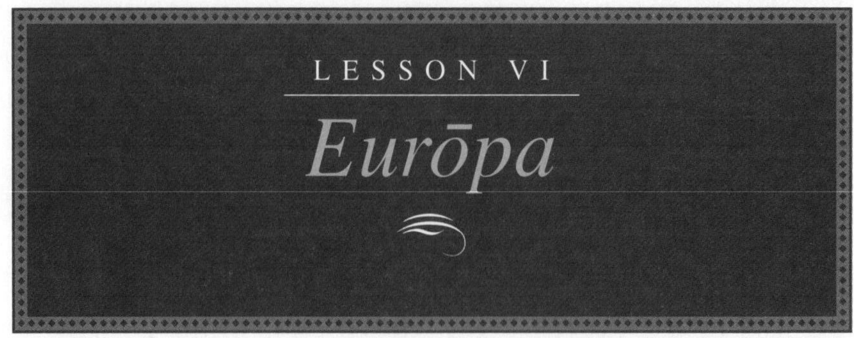

Ad Eurōpam nāvigābō; tōta familia nāvigābit. Nautae nāvem[1] novam parābunt. Magnam pecūniam ad Eurōpam portābimus. Cibum nōn parābimus, quod in nāvi[2] magna cōpia cibī bonī est.

Magnās undās spectābimus; sed aquam plānam, nōn magnās undās, amāmus. Ad īnsulam clāram Britanniam nāvigābimus. In Britanniā familia domum[3] rēgīnae spectābit. Ruīnās Rōmānās in Britanniā spectābō. Tum tōta familia ad Galliam nāvigābit. In Galliā rēgīna nōn est, sed familia multās pictūrās spectābit. Ruīnās Rōmānās in Galliā spectābō.

Tum ad Germāniam et ad Austriam ībimus.[4] Familia pictūrās et statuās in Germāniā et in Austriā spectābit, sed ruīnās Rōmānās spectābō. Tum ad Italiam ībimus. In Italiā tōta familia ruīnās Rōmānās spectābit.

Rēgīnās et pictūrās et statuās et terrās novās spectābō, sed ruīnās Rōmānās amō et semper[5] amābō.

[1] *ship* (acc. sing.)
[2] *ship* (abl. sing.)
[3] *house*
[4] *we shall go*
[5] *always*

QUESTIONS

1. Who is going to Europe?
2. Where can you find Roman ruins in Europe?
3. What does the speaker in this story especially like?

Grammar

The Future Tense

The *future* tense refers to something that *will* happen at some *future* time. In Latin, the future of the first conjugation is formed by adding the tense sign **–bi–** (which corresponds to *shall* and *will* in English) to the present stem and then attaching the same personal endings as in the present:

Wayne Rowe

Rome's empire outside Italy was divided into provinces (see map, pages 102-103). All of Gaul (ancient France) was finally made a Roman province by Julius Caesar in the first century B.C. This Roman amphitheater at Nîmes, France, is sometimes used for bullfights, not unlike the shows held there in ancient times.

SINGULAR	PLURAL
portā**bo**, *I shall carry*	portā**bimus**, *we shall carry*
portā**bis**, *you will carry*	portā**bitis**, *you will carry*
portā**bit**, *he, she, it will carry*	portā**bunt**, *they will carry*

NOTĀ·BENE

The future sign **–bi–** *drops the* **i** *before* **–ō** *in the first person singular and changes to* **–bu–** *before* **–nt** *in the third person plural.*

Aquam bonam laudābō.
I shall praise the good water.

Agricolae terram spectābunt.
The farmers will look at the land.

ORAL PRACTICE

1. Conjugate **labōrō** and **nāvigō** in the future tense, and translate.
2. Translate **labōrātis, portābit, nāvigāmus, parant, spectābitis.**

Prepositions

Prepositions are used in Latin much as they are in English. All prepositions in Latin are followed by either the accusative or ablative case. You must learn the case as you learn the meaning, just as you learn the gender of a noun. Some of the common prepositions you will want to use are:

ad (+ acc.), *to, toward*
prope (+ acc.), *near*
trans (+ acc.), *across*
cum (+ abl.), *with*
sine (+ abl.), *without*

Equus Annam ad viam portat.	*The horse carries Anna to the road.*
Cum agricolīs labōrābō.	*I shall work with the farmers.*

IN AQUAM IN AQUĀ

A few prepositions can take both the accusative and ablative cases, and the meaning changes somewhat. The most common one is **in**.

in (+ abl.), *in, on* **in** (+ acc.), *into*

In insulā est.	*She is on the island.*
In silvam aquam portat.	*She carries the water into the woods.*

AD AQUAM IN AQUAM

PRACTICE

1. Translate the following phrases into good English: **ad silvam, in Galliā, sine aquā**.
2. Give the Latin for the following: *with the slaves, across the island, into Italy.*

EXERCISES

A. Translate the following sentences while paying particular attention to the endings.

1. Ad silvam cibum portābunt.
2. Nunc carrum rēgīnae laudāmus.
3. Ad terram novam nāvigābimus.
4. Magnae undae ad īnsulam sunt.
5. Ubi magnam cōpiam cibī parābis?
6. Nautae ad īnsulam plānam nāvigābunt.
7. Anna ad familiam cōpiam aquae portābit.
8. Ubi undae erant, fōrma terrae plāna est.
9. Ad insulam cum regina navigābis.
10. Familia sine fortunā est.

B. Translate the words in italics into Latin.

1. Ad terrās novās (*we shall sail*).
2. Multōs carrōs (*he will prepare*).
3. Undās magnās (*they will look at*).
4. Ad familiam nautae pecūniam (*I shall carry*).
5. Numerus undārum magnus (*was*).

C. Identify the construction and provide the missing endings.

1. Est cōpia cib__ bon__ (*of the good food*).
2. Ubi sunt silv__ īnsul__ (*the islands*)?
3. Cōpiam pecūni__ (*of money*) parā__ (*we shall get*).
4. Familia naut__ (*sailor's*) ad īnsul__ nāvigā__ (*will sail*).
5. Agricolae terr__ plān__ (*the flat land*) amā__ (*will like*).

Scala/Art Resource, NY

The Romans used coinage from the early days of the republic. The denarius was a silver coin first minted in 187 B.C., though its use stopped in the A.D. 200s. The standard coin of the Roman Empire was the gold aureus. There were 25 denarii to one aureus. There were 10 asses to the denarius. A sesterce was a silver or bronze coin worth about a fourth of a denarius.

Vocabulary

Nouns

nau´ta, nau´tae, *m. sailor* (astronaut, nautical)
pecū´nia, pecū´niae, *f. money* (impecunious, pecuniary)
un´da, un´dae, *f. wave* (surround, undulate)

Adjective

tō´tus, tō´ta, tō´tum,[1] *whole, all* (totality)

Verb

nā´vigō, nāvigā´re, [nāvigā´vī, nāvigā´tus], *sail* (navigation, navy)

Adverbs

crās, *tomorrow* (procrastinate)
tum, *then*

Prepositions

ad (+ acc.), *to, toward, near* (adapt, adduce)
cum (+ abl.), *with*
in (+ acc.), *into* (incise)
sine (+ abl.), *without*
trāns (+ acc.), *across* (transact, transfer)

Latin for American Students

Did you know that Rome's equivalent to Wall Street was the ***Via Sacra****? Here the banking houses provided money-changing and money-lending services; handled deposits and checking accounts; sold bills of exchange on distant cities; negotiated loans; made sales, purchases, and investments for their clients; and collected debts. The banks also provided music and wine to customers while doing business!*

[1] The genitive singular of **tōtus** is irregular: **tō´tius, tō´tius, tō´tius.**

Word Studies

The vocabulary words in this lesson have provided the base for several words in English. Find the Latin root in each of the following words, look up the actual definitions, then use them in English sentences.

impecunious	procrastinate	navigable
inundated	nautilus	redundant

Prepositions are often used as prefixes. You can frequently figure out the meaning of an unfamiliar English word by breaking it down into its Latin prefix and root. Find the prefix and root of the following words and try to guess what they mean. Then look up each word and use it in an English sentence.

sinecure	transport	input
component	adopt	transformation

LESSON VII

Sunt Saturnalia

Anna et Clara beātae sunt quod Saturnālia sunt. Saturnālia diēs festī[1] est. Tōtae familiae Rōmānae Saturnum laudant. Saturnus deus est. Dominī et servī et fēminae et puellae celebrant et septem diēs[2] celebrābunt. Amīcī celebrant. Magna copia cibī est. Servī nōn labōrant. Amicī dōna[3] amicīs dōnant. Anna et Clara amīcae sunt. Anna Clarae dōnum[4] dōnat.

ANNA: Saturnālia celebrāre amō.

CLARA: Egō[5] etiam.

ANNA: Es mea amīca, Clara. Tibi[6] dōnum dōnō.

CLARA: Benignē, Anna. Pupa parva est! Pupās amō. Nunc dōnum tibi dōnō.

ANNA: Benignē, Clara. O, est pupa grāta etiam!

CLARA: Puellīs et feminīs pupās mōnstrābimus!

Anna et Clara amicīs pupās mōnstrant, sed amicīs pupās nōn mandant. Puellae cum curā pupās portant. Beātae sunt.

[1] *festival*
[2] *seven days*
[3] *gifts*
[4] *gift*
[5] *I*
[6] *to you*

QUESTIONS

1. Who was honored during the Saturnalia?
2. How did the Romans celebrate this holiday?
3. What was surprising about the life of the slaves during Saturnalia?

Latin for American Students

Did you know that Roman children often played with dolls made of rags, clay or wax, often with jointed arms and legs? Roman children also enjoyed hitching tame mice or rats to tiny carts, building model houses, riding on hobbyhorses, spinning tops, playing hide-and-seek and blindman's bluff, and rolling hoops with a stick. These hoops even had bits of metal attached to warn people in their way.

Grammar

The Dative Case

The *dative case* is used to indicate the *indirect object* of the verb. The indirect object is most commonly used after such verbs as *give, show, tell,* and *entrust*. In English, we often use the prepositions *to* or *for* to show this relationship. The preposition can be dropped in English, but the dative case is always used in Latin. Usually the dative case precedes the accusative case, giving a general Latin word order of: nominative, dative, accusative, verb.

Equō aquam dōnābō.	*I shall give water to the horse.* *I shall give the horse water.*
Nauta rēgīnae insulam mōnstrat.	*The sailor shows the island to the queen.* *The sailor shows the queen the island.*

NOTĀ·BENE

Because you are nearly always going to be giving, showing, telling, or entrusting something to or for someone, the dative case is nearly always a person or an animate object.

Alinari/Art Resource, NY

Festivals were an important aspect of Roman life, and women often played a very important part. The New Year festival was celebrated on March 1, when the Vestal Virgins lit a new fire in their temple. The Lupercalia, to celebrate the founding of Rome, was held in February and the Saturnalia, a huge festival that included gift-giving, was celebrated in December.

NOTĀ·BENE

Remember that after verbs of motion like "come" and "go," to is expressed in Latin by the preposition ad followed by the accusative.

1. HE WENT *TO THE CITY* AS FAST AS HE COULD (ACCUSATIVE WITH AD).

2. HE TOLD HIS STORY *TO THE OFFICER* AND SHOWED *HIM* HIS DRIVER'S LICENSE (DATIVES OF INDIRECT OBJECT).

ORAL PRACTICE

1. Give the dative of the following: **servus, agricolae, nauta, dominī.**
2. Put the following phrases in the dative: *to the horses, for the family, to the sailors, for the master.*
3. Tell which case you would use if you were translating the words in italics into Latin.
   a. Give *me* the horses.
   b. I showed *Anna* the book.
   c. I told my *friend* the whole story.
   d. We carried our bags to the *station.*
   e. He presented his library to the *president.*
   f. He told *me* how to go to the *wharf.*
   g. They moved to *California.*
   h. Do it for *me.*
   i. Show *him* to *me.*

EXERCISES

A. Translate the following sentences while paying particular attention to the endings.

1. Familiae pecūniam dōnābit.
2. Puellae litterās mandāmus.
3. Servō praedam nōn mōnstrābimus.
4. Amīcīs bonīs litterās mandābis.
5. Anna Clarae magnam pecūniam dōnābit.
6. Carrī ad silvam parvam aquam clāram portant.
7. Rēgīna puellae magnam pecūniam mandat.
8. Annae viās silvae mōnstrābō.

B. Identify the case needed for the words in italics, then translate into Latin.

1. (*To many lands*) nāvigābimus.
2. (*To the sailor*) litterās mandābō.
3. (*To the sailors*) viam mōnstrant.
4. (*To Anna*) fortūnam bonam nūntiābit.
5. (*To many families*) pecūniam dōnat.

C. Say what the following people are going to receive as gifts from the master at Saturnalia.

Anna parva / pupa grata — *Dominus Annae parvae pupam gratam donabit.*

1. agricola bonus / terrae planae
2. magna rēgīna / equus novus
3. antiquī amicī / pecūnia magna
4. clārus nauta / servus magnus
5. beāta familia / fortūna bona

Scala/Art Resource, NY

Young Roman girls often played with dolls, such as this one with jointed arms and legs. Dolls were often exchanged as gifts between friends at the Saturnalia celebrations.

Vocabulary

Nouns

amī´cus, amī´ci, *m. friend* (amicable)
do´minus, do´minī, *m. master* (dominant, dominate)
fē´mina, fē´minae, *f. woman, wife* (feminine, feminist)
li´ttera, li´tterae, *f. letter (of the alphabet); plural, a letter (epistle)* (literal, literary)[1]
prae´da, prae´dae, *f. loot, booty* (predator, prey)
pū´pa, pū´pae, *f. doll, little girl* (pupil, puppy)

Adjectives

amī´cus, amī´ca, amī´cum, *friendly* (amicable)
beā´tus, beā´ta, beā´tum, *happy, blessed* (beatific)
grā´tus, grā´ta, grā´tum, *pleasing, grateful* (grateful, gratitude)
me´us, me´a, me´um, *my*

[1] Except for *letter,* all the English derivatives have one *t,* based on an older spelling **lītera.**

Verbs

ce´lebrō, celebrā´re, celebrā´vī, celebrā´tus, *celebrate, honor* (celebration, celebratory)

dō´nō, dōnā´re, dōnā´vī, dōnā´tus, *give, present* (donate, pardon)

man´dō, mandā´re, mandā´vī, mandā´tus, *entrust* (mandate, mandatory)

mōn´strō, mōnstrā´re, mōnstrā´vī, mōnstrā´tus, *point out, show* (demonstrate, monstrance)

nūn´tiō, nūntiā´re, nūntiā´vī, nūntiā´tus, *announce, report* (pronunciation, renunciation)

pro´bō, probā´re, probā´vī, probā´tus, *test, prove, approve* (probation, probe)

Phrase

benig´nē, *thank you*

Word Studies

Try to see the relation between the meaning of the English derivative and the Latin word from which it comes, and then use the derivative in a sentence.

1. A "literary" man is a man of *letters;* a "literal" translation is one that is almost *letter for letter.*
2. A "mandate" is something *entrusted* to a person or a group, as the government of a weak nation.
3. A "novelty" is something *new.*
4. A person who is on "probation" is being *tested.*

In the same way explain a *familiar* friend, an *undulating* river, an *amicable* attitude, an interested *spectator*.

ITALIA
Scale of Miles
0 25 50 75 100
N
S
E
W
8°
10°
12°
14°
16°
18°
46°
44°
42°
40°
38°
36°
A L P E S
VENETIA
Mediolanum
Ticinus
Verona
Mantua
Aug. Taurinorum
GALLIA
Padus
LIGURIA
Trebia
Genua
APPENNINUS
MONS
Rubico
Ariminum
Metaurus
Pisae
Arnus
Florentia
Sentinum
UMBRIA
Aesis
Arretium
L. Trasumennus
Clusium
ETRURIA
PICENUM
Asculum
Volsinii
Falerii
Narnia
PAELIGNI
SABINI
FRENTANI
CORSICA
Aleria
Tarquinii
Feronia
Carsioli
Veii
Caere
Anio
MARSI
Tibur
Roma
Praeneste
Ostia
LATIUM
Tiberis
Antium
Fregellae
Circei
Formiae
Luceria
Bovianum
SAMNIUM
Aufidus
Beneventum
Cannae
APULIA
Capua
F. Caudinae
Cumae
CAMPANIA
Neapolis
Pompeii
Venusia
Brundisium
CALABRIA
Tarentum
LUCANIA
Paestum
Heraclea
SARDINIA
MARE TYRRHENUM
Caralis
MAGNA GRAECIA
BRUTTIUM
Croton
Locri
Rhegium
Messana
Mylae
ILLYRICUM
MARE HADRIATICUM
Ercte M.
Eryx M.
Panormus
AEGATES INS.
Drepana
Lilybaeum
SICILIA
Aetna M.
Catana
CALATHA I.
Hippo Zarytus
Agrigentum
Gela
Ecnomus
Syracusae
Utica
Carthago
Pr. Mercurii
Bagrada
COSSYRA
Pachynum Pr.
NUMIDIA
AFRICA

Rōmānī Galliam occupant et magnam praedam parant. Gallī silvīs fortūnās et familiās mandant. Rōmānī Gallīs magnās poenās parant. Poenae dūrae sunt. Tum memoria iniūriārum prōvinciam Galliam ad pugnam incitat. Gallī Rōmānīs nūntiant:

"Terram nostram[1] pugnīs occupātis. Praedam magnam ad Italiam multīs carrīs portātis. Poenae nostrae[1] dūrae sunt. Sed pugnābimus et victōriīs nostrīs[1] vītam[1] et pecūniam nostram servābimus. Iniūriīs et poenīs nōs[2] ad pugnam incitātis. Pugnāre parāmus. Familiīs nostrīs victōriās grātās nūntiābimus, sed victōriās grātās Rōmae nōn nūntiābitis."

Gallī diū et fortiter[3] pugnant, sed multae et clārae sunt victōriae Rōmānōrum. Pugnīs Gallī vītam et terram nōn servant.

Ubi est prōvincia Gallia? Gallōs accūsātis quod pugnāvērunt?[4] Animum Gallōrum nōn laudātis? Memoriae pugnās Gallōrum mandābitis?

[1] *our*
[2] *us*
[3] *long and bravely*
[4] *they fought*

QUESTIONS

1. What did the Gauls do with their families?
2. What did the Romans do to Gaul?
3. Why is France today considered a Latin country?

Latin for American Students

Did you know that Gaul before the rule of Caesar was divided into three regions named after the appearance of each regions' inhabitants? The region north of the Alps was called ***Braccata*** *because the men there wore long pants. The region south of the Alps was called* ***Togata*** *because the men wore togas and were Roman citizens.* ***Comata*** *was named for the men there who wore long hair.*

[1] In English we use the plural.

Explorer/Photo Researchers

Consisting of three tiers of arcades, the Pont du Gard in Nîmes, France, is a fine example of a Roman aqueduct. It was built in 19 B.C. over a deep gorge to carry water to a fresh-water source about 15 miles from the city.

Grammar

Ablative of Means

In Lesson V, you learned the first of several uses of the ablative case. In addition to expressing *place where,* the ablative is used to express the means or instrument by which something is done. This construction is called the *ablative of means.* In English, we almost always use the preposition *by* or *with* to express this, but in Latin, no preposition is used.

Litterīs victōriam nūntiant.	*They report the victory by (means of) a letter.*
Nauta gladiō pugnat.	*The sailor fights with (by means of) a sword.*

ORAL PRACTICE

Translate the phrases in italics into Latin: he was pushed *(by waves),* we carried the load *(with wagons).*

Adjectives as Substantives

In Latin, an adjective alone is often used to stand for what would be a noun plus an adjective in English. The translation depends on its gender and number, but generally you can substitute man (men), woman (women), or thing(s) along with the meaning of the adjective.

		MASCULINE	
bonus	*a good man*	**Rōmānus**	*a Roman (man)*
bonī	*good men, good people*	**Rōmānī**	*Roman men, Romans*
		FEMININE	
bona	*a good woman*	**Rōmāna**	*a Roman woman*
bonae	*good women*	**Rōmānae**	*Roman women*
		NEUTER	
bonum	*a good thing*	**novum**	*a new thing*
bona	*good things*	**nova**	*new things*

Rōmānī in īnsulā sunt.	*The Romans are on the island.*
Bonās laudō.	*I praise the good women.*

ORAL PRACTICE

Give the English for the following: **parvus, mala** (two ways), **āntiquī**.

EXERCISES

A. Translate the following sentences while paying particular attention to the endings.

1. Pugnīs īnsulam occupātis.
2. Cibō multās familiās servābitis.
3. Victōriīs vītam et prōvinciam servant.
4. Memoriā iniūriae nautās incitās.
5. Aquā vītam equōrum servābimus.
6. Puella memoriae litterās mandābit.
7. Litterīs magnam victōriam rēgīnae nūntiābit.

B. Put the words in italics into Latin, then translate the sentence.

1. (*With money*) nautās incitāmus.
2. (*To friends*) victōriam nūntiābō.
3. (*With care*) vītam amīcī servābō.
4. (*By the victory*) prōvinciam servābimus.
5. Memoria iniūriārum et poenārum gladiīs nautās (*arouses*).

C. Identify the construction, then supply the missing endings.

1. Pecūni__ nautās incitā__ (*I shall urge on*).
2. Serv__ (*of the slaves*) poenam nōn probāmus.
3. Aqu__ (*with water*) silvam serva__ (*they save*).
4. Victōri__ (*by victory*) prōvinciam servā__ (*they will save*).
5. Amīc__ (*to friends*) pecūniam dōnā__ (*I shall give*).

Vocabulary

Nouns

a´nimus, a´nimī, *m. soul, courage, mind* (animated, inanimate)
gla´dius, gla´dī,[2] *m. sword* (gladiator, gladiolus)
iniū´ria, iniū´riae, *f. injustice, wrong, injury* (injurious, injury)
memo´ria, memo´riae, *f. memory* (memorable, memorial)
poe´na, poe´nae, *f. punishment, penalty* (penal, penalize)
provin´cia, provin´ciae, *f. province* (provincial)
pug´na, pug´nae, *f. fight, battle* (pugnacious, repugnant)
victō´ria, victō´riae, *f. victory* (victorious)

Adjective

Gal´lus, Gal´la, Gal´lum, *Gallic (from Gaul)*

Verbs

in´citō, incitā´re, incitā´vī, incitā´tus, *urge on, arouse* (incitement)
oc´cupō, occupā´re, occupā´vī, occupā´tus, *seize* (occupant, occupation)
pug´nō, pugnā´re, pugnā´vī, pugnā´tus, *fight* (impugn, pugnacity)
ser´vō, servā´re, servā´vī, servā´tus, *save, guard* (conservation, preservation)

Word Studies

1. From what Latin words are *curator, reservoir, vitamin,* and *commemoration* derived?
2. Use the following words in a good English sentence that shows you know the Latin root of each: *penal, pugnacious, resuscitate, occupy, impugn.*

---

[2] Second declension nouns whose nominative ends in **–ius** regularly drop the **–i** from the stem in the genitive singular only.

LESSON IX
Cornēlia Nautam Servat

MĀTER[1]: Fīliae, fīliae, paene quīnta hōra est. Portāte aquam ad casam et cibum parāte. Anna, ubi est soror[2] tua Cornēlia?

ANNA: Aquam portābō, māter. Cornēlia in arēnā[3] est. Undās spectat.

MĀTER: Puella ignāva est! Anna, nūntiā Cornēliae cūram meam.

(Nunc quīnta hōra est.)

VOX[4] CORNĒLIAE: Māter! Pater![5] Adiuvāte!

MĀTER: Ēheu! Ēheu![6] Est vox Cornēliae. Fīlia mea exclāmat. Festīnāte!

(Māter et pater et Anna ad arēnam festīnant.)

CORNĒLIA: Spectāte—in undīs! Vir et puer sunt! Remum[7] longum prensant[8] sed sauciī sunt!

PATER: Ubi sunt vir et puer, Cornēlia? Mōnstrā eōs.[9]

(Cornēlia virum et puerum monstrat.)

CORNĒLIA ET ANNA: Festīnā, pater! Servā eōs!

MĀTER: Pater tuus ad virum et puerum natat. Eōs servābit.

ANNA: Spectāte! Pater virum et puerum et remum prensat. Nunc eōs ad arēnam reportābit.[10]

CORNĒLIA: Strāgulum[11] parābō. *(Cornēlia ad casam festīnat.)*

(Nunc decima hōra est. Cornēlia et Anna cibum parant.)

VIR: Fortūna nostra[12] bona erat et grātia nostra magna est.

PUER: Semper familiam tuam laudābimus.

PATER: Aliquandō[13] fīlia mea Cornēlia ignāva est, sed nōn hodiē. Mactē, Cornēlia!

[1] *Mother*
[2] *sister*
[3] *beach*
[4] *voice*
[5] *Father*
[6] *Alas!*
[7] *oar*
[8] *are clutching*
[9] *them*
[10] *will carry back*
[11] *blanket*
[12] *our*
[13] *sometimes*

QUESTIONS

1. Why was Cornelia's mother angry?
2. How were the man and boy saved?
3. How long did the whole incident last?

Grammar

Second Declension Nouns in *–r*

You have already learned about second declension nouns that end in **–us**, like **servus.** There is another group whose nominative ends in **–r.** These nouns have the same endings as the nouns in **–us** (except for the nominative singular), but they may or may not drop the vowel that precedes the **–r** in the stem. It is important to pay particular attention to these nouns in the genitive to see if the vowel is kept or dropped. Nouns in **–r** are declined as follows:

	vir, *man*		**ager,** *field*	
	SINGULAR	PLURAL	SINGULAR	PLURAL
NOMINATIVE	vir	virī	ager	agrī
GENITIVE	virī	virōrum	agrī	agrōrum
DATIVE	virō	virīs	agrō	agrīs
ACCUSATIVE	virum	virōs	agrum	agrōs
ABLATIVE	virō	virīs	agrō	agrīs

Note that **vir** retains the vowel before the **–r** and **ager** drops its **–e–**.

ORAL PRACTICE

1. Decline **puer** in the singular and plural.
2. Identify the case and number of the following (there may be more than one answer): **virō, anīmus, agrōrum, puer, virī, agrīs, dominōs, puerum.**

North Wind Picture Archives

The toga could only be worn by a Roman citizen. Up to the age of 14 or so, boys wore a toga with a purple stripe (toga praetexta), which they then exchanged for the all-white toga virilis or toga of manhood.

Present Imperative

The verbs you have studied so far have been either in the *infinitive form* or in the *indicative mood*. The indicative mood is used to make statements or ask questions. You have studied both the present indicative and the future indicative.

Commands are expressed in both Latin and English by the *imperative mood*.

In Latin, the present imperative singular is the same as the present stem of the verb: **portā,** *carry*. The plural is formed with the ending **–te: portāte,** *carry*. An imperative usually stands at or near the beginning of the sentence.

ORAL PRACTICE

1. Form the singular imperative of *fight, praise, report.*
2. Form the plural imperative of *give, sail, save.*

Latin for American Students

Did you know that Rome's equivalent to Broadway (New York City) was the ***Via Lata****? Traffic on this busy thoroughfare caused so much congestion that heavy vehicles were ordered to move only during the night. On the other hand, some busy streets in Rome were so narrow that residents had to knock on the inside of their doors before leaving, so as not to collide with passersby.*

C. M. Dixon

Servants and slaves accompanied their masters everywhere—visiting friends, doing errands, even going to the baths. They would make purchases at the direction of the master and carry the goods home afterward. This wallpainting is from the first century A.D.

C. M. Dixon

Upon their return home, servants took food purchases to the kitchen for preparation or storage. Fruits and fish were an important part of the Romans' diet. This boy appeared in a mosaic from Pompeii.

EXERCISES

A. Translate the following sentences while paying particular attention to the endings.

1. Mōnstrāte amīcīs viam.
2. Nunc quīnta hōra est; nāvigābimus.
3. Amā fīliam tuam et fīlia tua tē (*you*) amābit.
4. Servā pecūniam tuam et pecūnia tua tē (*you*) servābit.
5. Nautae vītam servōrum laudant et servī vītam nautārum laudant.

B. Give the imperative form of the words in italics. Use both the singular and plural if appropriate, then translate the entire sentence.

1. (*Show*) puerīs litterās meās.
2. (*Arouse*) servum et adiuvābit.
3. Puellae, (*look at*) equōs magnōs.
4. (*Entrust*) fāmam tuam fortūnae.
5. Nunc, nautae, ad prōvinciam (*hurry*).
6. (*Praise*), amīcī, fīliās bonās.
7. (*Help*) bonōs virōs.
8. (*Give*) pecūniam tuam amicīs.
9. (*Seize*) provinciam.
10. (*Save*) vītam puellae cibō.

C. Working with a partner, write a two-line dialogue following the model. The first person gives a command and the second person responds that it will be done. Remember to add any prepositions, as necessary, to make sense.

women / help / men

–Fēminae, adiuvāte virōs!
–Fēminae virōs adiuvābunt.

1. men / save / girls
2. slaves / get ready / wagon
3. farmer / work / fields
4. daughter / prepare / meal
5. sailors / hurry / island

Vocabulary

Nouns

a´ger, a´grī, *m. field* (agrarian, agriculture)
ca´sa, ca´sae, *f. house* (casino)
fī´lia, fī´liae, *f. daughter* (affiliate, filial)
hō´ra, hō´rae, *f. hour* (horary, hour)
pu´er, pu´erī, *m. boy* (puerile, puerilism)
vir, vi´rī, *m. man* (virile, virility)

Adjectives

de´cimus, de´cima, de´cimum, *tenth* (decimal, decimeter)
ignā´vus, ignā´va, ignā´vum, *lazy*
quin´tus, quin´ta, quin´tum, *fifth* (quintet, quintuplet)
sau´cius, sau´cia, sau´cium, *wounded, hurt*
tu´us, tu´a, tu´um, *your, yours* (referring to one person)

Verbs

adiu´vō, adiuvā´re, adiuvā´vī, adiuvā´tus, *help*
excla´mō, exclamā´re, exclamā´vī, exclamā´tus, *shout* (exclaim, exclamation)
festī´nō, festīnā´re, festīnā´vī, festīnā´tus, *hurry* (festinate)
na´tō, natā´re, natā´vī, natā´tus, *swim* (natant, natatorium)

Adverbs

ho´diē, *today*
pae´ne, *almost*
sem´per, *always*

Interjection

mac´tē, *well done!*

Word Studies

Like English, the Romance languages, which are derived from Latin, have also borrowed many words with little or no change. Compare the following list:

FRENCH	SPANISH	PORTUGUESE	ITALIAN
aimer	**amar**	**amar**	**amare**
ami	**amigo**	**amigo**	**amico**
bon	**bueno**	**bom**	**buono**
char	**carro**	**carro**	**carro**
famille	**familia**	**familia**	**famiglia**
forme	**forma**	**forma**	**forma**
heure	**hora**	**hora**	**ora**
lettre	**letra**	**letra**	**lettera**
province	**provincia**	**provincia**	**provincia**
terre	**tierra**	**terra**	**terra**

1. Judging from the Latin, what does each of these French, Spanish, Portuguese, and Italian words mean? Make a parallel column of English words.
2. What other words can you add to this list? Look back at your vocabulary lists for ideas.

"GOOD," ISN'T IT?

Glimpses of Roman Life

THE ETERNAL CITY

Although modern archaeology shows that the site of Rome was inhabited many centuries earlier, the Romans put the founding of their city in 753 B.C. The first settlement was on the Palatine Hill, named after Pales, the goddess of shepherds who was worshipped by the first settlers. As the city grew from a group of small village governments, it spread to the nearby hills and along the valleys between the banks of the Tiber River. In time it came to be known as the "City of the Seven Hills." These hills are neither high nor extensive; the Palatine is only 142 feet above the level of the Tiber River—about the height of a modern ten-story building.

Below the Palatine Hill was the valley that came to be known as the Forum Romanum. At first a marshy district, it became the market place of Rome, then the chief shopping and business district, and finally the civic center. The Forum finally evolved into a rectangular-paved space surrounded by temples, law courts, a senate house, and other public buildings. At one end was a speakers' platform called the *rostra* because it was ornamented with the beaks of ships (**rōstrum** = beak) captured in a war fought in the fourth century B.C.[1] Modern excavations have uncovered much of the Forum which was later known as Campo Vaccino.

The Palatine, because of its nearness to the Forum, became the residential district for statesmen and wealthy people and the temple district. The first emperors had their homes there. Eventually the whole imperial administration came to be centered on this hill during Augustus's rule, and the emperor's buildings covered it completely. So the hill that had been named for the protecting goddess of the shepherds who built their rude huts there came to be the site of *palatial* buildings. Thus, it happens that our word *palace* is derived from the name of the hill.

Another hill near the Forum, the Capitoline, got its name from the famous temple of Jupiter known as the Capitolium, because it was the "head" **(caput),** or main temple of that god. From this the Capitol in Washington, D.C., or any other state capitol building, gets its name. Also on the Capitoline was the temple of Juno Moneta. Why the goddess Juno was called Moneta is not certain.

[1] The fourth century B.C. (before Christ) covers 400–301 B.C.; the first, 100–1 B.C. Then comes the first century A.D., A.D. 1–100, etc.

In connection with this temple, a mint for coining money was later established, and thus from the word **monēta** we derive our words *money* and *mint*. The other seven hills were the Aventine, Caelian, Esquiline which was originally a pauper's graveyard and later a park, Quirinal, and Viminal. In the valley between the Palatine and the Aventine lay the Circus Maximus, a racecourse for chariots.

To the northwest of the Forum, in a bend of the Tiber River, stretched the Campus Martius, which enclosed a park and drill ground, and also was covered with temples, theaters, public baths, and other buildings. In the Middle Ages, this was the most densely populated district in Rome, as we can still see from its many narrow, twisting streets. Of the many temples, baths, and shops constructed here, only the Pantheon is visible today along with fragments of other buildings.

The streets of Rome were narrow and crooked and there existed over 200 of them. In the early days they were unpaved, but during the last part of the first century B.C. there was a program to beautify the city with paved streets and sidewalks.

In the early days the people of Rome got their water from wells, springs, and the Tiber River, which winds its way along one side of the city in the shape of the letter "s." About 313 B.C. Appius Claudius (the censor also

The Roman Forum, where business was transacted, laws were made, and a strong civilization took hold. The remains of the temple of Vesta are in the center, the three columns of the Temple of Castor are on the right with the Arch of Septimius Severus just behind it, and the remains of the Colosseum are in the background.

Vanni/Art Resource, NY

responsible for the Via Appia) built the first aqueduct, which brought pure water from springs about seven miles east of the city. Later, other aqueducts were built, some having their sources nearly forty miles away. Rome had 14 aqueducts at its peak and several are still in use today. There were many street fountains and eventually running water was piped into the public baths and many private houses of the wealthy.

For better administration the Emperor Augustus divided the city into fourteen regions, or wards. One feature of this arrangement was the reorganization and extension of the police and fire department (**vigilēs,** *watchmen*), the latter force numbering about 7,000. Earlier fire protection had been so poor that private fire companies were organized, but these companies were criticized for buying burning houses at bargain prices before they extinguished the fires.

In early days a wall known as the Servian Wall was built around the city for protection; parts of this wall may still be seen in the busy modern city. Rome soon outgrew this wall and in the third century A.D. the Emperor Aurelian constructed a new wall which had fifteen gates and still stands.

At its height, ancient Rome had a population of more than one million people. The modern city has been growing rapidly in recent years, and is once again the largest city in Italy.

Rome has been an important city for a longer time than any other city in the western world. It was first a kingdom, then a republic, and later the capital of the great Roman Empire. Then it continued its importance as the seat of the Catholic Church and in recent generations it has become also the capital of one of the leading nations of modern Europe. The name given to it during ancient times—"Eternal City" (**urbs aeterna**)—has been justified.

QUESTIONS

1. What is a civic center? Describe a modern one that you have visited and contrast it with that of ancient Rome.
2. Compare the development of Rome and that of Washington, D.C., or some other large city.
3. What factors cause a community to grow until it reaches the status of a city? A megalopolis?

Unit II Review
LESSONS V-IX

Vocabulary

Practice saying the following vocabulary words aloud with a partner. In addition to the meaning, for the nouns, give the genitive and gender; for the adjectives, give the three nominative forms; for the verbs, give the four principal parts; and for the prepositions, give the case they take.

Nouns

ager	fēmina	memoria	puer
amīcus	fīlia	nauta	pugna
animus	fōrma	numerus	pūpa
casa	gladius	pecūnia	rēgīna
cibus	hōra	poena	unda
cōpia	iniūria	praeda	victōria
cūra	littera	provincia	vir
dominus			

Adjectives

amīcus	decimus	meus	saucius
antiquus	Gallus	plānus	tōtus
beātus	grātus	quintus	tuus
clārus	ignāvus	Rōmānus	

Verbs

adiuvō	festīnō	natō	probō
celebrō	incitō	nāvigō	pugnō
dōnō	mandō	nūntiō	servō
exclāmō	mōnstrō	occupō	

Adverbs

benignē	etiam	paene	semper
crās	hodiē	postēa	tum

Prepositions

ad	in	sine	trāns
cum	prope		

Interjection

mactē

Grammar Summary

Nouns

Second Declension Nouns in *–r*

Second declension nouns that end in **–r** may or may not drop the vowel that precedes the **–r** in the stem. They are declined like **vir,** *man* or **ager,** *field.*

Case Uses

The Genitive Case. This genitive case is used to show possession.

gladius puerī	*the sword of the boy* *OR the boy's sword*
ager agricolārum	*the field of the farmers* *OR the farmers' field*

The genitive is used after the preposition *of.*

cōpia aquae	*a supply of water*

Unit II Review
LESSONS V-IX

The Dative Case. This case is used to indicate the *indirect object* of the verb. The indirect object is most commonly used after such verbs as *give, show, tell,* and *entrust*. In English, we often use the prepositions *to* or *for* to show this relationship. The preposition can be dropped in English, but the dative case is always used in Latin.

Pecūniam puellae dōnābō.	*I shall give money to the girl.* *I shall give the girl money.*

Accusative with Prepositions. Certain prepositions are followed by the accusative case.

Ad īnsulam natō.	*I am swimming toward the island.*

Ablative of *Place Where*. The ablative is used to show *where* something or someone is.

in silvā	*in the forest*

Ablative of Means. The ablative is used to express the means or instrument by which something is done. In English, we almost always use the preposition *by* or *with* to express this, but in Latin, no preposition is used.

Litterīs victōriam nuntiant.	*They report the victory by (means of) a letter.*
Nauta gladiō pugnat.	*The sailor fights with (by means of) a sword.*

Ablative with Prepositions. Certain prepositions are followed by the ablative case.

Virī cum agricolīs laborant.	*The men are working with the farmers.*

Adjectives

Adjectives as Substantives. In Latin, an adjective alone is often used to stand for what would be a noun plus an adjective in English.

Gallī pugnant.	*The Gauls are fighting.*

Verbs

The Future Tense. The future tense is formed in Latin by adding the tense sign **–bi** to the stem. The **–i** is dropped in the first person singular and the third person plural.

Agrōs spectābimus.	*We shall look at the fields.*
Equōs laudābunt.	*They will praise the horses.*

The Present Imperative. The present imperative is used to give commands. The singular is simply the present stem of the verb. The plural is formed by adding **–te** to the stem.

Adiuvā nautās!	*Help the sailors!*
Occupāte gladiōs!	*Seize the swords!*

Unit II Review
LESSONS V-IX

Unit Practice

Exercises

A. Decline **vīta mea, nauta malus** in the singular and plural.

B. State the case required and then give the following in Latin.

1. *level land* (direct object)
2. *your daughter* (possessive)
3. *little girls* (indirect object)
4. *my wagons* (means)
5. *large horses* (direct object)

C. This is a rapid-fire drill to be answered as quickly as you can.

1. Translate: **occupābō, mōnstrās, dōnā, amīcōrum, pecūniā, laudābunt, servāre, navigātis, incitant.**
2. Translate: *of the victory, with money, we report, he will entrust, you (sing.) will be showing, they give, he fights.*
3. Give the cases of nouns and adjectives and tenses of verbs: **iniūriīs, numerō, undās, pugnābunt, grātam, spectātis, bonō, tua, mandās.**

D. Working with a partner or in small groups, create a short story or dialogue (at least eight lines or sentences) using one or more of the following topics.

1. a fight between the Gauls and the Romans
2. a Saturnalia celebration
3. a letter to a friend who lives far away
4. an accident in which someone has been hurt

OB·REM·PVBLICAM·RESTITVTAM·IMPERIVMQVE·POPVLI·ROMANI
INSIGNIBVS·VIRTVTIBVS·EORVM·DOMI·FORISQVE

Unit III

Latin and the Romans

The Triumphal Arch of Septimius Severus was built in the Roman Forum in A.D. 203. Septimius Severus, backed by his army, marched into Rome in 193 and persuaded the Senate to confirm him as emperor after the murder of Pertinax. He led a successful campaign against the Parthians in 198 but died in an effort to conquer Scotland in 211.

LESSON X
Lingua Latīna

Lingua Rōmānōrum Latīna erat. Lingua patriae nostrae[1] nōn Latīna est, sed Anglica.[2] Linguā Latīnā scientiam[3] nostrae linguae augēmus. Lingua Latīna prīmō nōbīs[4] nova erat, sed nunc nōn terret. Disciplīna nōs[5] nōn terret, quod magistrum bonum habēmus. Linguam Latīnam semper in memoriā habēbimus. In Britanniā, in Italiā, in Galliā, in Americīs, in multīs terrīs et prōvinciīs multī magistrī linguam Latīnam nunc docent et semper docēbunt. In patriā nostrā lingua Latīna magnam fāmam habet. Magistrī magnum numerum discipulōrum docent. Disciplīna semper scientiam nostram[1] augēbit. Magistrī nōs probābunt, sī[6] cūram habēbimus, Patria nōs probābit et laudābit, sī scientiam et fāmam bonam parābimus.

[1] *our*
[2] *English*
[3] *knowledge*
[4] *to us*
[5] *us*
[6] *if*

QUESTIONS

1. Where is Latin taught?
2. Do many students study Latin? Why?
3. Do you agree that the study of Latin helps your knowledge of English and the Romance languages? Count the number of different Latin words in this passage from which an English word you know is derived.

Grammar

The Second Conjugation: Present and Future Tenses

The verbs you have studied in previous lessons all contain the stem vowel **–ā–** and belong to the first conjugation. Verbs that have the stem vowel **–ē–** in the present and future tenses belong to the *second conjugation.* The only difference from the first conjugation is in the stem vowel and in the first person singular present tense, which keeps the stem vowel: **doceō.**

PRESENT TENSE	
SINGULAR	PLURAL
doceō, *I teach, am teaching, do teach*	docēmus, *we teach, are teaching, do teach*
docēs, *you teach,* etc.	docētis, *you teach,* etc.
docet, *he, she, it teaches,* etc.	docent, *they teach,* etc.

FUTURE TENSE	
SINGULAR	PLURAL
docēbō, *I shall teach, shall be teaching*	docēbimus, *we shall teach,* etc.
docēbis, *you will teach,* etc.	docēbitis, *you will teach,* etc.
docēbit, *he, she, it will teach,* etc.	docēbunt, *they will teach,* etc.

NOTĀ·BENE

The present imperative of second conjugation verbs is formed according to the same rules as the first conjugation.
Tenē pūpam tuae fīliae.
Hold your daughter's doll.

Anna puerōs terret. *Anna frightens the boys.*
Disciplīnam nautārum augēbis. *You will increase the training of the sailors.*

ORAL PRACTICE

1. Conjugate **habeō** (*have, hold*) in the present tense and **augeō** (*increase*) in the future tense and then translate.
2. Give the singular imperative of *increase, teach;* give the plural imperative of *have, scare.*
3. Translate: *they will have, he increases, we show, he will teach, you* (pl.) *scare.*

C. M. Dixon

Roman children were taught by a magister, who was often a slave captured from one of the provinces. Young children learned reading, writing, and simple arithmetic. Older children, taught by a grammaticus, studied Greek, history, philosophy, and literature.

Latin for American Students

*Did you know that besides the **ludi** or **scholae** where basic instruction was given to both male and female Roman students, there were special schools for music, cooking, and barbering? However, no provision was made for formal training in certain subjects like law, administration, diplomacy, and military tactics. For practical on-the-job training, a young man would apprentice himself to an older man distinguished in one of these areas.*

EXERCISES

A. Translate the sentences into good English, while paying particular attention to the endings.

1. Docē linguās, Anna.
2. Multās linguās nōn docēbō.
3. Magnae undae servōs terrēbunt.
4. Magnae undae cūrās nautārum augent.
5. Victōria numerum servōrum nōn augēbit.
6. Pecūniam servāre est fortūnam augēre.
7. Prōvinciīs magnam victōriam patriae nūntiābimus.
8. Amīcus meus magnam pecūniam et parvam disciplīnam habet.

B. Identify the person, number, and tense required, then translate the words in italics into Latin.

1. Fīlia linguās (*will teach*).
2. Nautae Annam (*are scaring*).
3. (*Love*) linguam patriae tuae.
4. Cibum multum nōn (*we do have*).
5. (*Increase*) fortūnam tuam disciplīnā.
6. Memoriam Rōmae linguā Latīna (*we shall preserve*).
7. Patriam (*to seize*) et familiam meam (*to scare*) parābunt.

C. Say what the following people are doing today; then say that they will do it again **(iterum)** tomorrow, following the model. Add any prepositions you need to make sense.

fīlia / adiuvāre / sauciī — *Hodiē, fīlia sauciōs adiuvat. Crās, sauciōs iterum adiuvābit.*

1. nauta / navigāre / īnsula
2. agricola / laborāre / ager
3. magister / docēre / discipulī
4. dominī / spectāre / equī
5. servī / portāre / cibus
6. rēgīna / habēre / magna pecūnia
7. puerī / terrēre / puellae

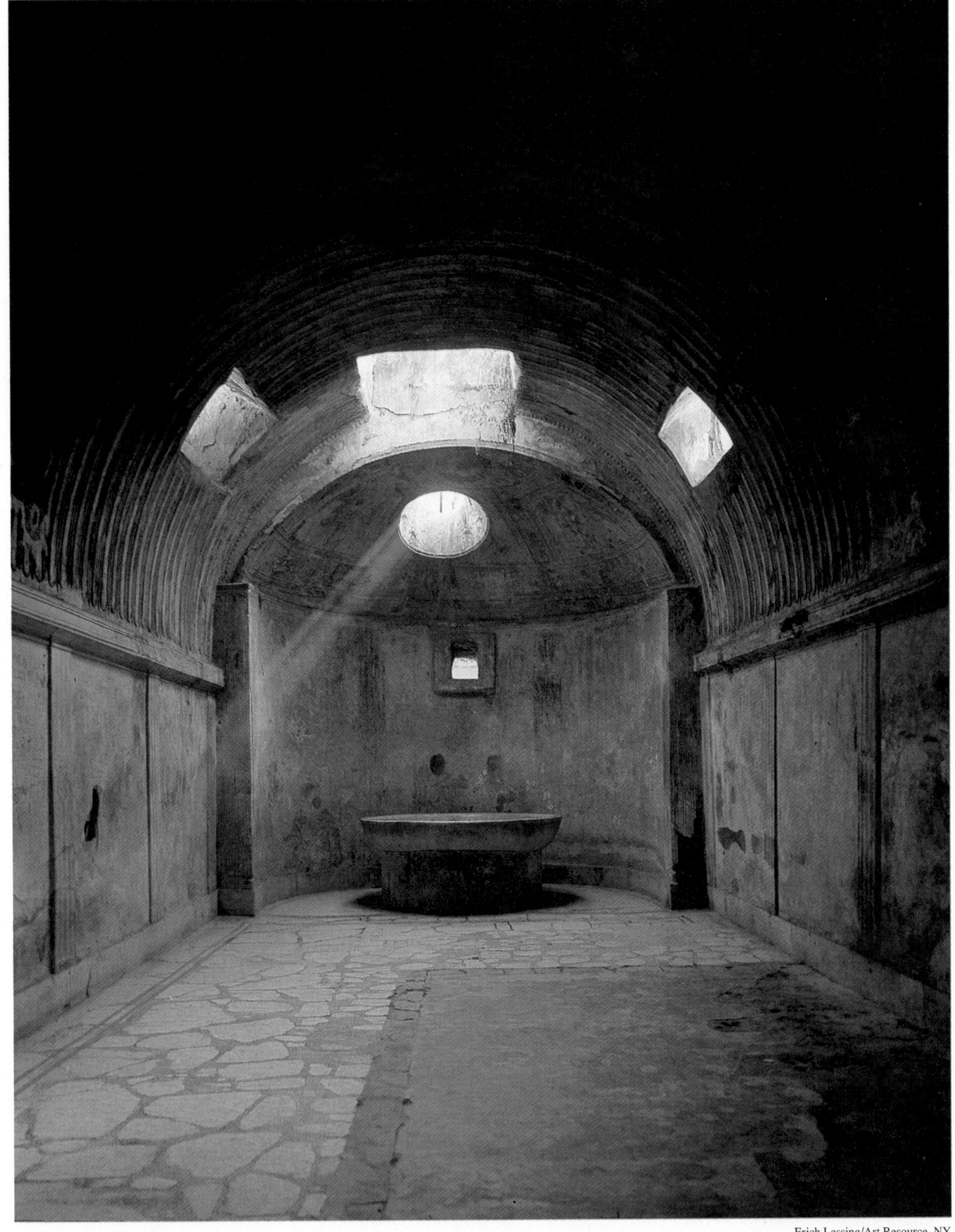

Erich Lessing/Art Resource, NY

Looking toward the water basin in a Roman bath in Pompeii. Romans used to meet here for bathing and conversation. This is one of the first baths uncovered after excavations at Pompeii began in the late eighteenth century.

Vocabulary

Nouns

disciplī´na, -ae,[1] *f. training, instruction* (discipline)

discipulus, -i, *m. student* (disciple)

lin´gua, -ae, *f. tongue, language* (bilingual, linguistic)

ma´gister, -trī, *m. teacher* (magisterial, magistrate)

pa´tria, -ae, *f. fatherland, country* (expatriate, patriotic)

Verbs

au´geō, augē´re, au´xī, auc´tus,[2] *increase* (auction, augment)

do´ceō, docē´re, do´cuī, doc´tus, *teach* (document, indoctrinate)

ha´beō, habē´re, ha´buī, ha´bitus, *have, hold* (habit, inhabitant)

ter´reō, terrē´re, ter´ruī, ter´ritus, *scare, frighten* (terrific, terrify)

Adverb

prī´mō, *at first* (prime, primitive)

Word Studies

1. From what Latin words are *accurate, doctrine, document* derived? When is the word *doctor* used to mean one who teaches? What is a *linguist*? What does the word *discipline* usually mean? What was its original meaning?
2. Which one of these words does not belong with the others? Why? *terrible subterranean deter terrified*
3. A number of Latin verb forms are preserved as English words. First conjugation: *veto, habitat, ignoramus, mandamus.* Second conjugation: *tenet.* Look them up in a dictionary to see if their meanings are the same.

---

[1] From now on only the genitive ending will be given.

[2] Note that the last two *principal parts* of second conjugation verbs are not quite so regular as those of the first conjugation.

LESSON XI
Britannia

Magna īnsula Britannia in amīcitiā Galliae manet. Caesar in Galliā pugnat et amīcitiam Britanniae et Galliae videt. Ibi māteriam et cibum parat et ad Britanniam nāvigat. Consilium habet. Ibi amīcōs Gallōrum pugnīs terret sed in Britanniā nōn manet. Īnsulam videt, nōn occupat, sed glōriam suam[1] auget. Semper prō[2] patriā et prō glōriā suā[1] labōrat. Caesar grātiam et amīcitiam Rōmānōrum meret,[3] quod magnae sunt victōriae. Multīs litterīs Rōmae victōriās nūntiat. Virīs praemia dōnat. Magna est grātia patriae quod Caesar patriam auget. Multam praedam carrīs et equīs ad patriam portat. Nunc Caesar magnam glōriam habet.

[1] *his*
[2] *for*
[3] *wins*

QUESTIONS

1. What did Caesar do to Britain?
2. Why did Caesar win the gratitude of his countrymen?

Michael Holford

Great detail and shading can be achieved with mosaic, as this representation of a sea god, probably Oceanus, shows. Notice that the claws that spring from the shaggy hair are not the usual lobster claws but those of some other sea beast. This mosaic dates from the last half of the second century A.D. *in Verulamium in England.*

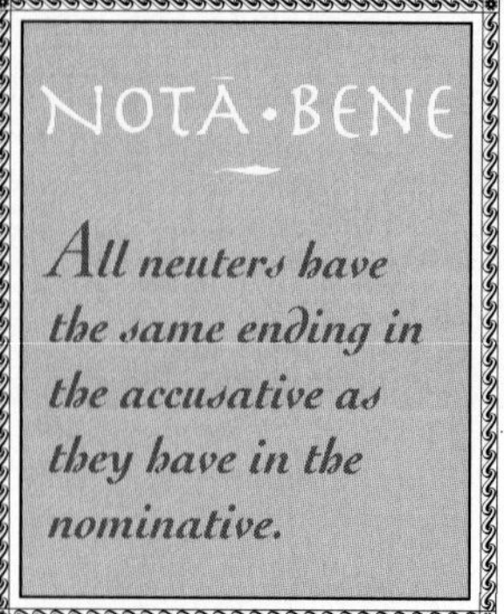

Grammar

Neuter Nouns of the Second Declension

The second declension contains, in addition to masculine nouns ending in **–us (–ius), –er,** and **–r,** neuter nouns ending in **–um (–ium).** The only difference, besides the nominative singular, between the neuter and the masculine nouns of the second declension is in the nominative and accusative plural, which both end in short **–a.**

Adjectives too have neuter forms. You have seen the nominative singular form in vocabulary lists since Lesson II. First and second declension adjectives share the same endings as first and second nouns. Remember that an adjective must agree in gender, number, and case with the noun it modifies. A typical second declension neuter adjective and noun are declined as follows.

	SINGULAR		PLURAL	
Nom.	signum	parvum	signa	parva
Gen.	signī	parvī	signōrum	parvōrum
Dat.	signō	parvō	signīs	parvīs
Acc.	signum	parvum	signa	parva
Abl.	signō	parvō	signīs	parvīs

PRACTICE

1. Decline **frūmentum bonum** and **praemium grātum.**
2. Identify the case and number of the following (there may be more than one answer): **magnōrum castrōrum, novō signo, multa praemia.**
3. Decline **amīcus tuus, vīta longa,** and **parvum praemium.**

Sentence Analysis

Before you write out an English translation of a Latin sentence or a Latin translation of an English sentence, you may find it helpful to do a brief analysis of each word in the sentence.

When translating from English to Latin, write above each noun the gender, number, and case required. Make sure all adjectives get the same notations. You also should check the verb and write out the person, number, and tense you need. When you write out your final sentence, insert any adverbs, prepositions, or conjunctions that are necessary.

The good man will give much grain to the little boys.

Your analysis should proceed like this:

1. You know that the subject of the sentence is *man,* so *man* is nominative. It is also masculine and singular. *Good* modifies *man* so it, too, is nominative, masculine, and singular.
2. *Give* is the verb. It is in the future tense, and must be singular and third person to agree with the subject, *man.*
3. *Grain* is the direct object of the verb *give,* so it is accusative; it is also singular and neuter. *Much* is modifying *grain,* so it is also accusative, neuter, and singular.
4. *Boys* is dative because it is the indirect object (after a verb of giving); also masculine and plural. *Little* must also be dative, masculine, and plural.

Now that you have all the information you need, it is much easier to translate into Latin without making a mistake. After you have done it a few times, it will become second nature.

Bonus vir multum frūmentum parvīs puerīs dōnābit.

Hadrian's Wall, an ancient fortified wall, crosses northern England at its narrowest point. After the Romans abandoned their attempt to conquer Scotland, the wall became the permanent northern boundary of the Roman empire as a barrier against the northern barbarians. Begun in A.D. 121, it stretched 73.5 miles. The wall varied from 6.5 to 11.5 feet thick and was 23 feet tall. It was protected on both sides by a ditch. Large portions of the wall are still standing.

National Trust/Art Resource, NY

You should perform the same analysis when translating from Latin to English. In this case, however, you may initially have more than one case noted for each noun, since some endings are repeated. Let's analyze the following sentence.

Agricolae ignāvī cōpiam frūmenti in prōvinciīs nōn augēbunt.

1. You know that **agricolae** could be genitive singular, dative singular, or nominative plural. Write down all three, until you can eliminate some of them.
2. **Ignāvī** could be genitive singular or nominative plural. Write them both down. Since it is positioned next to **agricolae** and has two out of three similar possibilities, it is probably modifying **agricolae,** but you cannot be positive yet.
3. **Cōpiam** can only be accusative singular, so it must be the direct object.
4. **Frūmentī** can only be genitive singular.
5. **In** is a preposition that can be followed by the accusative of *place to which* (meaning *into*) or by the ablative of *place where* (meaning *in* or *on*). Looking ahead to **prōvinciīs,** you know that the **–īs** ending can be dative plural or ablative plural. Since it is following a preposition that takes the ablative, it is likely that it is the ablative of *place where.*
6. **Augēbunt** is the verb. The **–nt** means that the subject has to be third person plural. The **–bu** indicates that it is in the future. **Nōn** makes it negative.

Now go back to the beginning of your analysis. Since **augēbunt** is not a verb that takes an indirect object, the dative possibility can be eliminated from **agricolae.** And since **augēbunt** requires a third person plural subject, and **agricolae** is plural, you can assume that **agricolae** is the subject and that **ignāvī** is modifying **agricolae.** English requires the verb to follow the subject, so we have so far:

The lazy farmers will not increase

Now you need your accusative direct object, **cōpiam.**

The lazy farmers will not increase the supply

This is not a complete sentence, so fill in with what you have left. The genitive singular makes sense because you need a supply *of* something. Finally, add the prepositional phrase.

The lazy farmers will not increase the supply of grain in the provinces.

Latin for American Students

Did you know that it took 14 million bushels of wheat a year to feed the people of Rome in Augustus's time, representing the produce of hundreds of miles of wheat fields? Most of the imported grain was specifically for the city of Rome. One third of it came from Egypt, and most of the rest from Sicily and North Africa and was unloaded at Ostia or the artificial harbor of Portus.

ORAL PRACTICE

1. Analyze the following English sentence: *On many islands, the women and men carry the queen's water.*
2. Analyze the following Latin sentence: **In castrīs Rōmānōrum, multōs equōs spectō.**

EXERCISES

A. Analyze the following sentences and translate.

1. Laudāte amīcitiam.
2. In viīs signa Rōmānōrum vidēbunt.
3. In silvīs māteriam vidēbis.
4. Nautae in terrā nōn manēbunt.
5. In viīs multōs servōs nōn videō.
6. Multās hōrās nōn habētis. Labōrāte!
7. Disciplīnā glōriam patriae augēbimus.
8. In patriā magnam pecūniam nunc habēmus.
9. Rēgīna virīs nūntiābit praemia.

B. Analyze and translate into Latin.

1. Remain and see my friends.
2. They will remain in the camp.
3. I shall see your daughter on the street.
4. By friendship you will increase your influence.
5. Through (by) injustice they will seize the land and grain of the province.

C. Answer the questions by substituting the words in parentheses for those in italics. Make all other necessary changes. Follow the model.

Castra Rōmānōrum in *Galliā* sunt? (non / Britannia)

Castra Rōmānōrum non sunt in Galliā sed in Britanniā.

1. Bonam cōpiam *frūmentī* habēbimus? (non / aqua)
2. Gloriam *virōrum* in provinciā celebrābitis? (non / agricola)
3. *Cōnsilia* fēminārum bona erant? (non / cībus)
4. Tuus *servus* gladiō pugnat? (non / fēmina)
5. Beātam *familiam* adiuvābimus? (non / amīcus)

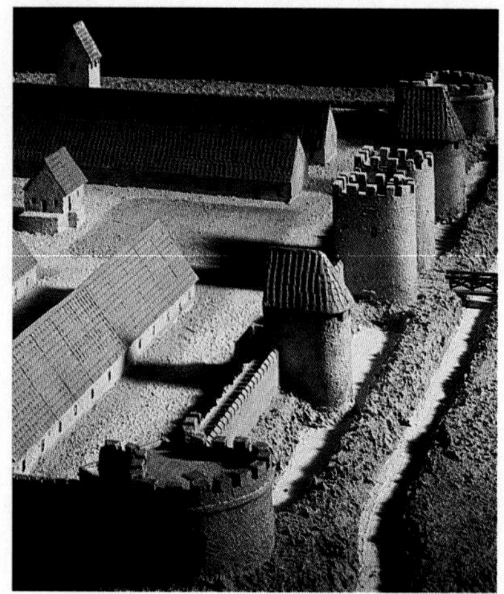

Erich Lessing/Art Resource, NY

Model of an auxiliary camp at Zwentendorf, Austria. This camp was big enough to house a Roman cohort of about 500 men. A cohort corresponded to a battle group in today's army, and was capable of independent operation, at least for a limited time. Ten cohorts made up a legion, the equivalent of an army division.

Vocabulary

Nouns

amīci´tia, -ae, *f. friendship*
an´nus, -i, *m. year* (annual, biennial)
cas´tra, -ōr´um, *n. pl. camp (pl. in form, sing. in meaning)*
cōnsi´lium, cōnsi´lī,[1] *n. plan, advice* (counsel)
frūmen´tum, -ī, *n. grain* (frumentaceous)
glō´ria, -ae, *f. glory* (glorify, glorious)
grā´tia, -ae, *f. gratitude, influence* (grateful, gratify)
mate´ria, -ae, *f. matter, timber* (material, materialism)
prae´mium, prae´mī, *n. reward* (premium)
sig´num, -ī, *n. sign* (significant)

Verbs

ma´neo, manē´re, mān´sī, mānsū´rus,[2] *remain* (manor, mansion)
vi´deo, vidē´re, vī´dī, vī´sus, *see* (provide, visual)

Adverb

i´bi, *there*

Word Studies

1. The following are Latin words of the **–um** and **–ium** type preserved in their original form in English:

SINGULAR	PLURAL	SINGULAR	PLURAL
addendum	*addenda*	*delirium*	*deliria* (or *–ums*)
	agenda	*dictum*	*dicta* (or *–ums*)
bacterium	*bacteria*	*maximum*	*maxima* (or *–ums*)
candelabrum	*candelabra*	*memorandum*	*memoranda* (or *–ums*)
curriculum	*curricula*	*minimum*	*minima* (or *–ums*)
datum	*data* (remember to say "**these** *data*")	*stratum*	*strata* (or *–ums*)

2. What is a *signatory* to a treaty? What is the difference between *biennial* and *semi-annual?*

[1] Nouns (not adjectives) that end in **–ium** usually shorten the **–ii** to **–i** in the genitive singular.
[2] This form in **–ūrus** instead of **–us** will be explained later.

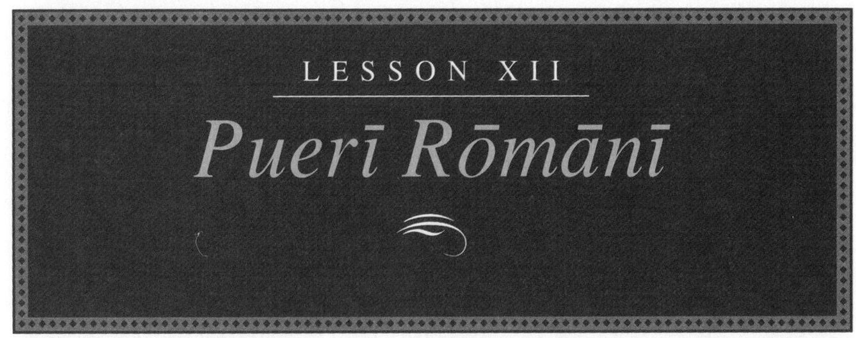

Lūcius, puer Rōmānus, in Viā Altā amīcum Mārcum videt.

LŪCIUS: Ubi est socius tuus Quīntus?

MĀRCUS: Ad īnsulam nāvigāvit.

LŪCIUS: Cūr ad īnsulam nāvigāvit?

MĀRCUS: Īnsulam amat. Ibi in aquā diū[1] manet; in silvā altā ambulat. In īnsulā multōs amīcōs habet.

LŪCIUS: Cūr nōn cum sociō tuō ad īnsulam nāvigāvistī? Cūr hīc[2] mānsistī?

MĀRCUS: In casā labōrāre dēbeō,[3] quod servōs liberāvimus.

LŪCIUS: Magnum numerum servōrum habēmus et semper habuimus. In casā, in viā, in silvā labōrant, māteriam portant, agricolae sunt. Servī grātiam nostram meruērunt, sed eōs[4] tenēbimus.

MĀRCUS: Quod servī nostrī agricolae bonī erant et semper labōrāvērunt eōs nōn tenuimus sed līberāvimus. Nunc amīcī et sociī sunt et amīcitiam eōrum[5] semper memoriā tenēbō.

[1] *a long time*
[2] *here*
[3] *I have to*
[4] *them*
[5] *their*

QUESTIONS

1. Where is Quintus?
2. Why isn't Marcus there?
3. Whose slaves have been freed?

Grammar

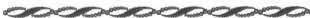

The Perfect Tense

In Latin, the *perfect tense* refers to things that happened in the past.

Viam spectāvimus.	*We have looked at the road.*
Magister puellās docuit.	*The teacher taught the girls.*
Romanī in Galliā pugnāvērunt?	*Did the Romans fight in Gaul?*

Servus laborat. A Roman wine shop. The slave carrying in the wine jars has hitched up his tunic, much as we "roll up our sleeves" for action. Because glass was expensive, clay jars of various sizes were used for liquids. From a relief sculpture in marble.

To form the perfect tense, you start with the perfect stem, and then add the perfect endings. The perfect stem is simply the third principal part of the verb, minus the **–i**.

THIRD PRINCIPAL PART	PERFECT STEM
portāvī	portāv–
docuī	docu–

The endings for the perfect tense are:

–ī	**–it**	**–istis**
–istī	**–imus**	**–ērunt**

The verbs **portāre** and **docēre,** conjugated in the perfect, look like this:

portāv**ī**, *I carried, I have carried, I did carry*	docu**ī**, *I taught, I have taught, I did teach*
portāv**istī**, *you carried,* etc.	docu**istī**, *you taught,* etc.
portāv**it**, *he carried,* etc.	docu**it**, *he taught,* etc.
portāv**imus**, *we carried,* etc.	docu**imus**, *we taught,* etc.
portāv**istis**, *you carried,* etc.	docu**istis**, *you taught,* etc.
portāv**ērunt**, *they carried,* etc.	docu**ērunt**, *they taught,* etc.

ORAL PRACTICE

1. Give the four principal parts of the following verbs: **amō, nūntiō, teneō, augeō**.
2. Conjugate the following in the perfect tense: **labōro, teneō, mereō, maneō, mōnstrō, augeō, habeō, videō**.
3. Translate: *he has praised, we entrusted, they scared, we did teach, I saw.*

EXERCISES

A. Translate the following sentences into good English.

1. Servō litterās mandāvī.
2. Multōs sociōs habuistis.
3. Agricola in terrā labōrābit.
4. Undae altae puellās terruērunt.
5. Cōpiam aquae clārae parāvistī.
6. Multōs servōs in casā vīdimus.
7. Agricolae, grātiam patriae meruistis.
8. Amīcus meus in prōvinciā nōn mānsit.

B. Translate the following sentences into Latin.

1. The slave held the horses.
2. We saw a large number of horses.
3. The farmers have got the food ready.
4. The girls will carry the food to the house.
5. My comrade has deserved my friendship.

Ronald Sheridan/Ancient Art & Architecture Collection

Roman slaves, like these who are threshing or sifting grain, worked for their Roman masters and lived with them as part of the familia. Slaves did not only do manual labor, but some also taught the master's children or served as a personal secretary to their master.

C. Tell a friend what you saw or did when you visited the following places. (You may want to create an English sentence first, then analyze and translate it into Latin.) Then your friend asks if you truly **(vērō)** did it.

Gallia / castra / Romani / spectare — *–In Galliā castra Rōmānōrum spectāvī.* *–Vērō castra Rōmānōrum spectāvistī?*

1. Sicilia / agricolae / labōrāre
2. īnsula / parvae puellae / terrēre
3. Britannia / equī magnī / vidēre
4. Ītalia / nauta / nāvigāre
5. Corsica / puer saucius / adiuvāre

Vocabulary

Nouns

so´cius, so´cī,[1] *m. ally, comrade* (associate, social)

Adjectives

al´tus, -a, -um,[2] *high* (altimeter, altitude)

bar´barus, -a, -um, *foreign (as a noun, foreigner)* (barbaric, barbarous)

Verbs

am´bulō, ambulā´re, ambulā´vī, ambulā´tus, *walk* (amble, ambulatory)

ēvo´cō, ēvocā´re, ēvocā´vī, ēvocā´tus, *summon, call out* (evoke, vocation)

lī´bero, līberā´re, līberā´vī, līberā´tus, *free* (liberal, liberator)

me´reō, merē´re, me´ruī, me´ritus, *deserve, earn* (merit, meritorious)

te´neō, tenē´re, te´nuī, ten´tus, *hold, keep* (retain, retentive)

Adverb

cūr, *why*

---

[1] Nouns (not adjectives) that end in **–ius** usually shorten **–iī** to **–ī** in the genitive singular: **so´ciī** becomes **so´cī**, and the accent is not changed. The nominative plural always ends in **–iī: sociī.**

[2] Now that you are familiar with the adjective forms, only the nominative endings will be given.

Latin for American Students

Did you know that the Romans considered the Greeks to be barbarians, yet they were aware that the Greeks were their cultural superiors? This love-hate relationship was central to Roman social life and history. The Greeks provided a great deal of the art, architecture, medicine, and teaching to the Roman world and all Greek items were fashionable among the educated Romans.

Word Studies

1. From their meanings tell which of the following words come from **servāre** and which from **servus:** *serf, conserve, serve, servant, reserve.*
2. What does the derivation tell us about the meaning of *social, social service, social security, socialism*? What is an *equestrian*? A *copious* portion? A *nautical* mile?
3. These names were in common use among the Romans: August, Augustus, *venerable;* Rufus, *red-haired;* Victor, *conqueror;* Vincent **(vincēns),** *conquering.*
4. Other Roman names still used in English include: Emil and Emily **(Aemilius, Aemilia);** Cecilia **(Caecilia);** Claudia; Cornelius, Cornelia; Horace **(Horātius);** Julius, Julia; Lavinia; Mark **(Mārcus);** Marcia; Paul **(Paulus).**

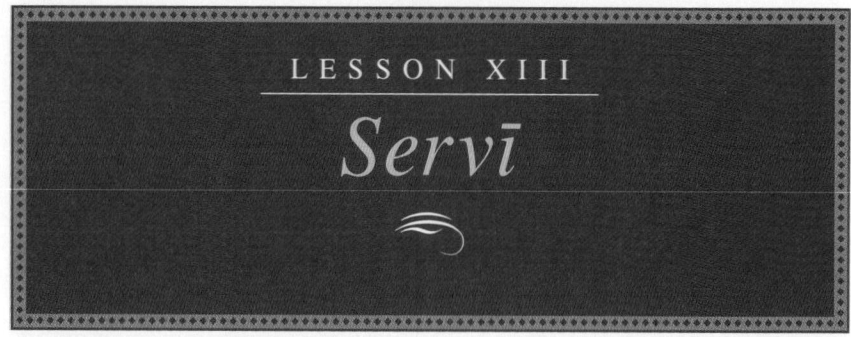

LESSON XIII

Servī

Servī Rōmānī erant captīvī. Rōmānī multīs pugnīs singulās terrās occupāvērunt, et magnus erat numerus captīvōrum. Captīvōs ē Graeciā, ē Galliā, ex Asiā, ex Āfricā in Italiam mōvērunt. In familiā Rōmānā erant multī servī, bonī et malī.

Servī aquam in casās portāvērunt; medicī et agricolae erant; dē vītā, dē glōriā, dē amīcitiā docuērunt. Multī clārī Graecī erant servī et amīcī Rōmānōrum. Litterae[1] Rōmānōrum memoriam servōrum servāvērunt. Poena servī malī magna erat. Servōs bonōs multī Rōmānī līberāvērunt.

In quādam[2] casā Rōmānā Maximus servōs vocāvit: "Mārce et Statī,[3] hōra quīnta est; portāte singulī māteriam dē silvā; Cornēlī, vocā socium tuum et movēte carrum ā viā et equōs ab aquā. Tum parāte cēnam; amīcōs meōs in Altā Viā vīdī et ad cēnam vocāvī."

Servī māteriam portāvērunt, carrum et equōs mōvērunt. Tum cibum parāvērunt et ad mēnsam portāvērunt. Post[4] cēnam amīcī mānsērunt, et Maximus amīcīs pictūrās mōnstrāvit. Interim[5] servī in culīnā[6] labōrāvērunt. Tum amīcī Maximī servōs laudāvērunt et eīs[7] pecūniam dōnāvērunt. Maximō singulī "valē" dīxērunt.[8]

[1] *literature*
[2] *a certain*
[3] *Statius (Stā´shius)*
[4] *after*
[5] *in the meantime*
[6] *kitchen*
[7] *to them*
[8] *said*

QUESTIONS

1. How and where did the Romans get their slaves?
2. Name four things that the slaves did.
3. To how many slaves does Maximus refer?

Grammar

The Vocative Case

In Latin, the *vocative* case is used to address a person. It generally has the same form as the nominative, except that the vocative singular of **–us** nouns and adjectives of the second declension ends in **–e** (in **–ius** nouns, **–ie** becomes **–ī**):

Spectāte undās, parve Lūcī et parva Claudia.	*Look at the waves, little Lucius and little Claudia.*
Līberā captīvōs, amīce Mārce.	*Free the captives, friend Marcus.*

NOTĀ·BENE

Unless it is emphatic, the vocative rarely stands first in the sentence.

ORAL PRACTICE

1. Give the vocative forms of the following: **Marcus, agricolae, Cornēlia, Quintus, Tullius, Anna.**
2. Translate the following into Latin using the vocative case: *Slave!, Maximus!, Clara!, Men and women!, Publius!*.

Ablative of Place From Which

As you know, the ablative case can be used to fulfill several functions in a sentence. The *ablative of place from which* uses one of three prepositions, together with the ablative, to express the concept *from:*

ā, ab	*away from (the outside)*
de	*from, down from*
ē, ex	*out from (the inside)*

Tombstone of Q. Fabius Diogenes and Fabia Primigenia, who shared 47 years together. It was set up by their freedmen, freedwomen, and slaves (familia). Obviously, these freedmen and slaves thought highly of their former master and mistress, who lived in Cumae.

NOTĀ·BENE

The short forms, ā and ē, are used when the next word begins with a consonant (except h).

Ā viā ambulant.	*They are walking away from the road.*
Fēminae dē Galliā vēnērunt.	*The women came from Gaul.*
Ē silvā ambulāvit.	*He walked out of (from) the forest.*

ORAL PRACTICE

Give the Latin for the following phrases: *out of the water, away from the house, from Italy, away from the table, from the island.*

EXERCISES

A. Translate the following sentences into good English.

1. Vocā, Mārce, servōs ē casā.
2. Sociī equōs ē Viā Quīntā movēbunt.
3. In malā fortūnā bonōs amīcōs habuimus.
4. Movē, Cornēlī, carrōs singulōs dē silvā altā.
5. Portāte, captīvī, māteriam dē silvīs ad aquam.
6. Servī malī multam praedam ab īnsulīs portāvērunt.

B. Translate the following sentences into Latin.

1. We have called the girls to dinner.
2. My daughter had a large number of friends.
3. Brutus, move the prisoners from the island.
4. One at a time they sailed from the island to the new land.

C. Tell the following people to move something from somewhere. Follow the model below.

Anna / rana / aquā *Movē, Anna, ranam ex aquā.*

1. Marcus / carrus / silva
2. Clara / pūpa / mensa
3. Servī / familia / casa
4. Quintus / captīvī / castra
5. Medicus / sauciī / via

Latin for American Students

Did you know that adaptations of some Roman medical treatments are used in modern medicine? People with contagious diseases were quarantined in isolation for forty days; a form of cauterization was practiced with a red hot stone held against a wound or snakebite; burnt sea sponge was prescribed for goiter (now we realize that it contains iodine); and smallpox innoculation and blood transfusion procedures were known.

Erich Lessing/Art Resource, NY

Relief of a food shop at Ostia showing chickens, apples, and caged rabbits (lower right). The monkeys seem to be there to attract customers.

Vocabulary

Nouns

captī´vus, -ī, *m. prisoner* (captivate, captivity)
cē´na, -ae, *f. dinner* (cenacle)
medicus, -ī, *m. doctor* (medical, medicine)
men´sa, -ae, *f. table*

Adjective

sin´gulī, -ae, -a, *one at a time (always plural)* (single, singular)

Verbs

mo´veō, movē´re, mō´vī, mō´tus, *move* (motion, motive)
vo´cō, vocā´re, vocā´vī, vocā´tus, *call* (evocative, vocal)

Prepositions

ā, ab (+ abl.), *from, away from* (abduct, abjure)
dē (+ abl.), *from, down from, about* (decalcify, derive)
ē, ex (+ abl.), *from, out of, out from* (exfoliate, export)

Word Studies

Many Latin words are formed by joining prefixes (**prae** = *in front;* **fīxus** = *attached*) to root words. These same prefixes, most of which are prepositions, are those chiefly used in English. With these prefixes we are continually forming new words.

Examples of the prefixes **ab–, dē–** and **ex–** are:

ab– (abs–, ā–): *a-vocation, ab-undance, abs-tain*
dē–: *de-fame, de-form, de-ter, de-viate, de-portation*
ex– (ē–, ef–): *ex-alt, ex-patriation, ex-pect* (from **spectō**), *e-voke, ex-president*

1. Define the words above according to prefix and root. For root words, see earlier lesson vocabularies.
2. Distinguish the meanings of *vocation* and *avocation.*

Ā VIĀ — DĒ SILVĀ — EX AQUĀ

LESSON XIV

Aristotelēs et Alexander

[1] *Aristotle* (nominative)
[2] *king of Macedonia*
[3] accusative
[4] dative
[5] *Homer*
[6] *Achilles* (genitive, hero of Homer's *Iliad)*
[7] *anger*
[8] *owe*
[9] *he will be*

Aristotelēs[1] magister bonus multōrum virōrum erat. Philosophiam et scientiam nātūrālem docuit. Aristotelēs erat clārus et bonus magister, Philippus, rēx Macedoniae,[2] Aristotelem[3] probāvit.

Philippus fīlium habuit, Alexandrum, puerum bonum et amīcum. Philippus clārō magistrō Aristotelī[4] puerum Alexandrum mandāvit:

"Docē fīlium meum, philosophe."

Aristotelēs semper amīcus Alexandrō erat, et Alexandrum nōn terruit. Aristotelēs Alexandrum dē philosophiā et dē Homērō,[5] poētā clārō, docuit. Alexander Homērum amāvit et laudāvit, sed philosophia erat disciplīna dūra et longa.

In agrō Alexander equum novum habuit. Alexander agrum et equum spectāvit, et Aristotelī nūntiāvit:

"Vidē, magister, agrum grātum. Casam tuam nōn amō. Docē mē in agrō. Puer sum, nōn vir. Puer līber sum, fīlius Philippī, nōn captīvus tuus. In agrō Homērum et glōriam virī magnī Achillis[6] memoriae mandābō."

Aristotelēs in agrō Alexandrum docēre parat. Sed ubi est puer Alexander? Alexander ad silvam equum incitat. Līber est!

Magna erat īra[7] Philippī, sed in philosophō amīcō nōn erat īra. Philippō Aristotelēs nūntiat:

"Puer nōn malus est. Puerī nostrī sacrī sunt; puellae nostrae sacrae sunt. Puerīs nostrīs magnam reverentiam dēbēmus.[8] Alexander bonus est, magnus erit."[9]

Et erat Alexander magnus. Multās terrās occupāvit. Semper fāmam Achillis[6] memoriā tenuit.

Erich Lessing/Art Resource, NY

A full-size statue of Alexander the Great, king of Macedonia 356-323 B.C. Alexander III, the first king to be called "the Great," was one of the greatest miliary leaders in history. He extended the Macedonian empire from Greece to India, was accepted as a pharoah in Egypt, and conquered the Persian empire, defeating Darius III. This is an idealized image as he was short and rather plain-looking.

QUESTIONS

1. What did Aristotle teach?
2. What promise did Alexander make to Aristotle? Did he keep it?

NOTĀ·BENE

Remember that adjectives agree with their nouns in gender, number, and case, but not always in endings: **puer bonus, nauta līber.**

Grammar

The Second Declension: Adjectives in *–r*

Like nouns, there are adjectives of the second declension whose stems end in **–r.** By learning the three nominative forms, you will know whether to keep or drop the **–e** in the stem. Adjectives that retain the **–e** are declined like **līber,** *free*. Those that drop the **–e** are declined like **noster.** Examples are:

	SINGULAR		PLURAL	
Nom.	ager	noster	agrī	nostrī
Gen.	agrī	nostrī	agrōrum	nostrōrum
Dat.	agrō	nostrō	agrīs	nostrīs
Acc.	agrum	nostrum	agrōs	nostrōs
Abl.	agrō	nostrō	agrīs	nostrīs
	SINGULAR		PLURAL	
Nom.	vir	līber	virī	līberī
Gen.	virī	līberī	virōrum	līberōrum
Dat.	virō	līberō	virīs	līberīs
Acc.	virum	līberum	virōs	līberōs
Abl.	virō	līberō	virīs	līberīs

Latin for American Students

Did you know that giving a slave his freedom could mean that he could become a Roman citizen? In other words, he was entitled to inherit part or all of his former master's estate and his sons were even eligible for the senate, knighthood, or the top ranks of the army. The manumission of slaves made upward social mobility possible within the rigid Roman hierarchical society.

ORAL PRACTICE

1. Decline **magister novus, puella lībera.**
2. Translate **equīs, agrum, virō, nostrī, līberōs, sacrā, plānōrum, singulī, casārum.**

The Present Tense of Sum

The verb *to be* is irregularly formed in English and Latin, as well as in other languages, and so does not belong to one of the "regular" conjugations. The principal parts of **sum** are **sum, esse, fuī, futūrus.** The present indicative is conjugated as follows:

The Metropolitan Museum of Art, Purchased with special funds and gifts of friends of the Museum, 1961 (61.198).

Classical themes were particularly popular during the 15th to 18th centuries (the Renaissance). The great Dutch artist Rembrandt painted "Aristotle Contemplating the Bust of Homer" in 1653, showing Aristotle dressed in the costume of that time but Homer in ancient garb.

sum, *I am*	sumus, *we are*
es, *you are*	estis, *you are*
est, *he, she, it is*	sunt, *they are*

Sum is a linking verb, so it does not have a direct object.

ORAL PRACTICE

Give the Latin in the proper case for the underlined words, telling which is a predicate nominative and which is a direct object.

1. They are sailors.
2. We are settlers.
3. They move the prisoners.
4. He is a slave.
5. I teach my friend.
6. You are boys.

EXERCISES

A. Translate the following sentences into good English.

1. Incitā, Mārce, equum ad agrum.
2. Magister noster linguam clāram docet.
3. Memoria clārōrum nostrōrum virōrum sacra est.
4. Magister tuus puerō malō pecūniam nōn dōnāvit.
5. In Americā magnōs agrōs et virōs līberōs vidēbitis.
6. Virī nostrī agrōs sociōrum amīcōrum nōn occupāvērunt.

B. Translate the following sentences into Latin.

1. Give Anna the boy's money.
2. In the provinces, we are free.
3. A friend of my son teaches boys.
4. I saw many horses in the fields of our friends.
5. The men moved the timber out of the forest with horses.
6. You are our little boy.

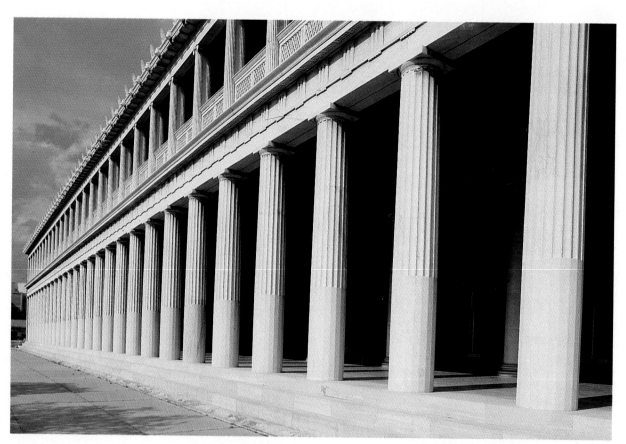

Ronald Sheridan/Ancient Art & Architecture Collection

The reconstructed Stoa of Attalus in Athens, 2nd century B.C. currently houses many beautiful Greek antiquities. The stoa was a long covered hall with an open colonnaded front and shops or a closed wall in back. They were frequently built around important buildings and surrounded the agora, or Greek marketplace.

C. Make up sensible answers to the following questions using the word in parentheses. Make all necessary changes. Follow the model below.

Marcus tuus filius est? (sīc) *Sīc, Marcus meus filius est.*

1. Ubi natāvistis? (aqua)
2. Rana in aquā est? (mensa)
3. Meum equum vīdistī? (silva)
4. Cūr ē silvā movistī? (ranae)
5. Ubi tua familia habitāvit? (Britannia)
6. Līber esse amās? (sīc)

Vocabulary 

Nouns

colō´nus, -ī, *m. settler* (colonial, colonize)
fī´lius, fi´lī, *m. son* (affiliated, filial)

Adjectives

lī´ber, lī´bera, lī´berum, *free* (liberal, liberated)
nos´ter, nos´tra, nos´trum, *our* (nostrum)
sa´cer, sa´cra, sa´crum, *sacred* (consecrate, sacrifice)

Verbs

ha´bitō, habitā´re, habitā´vī, habitā´tus, *live* (habitat, inhabitable)
mi´grō, migrā´re, migrā´vī, migrā´tūrus, *depart* (immigrant, migration)
sum, esse, fu´ī, futū´rus, *be* (essence, future)

Word Studies

1. Several Latin nouns and adjectives of the **–er** type are used in English: *arbiter, cancer, minister, vesper, integer, miser, neuter, sinister.*
2. **Assimilation.** Some prefixes change their final consonants to make them like the initial consonants of the words to which they are attached. This is called *assimilation* (**ad** = *to;* **similis** = *like*).

   The prefix **ad–** is generally assimilated. Identify the roots and define the following words—all of them formed from Latin words in the earlier vocabularies: *ac-curate, af-filiate, al-literation, an-nounce, ap-paratus, a-spect, as-sociate, ad-vocate.*

   Additional examples are: *ab-breviate, af-fect, ag-gressive, ac-quire, ar-rogant, at-tend,* and the word *as-similation* itself.

OCEANUS ATLANTICUS
MARE GERMANICUM
MARE SUEVIC
HIBERNIA
BRITANNIA
Eboracum
Londinium
Saxones
Albis
Visu
Rhenus
GERMANIA
Belgae
Sequana
Remi
Matrona
Lutetia
Liger
GALLIA
Celtae
Genua
Lugdunum
Helvetii
ALPES
RAETIA
NORICUM
PANNONIA
Garumna
AQUITANIA
Rhodanus
Mediolanum
Padus
Genua
PYRENAEI
Narbo
Massilia
Rubico
ILLYRICUM
Numantia
Hiberus
HISPANIA
Tagus
LUSITANIA
Tarraco
CORSICA
Roma
ITALIA
Ostia
Saguntum
Anas
Neapolis
Pompeii
Cannae
Dyrrachium
Tarentu
Corduba
Gades
BALEARES
SARDINIA
Nova Carthago
MARE
Utica
SICILIA
Aetna
Syracusae
Carthago
Zama
MAURETANIA
AFRICA
NUMIDIA
MELITA
Thapsus
ATLAS
MEDI
Leptis Magna
Roman Walls
Roman Territory 264 B.C. Before Punic Wars
Added Territory 238-201 B.C. After First and Second Punic Wars
Added Territory 133 B.C.
Added Territory 44 B.C. Death of Caesar
Added Territory 14 A.D. Death of Augustus
Added Territory Second Century A.D.
20°
10°
0°
10°
50°
40°
30°
0°
10°

IMPERIUM ROMANUM
SARMATIA
Tanais
SCYTHIA
DACIA
Danuvius
MOESIA
THRACIA
PONTUS EUXINUS
CAUCASUS
MARE CASPIUM
Bosporus
Byzantium
BITHYNIA
PONTUS
ARMENIA
Phillipi
Thessalonica
Troia
GALATIA
Pharsalus
ASIA
CAPPADOCIA
PARTHIA
Mare
Corinthus
Athenae
Aegaeum
Sparta
PAMPHYLIA
CILICIA
LYCIA
RHODUS
Antiochia
MESOPOTAMIA
ASSYRIA
Euphrates
Tigris
PHOENICIA
Palmyra
SYRIA
Damascus
Babylon
CRETA
CYPRUS
Tyrus
PALAESTINA
Hierosolyma
Cyrene
Alexandria
ARABIA
AEGYPTUS
Nilus
Scale of Miles
0 100 200 300 400 500
30° 40° 50° 60°

Glimpses of Roman Life

SLAVERY

In the earliest days the Romans had few slaves, but as prosperity and colonization spread they came to increasingly depend on them. Slaves did much of the work on the farms and in the trades and businesses that were developing. Slaves worked as unskilled laborers, mechanics, artisans, carpenters, bricklayers, seamen, and assistants to merchants and shopkeepers. Many slaves were prisoners of war, won in battles with foreign nations. Some of those who came from less developed countries may actually have profited from their exposure to Roman culture. But many from Greece and the Near East were more knowledgeable than their masters as a result of their background and early education. They became the teachers, doctors, musicians,

Scala/Art Resource, NY

Actors in Roman plays wore masks to indicate the type of part being played. Women's roles were played by men. Most of the actors were slaves or freedmen.

actors, and bookkeepers in Roman society. Although the educated and skilled slaves were given much personal freedom, they were still the master's property, and could be bought and sold at will. A highly educated slave might cost as much as $12,000 at today's prices, a trained farm worker slightly more than $1,000, a common laborer much less; physical strength, beauty, education, and skills were attributes highly sought after. The slave was generally of the same race as his or her master.

Wealthy Romans kept large numbers of slaves, many of whom had specialized tasks in the household (**familia urbana**). One might be in charge of polishing the silver, another of writing letters, and another of announcing the guests or the hour of the day. Great landholders sometimes had hundreds of slaves on their estates—a class of slaves called **familia rustica**—where they tended the herds and did the work of growing grapes, olives, or wheat.

The lot of the slave was not always so hard as we might imagine. The businesslike Romans realized that a slave was valuable property, although he was often mistreated by a cruel master or by a foreman who might himself be a slave. Disobedient slaves were punished in various ways. The master had the legal right to kill a slave, but naturally he was not often inclined to do so, as he would be destroying his own property. Flogging with a lash was a common punishment for minor offenses. Another more feared punishment was to send a city slave to the farm or to the mines, where the work was harder. Runaway slaves were branded on the forehead with the letter *F*, for **fugitīvus** when they were caught. Sometimes a former runaway slave wore a metal collar around the neck on which was inscribed the name of his owner. In 73–71 B.C. a slave named Spartacus led a mass revolt that seriously disturbed the peace of southern Italy until it was ruthlessly suppressed.

On the other hand, some slaves and their masters became close friends. A fine example of the close relationship between master and slave is that of Cicero and his secretary Tiro, a brilliant man who invented a system of shorthand. Many of Cicero's letters show the great affection and esteem he had for Tiro.

Most slaves were given an allowance, and the thrifty slave could hope to save enough in the course of years to buy his own freedom. Masters often granted freedom or manumitted their slaves out of gratitude for services rendered, many from a genuine feeling that slavery was evil. Others freed their slaves in their wills and left them a sum of money to begin a new life.

A few of these freedmen became very rich and influential. From the time of the Emperor Augustus in the first century A.D. until the rule of Hadrian, some freedmen took over highly important secretaryships in the imperial administration. Narcissus, the freedman secretary of the Emperor Claudius, made a tremendous fortune. He was even sent to hasten the Roman invasion of Britain in A.D. 48.

Scala/Art Resource, NY

Rich color and elaborate design are typical of later Roman art. Here we see a wall painting from the house of Lucrezio Frontone at Pompeii.

QUESTIONS

1. What differences are there between Roman slavery and that which once existed in the New World?
2. Does slavery still exist today? In the same form as in the Roman world or is it different?

Unit III Review
LESSONS X-XIV

Vocabulary

Nouns

amīcitia	cōnsilium	grātia	mensa
annus	disciplīna	lingua	patria
captīvus	discipulus	magister	praemium
castra	fīlius	māteria	signum
cēna	frūmentum	medicus	socius
colōnus	glōria		

Adjectives

altus	līber	sacer	singulī
barbarus	noster		

Verbs

ambulō	habeō	mereō	teneō
augeō	habitō	migrō	terreō
doceō	līberō	moveō	videō
ēvocō	maneō	sum	vocō

Adverbs

cur	ibi	primō

Prepositions

ā, ab	dē	ē, ex

Word Studies

1. Give prefix and Latin root word from which the following words are derived, and define: *defame, approve, advocate, invocation, immigrant, emigrant, avocation, vocation, deter.*

2. Choose the word in parentheses that most nearly gives the meaning of the italicized word. Tell why you selected it.
   a. *amicable* relations (friendly, social, free, hostile)
   b. a *puerile* act (poor, childish, manly, effeminate)
   c. a *docile* creature (wild, untamed, stubborn, easily taught)
   d. an animal's *habitat* (habit, appearance, living place, color)
   e. a *migratory* bird (singing, wandering, tame, nocturnal)

Grammar Summary

Nouns

Second Declension Neuter

Neuter nouns of the second declension end in **–um** in the nominative singular. They share the same second declension endings as the masculine nouns, except that the nominative singular and plural end in **–a**.

Nautae bonum cōnsilium dōnāvit.	*He gave the sailor good advice.*

The Ablative of Place From Which

The ablative is used with certain prepositions (**ab, ex, dē**) to express movement *from* a place. **Ab** is shortened to **ā** and **ex** to **ē** before a consonant.

Ā Romā migrāvit.	*He departed from Rome.*

Unit III Review
LESSONS X-XIV

The Vocative Case

The vocative case is used to address people directly. It has the same endings as the nominative except for second declension masculine nouns ending in **–us** and **–ius**. In this case, the **–us** changes to **–e** and the **–ius** changes to **–i**.

Nāvigā ad īnsulam, Marce.	*Sail to the island, Marcus.*
Servā tuam pecūniam, fīlī.	*Save your money, son.*

Adjectives

Like second declension nouns that end in **–r**, adjectives share the same endings. It is important to learn all three nominative forms in order to know whether the vowel is kept or retained in the stem.

Nostra fīlia in casā est.	*Our daughter is in the house.*
Nautae sunt līberī.	*The sailors are free.*

Verbs

Second Conjugation: Present and Future Tenses

Verbs that belong to the second conjugation have an **–e** in their present stem. The first principal part always ends in **–eō** and the infinitive always ends in **–ēre**.

In casā manēbimus.	*We shall remain in the house.*
Magister scientiam docet.	*The teacher teaches science.*

The Perfect Tense

The perfect tense is formed by adding the perfect endings (**–ī, istī, –it, –imus, –istis, –ērunt**) to the perfect stem. To find the perfect stem, drop the **–ī** from the third principal part. To translate it, use the *–ed* form of the verb, or the helping verbs *have* or *did*.

Trans īnsulam ambulāvisti.	*You walked across the island.*

The Verb To Be

The verb *to be* is rendered in Latin by **sum, esse, fuī, futūrus**. It is irregular in the present tense (**sum, es, est, sumus, estis, sunt**). It is also a linking verb, which means it never takes a direct object. Nouns that follow a linking verb are in the predicate nominative.

Medicus bonus vir est.	*The doctor is a good man.*

Sentence Analysis

It is a good idea to break down a sentence into individual words and identify the attributes of each before translating. This means that for nouns and adjectives, the gender, number, and case are important; for verbs, the person, number, and tense are important.

Unit Practice

Oral Practice

1. Decline **socius noster, agricola novus, signum nostrum**.
2. Conjugate in full and translate: **migrō** in the present, **maneō** in the perfect, **doceō** in the future.
3. What forms are **tenent, socī, tenuistis, fīliī, docēbitis, linguīs, fīlī, habēbis, habitāre, amīce?**
4. Translate into Latin: *he increases, they have, we have lived, he taught, I shall remain, they are calling, you* (sing.) *deserve, we work, you* (plur.) *will see, call out* (sing.), *walk* (plur.).

Exercises

A. Choose the right words in the parentheses to complete the sentences correctly. Identify the construction and translate.

1. Agrī sunt (magnī, magnōs).
2. Agricola (agrōs, agrī) habet.
3. Agricolae (in agrōs, in agrīs) labōrant.
4. In īnsulā (multī colōnī, multōs colōnōs) vidēbō.
5. In patriā nostrā (multās, multōs) agricolās habēmus.

B. Fill in the blanks and then translate the sentences into good English.

1. Agricola est bon__.
2. Portā aquam, serv__.
3. Colōnī multōs servōs habu__.
4. Amīcī meī sunt mult__ et bon__.

C. Working with a partner or in a small group, write about a trip. Indicate where you went, what you saw, and what you did. Use your imagination. You may want to include some of the following information.

1. To get there you sailed across the water. You also needed a cart and horse; maybe some servants helped you.
2. You saw evidence of old Roman camps, including an area where doctors helped the wounded.
3. New settlers now live where the queen kept her supplies of food, grain, and water.
4. You could tell that the life of the settlers was hard but good because the houses were big; probably the families were also big.
5. You are happy that you went because you have many good memories.

Erich Lessing/Art Resource, NY

Unit IV

Roman Social Life

This is the house of Poseidon and Amphitrite in Herculaneum, a town near Pompeii that was covered by volcanic ash during the eruption of Mt. Vesuvius in August, A.D. 79. From this view, we see the front portion of the house called the atrium. Here, guests were received and meals often served. It was common for the wealthy to recline on benches covered with pillows. A table with food would be set in the middle of the room. In the back wall is the lararium, or the shrine where the statuettes of the Lares, the household gods, were kept.

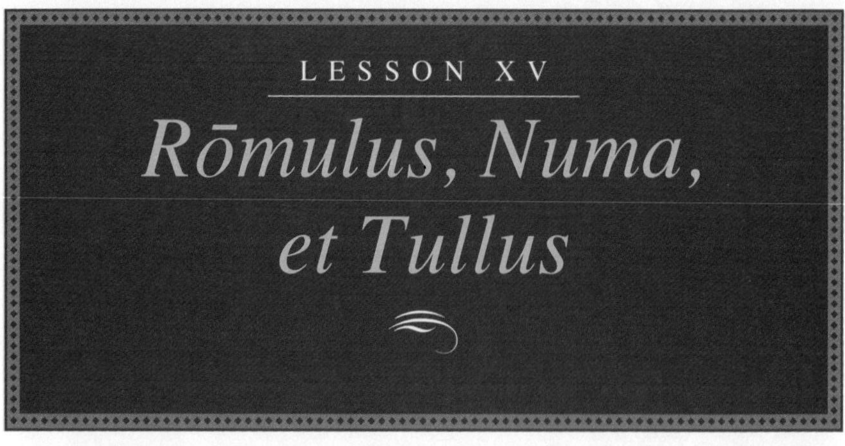

Prīmus rex[1] Rōmae Rōmulus fuit. Armīs et consiliīs bonīs glōriam Rōmae auxit. Virī et fēminae Rōmulum amāvērunt quod multīs familiīs asȳlum[2] dōnāvit et ad victōriam sociōs incitāvit. "Rōma magna erit," inquit[4] Rōmulus. "Clārī eritis."

Secundus rex Rōmae fuit Numa Pompilius. Numa bellum nōn amāvit. Deam Ēgeriam amāvit. Ēgeria Numam dē cūrīs sacrīs docuit. Tum rex Rōmānōs docēre mātūrāvit. "Deī amīcī Rōmae erunt," inquit Numa, "sī[3] bonī et grātī erimus. Multam grātiam deīs habēre dēbēmus."

Tertius rex Rōmae fuit Tullus Hostīlius. Concordiam nōn amāvit et reverentiam[4] parvam habuit. Tullus multa bella mōvit. Officia sacra nōn complēvit.[5] In extrēmīs,[6] Tullus inquit, "Bonus vir et rex ero." Sed Iuppiter nōn probāvit et vītam Tullī occupāvit.

[1] *king*
[2] *refuge, asylum*
[3] *if*
[4] *reverence*
[5] *he did not fulfil*
[6] *in his final hours*

QUESTIONS

1. Why was Romulus a popular king?
2. How did King Numa learn so much about the gods?
3. What did King Tullus neglect?

Grammar

The Future and Perfect of *Sum*

The future tense of **sum**, like the present tense, is slightly irregular.

er**ō**, *I shall be*	er**imus**, *we shall be*
er**is**, *you will be*	er**itis**, *you will be*
er**it**, *he, she, it will be*	er**unt**, *they will be*

AKG/Photo Researchers

A marble relief of Romulus and Remus. According to legend, these twins were the offspring of Mars and Rhea Silvia. Ordered to be exposed by a usurper to the throne, they were nursed by a she-wolf until they were found and raised by a shepherd. After an omen proclaimed Romulus to be the rightful ruler, he killed Remus and became the first of Rome's seven kings, ruling from 753-716 B.C.

The perfect tense, however, is perfectly regular.

fuī, *I have been*	fuimus, *we have been*
fuistī, *you have been*	fuistis, *you have been*
fuit, *he, she, it has been*	fuērunt, *they have been*

ORAL PRACTICE

1. Translate into English: **es, erit, fuērunt, sunt, erimus, fuistī.**
2. Translate into Latin: *we have been, you (pl.) are, I am, she has been, you (s.) will be, they will be.*

Uses of the Infinitive

You have learned that the present infinitive is the second principal part of the verb and that it is used to find the present stem. You have also used it several times to complete the meaning of the conjugated verb. In this case, the infinitive is actually the *direct object* of the verb.

Ad Ītaliam nāvigāre parat.	*He is preparing to sail to Italy.*
In silvā ambulāre amāmus.	*We love to walk in the woods.*

A Nike, or Victory statue, was a common theme throughout the Roman empire. They were found in major government buildings, always showing a person with spread wings and flowing robes.

Ronald Sheridan/Ancient Art & Architecture Collection

NOTĀ·BENE

The infinitive is always neuter and singular.

The infinitive can also be used as the *subject* or the *predicate nominative* of the sentence. Sometimes *it* is used in English to make the translation smoother.

Amīcōs habēre est grātum.	*To have friends is pleasing.*
Vidēre est crēdere.	*To see is to believe.*
Bonum erat Annam vidēre.	*It was good to see Anna.*

ORAL PRACTICE

Translate the phrases in italics and state whether you are using the infinitive as a subject, predicate nominative, or direct object: I deserve *to help; To be free* is great; He prepared *to depart;* It is pleasing *to announce* good things.

The Ablative of Accompaniment

Another construction you have been using for several lessons now is the ablative of accompaniment. The preposition **cum** + *the ablative* is used to express *with* or *together with.*

Anna cum nautā ambulāvit.	*Anna walked with the sailor.*
Cum multīs virīs nāvigābit.	*He will sail with many men.*

ORAL PRACTICE

Decide which construction is needed in the following sentences: the ablative of accompaniment or the ablative of means.

1. Come with me.
2. Play with us, Jane.
3. John wrote with ink.
4. Anna is with the teacher.
5. George fought with snowballs.
6. You can play with these toys, Mike.

NOTĀ·BENE

Remember that to show the means by which or with which something is done, use the ablative of means (with no preposition). Use the ablative of accompaniment when with means accompaniment or association.

VIRŌ PUGNAT. (THE MAN IS USED AS A WEAPON.)

CUM VIRŌ PUGNAT.

EXERCISES

A. Translate the following sentences into good English.

1. Puellae et puerī cēnam bonam parāre dēbent.
2. Multōs equōs cum agricolīs in agrīs vidēre grātum fuit.
3. Pecūniam habēre est multās cūrās habēre.
4. Rēgīnae praemium nostrum mōnstrāre mātūrāmus.
5. Bonum erit concordiam et auxilium in bellō habēre.
6. Nūntiī praemiīs animōs nautārum incitāre parābunt.
7. Cum nostrīs sociīs signa et arma ad terram novam portāre mātūrāvimus.

B. Translate the words in italics into Latin.

1. Es (*my friend*).
2. Erit (*a farmer*).
3. Erat (*a sailor*).
4. Fuimus (*comrades*).
5. Erunt (*our friends*).

C. Translate the following sentences into Latin.

1. It is bad to owe money.
2. Farmers, hasten to increase the supply of grain.
3. We ought to report the plan of war to the men.
4. It was pleasing to see the courage and harmony of the colonists.
5. The messenger will hasten to report the victory to the fatherland.

D. Marcus and Cornelia have many things to do. Some of the things they did yesterday **(herī)**, some they are doing today **(hodiē)**, and some will be put off until tomorrow **(crās)**. Work with a partner to create a dialogue as they go through their list.

announce the good news to the family — Marcus–*Bona nova familiae nūntiāvistī?*

Cornelia–*Bona nova familiae crās nūntiābō.*

OR Cornelia–*Bona nova familiae hodiē nūntiō.*

OR Cornelia–*Bona nova familiae herī nūntiāvī.*

1. prepare a big dinner
2. work with the servants in the house
3. give the gift to your teacher
4. earn much money
5. show the new horses to the farmer

Latin for American Students

*Did you know that the march of a Roman footsoldier was about twenty miles a day? During the march, he carried a backpack called a **sarcina** which contained food for fifteen days, an ax, leather thong, chain, saw, basket, hook, pots, and two stakes used in the making of an evening camp. The soldier also carried his helmet, javelin, shield, and sword. The entire **sarcina** usually weighed about sixty-five pounds.*

Vocabulary

Nouns

arma, -ōrum, *n. pl. arms, weapons*	(arms, army)
auxilium, auxilī, *n. aid, help*	(auxiliary)
bellum, -i, *n. war*	(bellicose, belligerent)
concordia, -ae, *f. harmony*	(accord, concord)
dea, -ae, *f. goddess*	(adieu, deity)
deus, -i, *m. god*	(deify, deism)
nūntius, nūntī, *m. messenger*	(announce, denounce)
officium, officī, *n. duty, office*	(official, officiate)

Adjectives

secundus, -a, -um, *second*	(secondary, secondo)
tertius, -a, -um, *third*	(tercet, tertiary)

Verbs

dēbeo, dēbēre, dēbuī, dēbitus, *ought, owe*	(debtor, indebtedness)
inquit,[1] *he, she said*	
mātūrō, mātūrāre, mātūrāvī, mātūrātus, *hasten*	(mature, maturity)

Word Studies

1. What is meant by large *armaments?* When is a person called *bellicose?* What is an *auxiliary* engine on a yacht? What is a *debenture?* a *debit?* a *premature* judgment?
2. The preposition **in,** used as a prefix, is very common in English derivatives. Define the following which are formed from words found in recent vocabularies: *in-gratiate, in-habitant, in-spect, in-undate, in-voke, in-form.*
3. Define the following words: *im-migrant, im-port.* Other examples of assimilation are *il-lusion, ir-rigate.* Words that have come into English through French often have **en–** or **em–** for **in–** or **im–:** *enchant, inquire,* or *enquire.* Our word *envy* comes from Latin **in-vidia** (from **in-videō,** *look into* or *against, look askance at).*

What is meant by a *colonial* period of a nation's history? What is a *magnanimous* person? What is the difference between *immigration* and *emigration?*

[1] This is a defective verb in the perfect tense; only the third person singular is common.

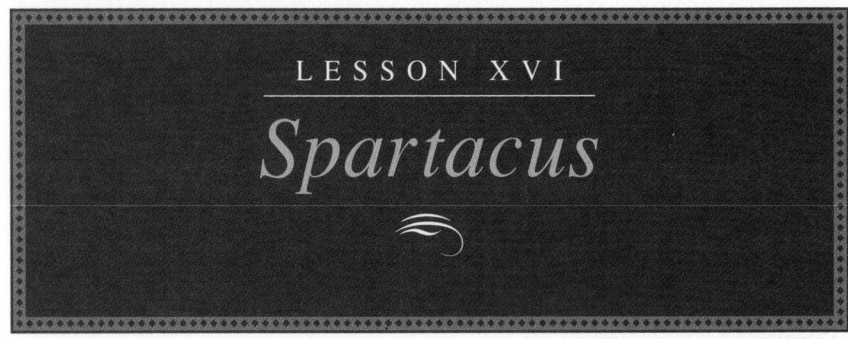

LESSON XVI
Spartacus

Spartacus fuit clārus servus, captīvus Rōmānōrum. Sociōs ēvocāvit et ad bellum incitāvit: "Ō sociī, Rōmānī nōn sunt aequī. Puer eram in oppidō meō, et vīta grāta semper erat. Magna erat concordia in patriā nostrā. Populus aequus erat. Silvās magnās et agrōs lātōs amāvī. Dominum nōn habuī; līber ibi fuī. Vērum amīcum habuī, puerum bonum et grātum. Sed Rōmānī patriam meam occupāvērunt; mē et amīcum meum ex patriā portāvērunt. Nunc post multōs annōs vir sum et in arēnā pūblicā pugnō. Hodie in hōc[1] oppidō virum quem[2] nōn cognōvī[3] occīdī[4] —et erat amīcus meus! Estisne virī? Populum Rōmānum et dominōs malōs nōn amātis. Iniūriās nōn merēmus. Causa nostra est aequa. Nōnne nunc hōra est? Ad arma! Pugnāte! Animum vestrum mōnstrāte! Vocāte sociōs vestrōs ad auxilium! Servōs līberābimus, līberī erimus, ad patriam nostram sacram migrāre mātūrābimus et ibi in agrīs nostrīs labōrābimus et in concordiā habitābimus."

[1] *this*
[2] *whom*
[3] *I recognized*
[4] *I killed*

QUESTIONS

1. What happened to Spartacus and his boyhood friend?
2. How did the friend die?

Grammar

Asking Questions

In Latin, as in English, there are two main types of questions: information questions and yes/no questions. To ask an information question in Latin, you use an interrogative pronoun, adjective, or adverb.

Ubi est Ītalia?	*Where is Italy?*
Quis in viā ambulat?	*Who is walking in the street?*
Quid spectās?	*What are you watching?*
Cūr exclāmāvistī?	*Why did you shout?*

E.T. Archives, London/SuperStock

Seating 50,000 people, the Colosseum was used for a variety of public entertainment, including gladiatorial contests between Roman slaves who had been trained to fight. Spartacus was one of the most famous Roman gladiators. In hot weather, large awnings were stretched over the top of the Colosseum to provide shade. In the foreground are columns of the Temple of Venus.

To ask a yes/no question, you add **–ne** to the end of the first word in the sentence. If you expect the answer to be *yes,* begin the sentence with **nōnne**. If you expect the answer to be *no,* begin the sentence with **num**.

Marcusne Clāram amat?	*Does Marcus love Clara?*
Nōnne Marcus Clāram amat?	*Marcus loves Clara, doesn't he?*
Num Marcus Clāram amat?	*Marcus doesn't love Clara, does he?*

ORAL PRACTICE

Ask the following questions in Latin. *Is the field wide? Where is your town? He prepared the dinner, didn't he? What are they carrying?*

Vir et femina. Even everyday people played a part in Roman art, as did this couple in fragment of a piece of gilded glass from the bottom of a plate.

Erich Lessing/Art Resource, NY

Conjunctions

There are several ways to connect your ideas in Latin. Using more than one will make your writing and conversation more interesting. You are already familiar with **et**. Another way to say *and* is to use **atque**, which also means *and also.* **Et...et** is the way to say *Both...and.* Finally, you can attach **–que** to the end of the second word in a pair of words as the equivalent of *and.*

Magister puerōs puellāsque docet.	*The teacher teaches girls and boys.*
Et equum et carrum habeō.	*I have both a horse and a wagon.*

ORAL PRACTICE

Translate the words in italics into Latin in two or more ways: *I saw the farmer and the sailor; The Gauls and the Romans* are fighting; They deserve *fame and rewards.*

Apposition

1. **Dominum meum, Lūcium Cornēlium, exspectō,** *I am waiting for my master, Lucius Cornelius.*
2. **Nautīs, amīcīs nostrīs, pecūniam dōnāvimus,** *We gave money to the sailors, our friends.*

You will note that **Lūcium Cornēlium** (1) identifies the object **dominum** and stands in direct relation to it, and is in the accusative like **dominum. Amīcīs nostrīs** (2) identifies **nautīs,** the indirect object, and is in the dative. No verb is involved. This construction is called *apposition.* A noun in apposition with another noun (or pronoun) is in the same case as that other noun (or pronoun).

ORAL PRACTICE

Translate the words in italics into Latin: I saw John, my *friend.* Have you heard the story of Spartacus, the *slave?* We lived in England, a large *island.* I told it to Mr. Jones, *my teacher.*

Spartacus, a Thracian gladiator, led an uprising of 90,000 Italian fugitive slaves in 73 B.C. *He defeated the Romans seven times, and was finally killed in a battle against Crassus at Lucania in 71* B.C.

THE GRANGER COLLECTION, New York

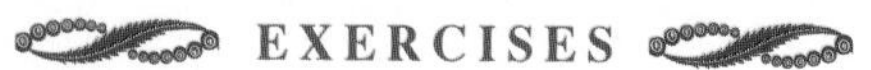

A. Answer the following questions in Latin.

1. Eurōpane est in Italiā?
2. Estne Italia īnsula?
3. Ubi est Rōma?
4. Estne Italia prōvincia?
5. Nōnne Marcus puer est?
6. Cūr Anna cum Clārā pugnat?
7. Et Marcum et Quintum vīdistī?

B. Rewrite the following sentences using the word in italics in apposition to the appropriate word in the sentence.

1. In oppidō, Rōmulum vidī. *(magister)*
2. Amīcī meī dōnum dōnāvī. *(Cornelius)*
3. In Britannia habitāvimus. *(magna insula)*
4. In Hispaniā, Isabellam spectāvī. *(rēgīna)*

C. Work with a partner to create a dialogue based on the following cues. Translate your dialogue into Latin, then act it out.

1. You greet each other.
2. You ask where your friend is going. **(ambulō)**
3. He/she is going to the Forum. **(Forum)**
4. You ask why he/she is going there.
5. He/she says that a messenger will announce the news.
6. You ask if the news is about **(dē)** the war in Gaul.
7. He/she says yes.
8. You decide to go with your friend **(tēcum)**.

Latin for American Students

*Did you know that the major newspaper of the ancient Romans was written on a series of tall boards attached to pillars in the Forum? The **Acta Dicturna** (Daily Happenings) posted the latest news from war fronts, the provinces, different sections of Rome, senate proceedings and government regulations, and news of personal interest. There were also "For sale" and "For rent" sections of the newspaper.*

Vocabulary

Nouns

causa, -ae, *f. cause, reason, case* (because, causal)
oppidum, -ī, *n. town*
populus, -ī, *m. people* (populace, popular)

Adjectives

aequus, -a, -um, *even, just, calm* (equality, equate)
lātus, -a, -um, *wide* (latitude, latitudinarian)
pūblicus, -a, -um, *public* (publican, publish)
vērus, -a, -um, *true* (verify, verity)
vester, vestra, vestrum,
your (referring to two or more persons)

Pronouns

quis, *who?*
quid, *what?* (quid pro quo)

Preposition

post (+ acc.), *after* (of time), *behind* (of place) (postdate, posterior)

Conjunctions

atque, *and, and also*
et...et, *both...and*
-que (joined to second word), *and*

Word Studies

1. What is *popular* government? Use *depopulate* in a sentence. What is meant by the sentence: "I listened to his attacks with *equanimity*"? Give three more derivatives of **aequus**.
2. Give three derivatives each from **nūntiō, portō, spectō,** and **vocō** by attaching one of the prefixes **ad–, dē–, ex–,** or **in–**.

LESSON XVII

Patrōnus et Clientēs[1]

In ātriō multī clientēs exspectant. Patrōnus, vir clārus, mox aderit.[2] Interim clientēs dē officiīs agunt. Patrōnum laudant quod amīcus et generōsus est.

CLIENS PRĪMUS: Salvē, amīce! Vīdistīne patrōnum nostrum?

CLIENS SECUNDUS: Minimē. Multa officia habet et in tablīnō labōrat.

CLIENS PRĪMUS: Parvum ōtium[3] habet quod prō aliīs[4] vītam agit. Cūrae aliōrum virōrum semper eum[5] movent.

CLIENS SECUNDUS: Ab officiīs novīs et dūrīs numquam cēdit. Nōnne saepe auxilium ad familiās nostrās mīsit?

CLIENS PRĪMUS: Sīc. Ergo[6] grātum est eum laudāre et grātiā nostrā fāmam eius[7] augēre.

Nunc patrōnus accedīt et virōs in ātrio salūtat.[8] Sportulās portat. In sportulīs cibum et pecūniam posuit. Sportulae sunt praemia. Quod clientēs fīdī[9] fuērunt, patrōnus sportulās ad familiās mittit.

Aliquandō[10] clientēs patrōnum spectant dum[11] causās in Forō agit. Aliquandō patrōnus clientēs[12] dēfendit. Aliquandō ad cēnam clientēs vocat. Nōn servī sunt, sed patrōnus paene dominus est. "Manus manum lavat."[13]

1 *a patron and his clients*
2 *he will be present*
3 *leisure*
4 *for others*
5 *him*
6 *therefore*
7 *his*
8 *greets*
9 *faithful*
10 *sometimes*
11 *while*
12 *clients*
13 *"One hand washes the other."*

QUESTIONS

1. What do the clients take home from the visit to their patron?
2. In what other way did Roman patrons provide for their clients?

Grammar

The Third Conjugation

Verbs of the *third conjugation* have the stem vowel **–ĕ–**. In the present tense, the short vowel **–ĕ–** of the third conjugation changes to **–ĭ–** in several places. Conjugate **pōnō, pōnere, posuī, positus,** *put, place*.

North Wind Picture Archives

This artist's reconstruction of an ancient Roman house is based on existing archaeological remains in Pompeii. The view looks through its atrium (note its basin) and the owner's office into the peristyle. At the right is a balcony leading into the second floor rooms. The lower sections of some columns are painted red to hide fingerprints!

PRESENT TENSE		PRESENT IMPERATIVE	
pōnō	pōnimus	pōne	pōnite
pōnis	pōnitis		
pōnit	pōnunt		

The perfect tense is conjugated regularly.

PERFECT TENSE	
posuī	posuimus
posuistī	posuistis
posuit	posuērunt

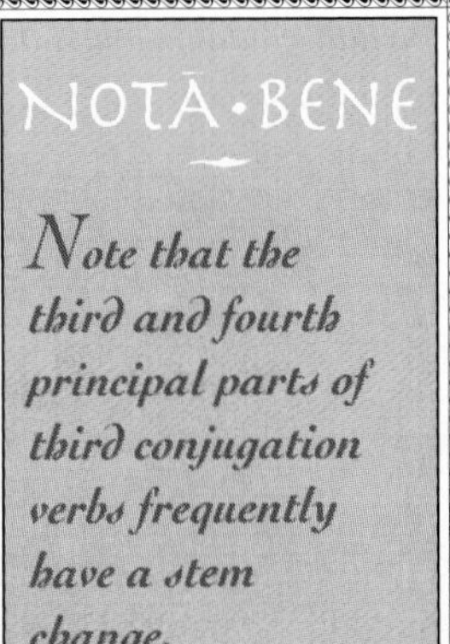

NOTĀ·BENE
Note that the third and fourth principal parts of third conjugation verbs frequently have a stem change.

ORAL PRACTICE

1. Conjugate **agō** and **dēfendō** in the present and perfect tenses.
2. Form the present imperative, singular and plural, of **cēdō, mittō, agō.**
3. Give the Latin for *he departs, he moves, he hastens, we are defending, you* (plur.) *approach.*

EXERCISES

A. Translate the following sentences into good English.

1. Litterāsne ad amīcōs vērōs mīsistī?
2. Semper, puerī, agite vītam bonam.
3. Equōsne tuōs, Cornēlī, in aquam agis?
4. Ubi praedam pōnitis? In viā praedam pōnimus.
5. In Americā, patriā nostrā, semper habitābimus.
6. Ad īnsulam cessimus et castra dēfendere parāvimus.

B. Translate the following sentences into Latin.

1. Is he not living a long life?
2. Send aid to our allies, the Roman people.
3. It is the duty of the prisoner to work in the fields.
4. We ought to increase the number of settlers in the province, shouldn't we?
5. The slave, a prisoner of the Romans, is preparing to put the grain into the wagon soon.

C. Working with a partner, imagine you are having a discussion with a Roman. Describe your family's house and have your (Roman) partner describe his or her house. You may find the following words and prepositions helpful.

ROOMS	PREPOSITIONS
ātrium, *entry hall*	**apud mē,** *at my house*
cubiculum, *bedroom*	**ante** (+ acc.), *in front of, before*
culīna, *kitchen*	**post** (+ acc.), *behind, after*
peristȳlium, *courtyard (porch)*	**super** (+ acc.), *above*
impluvium, *pool*	**sub** (+ abl.), *below*
tablīnum, *den, study*	**prope** (+ acc.), *near*
trīclīnium, *dining room*	

In this section of a Roman house, you can visualize the rectangular shape as you enter from the right into the vestibule. Guests were received in the atrium and the master of the house often had his office in the tablinum. Often an impluvium would be found in the center of the peristyle.

North Wind Picture Archives

SECTION OF A ROMAN HOUSE

Latin for American Students

Did you know that many of our common and useful pieces of furniture were unknown to the Romans? No mirrors hung on their walls; there were no chests of drawers, desks, or writing tables; no glass door cabinets to show objects of value and beauty. Even the houses of the wealthy were simply furnished with essential items like chairs, tables, couches, chests, wooden cabinets with doors, olive oil lamps, and an occasional brazier for heating rooms.

Vocabulary

Nouns

ātrium, ātrī, *n. entry hall* (atrium)
sportula, -ae, *f. small gift-basket*
tablīnum, -ī, *n. study, den*

Verbs

accēdō, accēdere, accessī, accessūrus, *approach* (accede, access)
agō, agere, ēgī, āctus, *do, drive, discuss, live, spend (time)* (action, active)
cēdō, cēdere, cessī, cessūrus, *move, retreat, yield* (concession, secede)
dēfendō, dēfendere, dēfendī, dēfēnsus, *defend* (defensive, indefensible)
excēdō, excēdere, excessī, excessūrus, *depart* (excess, excessive)
exspectō, exspectāre, exspectāvī, exspectātus, *look out for, await* (expect, expectation)
mittō, mittere, mīsī, missus, *let go, send* (missile, transmit)
pōnō, pōnere, posuī, positus, *put, place* (position, positive)

Adverbs

interim, *meanwhile*
mox, *soon*
numquam, *never*
saepe, *often*

Word Studies

1. Here are some Latin phrases commonly used in English:
   multum in parvo, *much in little*
   de novo, *anew,* literally, *from a new* (start)
   In Memoriam, *To the memory (of).*
   Tennyson used this as a title for a poem.
   ex animo, *from the heart* (sincerely)
   Experientia docet, *Experience teaches.*
   ad infinitum, *to infinity,* i.e., without limit
   ad astra per aspera, *to the stars through difficulties*
   (used by Kansas as its state motto)

2. Can you think of other literary or musical works or state mottoes that are in Latin? What do they mean in English?

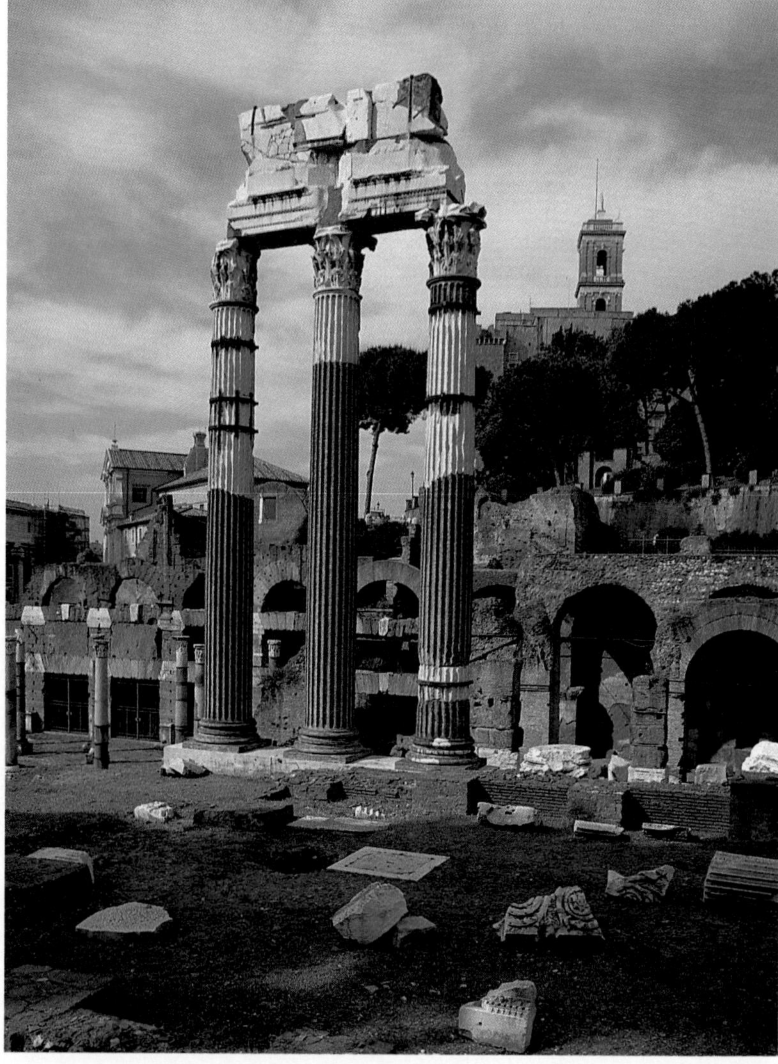

Larry Lee/Westlight

In the Forum of Julius Caesar, we see the three columns of the Temple of Venus Genetrix. In the background are the arched remains of the numerous shops that prospered during Roman times. The Forum of Julius Caesar is located a short distance from the Roman Forum.

LESSON XVIII
Rōmānī

Quondam[1] Rōma, oppidum Italiae, parva erat. Rōmānī, populus firmus, oppidum mūnīvērunt quod arma capere et patriam dēfendere parāvērunt. Victōriīs magnīs patriam servavērunt et auxērunt. Ex multīs terrīs praedam ēgērunt. Deīs grātiās ēgērunt et templa magna et alta fēcērunt. Magna praemia Rōmānī meruērunt et accēpērunt, quod officium fēcērunt. Magnum numerum colōnōrum in aliās[2] terrās mīsērunt. Multās terrās barbarās cēpērunt, prōvinciās fēcērunt et aequē[3] rēxērunt. Barbarī linguam Latīnam accēpērunt. Rōmānī frūmentum ex aliīs[2] terrīs in Italiam portāvērunt. Ad Britanniam, Hispāniam, Āfricam, Graeciam, Asiam nāvigāvērunt et oppida mūnīvērunt. Rōma multōs annōs multōs populōs rēxit.

Nunc Rōma magna et pulchra est. Multī ad Italiam veniunt et viās antīquās et templa pulchra inveniunt. Mātūrābisne in Italiam venīre et ruīnās Rōmānās invenīre?

[1] *once*
[2] *other*
[3] *justly*

QUESTIONS

1. Why were the Romans rewarded?
2. What do visitors to Italy see?

Latin for American Students

Did you know that one of the oldest and most famous priest colleges of Rome was located in the temple dedicated to Vesta, the goddess of the hearth? The worship of this goddess was directed by six women called ***Virgines Vestales*** *(Vestal Virgins) who tended the sacred fire on the altar and took part in Roman festivals. Each Vestal spent ten years learning her duties, ten years performing them, and then ten years training younger women.*

Grammar

Third (–iō) and Fourth Conjugation Verbs

In a few important verbs of the third conjugation, a short **–ĭ–** is inserted before the stem vowel in the first person singular and in the third person plural of the present tense. They are often called **"–iō** verbs" of the third conjugation and are conjugated like **capiō,** *take.*

But most verbs ending in **–iō** belong to the *fourth conjugation* and have a stem vowel long **–ī–.** They retain this long **–ī–** throughout their conjugation except where long vowels are regularly shortened. Fourth conjugation verbs are conjugated like **mūniō,** *fortify.*

THIRD CONJUGATION		FOURTH CONJUGATION	
capiō	capimus	mūniō	mūnīmus
capis	capitis	mūnīs	mūnītis
capit	capiunt	mūnit	mūniunt

The imperative shows similar differences: **cape, capite;**[1] **mūnī, mūnīte.** The perfect tense is conjugated regularly.

ORAL PRACTICE

1. Conjugate in the present tense: **accīpiō, capiō, veniō.**
2. Give the present imperatives of: **mūniō, faciō, incipiō.**
3. Conjugate in the perfect tense: **inveniō, incipiō, faciō.**

Word Sense and Idiomatic Expressions

Few words in any language have exactly the same meaning at all times. Verbs are particularly prone to having different shades of meaning. These differences can be affected by the context or by another word in the sentence. Although it is important to know the general meaning of a word, it is just as important to know alternate meanings in order to make your English translation sound better. Let's look at one verb, **agō,** to see how its meaning can vary.

equum agere, *to drive a horse*
praedam agere, *to carry off loot*
multum agere, *to do much*
grātiās agere, *to give thanks* (+ dat.)
causam agere, *to plead a case*
vītam agere, *to live a life*
dē officiīs agere, *to talk about duties*

[1] The imperative singular of **faciō** is **fac.**

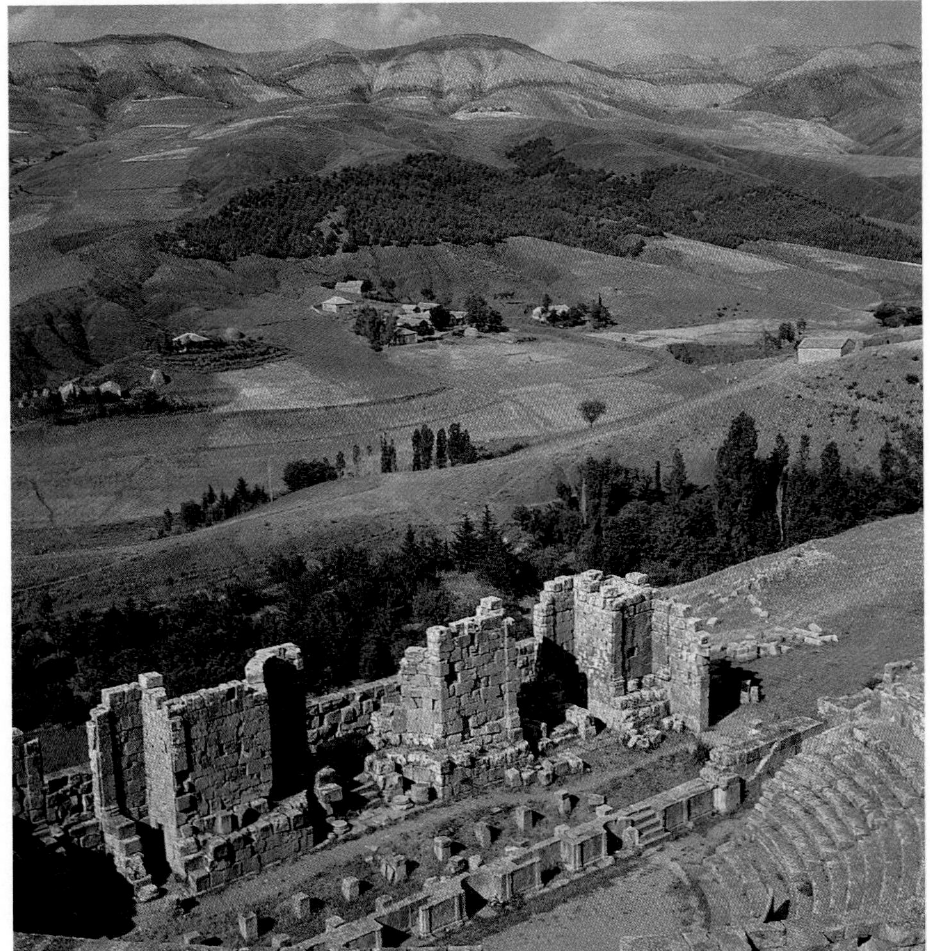

G. Ricatto/SuperStock

These well-preserved theater ruins in Djemila, Algeria, show once again the far-flung influence of the Romans throughout the Mediterranean area. In some parts of the world, the theaters are still used today to stage plays.

A verb can also have a completely different meaning from the general one when combined with a specific word. These are called *idiomatic expressions*. Some common examples include:

grātiam habēre, *to feel grateful*
bellum gerere, *to wage war*
castra pōnere, *to pitch camp*
viam mūnīre, *to build a road*
memoriā tenēre, *to remember*
cōnsilium capere, *to adopt a plan*

ORAL PRACTICE

Translate the phrases in italics: The men *pitched camp* in the field; I *felt grateful* for their help; The patron *is pleading a case* for his client; *You will remember* this day always.

EXERCISES

A. Translate the following sentences into good English.

1. Castra mūniunt et virōs ēvocant.
2. Ubi estis, puerī et puellae? Venīmus, magister.
3. Nōnne aequum est semper amīcōs dēfendere?
4. In agrīs frūmentum, magnum auxilium, invenīmus.
5. Virī singulī praemia accipiunt, quod officium fēcērunt.
6. Mārcus multum agit. In agrīs equōs agit, in bellō praedam agit, in forō causās agit, amīcō pro cēnā grātiās agit, cum amīcīs dē officiīs agit. Vītam bonam agit.

B. Translate the following sentences into Latin.

1. We are pitching the camp.
2. It is pleasing to find money.
3. We did not find our friend Marcus.
4. Marcus is not receiving a reward because he did not come.
5. A beautiful queen rules the people.

C. Ask questions from the following answers. Then work with a partner to ask and answer the questions. (There may be more than one correct answer or question.)

Caesar in Gallia bellum gessit. *Ubi Caesar bellum gessit?*

1. Patrōnus dē officiīs ēgit.
2. Bonam fortūnam meam memoriā tenet.
3. Bellum gessērunt in provinciīs.
4. Sīc, rēgīnae grātiās ēgimus.
5. Minimē, malī praedam nōn agunt.
6. Virī in agrīs castra posuērunt.

Wayne Rowe

Probably no one is more immediately associated with Rome and the Roman civilization than Augustus Caesar, the first Roman emperor (27 B.C.–14 A.D.). Such heroic-looking statues dotted Rome to emphasize for its residents and visitors the greatness and power of the empire.

Vocabulary

Noun

templum, -ī, *n. temple* (contemplate, temple)

Adjective

pulcher, -chra, -chrum, *beautiful* (pulchritude, pulchritudinous)

Verbs

accipiō, accipere, accēpī, acceptus, *receive* (accept, acceptable)

capiō, capere, cēpī, captus, *take, seize* (captive, capture)

faciō, facere, fēcī, factus, *do, make* (efficient, manufacture)

gerō, gerere, gessī, gestus, *carry on* (belligerent, gerund)

incipiō, incipere, incēpī, inceptus, *take to, begin* (inception, incipient)

inveniō, invenīre, invēnī, inventus, *find, come upon* (invent, invention)

mūniō, mūnīre, mūnīvī, mūnītus, *fortify* (muniment, munitions)

regō, regere, rēxī, rēctus, *rule, reign, guide* (regal, regent)

veniō, venīre, vēnī, ventūrus, *come* (convene, convention)

Preposition

prō (+ abl.), *for, in behalf of, in front of, before* (proactive, prolapse)

Word Studies

The preposition **cum** is often used as a prefix in Latin and English but always in the assimilated forms **com–, con–, col–, cor–, co–.** In compounds it usually means *together* rather than *with.*

Define the following words, all formed from verbs which you have studied: *convoke, collaborate, commotion, convene.* What is a political *convention?*

Give five other English words formed by attaching this prefix to Latin verbs, nouns, or adjectives already presented and studied.

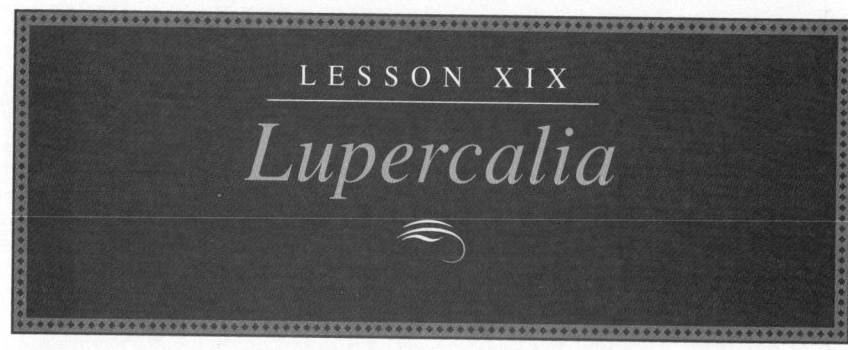

[1] *this*
[2] *whom*
[3] *herds, flocks*
[4] *fertility* (gen. pl.)
[5] *fertility* (acc. sing.)
[6] *February* (atonement month)
[7] *to him*
[8] *dog*
[9] *called*
[10] *names*
[11] *love notes*
[12] *love*

Rōmānī feriās amāvērunt. Tōtōs deōs et tōtās deās celebrāre amāvērunt. Hoc[1] fēcērunt quod deī et deae Rōmānōs adiuvāvērunt et defendērunt. Ūnus deōrum quem[2] celebrāre amāvērunt Faunus erat. Faunus erat deus pecorum[3] et fertilitatis.[4] Rōmānī fertilitatem[5] feminārum et pecorum et agrōrum dēfendere amāvērunt. Faunum mense[6] Februariō celebrāvērunt.

Faunus erat deus in silvā, sed in oppidō Rōmānī Faunum Lupercum appellāvērunt. Lupercum in templō in Palatinō adorāvērunt. Ut celebrent Lupercum, eī[7] caprōs et ūnum canem[8] sacrificāvērunt. Tum adulescentulī, Lupercī appellatī,[9] flagella coriō caprī fēcērunt. Tum circum Palatinum cum flagellīs cucurrērunt. Fēminās flagellīs ferīvērunt.[1] Tum fēminae multōs līberōs habēbunt.

Fēminae nomina[10] in epistulā amātōriā[11] scripsērunt. Epistulās amātōriās in urnā posuērunt. Vir epistulam amātōriam cēpit. Tum amīcitiam et amōrem[12] fēminae petīvit.

QUESTIONS

1. Why was the god Faunus so important to the Romans?
2. What did the young men do during the festival?
3. What did the young women do?

Grammar

Formation of Adverbs

In English, adverbs are regularly formed by adding *–ly* to an adjective.

clear	clearly
free	freely

[1] The women were touched, not hit by the whips. Women who wanted to get pregnant deliberately got in the way.

Although animal sacrifice was common throughout much of the ancient world, it was much less so with the Romans. This Pompeiian altar, though, depicts a scene from a sacrifice, possibly from a Lupercal celebration.

In Latin, adverbs are regularly formed from first and second declensions by adding **–ē** to the stem.

clārus	clārē
līber	līberē

ORAL PRACTICE

1. Form adverbs from: **publicus, grātus, beātus, ignāvus.**
2. Translate into Latin: *truly, beautifully, equally.*

Numbers

In Latin, only the numbers *one, two,* and *three* are declined and therefore agree in gender, number, and case with the noun they modify. All the others have only one indeclinable form.

	unus			duo		
Nom.	ūnus	ūna	ūnum	duo	duae	duo
Gen.	ūnīus	ūnīus	unīus	duōrum	duārum	duōrum
Dat.	ūnī	ūnī	ūnī	duōbus	duābus	duōbus
Acc.	ūnum	ūnam	ūnum	duōs	duās	duo
Abl.	ūnō	ūnā	ūnō	duōbus	duābus	duōbus

In the declension of *three,* the masculine and feminine have the same forms.

	tres	
Nom.	trēs	tria
Gen.	trium	trium
Dat.	tribus	tribus
Acc.	trēs	tria
Abl.	tribus	tribus

Other numbers you may wish to use are:

quattuor IV	**octō** VIII	**duodecim** XII
quinque V	**novem** IX	**vīgintī** XX
sex VI	**decem** X	**centum** C
septem VII	**ūndecim** XI	**mille** M

ORAL PRACTICE

Answer the following questions with a number in Latin. *How many lessons were in Unit I of this textbook? How many in Unit II? How many people are in your family? What is the number of the grade you are in? How many students are in your class?*

Word Order

You know that the words in a Latin sentence show their connection with one another by means of endings, regardless of position (unlike English). They may be shifted rather freely without obscuring the relationship. The more or less normal order is:

Nominative › Genitive › Ablative › Dative › Accusative › Adverb › Verb (noun/adjective)

To summarize:

1. Adjectives, including possessive adjectives, usually follow nouns, but adjectives that indicate quantity and size usually precede: **virī bonī, multa pecunia, amicus meus**.
2. A genitive most often follows its noun.
3. An indirect object (dative) comes before the direct object (accusative).
4. The verb generally goes last, although a linking verb is often found in the middle of a sentence.

NOTĀ·BENE

Generally speaking, when the word order is shifted, it is done for emphasis.

EXERCISES

A. Translate the following sentences into good English.

1. Magnum fuit praemium nostrae victōriae.
2. Invēnī in viā pecūniam, sed nōn cēpī.
3. Ubi sunt quattuor caprī tuī, Marce?
4. Vocā virōs ad arma, Mārce, et mūnī agrōs plānos.
5. Adulescentulī ad agrum altum vēnērunt et magnam silvam clārē vīdērunt.
6. Decem equōs habēre dēbēmus, sed trēs nunc habeō.
7. Magister tuus concordiam nōn fēcit, quod malī sunt puerī.

B. Translate the following sentences into Latin.

1. Great is the fame of our teacher.
2. Have you seen the two little whips?
3. Are you coming to our friend's dinner?
4. The children love to run to the Forum.
5. The teacher taught the boys and girls science.

C. Working with a partner, write a short letter to a friend in a neighboring Roman province telling him or her about the Lupercalia celebration in your town. Include as much information as possible, including where it took place; how many young men and women were involved; how many goats were sacrificed, etc.

Vocabulary

Nouns

adulescentulus, -ī, *m. young man* (adolescence, adolescent)
caper, caprī, *m. goat* (caper, capriole)
corium, corī, *n. skin, leather* (currier, excoriate)
feriae, -ārum, *f. pl. holiday* (fair)
flagellum, -ī, *n. whip* (flagellate)
līberī, -ōrum, *m. pl. children*

Verbs

adōrō, adōrāre, adōrāvī, adōrātus, *worship* (adoration, adore)
appellō, appellāre, appellāvī, appellātus, *call, name, address* (appeal, appellation)
currō, currere, cucurrī, cursūrus, *run* (current, curriculum)
ferio, ferīre, ferīvī, ferītus, *hit, strike*
petō, petere, petīvī, petītus, *seek, attack, aim at, ask (for)* (compete, petition)
sacrificō, sacrificāre, sacrificāvī, sacrificātus, *sacrifice* (+ dat.) (sacrificial)
scrībō, scrībere, scripsī, scriptus, *write* (inscribe, scribble)

Preposition

circum (+ acc.), *around* (circumnavigate, circumspect)

Word Studies

Explain the following Latin expressions: **post scriptum, cave canem, ē plūribus ūnum, multum in parvō, semper parātus, amor caecus est, festīna lentē.**

Latin for American Students

Did you know that goat's meat was often eaten only by the lower classes in Rome? The consumption of beef was considered a luxury and ordinary citizens only ate beef on special occasions as a result of animal sacrifices at festivals. Pork was the choicest domestic meat and was widely used by both the wealthy and the poor. Evidence of this popularity is shown in the many Latin words for pig like **sus, porcus, porca,** *and* **aper.**

Scala/Art Resource, NY

The Pantheon, built from A.D. *118-128, is the best preserved of all Roman buildings. Constructed during the reign of Hadrian, it is an immense round temple with a dome. The inside diameter is 142′ and the walls are 20′ thick. The proportions are such that if the dome were a sphere, it would just "kiss" the floor. The only window in the building is the round oculus at the top of the dome—an open hole 30′ in diameter which lets in both light and rain, some of the god's major gifts to humankind. The sphere is also a symbolic reference to all the gods and goddesses in the heavens.*

Glimpses of Roman Life

SIGNS OF THE TIMES

Perhaps nothing gives us quite so intimate a glimpse of a civilization as its signs and posters on walls, in windows, and on posts. We are fortunate in being able to catch such a glimpse of the everyday life of ancient cities through the signs found at Pompeii and Herculaneum, two cities near Naples that were buried by a shower of volcanic ash and mud from Mt. Vesuvius in A.D 79. For more than two hundred years excavation has been going on in the ruins, and hundreds of notices painted or scratched on walls have been uncovered. Among them are the scribblings of small children, who practiced writing the alphabet. In the women's waiting room of the Forum Baths in Herculaneum, the Latin alphabet as far as the letter Q is written on the wall. Sometimes the writer started a fable, as "Once upon a time a mouse...." Sometimes lines were quoted from Vergil and other poets. In a shop in Herculaneum, a quote from Diogenes, a Greek philosopher, is neatly written in Greek. A kind of "pig Latin" is represented by **anumurb** for **urbānum**, like "eesay" for "see."

In Pompeii, there are messages to sweethearts; in one, greetings are sent to a girl whom the lover calls his "little fish." Another girl is called the "queen of Pompeii," evidently meaning the beauty queen. To another, who is unnamed, there is merely the message **Venus es.** Several run like this: **Helena amātur ā Rūfō,** "Rufus loves Helen." But another tells about a girl who cannot stand a certain boy. In the House of Telephus in Herculaneum, someone has penned: "Portumnus loves Amphianda, Januarius loves Veneria, We pray Venus that you should hold us in mind—this we only ask you."

Some of the messages are not very complimentary: "thief" occurs several times. One reads: **Stronnius nīl scit,** "Stronnius knows nothing." In another, one person says hello to another and adds: **Quid agit tibi dexter ocellus?** "How is your right eye?"—apparently having some fun about a black eye. The owners of houses in Pompeii tried to keep away idlers by such signs as: **Ōtiōsīs locus hic nōn est. Discēde, morātor,** "This is no place for idlers. Go away, loafer."

Sometimes there are New Year's greetings or holiday greetings (**Iō Sāturnālia).** In some cases a record is kept of special events such as a birthday or the arrival of the emperor. One writer indicates that he has a cold. One says that he (or she) baked bread on April 19; another that he put up olives on October 16; still another tells of setting a hen on April 30. One wall lists daily expenditures for cheese, bread, oil, and wine. In what appears to be a laundry list, a tunic and a cloak on April 20, underwear on May 7, two tunics on May 8 are mentioned. No wonder that some unknown writer scribbled: "Wall, I wonder that you have not collapsed from having to bear the tiresome stuff of so many writers."

When we come to formal notices, we find that election posters play a prominent part. Advertising in Pompeii was less restrained than in Herculaneum and both politicians and shopkeepers went in for the "hard sell." These ask support for this man or that because he is deserving or respectable or honest or because he delivers good bread, etc. The supporters include teamsters, tailors, barbers, dyers, and many other groups. One inscription advocates giving away the money in the public treasury!

Another group of notices advertises the shows of gladiators, similar to our prize fights. Besides mentioning the number of matches, they often name other attractions for the fans, such as awnings for sun protection, sprinklers for dust control, animal fights, and athletic contests.

Hotels and shops advertised frequently. One hotel in Pompeii offers a dining room with three couches and all conveniences **(commodīs).** In an apartment house **(īnsula),** shops on the ground floor are offered from July 1, and luxurious (**equestria,** suitable for a rich man) upstairs apartments; the advertisement suggests to "see agent of the owner." A wine shop in Herculaneum advertised its different wines with a depiction of the god Bacchus and the expression, "Come to the sign of the bowls! [of wine]."

Signs in Pompeii and Herculaneum offer rewards for return of lost or stolen articles. On one Pompeiian sign a man says that he found a horse on November 25 and asks the owner to claim it on a farm near the bridge.

Ronald Sheridan/Ancient Art & Architecture Collection

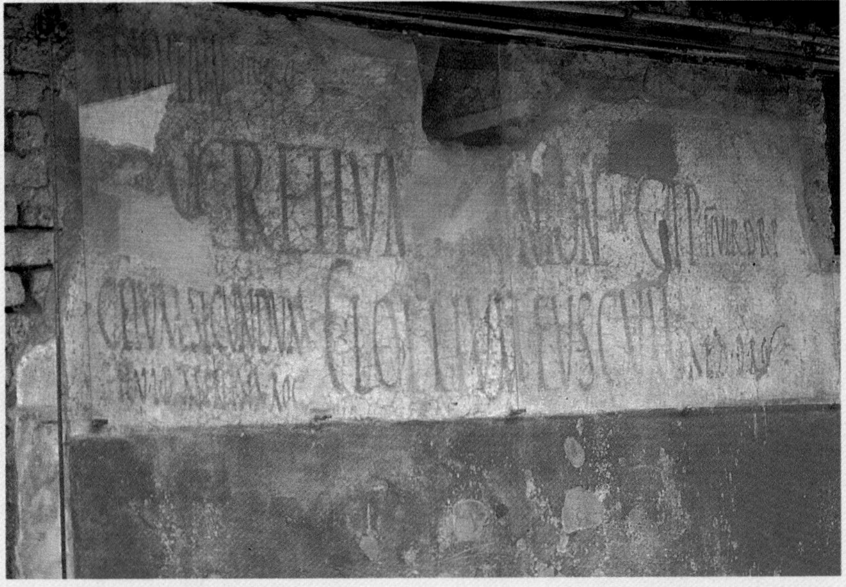

Election posters and notices of gladiatorial shows on a house front in Pompeii. They note that Lucretius Satrius furnishes 20 pairs of gladiators and his son 10 pairs.

Unit IV Review
LESSONS XV-XIX

Vocabulary

Nouns

adulescentulus	caper	feriae	oppidum
arma	causa	flagellum	populus
ātrium	concordia	līberī	sportula
auxilium	corium	nūntius	tablīnum
bellum	dea	officium	templum
	deus		

Adjectives

aequus	publicus	secundus	vērus
lātus	pulcher	tertius	vester

Verbs

accēdō	currō	gerō	petō
accipiō	debeō	incipiō	pōnō
adōrō	dēfendō	inquit	regō
agō	excēdō	inveniō	sacrificō
appellō	exspectō	mātūrō	scrībō
capiō	faciō	mittō	veniō
cēdō	feriō	mūniō	

Pronouns

quid quis

Conjunctions

atque et...et -que

Adverbs

interim mox numquam saepe

Prepositions

circum post pro

Word Studies

1. Give the prefix and Latin root word from which the following are derived: **excipiō, adigō, ērigō, afficiō;** *allocation, depopulate, exigency, efficient, accessory.*
2. Make Latin words out of **ad–** and **capiō, in–** and **pōnō, ad–** and **teneō, dē–** and **mereō.**
3. The first word in each of the following lines is a Latin word. Pick the correct derivative from the English words that follow it.

pōnō	pone	pony
	exponent	put
mittēmus	mitten	meet
	send	remit
populus	poplar	population
	pope	pop
capit	cap	cape
	decapitate	recipient
aequum	equestrian	equine
	equity	equip

Unit IV Review
LESSONS XV-XIX

Grammar Summary

Future and Perfect of *Sum*

Sum is irregular in the present and future, but regular in the perfect.

Līberī erunt bonī.	*The children will be good.*
Beātī fuimus in nostrā casā.	*We have been happy in our house.*

Uses of the Infinitive

The infinitive can be used as the subject of a sentence, as a predicate nominative, or as a direct object. It is always neuter and singular.

Ferīre magistrōs est malum.	*To hit teachers is bad.*
Annae litterās scrībere incēpī.	*I began to write a letter to Anna.*

The Third Conjugation

The third conjugation is characterized by an infinitive ending in **–ere**. The present tense and the present imperative show some additional spelling changes. The perfect tense is regular. Third conjugation verbs whose first principal part ends in **–iō** retain the short **–ĭ** in the first person singular and the third person plural.

Caesar bellum in Galliā gerit.	*Caesar is waging war in Gaul.*
Terrās novās petunt.	*They seek new lands.*
Currite ad oppidum, puerī!	*Run to the town, boys!*
Adulescentulī caprōs capiunt.	*The young men are taking the goats.*

The Fourth Conjugation

The fourth conjugation verbs all have an **–iō** in the first principal part and the present infinitive ends in **–īre**. They are conjugated regularly, except that a **–u** is inserted in the third person plural.

Ad templum venimus.	*We are coming to the temple.*
Viās in Galliā mūnīvērunt.	*They built roads in Gaul.*

Ablative of Accompaniment

Accompaniment is expressed by using the preposition **cum** + ablative.

Clāra cum Anna cucurrit.	*Clara ran with Anna.*
Cum līberīs ambulāvimus.	*We walked with the children.*

Unit IV Review
LESSONS XV-XIX

Asking Questions

There are two kinds of questions: information questions and yes/no questions. To ask an information question, begin your sentence with an interrogative adverb or pronoun. To ask a yes/no question, add **–ne** to the end of the first word. If you expect the answer to be *yes*, begin with **nōnne**; if you expect a *no* answer, begin with **num**.

Cūr celebrātis?	*Why are you celebrating?*
Patriamne tuam amās?	*Do you love your native land?*
Nōnne prō Rōma pugnās?	*You are fighting for Rome, aren't you?* OR *Aren't you fighting for Rome?*

Formation of Adverbs

Adverbs are formed from first and second declension adjectives by adding **–ē** to the stem.

Līberē vītam agere amāmus.	*We like to live freely.*

Numbers

Only the numbers one, two, and three are declined. All others are indeclinable.

Duōs equōs habeō.	*I have two horses.*
Octō līberōs habent.	*They have eight children.*

Unit Practice

Noun and Adjective Drill

1. Decline **multum auxilium, populus clārus, concordia vēra**.
2. Provide the Latin singular and plural of the following in the cases indicated:

nom.: *my duty*	dat.: *a good goat*
abl.: *our friend*	gen.: *a sacred land*
acc.: *a small child*	nom.: *a just man*

Verb Drill

A. Decide which form of **sum** translates the English in the first column:

1. *they were*	fuimus	sunt
	erant	sumus
2. *you will be*	erō	eris
	estis	fuistis
3. *you are*	eris	fuistī
	fuistis	es
4. *he was*	erant	erat
	erit	fuērunt
5. *we are*	sunt	sumus
	estis	erimus
6. *they will be*	erunt	erant
	erit	sunt
7. *we were*	erant	erimus
	sumus	fuimus

Unit IV Review
LESSONS XV-XIX

B. Give the third plural of the following verbs in the present, future, and perfect:

1. **sum**
2. **exspectō**
3. **dēbeō**
4. **mātūrō**
5. **ēvocō**

C. Translate the verb forms. Provide the tense, person, and number.

1. **regunt**
2. **pōnit**
3. **erunt**
4. **mātūrātis**
5. **mīsit**
6. **fuit**
7. **fēcistī**
8. **es**
9. **exspectābimus**
10. **eris**
11. **dūxērunt**
12. **invenīmus**
13. **veniunt**
14. **accēdit**
15. **laudābunt**

D. Translate into Latin:

1. *he will be*
2. *I fortified*
3. *they approached*
4. *you* (sing.) *worship*
5. *we are*
6. *they do*
7. *they received*
8. *you* (plur.) *came*
9. *we shall be*
10. *they will hasten*
11. *they will be*
12. *he seeks*
13. *we are defending*
14. *he departed*
15. *he takes*

E. Reread the *Glimpses of Roman Life*. Then work with a partner or in a small group and create similar slogans, sayings, and graffiti in Latin that would be appropriate now. Use your imagination!

Scala/Art Resource, NY

Unit V

Roman Myths and Legends

You may recall that according to legend, Romulus and Remus were the twin sons of Mars and the Vestal Virgin Rhea Silvia. When the babies were thrown into the Tiber River, they were miraculously saved by a she-wolf, who nursed them until they were found later by shepherds. Upon reaching adulthood, Romulus killed his brother in a quarrel and became the founder of Rome. This famous bronze of the wolf dates from Etruscan times (fifth century B.C.*).*

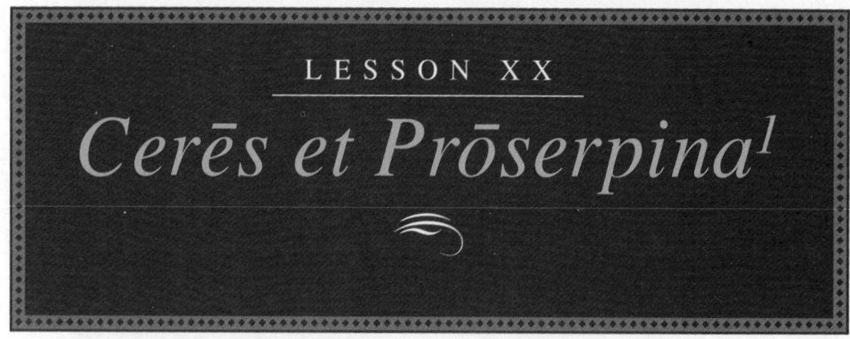

Cerēs, dea frūmentī, et fīlia Prōserpina in Siciliā habitāvērunt. Quondam[2] Prōserpina et aliae[3] puellae in agrīs erant. Locum commodum invēnērunt et flōrēs[4] variōs lēgērunt. Ōtium grātum erat; magnum erat studium puellārum.

Plūtō, deus īnferōrum,[5] Prōserpinam vīdit et amāvit. Equōs incitāvit et ad locum ubi puellae erant accessit. Puellae fūgērunt. Prōserpina fugere mātūrāvit, sed Plūtō valuit et eam[6] cēpit, in carrō posuit, ad īnferōs dūxit.

Cerēs nocte[7] ex agrīs vēnit. Fīliam exspectāvit, sed Prōserpina nōn vēnit. Magna erat cūra deae. Ad multa loca, ad terminōs terrae Cerēs accessit. Ōtium nōn invēnit.

Quod Cerēs Prōserpinam nōn invēnit, in agrīs nōn labōrāvit. Flōrēs nōn erant, frūmentum in agrīs nōn erat. Populus vītam dūram ēgit et deam accūsāvit quod pretium cibī magnum erat. Multī agricolae dīxērunt:

"Quid agēmus? In agrīs labōrāmus sed frūmentum nōn habēmus. Nōn valēmus. Deī nōn aequī sunt; officium nōn faciunt."

Iuppiter, quī deōs et virōs regit, iniūriās populī vīdit et deae agrōrum nūntiāvit:

"Prōserpina valet sed Plūtō eam habet. Mercurium nūntium ad īnferōs mittam. Mercurius fīliam tuam ad tē[8] dūcet. Sed nōn semper in terra Prōserpina manēbit. Ita commodum erit: partem[9] annī in terrā, partem sub terrā aget."

Ita Iuppiter concordiam effēcit. Cerēs fīliam accēpit. Prōserpina partem annī in terrā, partem sub terrā ēgit. Cum[10] lībera in terrā est, multōs flōrēs et magnam cōpiam frūmentī vidēmus, quod Cerēs grāta in agrīs est et magnum est studium deae. Sed cum Prōserpina ad īnferōs excēdit, Cerēs trīstis[11] est, et flōrēs variī nōn sunt.

[1] *Prosérpina*
[2] *once*
[3] *other*
[4] *flowers*
[5] *those below,* i.e., the ghosts of the dead in Hades
[6] *her*
[7] *at night*
[8] *you*
[9] *part* (acc. sing.)
[10] *whenever*
[11] *sad*

QUESTIONS

1. What was Proserpina doing when Pluto came?
2. What happened to the flowers after Proserpina left?
3. On what terms did Proserpina go back to her mother?

Both this woodcut of Pluto kidnapping Proserpina as well as the smaller one on the next page were illustrations from an edition of Ovid. This one was printed in 1501.

Grammar

Third Conjugation: Future

You know that the future sign of verbs of the first and second conjugations is **–bi–**. The future sign of verbs of the third and fourth conjugations, however, is long **–ē–**. The **–ō** verbs of the third conjugation substitute this long **–ē–** for the stem vowel, **–ĕ–**, except in the first person singular **(–am)**.

pōn**am**	pōn**ēmus**
pōn**ēs**	pōn**ētis**
pōn**et**	pōn**ent**

ORAL PRACTICE

1. Conjugate **dūcō, legō** in the future.
2. Conjugate **mittō** in the present, **cēdō** in the future, and **dēfendō** in the perfect.
3. Provide the form of **fūgit, valēbis, efficit, dūcēmus, docēmus, accipitis, mūniunt, migrāvit, agent.**

EXERCISES

A. Translate the following sentences into good English.

1. Cēdētisne puerīs malīs?
2. Valēsne, fīlia mea? Valeō.
3. Captīvī ab oppidō in silvās lātās fugiunt.
4. Litterās ad Mārcum, amīcum meum, mittam.
5. Puerī bonī ex studiīs magnam fāmam accipiunt.
6. Virī ex oppidō nōn excēdent sed puellās dēfendent.
7. Multās hōrās in ōtiō nōn agēmus sed semper labōrābimus.

B. Translate the following sentences into Latin.

1. They fortify the camp.
2. They will rule the province.
3. Did you approve the shape of the wagon?
4. It is not convenient to send a letter.
5. We shall remain in the town and send a messenger.

C. The story of Ceres and Proserpina is part of Roman mythology. Mythology was important to the Romans as a means of explaining events or teaching a lesson as do our fairy tales. Working in a small group, relate a short version of the story of Little Red Riding Hood in Latin. You may find the following vocabulary handy.

lūpus, -ī, *m. wolf*
avia, -ae, *f. grandmother*
oculus, -ī, *m. eye*
nāsus, -ī, *m. nose*
ōs, ōris, *n. mouth*
edō, ēsse, ēdī, ēsus, *eat*
interficiō, interficere, interfēcī, interfectus, *kill*

1. She took a gift basket.
2. She put food into the basket.
3. She departed and collected flowers on the way.
4. She saw a wolf and fled.
5. The wolf hastened to grandmother's house.
6. The wolf ate grandmother.
7. The girl approaches grandmother's house in the woods.
8. She comments on how big grandmother's eyes, nose, and mouth are.
9. The wolf hastens out of the bedroom.
10. The little girl shouts and flees and a man runs out of the forest.
11. The man is strong and he kills the wolf with a sword.

This woodcut, from a 1539 edition of Ovid, portrays Pluto and his horse in dark tones, presumably because he was the god of the underworld.

Vocabulary

Nouns

locus, -ī, *m. place; in plural,* **loca, -ōrum,** *n.* (local, location)

ōtium, ōtī, *n. leisure* (otiose)

pretium, pretī, *n. price* (appreciate, precious)

studium, studī, *n. eagerness, interest; pl. studies* (studio, studious)

terminus, -ī, *m. end, boundary* (exterminate, terminal)

Adjectives

commodus, -a, -um, *suitable, convenient* (accommodate, commodious)

varius, -a, -um, *changing, varying* (variable, variety)

Verbs

dīcō, dīcere, dixī, dictus, *say, tell* (dictionary, dictum)

dūcō, dūcere, dūxī, ductus, *lead, draw* (aqueduct, reduce)

efficiō, efficere, effēcī, effectus, *make (out), bring about* (effect, effective)

fugiō, fugere, fūgī, fugitūrus, *run away, flee* (fugitive, refugee)

legō, legere, lēgī, lectus, *collect, gather, pick, read* (collection, elect)

valeō, valēre, valuī, valitūrus, *be strong, be well* (valiant, valid)

Adverb

ita, *so*

Erich Lessing/Art Resource, NY

Ceres, the goddess of grain and the harvest, is often shown with food items, as she is here, carrying a fruit basket and accompanied by a wild boar.

Word Studies

1. What are *commodities* and why are they so called? Why does a good student "pursue" his or her *studies*? Can you explain the word *cereal*? Give three more derivatives of **varius**.
2. Here are some Latin phrases in English:
   auxilio ab alto, *by aid from (on) high*
   victoria, non praeda, *victory, not loot*
   Montani semper liberi, *Mountaineers (are) always free* (motto of the state of West Virginia).
   ex officio, *out of (as a result of) one's duty or office;* for example, a president of an organization may be a member of a committee *ex officio* as a result of his office as president.

Latin for American Students

Did you know that the Romans often celebrated holidays as many as 132 days each year during the rule of Augustus? Popular forms of holiday entertainment were the games, circus, or the theater. The great public games ***(ludi)*** *were free entertainments originally provided by the state to honor a god or goddess. They consisted of* ***ludi scaenici*** *(dramas and comedies at theaters),* ***munera gladiatoria*** *(staged combat between gladiators), and* ***ludi circenses*** *(chariot races and other exhibitions in a circus).*

Ronald Sheridan/Ancient Art & Architecture Collection

Magister discipulum tardum terret. While one boy begins to read from his roll, the teacher rebukes a latecomer. From a sculptured relief now in Treves, Germany.

Multa dē clārīs Rōmānīs ā magistrō tuō audiēs et ex librīs trahēs. Venīte, puerī et puellae! Nunc audiētis fābulam novam dē magistrō Orbiliō et dē discipulō eius[1] Quīntō.

Orbilius grammaticus dūrus erat; saepe discipulōs tardōs poenā afficiēbat. Quīntus saepe tardus erat, quod in viīs Rōmānīs pater eius[1] multa dē vītā mōnstrābat.

In scholā Orbilius discipulīs nūntiāvit: "Librī vestrī multa adiectīva[2] continent, quae litterīs *–ōsus* fīniuntur.[3] Litterae *–ōsus* sunt signum plēnitūdinis.[4] Spectāte; mōnstrāre incipiam:

"Verbum—verb-ōsus. Liber multa verba continet. Liber est plēnus verbōrum. Liber verbōsus est. Spectāte.

"Glōria—glōri-ōsus. Patria magnam glōriam accipiet. Patria plēna glōriae erit. Patria glōriōsa erit. Spectāte.

"Iniūria—iniūri-ōsus. Bellum plēnum iniūriārum est. Bellum iniūriōsum est.

"Sed ubi est Quīntus Horātius? Tardusne est? Nōnne est semper tardus? Studiōsus nōn est—ōtiōsus est. Poenā Quīntum afficiam—multās plāgās[5] dōnābō."

Et poenā nōn grātā miserum Quīntum affēcit. Sed nunc Orbilius famōsus est. Cur? Quod tardus discipulus Quīntus erat Quīntus Horātius Flaccus, clārus poēta Rōmānus. Posteā Horātius poēta magistrum Orbilium "plāgōsum Orbilium" in librō appellāvit, quod Orbilius plēnus plāgārum fuerat.[6] Quod Horātius verbum novum "plāgōsum" invēnit, multī discipulī plāgōsum Orbilium memoriā tenuērunt et semper tenēbunt.

[1] *his*
[2] *adjectives*
[3] *which end with the letters* **–ōsus**
[4] *of fullness*
[5] *whacks* (with a stick or whip)
[6] *had been*

QUESTIONS

1. What would be a good name for Orbilius today?
2. What English derivatives can you form by adding **–ōsus** to **victōria, cōpia, cūra**?

Grammar

The Future of Third (–iō) and Fourth Conjugation Verbs

Verbs of the third (**–iō**) and fourth conjugations form the future by adding **–ē–** (**–a–** in the first person singular) and the personal endings directly to the present stem. The long **–ī–** of the fourth conjugation stem is shortened.

THIRD CONJUGATION (**–iō**)		FOURTH CONJUGATION	
capiam	capiēmus	mūniam	mūniēmus
capiēs	capiētis	mūniēs	mūniētis
capiet	capient	mūniet	mūnient

ORAL PRACTICE

1. Give the future tense of **incipiō** and **audiō.**
2. Give the Latin for *they will affect, we shall hear, you* (plur.) *will receive, they will draw, it will contain.*
3. Tell the form of **inveniētis, audīs, faciam, vidēbunt, parāvistī.**

Equi carrum ducunt. Carriages could be large or small, depending on one's wealth. Obviously this person was rich enough to allot two horses to the carriage, instead of working in the fields. Stone relief from a sarcophagus, second century A.D.

C. M. Dixon

EXERCISES

A. Translate the following sentences into good English.

1. Equī carrōs agricolārum tardē trāxērunt.
2. Carrī magnam cōpiam frūmentī continent.
3. Equōs in locō lātō et commodō continēbimus.
4. Magister tardōs puerōs poenā pūblicē afficiet.
5. Nautae nostrī ex aquā virōs trahent et servābunt.
6. Colōnī ex agrīs frūmentum portābunt et magnam pecūniam accipient.

B. Translate the following sentences into Latin.

1. Will you come to my house?
2. We shall save the people with food.
3. Anna, a friendly girl, will receive a book.
4. The late boys will not hear the words of the famous man.
5. The boys will not receive a reward because they are late.

C. Working in a group of three (a **magister** and **duo discipulī**), create a dialogue based on the following cues. Then act it out in class.

MAGISTER: Where is ... (Discipulus 1)?

DISCIPULUS 2: He/she is coming. He/she is late.

DISCIPULUS 1: Did you hear the news?

MAGISTER: What did you hear?

DISCIPULUS 1: A famous poet (**poēta, -ae,** *m.*) is coming. He will come tomorrow.

DISCIPULUS 2: What will he do?

DISCIPULUS 1: He will tell the people and students about (**dē**) poetry (**poētica, -ae,** *f.*).

DISCIPULUS 2: Why will he do this (**hoc**)?

DISCIPULUS 1: He likes to write poetry.

DISCIPULUS 2: Will he teach the students to write poems?

MAGISTER: Yes. He will do this. You all must (ought) come to school tomorrow.

Ronald Sheridan/Ancient Art & Architecture Collection

Discipulus ludum parat. A young Roman schoolboy carries his tablet and stylus to school, ready to listen to his teacher.

Latin for American Students

*Did you know that the Romans adopted Greek ideas of education beyond the elementary level? Schools were established soon after the Punic Wars in which the curriculum was based on study of the Greek poets. The main subject was **grammatica** which included both Latin and Greek grammar, literature, and some literary criticism. Students were also taught geography, mythology, antiquities, history, and ethics by the **grammaticus** (teacher).*

Vocabulary

Nouns

grammaticus, -ī, *m. school teacher*	(grammar, grammarian)
liber, librī, *m. book*	(libel, library)
schola, -ae, *f. school*	(scholar, scholastic)
verbum, -ī, *n. word*	(verbal, verbose)

Adjectives

firmus, -a, -um, *strong, firm*	(affirmation, confirm)
miser, -era, -erum, *poor, wretched*	(miserable, misery)
perpetuus, -a, *-um, constant*	(perpetual, perpetuity)
tardus, -a, -um, *late, slow*	(retard, tardy)

Verbs

afficiō, afficere, affēcī, affectus, *affect, afflict with*	(affection, affective)
audiō, audīre, audīvī, audītus, *hear*	(audience, auditorium)
contineō, continēre, continuī, contentus, *hold (together), contain*	(content, tenure)
trahō, trahere, trāxī, tractus, *draw, drag*	(attraction, tractor)

Word Studies

Most prefixes are also used as prepositions, but a few are not. **Re–** is used only as a prefix in both Latin and English; it means *back* or *again.* It sometimes has the form **red–**, especially before vowels. Examples: ***re*tineō**, *hold* ***back;*** ***re*ficiō**, *make* ***again;*** ***red*igō**, *drive* ***back.***

In English, **re–** is freely used with all sorts of words: *remake, revisit, rehash, refill.*

Give seven examples of the prefix **re–** in English words derived from Latin. What are the meanings of *revoke, incipient, refugee, audition?*

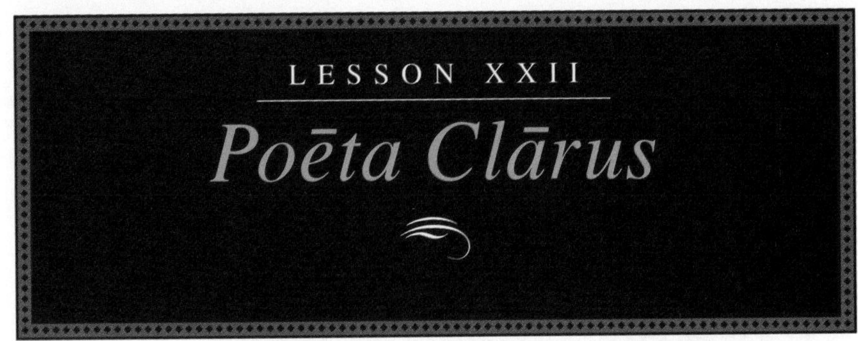

LESSON XXII
Poēta Clārus

Quondam puer parvus Pūblius prope Mantuam, oppidum Italiae, habitābat. Fīlius agricolae erat. In agrīs Pūblius nōn labōrābat, quod numquam valuit, sed agrōs, silvās, frūmentum, equōs amābat. In lūdō multōs librōs legēbat, multās fābulās dē glōriā patriae et dē locīs clārīs Italiae audiēbat, verba sententiāsque magistrī memoriā tenēbat.

Reliquī puerī in patriā mānsērunt, sed Pūblius, nunc vir, in urbe[1] Rōmā studia coluit.[2] In Forō Rōmānō verba numquam fēcit, quod timidus erat et populus eum[3] terrēbat. Bella armaque semper fugiēbat, concordiam ōtiumque amābat. Agrōs et casam familiae āmīsit, sed auxiliō amīcōrum recēpit. Magnam gratiam amīcīs semper habēbat. Amīcōs nōn multōs sed firmōs habēbat. Tum carmina[4] varia dē agrīs agricolīsque scrībere incēpit. Tardē scrībēbat multumque labōrābat, sed nōn multa carmina effēcit. Posteā magnum carmen[5] dē bellō Troiānōrum et dē glōriā Rōmae scrīpsit.

Audīvistisne dē Pūbliō, puerī puellaeque? Erat Pūblius Vergilius Marō,[6] poēta clārus Rōmānus, quī reliquōs poētās Rōmānōs superāvit. Lēgistis legētisque fābulam pulchram Vergilī dē Aenēā.

[1] *city*
[2] *cultivated, carried on*
[3] *him*
[4] *songs, poems* (acc. pl.)
[5] *song, poem* (acc. sing.)
[6] Nominative singular

QUESTIONS

1. What did Vergil prefer to do as a boy?
2. Why did Vergil never become an orator?
3. What did Vergil write about?

Grammar

The Imperfect Tense

The Latin *imperfect* tense is called imperfect because it often represents incomplete or repetitive actions in the past. It is formed by adding the tense sign **–bā–** to the present stem and then attaching the personal endings, which you already know. It is translated into English by *was, were, used to.*

It may seem that boys received more attention than girls in the ancient world, but this man's daughter was very important to him, since her image walking along with him is carved on this sarcophagus.

Erich Lessing/Art Resource, NY

NOTĀ·BENE

All four conjugations are conjugated the same way in the imperfect.

SINGULAR	PLURAL
portā**bam**	portā**bāmus**
portā**bās**	portā**bātis**
portā**bat**	portā**bant**

In silvā ambulābāmus.	*We used to walk in the woods.*
Discipulōs docēbat.	*He was teaching the students.*
Multōs librōs legēbās.	*You used to read many books.*

Latin for American Students

Did you know that Rome had 28 public libraries by the 4th century A.D.? In a typical library, there was a podium three steps above the floor to support the books in their niches. A row of columns divided these wall spaces into alcoves. Many townhouses of the wealthy also contained large private collections of books, although some individuals only displayed their books as expensive acquisitions.

The imperfect of **sum** is irregular, but you are already familiar with the third person singular and plural.

eram	**er**āmus
erās	**er**ātis
erat	**er**ant

NOTĀ·BENE

Note that the first person singular ends in –m, not –o.

Tardī semper erāmus.	*We were always late.*

A. Translate the following sentences into good English.

1. Multōsne librōs lēgistis?
2. Puellae puerīque litterās scrībēbant.
3. In casam veniēbam; ibi amīcum meum vīdī.
4. Mārcus amīcum vocābat sed amīcus nōn vēnit.
5. Multōs equōs in viīs vidēbāmus, sed nunc ubi sunt equī?
6. Multī virī in agrīs habitābant sed nunc ad oppida migrāvērunt.

Scala/Art Resource, NY

This mosaic illustrates the hunters' grain carts, loaded with grain to sustain the men on a long hunt. Note the subtle shadings that can be achieved with the small pieces of tile.

B. Translate the following sentences into Latin.

1. Have you never received letters?
2. We were leading the horses to water.
3. We kept waiting but they did not come.
4. Marcus, did you read about the causes of the war?
5. Marcus came to dinner but the rest of the boys did not come.

C. Work with a partner to ask questions and answer them, following the cues.

1. What were you doing in your bedroom? —I was reading a book.
2. What were you doing in the fields? —I was working with the farmers.
3. What were Clara and your friend doing in the den? —They were writing letters.
4. What were the servants doing in the kitchen? —They were preparing dinner.
5. What were you doing in the entrance hall? —I was waiting for my friend.

Vocabulary

Nouns

lūdus, -ī, *m. school, game, play*

poēta, -ae, *m. poet* (poetaster, poetry)

sententia, -ae, *f. saying, motto, feeling* (sentence, sententious)

MEDIATOR AND BELLIGERENTS

Adjectives

medius, -a, -um, (mediator, medium)
middle, middle of

reliquus, -a, -um, (relic)
remaining, rest (of)

Verbs

āmittō, āmittere, āmīsī, āmissus,
lose, let go, send away

conveniō, convenīre, convēnī, conventūrus, *come together* (convene, convention)

convocō, convocāre, convocāvī, convocātus, *call together* (convocation)

redūcō, redūcere, redūxī, reductus, *lead back* (reduce, reduction)

superō, superāre, superāvī, superātus, *conquer, excel* (superable, superably)

Prepositions

prope (+ acc.), *near*

sine (+ abl.), *without* (sinecure)

Adverb

quondam, *once (upon a time)*

Word Studies

Often a careful *inspection* of a familiar English word will reveal an *unexpected aspect* of meaning. A "sentence" in grammar is a single complete *opinion* or expression. A judicial "sentence" is a judge's *opinion.* A "convention" *comes together* in an "auditorium" to *hear* the speaker. A "mediator" settles disputes by taking a *middle* position. A spiritualistic "medium" is supposed to take a *middle* position between the unseen spirit and the "audience" who *hear.* A "studious" person is one who is *eager* to learn. An "alarm" is a call to *arms* **(ad arma)**. To "repatriate" a person is to bring him or her *back* to his or her *fatherland.*

What is a *convocation? Verbosity?* An *audition?*

[The Trojan War was fought more than three thousand years ago at Troy, in Asia Minor near the Dardanelles in what is now Turkey. The story of the war is told by the Greek poet Homer in the *Iliad*. Vergil, the Roman poet, tells part of the story in his *Aeneid* and goes on to tell of the Trojan Aeneas, said to be the son of the goddess Venus. After the fall of Troy Aeneas eventually reached Italy and, according to the story, he and his companions were the ancestors of the Romans.]

Troiānī cum Graecīs multōs annōs bellum gessērunt. Graecī Troiam occupāvērunt. Aenēās Troiānus arma cēpit et cum multīs virīs oppidum dēfendere mātūrāvit. Sed Venus dea, māter Aenēae,[1] eum[2] in mediō oppidō invēnit et verba fēcit:

"Audī sententiam meam. Tenē memoriā familiam tuam. Convocā familiam et amīcōs firmōs et fuge. Novam patriam inveniēs. Cēde fortūnae. Deī Troiānōs poenā dūrā afficient."

Cōnsilium Aenēās nōn grātē audīvit sed officium fēcit. Virōs redūxit et amīcōs convocāvit. Amīcī convēnērunt et excēdere parāvērunt. Tum Aenēas ex oppidō patrem[3] portāvit et fīlium parvum dūxit. Cum multīs servīs et sociīs fūgit. Singulī in locum commodum convēnērunt et ibi castra posuērunt. Māteriam ex silvā portāvērunt et nāvēs[4] parāvērunt. Tum nāvēs in aquam trāxērunt et undīs mandāvērunt et migrāvērunt. Ad multās īnsulās et terrās novās vēnērunt sed patriam novam nōn invēnērunt. Vītam dūram ēgērunt. Īra Iūnōnis,[5] rēgīnae deōrum, hoc[6] effēcit.

In īnsulā Crētā castra posuērunt. Tum in mediō somnō Aenēās Penātēs[7] vīdit et sententiam audīvit:

"Crēta patria vestra nōn erit. Excēdite, Troiānī. Locus est quem[8] Graecī Hesperiam, aliī Italiam vocant. Ibi terminum cūrārum perpetuārum inveniētis. Ibi in ōtiō et concordiā habitābitis et magnum oppidum pōnētis et mūniētis."

Ita Troiānī cōnsilium novum cēpērunt. Castra mōvērunt et ad Italiam nāvigāvērunt.

[1] Aeneas (gen. sing.)
[2] *him*
[3] *father*
[4] *ships*
[5] *of Juno*
[6] *this*
[7] *household gods* (acc. pl.)
[8] *which* (acc.)

The Bettmann Archive

Mosaic showing the Roman poet Vergil holding a papyrus roll on which is written one of the opening lines of the ***Aeneid****: "Musa mihi causas memoria..." On either side are two of the nine Muses, who were the goddesses associated with the arts. Why do you think the Muses are shown in this mosaic?*

QUESTIONS

1. What did Venus tell Aeneas to do?
2. Whom does Aeneas take with him from Troy?
3. Why didn't Aeneas stay in Crete?

Grammar

The Perfect Passive Participle as Adjective

The fourth principal part of the verb is called the *perfect passive participle*. It is used to form certain tenses that you will learn later and is often used as an adjective. Generally, the perfect passive participle is translated as the past tense of the verb. (It is the third form of the verb in English.) Like all adjectives, it must agree in gender, number, and case with the noun it modifies.

Īnsula Sicilia appellāta est prope Ītaliam.	*The island called Sicily is near Italy.*
Portātus in undīs, nauta terram pervēnit.	*Carried on the waves, the sailor reached land.*

Sicily was the first land outside of Italy to become Roman territory (241 B.C.).

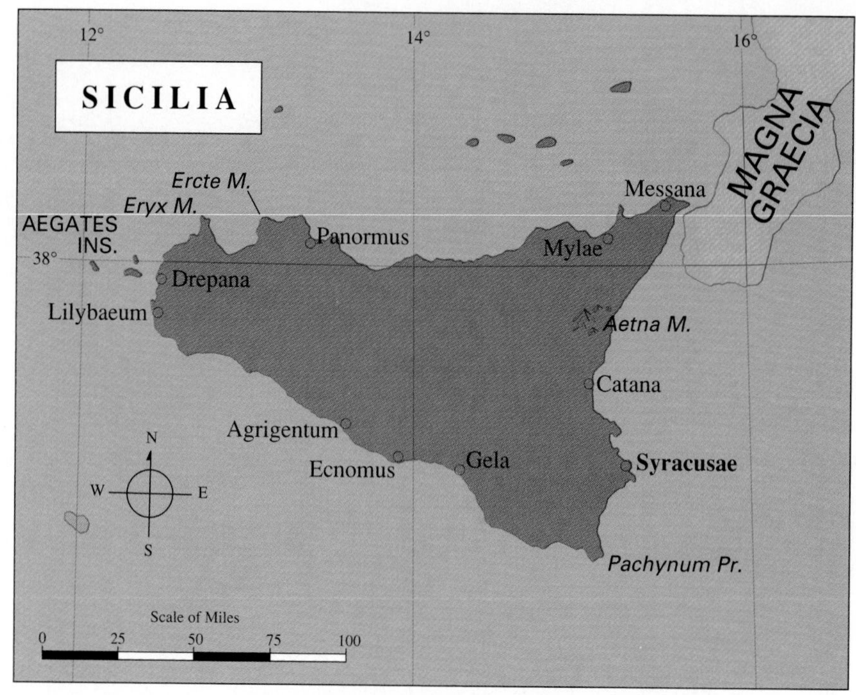

ORAL PRACTICE

1. Give the perfect passive participle of the following verbs: **videō, parō, adiuvō, doceō.**
2. Give the Latin for the following (all nominative forms): *warned, known, called out, loved, sent.*

EXERCISES

A. Translate the following sentences into good English.

1. Puerōsne territōs ex mediā silvā in oppidum redūcam?
2. Virī ex multīs terrīs convenient et verba facient.
3. Rōmānī multās longās viās in Italiā mūnīvērunt.
4. Puerōs singulōs convocābimus et sententiās audiēmus.
5. Pōnite castra, puerī, in agrīs, et ibi agite līberam vītam.
6. Magistrō nostrō grātiam habēmus et līberē grātiās agēmus.

B. Translate the following sentences into Latin.

1. The boys will find water and pitch camp.
2. We ought to feel grateful to your friends.
3. The young men, called Lupercī, ran around the Palatine.
4. The girls feel grateful and will thank the teacher.
5. We shall remember the teacher's words about duty.
6. You will not lead your comrades back to your fatherland.
7. Seen from the town, the fields were wide.

C. Work with a partner to translate the following story and to learn more about the **Larēs** *(m., nom. and acc. pl.)* and **Pēnatēs** *(m., nom. and acc. pl.)* of the Romans.

Aeneas heard the Penates in (his) sleep. They said, "Depart from Crete." Thus warned, he heard them **(eōs)** and he did his duty. The Lares and Penates were not big gods, but small. A Roman family had two Lares and two Penates. The Lares and Penates protected **(dēfendō)** the family. The whole family worshipped the Lares and Penates because the gods protected the family's food and fortune. The family gave food from the meals to the gods. If **(si)** a family departed from the house to a new house, they took the Lares and Penates with them **(sēcum)**.

Latin for American Students

Did you know that the Romans often used the following words to express emotion in their everyday speech? These exclamations included ***hem*** *to call attention,* ***evax*** *for joy,* ***ha*** *and* ***he*** *for laughter,* ***heu*** *and* ***eheu*** *for grief,* ***vah*** *for wonder,* ***euge*** *for praise;* ***au, st,*** *and* ***pax*** *for silence,* ***apage*** *for aversion,* ***hui*** *for scorn;* ***o, oh,*** *and* ***proh*** *for exclamation,* ***atat*** *for fear, and* ***eho, io,*** *and* ***ho*** *for calling.*

Werner Forman/Art Resource, NY

Every Roman home had a special area set aside to place its household gods, the Lares. Off the courtyard of this large home, the images are displayed in a recess in a wall behind the altar.

Vocabulary

Nouns

fīnitimus, -i, *m. neighbor*
īra, -ae, *f. anger* (ire)
proelium, proelī, *n. battle*
somnus, -ī, *m. sleep* (somnambulant, somnolent)

Adjectives

fīnitimus, -a, -um, *neighboring*
paucī, -ae, -a, *a few, few* (paucity)

Verbs

committō, committere, commīsī, commissus, *join together, commit, entrust* (commission, commitment)
  proelium committō, *begin battle*
moneō, monēre, monuī, monitus, *warn, advise* (admonish, premonition)
perveniō, pervenīre, pervēnī, pervenūrus, *arrive*
properō, properāre, properāvī, properātūrus, *hasten*
sciō, scīre, scīvī, scītus, *know* (omniscient, science)

Conjunctions

aut, *or*
aut...aut, *either...or*

Word Studies

DEFICIT

1. How did the *Mediterranean* Sea get its name? The English word *deficit* preserves the third person singular present of Latin **dēficiō.**
2. Here are some Latin phrases in English:
   magnum bonum, *great good*
   via media, *a middle way or course*
   amicus curiae, *a friend of the court*
   consilio et armis, *by counsel and by arms*

[Ulysses (or Odysseus) was a Greek who fought in the Trojan War. His many wanderings before he returned home to Ithaca, an island west of Greece, are described by the Greek poet Homer in the *Odyssey*.]

Ulixēs, dux Graecus quī[1] in bellō Troiānō pugnāverat, post pācem ad Ithacam ubi habitāverat, properāvit. Sed multa mala miser sustinuit nec salūtem invēnit. Cūrīs dūrīs pressus, decem annōs in multīs terrīs ēgit.

Post pācem ā Troiā cum multīs mīlitibus Ulixēs migrāverat. Ad terram Lōtophagōrum[2] accessit. Paucī mīlitēs Graecī lōtum ēdērunt[3] et amāvērunt; et ducem et sociōs nōn memoriā tenuērunt. Ulixēs mīlitēs ad nāvēs[4] redūxit, nāvēs undīs commīsit.

Tum ad Siciliam ventīs āctus est. In Siciliā habitāvērunt Cyclōpēs, hominēs altī et dūrī quī singulōs oculōs[5] habuērunt. Neque lēgēs deōrum neque hominum timuērunt. Ulixēs cum paucīs nautīs in hōc[6] locō frūmentum petīvit. Magnam speluncam[7] invēnērunt. Magnam cōpiam frūmentī continuit. Tum vēnit Cyclōps appellātus Polyphēmus. Ovēs[8] in spēluncam ēgit. Polyphēmus Graecōs vīdit et clāmāvit: "Ā quō[9] locō venītis? Quī hominēs estis? Quid petitis?" Ulixēs respondit: "Graecī sumus. Nēmō[10] sum. Auxilium tuum petimus."

Polyphēmus duōs hominēs cēpit et ēdit; tum somnum cēpit. Reliquī Graecī sude[11] oculum Polyphēmī pressērunt, quī clāmāvit et sociōs ēvocāvit. "Quid est?" rogant. "Quis tē vulnerāvit?" Polyphēmus dixit: "Nēmō mē vulnerāvit." Itaque reliquī Cyclōpēs discessērunt. Polyphēmus Graecōs petīvit sed nōn invēnit quod sub ovibus ligātī ex spēluncā excessērunt. Līberātī ad nāvēs properāvērunt atque ibi salūtem invēnērunt.

[1] *who*
[2] *Lotus-eaters*
[3] *ate the lotus*
[4] *ships*
[5] *eye*
[6] *this*
[7] *cave*
[8] *sheep*
[9] *what*
[10] *No-man*
[11] *with a stake*

QUESTIONS

1. How long did it take Ulysses to reach home?
2. Why didn't the other Cyclopes help Polyphemus?
3. What other expressions are more current today to describe a "lotus-eater"?

Ulixes sub ova ligatus ex spelunca excessit. From a Greek vase dating from 475 B.C. This type of vase painting is called red-figured because the subjects were left in the natural red color of the clay, and a black background was painted in around them.

Anonymous Gift in memory of L. D. Caskey, Courtesy, Museum of Fine Arts, Boston

Grammar

NOTĀ·BENE

The dative and ablative plural are alike, as is true in all declensions. The nominative and accusative plural also are alike in the third declension.

The Third Declension: Masculine and Feminine Nouns

In nouns of the *third declension* the genitive singular ends in **–is.** Like other nouns, you find the base by dropping the genitive singular ending. All three genders occur in nouns of the third declension; no general rule for gender can be given. The gender, as well as the nominative and genitive singular, must be learned from the vocabulary. Masculine and feminine nouns are declined alike:

	mīles, *soldier*		**lex,** *law*	
Nom.	mīles	mīlitēs	lēx	lēgēs
Gen.	mīlitis	mīlitum	lēgis	lēgum
Dat.	mīlitī	mīlitibus	lēgī	lēgibus
Acc.	mīlitem	mīlitēs	lēgem	lēgēs
Abl.	mīlite	mīlitibus	lēge	lēgibus

Et Ulixēs et Aeneās dūcēs erant.	*Both Ulysses and Aeneas were leaders.*
Fēminae cum hominibus veniunt.	*The women are coming with the men.*

Latin for American Students

Did you know that Roman soldiers were required to make a regular or fortified camp every night while on the march? This was done to avoid the ever-present possibility of a surprise attack by the enemy. The disciplined Roman army also never engaged in battle until they were fully entrenched. Such practices made the Roman legion an extremely capable fighting force in the ancient world.

ORAL PRACTICE

1. Decline **homō magnus, pāx aequa.**
2. Give the form of **salūtem, ducum, māteriā, mīlitibus, lēgī, rēgīnae, ducem, mīlite.**

EXERCISES

A. Translate the following sentences into good English.

1. Sine pāce vīta dūra est.
2. Dux mīlitēs ad pugnam dūxit.
3. Ibi valet populus ubi lēgēs valent.
4. Salūtem patriae in armīs mīlitum nostrōrum pōnimus.
5. Sine bellō pācem et ōtium et salūtem habēbimus.
6. Magna est glōria mīlitum; bellō pressī nōn cessērunt.

Scala/Art Resource, NY

Ulysses and his companion escaping from the Cyclops, Polyphemus. From a painting by Tibaldi.

B. Translate the following sentences into Latin.

1. The prepared soldiers began battle.
2. "Safety first!" is a good motto on the roads.
3. The people praised the peace plan.
4. The boys and girls sent many books to the soldiers.

C. Both Aeneas and Ulysses encountered good and bad experiences during the Trojan War and afterwards. Working with a partner or in a small group, pretend you were a soldier (either Greek or Trojan) and write a journal entry (similar to the following fictitious entry) about your experiences during this period of history.

We fought for ten years. Our leaders were great men; they were strong and they helped all the soldiers to withstand many injuries. The Trojans/Greeks pressed hard, but we took many victories. I will always remember my friends. After many battles and many wounds, there was peace. Then we sailed from Troy. We saw many foreign people and they aroused our spirits and memories of our houses. To find my house soon will be a blessed thing.

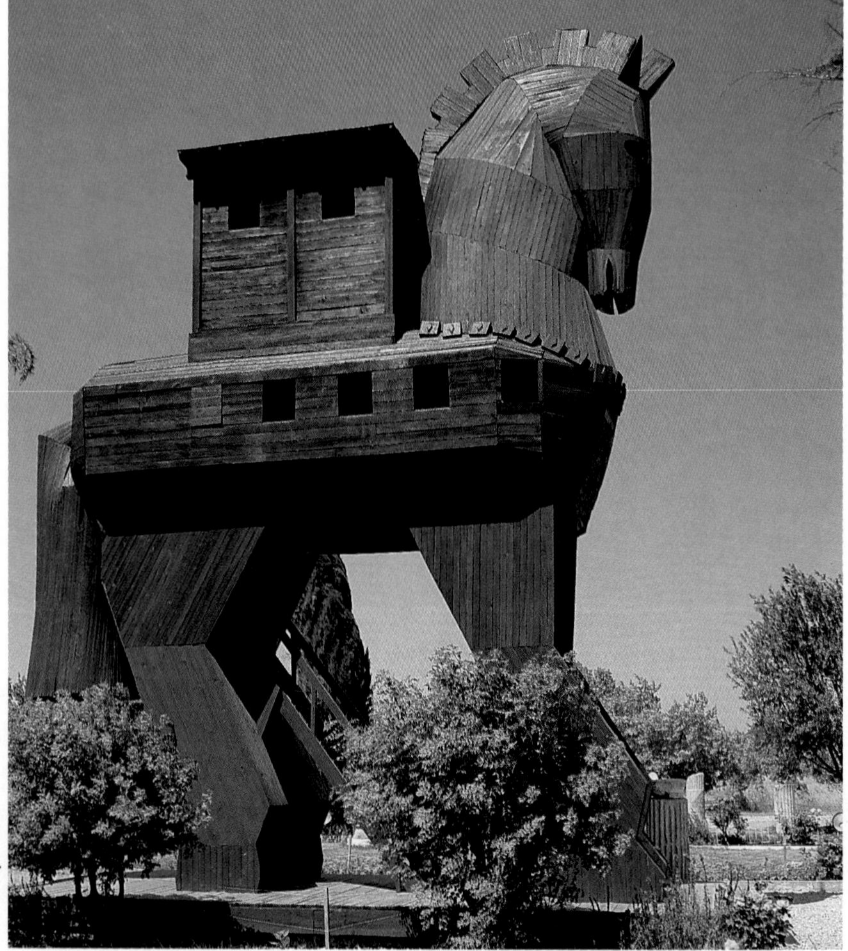

S. Vidler/SuperStock

The Trojan Horse was so large that the Trojans had to tear down parts of the fortification walls, which had protected them for ten years, in order to bring it into the city. At night, the Greeks hidden inside crept out and set fire to many parts of the city.

Vocabulary

Nouns

dux, ducis, *m. leader, general* (conductor, conduit)
homō, hominis, *m. man, human being* (homicide, hominid)
lex, lēgis, *f. law* (legal, legislature)
mīles, mīlites, *m. soldier* (militant, military)
pax, pācis, *f. peace* (pacifist, pacify)
salūs, salūtis, *f. health, safety* (salubrious, salutary)

Verbs

clāmō, clāmāre, clāmāvī, clāmātus, *shout, cry out* (claim, clamor)
premō, premere, pressī, pressus, *press, press hard* (impression, pressure)
rogō, rogāre, rogāvī, rogātus, ask, ask for (interrogate, interrogative)
sustineō, sustīnēre, sustinuī, sustentus, *hold up, maintain, withstand* (sustain)
vulnerō, vulnerāre, vulnerāvī, vulnerātus, *wound* (invulnerable, vulnerable)

Conjunction

neque...neque, *neither...nor*

Word Studies

1. Explain *illegal, impressive, depression, ducal, militant.* To *salute* a person is to wish him or her *health,* as we say "*good* morning," not "*bad* morning." To *pay* a person is to *pacify* him or her. What is a *pacifist*?
2. Four states have towns named *Ithaca.* Can you name these states? Four states have towns named *Ulysses.* Can you name these states? Why do you think that iron and steel works in San Francisco, Oakland, and Pittsburgh have the name *Cyclops?*
3. Here are some Latin phrases in English:
lex scripta, *the written law*
pax in bello, *peace in* (*the midst of*) *war*
novus homo, *a new man* (in politics); hence, *an upstart*
Dux femina facti, *A woman* (*was*) *leader in* (*of*) *the deed.*

NOTĀ·BENE

When two subjects are connected by **neque...neque** *or* **aut...aut,** *the verb agrees with the nearer subject.*
Neque puerī neque puella in silvā est.
Neither the boys nor the girl is in the forest.

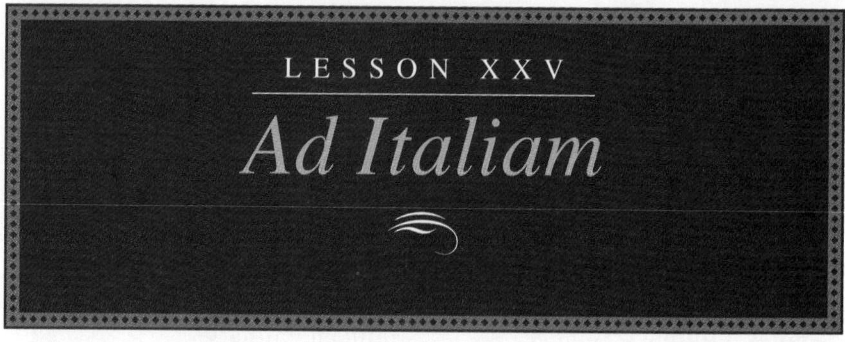

LESSON XXV
Ad Italiam

[Now that you know some of the experiences of Ulysses, the Greek, after the Trojan War, let's return to Aeneas, the Trojan, and his travels throughout the Mediterranean.]

In magnīs undīs nāvēs[1] Troiānōrum volvuntur. Sed Troiānī ex mediīs undīs servantur et ad Actium[2] properant; ibi inveniunt Helenum Troiānum, quī[3] terram regēbat. Helenus Troiānōs convocat et verba pauca facit:

"Longa est via ad Italiam, ad quam[4] accēdere parātis. Accēdite ad Siciliam et nāvigāte ab Siciliā ad Italiam fīnitimam. Dūrum est semper nāvigāre, sed Fāta viam invenient."

Sententia Helenī grātē accipitur, et Aenēās Helenō grātiās agit. Castra moventur nāvēsque[1] undīs committuntur. "Italiam, Italiam videō!" clāmat nauta et terram mōnstrat. In terrā equī clārē videntur. "Signum proelī sunt equī," dīcit Anchīsēs;[5] "equīs bellum geritur. Proelium committere nōn dēbēmus." Nōn ibi manent sed ad Siciliam fīnitimam properant. Aetna eōs[6] terret et ab Siciliā fugiunt.

Tum Iūnō, rēgīna deōrum, quae[7] Troiānōs nōn amāvit, ad Aeolum, quī ventōs regit et continet, venit dīcitque:

"Sī ventī dūrī in nāvēs[8] Troiānōrum mittentur, magnam grātiam habēbō et magna praemia tibi[9] dōnābō."

Aeolus ventōs in nāvēs mittere mātūrat. Altīs undīs Troiānī terrentur. Arma virīque in undīs sunt. Tum Neptūnus, deus undārum, ventōs audit et ad locum venit ubi nāvēs sunt. Īra Neptūnī magna est; ventī lātē fugiunt. Paucī Troiānī āmittuntur; reliquī ad terram fīnitimam veniunt et servantur. Sed in quā[10] terrā sunt? Nōn sciunt. Sed castra pōnere nōn dubitāvērunt.

[1] *ships*
[2] *Actium (Ak´shium)*
[3] *who*
[4] *which*
[5] father of Aeneas; pronounced *Ankī´sēs*
[6] *them*
[7] *who*
[8] *ships*
[9] *to you*
[10] *what*

QUESTIONS

1. Where does Helenus tell the Trojans to go?
2. What does Juno ask Aeolus to do?
3. What does Neptune do?

Vanni/Art Resource, NY

Ira Neptuni magna est. Neptune, god of the seas, drives the winds away from the Trojan ships and causes Aeneas and his followers to land in several places in the Mediterranean before finally arriving in Italy.

Grammar

The Active and Passive Voice

All of the verb forms you have learned until now have been in the *active voice,* which means that the subject performs the action.

Vir militēs dūcet.	*The man will lead the soldiers.*
Feminae līberōs vocant.	*The women are calling the children.*

When the subject is acted upon rather than doing the action, it is in the *passive voice*.

Mīlitēs dūcentur.	*The soldiers will be led.*
Līberī vocantur.	*The children are being called.*

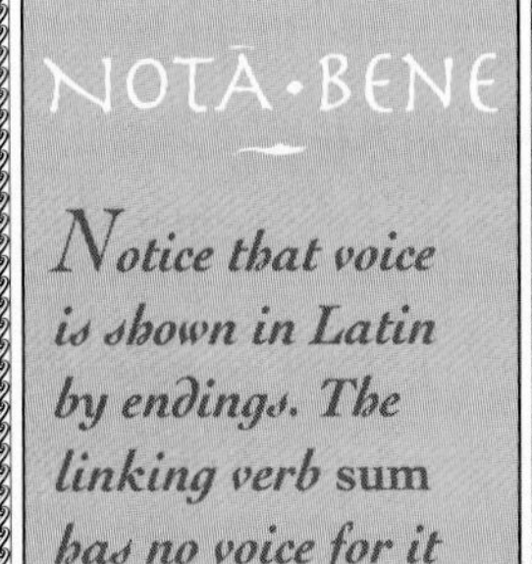

NOTĀ·BENE

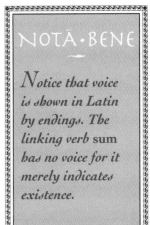

Notice that voice is shown in Latin by endings. The linking verb sum *has no voice for it merely indicates existence.*

> **NOTA·BENE**
>
> Faciō *does not form its passive this way, although its compounds do.*

In Latin it is not difficult to distinguish active and passive.

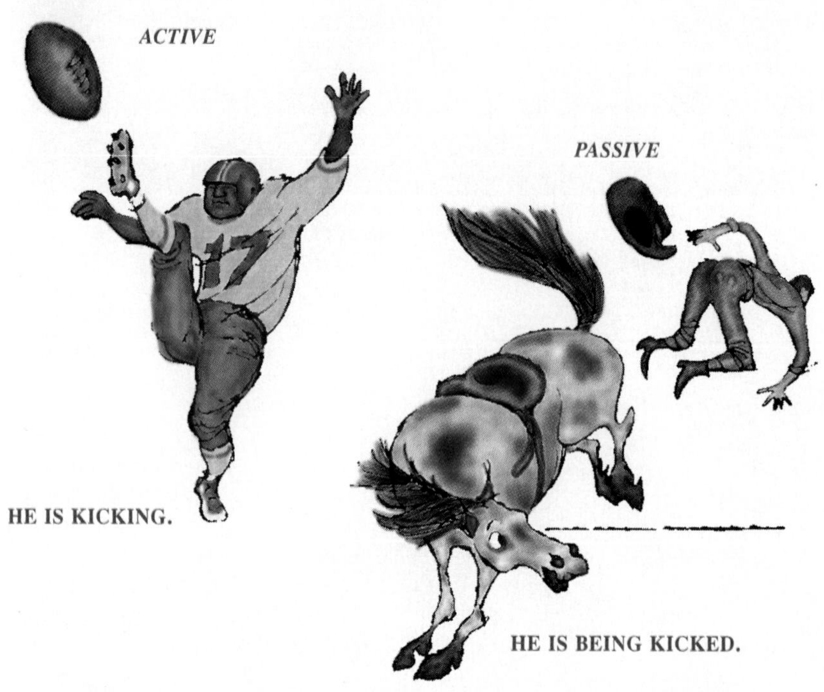
ACTIVE
PASSIVE
HE IS KICKING.
HE IS BEING KICKED.

ORAL PRACTICE

Identify whether each of the following verbs is active or passive: *he called, we were cold, he was laughing, they were found, you are being beaten, he is fighting, they will be scolded, he will praise, you will be invited, it was being written, we were reading, she was sent.*

In Latin the passive voice of all four conjugations is formed by adding the passive personal endings to the present stem:[1]

PASSIVE ENDINGS	
–r	**–mur**
–ris	**–minī**
–tur	**–ntur**

PRESENT PASSIVE	
port**or**, *I am carried*	portā**mur**, *we are carried*
portā**ris**, *you are carried*	portā**minī**, *you are carried*
portā**tur**, *he is carried*	port**antur**, *they are carried*

[1] But in forms ending in **–ō** in the active (as **portō** and **portābō**), the passive ending **–r** is *added to,* not *substituted for,* the active ending.

Similarly **doceor, pōnor, capior, mūnior.**

IMPERFECT PASSIVE

docēbar, *I was being taught*	**docēbāmur**, *we were being taught*
docēbāris, *you were being taught*	**docēbāminī**, *you were being taught*
docēbātur, *he was being taught*	**docēbantur**, *they were being taught*

Similarly **portābar, pōnēbar, capiēbar, mūniēbar.**

FUTURE PASSIVE

capiar, *I shall be taken*	capiēmur, *we shall be taken*
capiēris, *you will be taken*	capiēminī, *you will be taken*
capiētur, *he will be taken*	capientur, *they will be taken*

Similarly **portābor, docēbor, pōnar, mūniar.**

NOTĀ·BENE

The word being *is important in the English translation since it underscores the incomplete nature of the imperfect.*

NOTĀ·BENE

Notice that r *occurs in five of the six passive endings.*

ORAL PRACTICE

1. Conjugate **accipiō** in the present passive, **dēfendō** in the imperfect passive, and **invenīo** in the future passive.
2. Translate into Latin: *we shall be called, he is being taught, it is not approved, they were being sent, it will be received, he will be heard, you* (sing.) *are moved, they are ruled, you* (plur.) *will be seen, we are awaited.*

David Nunuk/Westlight

The Lincoln Memorial in Washington, D.C. The strength and simplicity of the Doric temple are especially appropriate for a building honoring a strong and simple man.

EXERCISES

A. Translate the following sentences into good English.

1. Amā fīnitimum tuum.
2. Litterae in ōtiō scrībentur.
3. Reliquī nautae ad prōvinciam mittentur.
4. Rōmānī proelium cum barbarīs nunc committunt.
5. Paucī virī in fīnitimīs agrīs oppidīsque vidēbantur.
6. Multa praemia reliquīs puerīs puellīsque dōnābuntur.
7. Captīvī ad oppidum redūcentur et proelium committētur.

B. Translate the following sentences into Latin.

1. Few books were being read in camp.
2. They will find food in the house.
3. Food will be found in the kitchen of the house.
4. The rest of the men will be sent to the island.
5. Are the rest of the boys working in the fields?

C. Some Roman soldiers are preparing to do battle with the enemy. Work with a partner to create a dialogue based on the following cues. You may want to add extra items for the soldiers to think about.

1. —Is Marcus prepared? —No, but he will be prepared tomorrow.
2. —Are the soldiers leading? —No, but the soldiers will be led tomorrow.
3. —Is the camp being pitched? —No, but the camp will be pitched tomorrow.
4. —Is the food being collected? —No, but the food will be collected tomorrow.
5. —Is the water ready? —No, but the water will be ready tomorrow.
6. —Are the gods being worshipped? —No, but they will be worshipped tomorrow.

Latin for American Students

Did you know that the average pay of a Roman footsoldier was about twelve to fifteen cents a day? This amount was about fifty dollars annually out of which the cost of food and military equipment was deducted. His uniform of a woolen tunic, leather armor and half-boots, and raingear was also deducted from his salary. The spoils of war: plunder from captured cities, ransoms from spared cities, and returns from the sale of war prisoners, were also part of the soldier's wages.

Vocabulary

Nouns

caelum, -ī, *n. sky*
campus, -ī, *m. field* (camp, encampment)
natūra, -ae, *f. nature* (supernatural, unnatural)
perīculum, -ī, *n. danger* (imperil, perilous)
praesidium, praesidī, *n. guard, protection*
ventus, -ī, *m. wind* (vent, ventilate)

Adjective

parātus, -a, -um, *ready, prepared*

Verbs

dubitō, dubitāre, dubitāvī, dubitātus, *hesitate, doubt* (doubtful, indubitably)
spērō, spērāre, spērāvī, spērātus, *hope (for)* (desperate)

Preposition

sub, *under* (+ acc. *with verbs of motion;* + abl. *with verbs of rest or position*) (subhuman, submarine)

Word Studies

We have seen how Latin and English words are formed from others. It is important to recognize the roots that words have in common. Note the relationship and review the meanings of the following words that have occurred in earlier vocabularies:

1. **amīcus** and **amīcitia**
2. **nāvigō** and **nauta**
3. **nūntiō** and **nūntius**
4. **capiō** and **captīvus** (a "captive" is one who is *taken*)
5. **pugna** and **pugnō**
6. **puer** and **puella**
7. **habeō** and **habitō** (to "inhabit" a place is to keep on *having* it)

Try to associate new Latin words with those you have already studied, as well as with English derivatives which you find.

Towns named *Neptune* are in New Jersey and Tennessee; *Neptune Beach* is in Florida. The four cities in the United States which have more firms named *Neptune* listed in their telephone directories than other cities are New York, Boston, Seattle, and Los Angeles. Why do you think this name is popular in these cities?

Glimpses of Roman Life

DRESS AND APPEARANCE

Probably the most obvious difference between ancient and modern clothing was that civilized men did not wear long pants. These garments were worn only by barbarians. After the barbarians invaded the Roman Empire, their dress became the fashion for all of Europe. The same is true of the mustache (without beard). No early Roman citizen ever wore one, and it was just as much the mark of the barbarian as long pants were. Most Roman men were smooth shaven until the second century A.D., when beards and hair worn across the forehead came into fashion.

Over a sort of pair of trunks, Roman men wore a long shirt called a **tunica,** made of white wool, as an outer garment. Senators and knights had crimson stripes down the front and back, the senators' stripes being broader than those of the knights. A belt was worn around this, and the upper part was bloused out over the belt. When a Roman was engaged in some active occupation, he pulled his tunic up to his knees. In the house, the tunic was usually sufficient clothing.

Over the tunic the Roman citizen might wear a toga. This garment was the official dress of Roman citizens, and only citizens were allowed to wear it as a symbol of Roman citizenship. It was made of white wool. The toga worn by boys and government officials had a crimson border. When boys grew up, they changed to the plain white toga. Important citizens always wore this garment when appearing in public, but the ordinary Roman wore it much less frequently. The poorer classes and slaves wore only a tunic. For parties and special occasions, brightly colored togas were often worn.

The toga was really a sort of blanket which was thrown over the left shoulder, pulled across the back and under the right arm, and again thrown over the left shoulder. It was not fastened in any way, and it must have been quite a trick to learn to wear it properly!

Roman women also wore a tunic. Over this the married women wore a **stola,** a long dress with a protecting band sewn around the bottom. A **stola** for parties often had embroidery around the hem. For street wear a shawl often reaching down to the ankles, called a **palla,** was added.

Wool was the chief material for clothing; next came linen. Silk was rare and expensive and ranked with gold in value; cotton, which was imported from the East, was almost unknown.

Erich Lessing/Art Resource, NY

The fact that the ancient Roman matron in the modern-looking wicker chair has three hairdressers testifies to her wealth and position. The mirror shown was probably of highly polished bronze. The girl in the middle holds a jar of unguents. This relief is now in Treves, Germany.

In the house men and women wore sandals without heels or slippers; outdoors they wore shoes. The shoes of officials were red. No stockings were worn, although in cold weather old and sickly people sometimes wound cloth around their legs.

Hats were rarely worn, except on journeys. Such as there were had broad brims and were flat. Women often wore ribbons and elaborate pins in their hair. Styles in hairdressing changed constantly as they do in modern times, but women did not cut their hair short.

Both men and women of the richer classes wore rings, usually made of gold. Women also occasionally wore a decorative pin, or **fibula,** to fasten tunics or shawls. They were often decorated with semi-precious stones and cameos. Women also wore necklaces, chains, bracelets, and earrings.

Cosmetics and perfumes also played an important role in the lives of the wealthy Romans. For example, the women of the Roman upper class often blackened their eyelids, eye lashes, and eyebrows with kohl. Henna was used to dye the nails and, often, the palms and soles of the feet. White lead or chalk whitened the face while rouge was applied to the cheeks and lips. Balsam perfume and rosewater were popular with both men and women.

QUESTIONS

1. What was the distinctive garment of Roman men? Of women?
2. When did the Roman men begin to grow mustaches and wear long pants?

Unit V Review
LESSONS XX-XXV

Vocabulary

Nouns

caelum, lūdus, proelium
campus, mīles, salūs
dux, nātūra, sententia
fīnitimus, ōtium, schola
grammaticus, pax, somnus
homō, poēta, studium
īra, perīculum, terminus
lex, praesidium, ventus
līber, pretium, verbum
locus

Adjectives

commodus, miser, reliquus
fīnitimus, paucī, tardus
firmus, parātus, varius
medius, perpetuus

Verbs

afficiō, convocō, moneō, spērō
āmittō, dīcō, perveniō, superō
audiō, dubitō, premō, sustineō
clāmō, dūcō, properō, trahō
committō, efficiō, redūcō, valeō
contineō, fugiō, rogō, vulnerō
conveniō, legō, sciō

Adverbs

ita, posteā, quondam

Prepositions

prope, sub

Conjunctions

aut, aut . . . aut, neque . . . neque

Grammar Summary

Third Declension Masculine and Feminine

The third declension contains many important nouns of all three genders. The third declension is characterized by a genitive singular ending of **–is**.

Pacem habēre amāmus.	*We love to have peace.*
Gladium mīlitis vīdī.	*I saw the sword of the soldier.*

Third Conjugation Future

The third conjugation forms the future tense by dropping the **–o** from the first principal part and inserting the tense sign **–e–** and the personal endings. The first person singular has an **–a–**.

Mīlites dūcam.	*I shall lead the soldiers.*
Tōtam Ītaliam regēs.	*You will rule all Italy.*

Unit V Review
LESSONS XX-XXV

Future of Third –iō and Fourth Conjugation Verbs

The future tense of third conjugation **–iō** and fourth conjugation verbs is formed the same way. Drop the **–ō** from the first principal part and add the **–e–** and personal endings. Remember that these verbs retain the **–i–** in the stem.

Caprōs ad agrōs capiet.	*He will take the goats to the fields.*
Ad oppidum crās veniēmus.	*We shall come to town tomorrow.*

The Imperfect

The imperfect tense is used to describe actions that are incomplete or repeated in the past. It is formed for all conjugations by adding the tense sign **–ba–** to the present stem, then adding the personal endings.

Larēs et Pēnatēs laudābāmus.	*We were praising the Lares and Penates.*
Litterās docēbās.	*You used to teach literature.*

Perfect Passive Participle as Adjective

The fourth principal part is called the perfect passive participle. It is often used as an adjective and must agree in gender, number, and case.

Puerī territī ē silvā cucurrērunt.	*The frightened boys ran out of the forest.*
Cibum parātum ēdimus.	*We ate the prepared meal.*

The Passive Voice

The passive voice is used to show that the subject of the sentence is receiving the action of the verb, rather than doing it. The present, imperfect, and future tenses are formed like the active voice, but a different set of personal endings is used.

In proelium vocātur.	*He is called into battle.*
Ā magistrō monēbantur.	*They were warned by the teacher.*

Unit Practice

Oral Form Drill

1. Form and translate adverbs from **lātus, līber,** and **perpetuus.**
2. Conjugate **trahō, incipiō,** and **audiō** in the future, active and passive.
3. Translate into English: **gerit, geret, incipient, incipiunt, līberābō, fugiam, audīris, audiēris, afficiuntur, mittentur, convēnimus, continēbitur, convocābuntur, invenientur.**

Unit V Review

LESSONS XX-XXV

4. Provide the Latin for: *they will hear, they will be heard, I shall see, I shall be seen, he will begin, she will be wounded, we shall be called together, it will draw, they will be led back, he was being taught, you* (sing.) *will write, you* (plur.) *will be affected.*
5. Give the Latin for the following in the singular and plural in the case required: *great interest* (nom.), *a good price* (gen.), *varying opinion* (dat.), *a small guard* (acc.), *a neighboring place* (abl.).

Sentence Drill

A. Translate the words in italics into Latin.

1. (*We are called*) amīcī bonī.
2. Multī mīlitēs post proelium (*will be wounded*).
3. Patria (*will be saved*) quod valet.
4. Verba magistrī in lūdō (*are heard*).
5. Puer ex aquā mox (*will be dragged*).
6. Multa bella in Galliā (*were being carried on*).

The Forum as it was: Temples of Vesta and Castor, Basilica Julia; above, on the Capitoline Hill, Temple of Jupiter; at the end of the open Forum are the Rostra, other temples, and Tabularium. The scene portrayed in the reconstruction is a triumphal procession moving up to the Capitoline.

A.K.G., Berlin/SuperStock

B. Translate these sentences into Latin.
1. Few find peace and safety.
2. The men will receive aid.
3. The boy scares the horses.
4. Many will never read my words.
5. The teacher will praise the girls.

C. Work in a small group to write a letter to an imaginary friend in ancient Rome explaining what clothing styles are worn today in the United States. Compare your letter with what you have read in the *Glimpses of Roman Life* section. Or, pretend you are writing to a penpal and describe yourself and the clothing you wear in Latin. You may find the following vocabulary useful.

gero, gerere, gessī, gestus OR **gestō, gestāre, gestāvī, gestātus**, *wear*

stola, -ae, *f. dress*
subucula, -ae, *f. undershirt*
tunica, -ae, *f. shirt*
brācae, -ārum, *f. pl. pants*
calceus, -ī, *m. shoe*
solea, -ae, *f. sandal*
torques, -is, *m. necklace*
armilla, -ae, *f. bracelet*
anūlus, -i, *m. ring*
inaurēs, -ium, *f. pl. earrings*
vestis, -is, *f. clothes*
comae, -ārum, *f. pl. hair*
gestus, -a, -um, *worn (—by* **ā/ab** + abl.*)*
crispus, -a, -um, *curly*
rūfus, -a, -um, *red-headed*
flāvus, -a, -um, *golden yellow*
caerūleus, -a, -um, *blue*
ater, -tra, -trum, *black*
albus, -a, -um, *white*
ruber, -bra, -brum, *red*
fuscus, -a, -um, *brown*

Word Studies

1. Define the following words according to derivation: *relic, digest, Mr., doctor, libel, audio-visual, mediation, retardation.* Look up the words in the dictionary if necessary.
2. Give the prefix and Latin root word from which the following are derived: **redigō, concipiō, attrahō, committō**; *respect, component, incorrigible, exhibit.*

Scala/Art Resource, NY

Unit VI

The Founding of Rome

The poet Vergil (70-19 B.C.) is known as one of the world's greatest writers. His masterpiece was the ***Aeneid****, an epic poem that tells of the wanderings of the Trojan Aeneas and his attempts to find a new home after the capture of Troy by the Greeks in the twelfth century B.C. It also describes Aeneas' arrival in Italy where his descendants were said to have founded Rome. In this painting by Jules Guérin (1866-1946), we see Aeneas and Queen Dido in the palace at Carthage.*

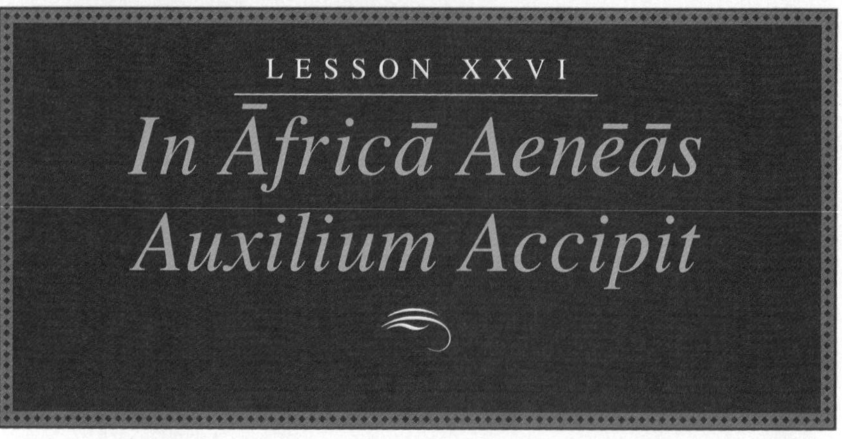

LESSON XXVI

In Āfricā Aenēās Auxilium Accipit

Aenēās sociōs convocāvit et verba fēcit:

"In terrā nōn nōtā sumus. Sed deī praesidium nostrum sunt. Deīs vītam committite. Neque terra neque aqua nōs[1] terret. Inveniēmus viam aut faciēmus. Italia nostra erit. Ibi et terminus malōrum nostrōrum et ōtium perpetuum ā Troiānīs invenientur. Ibi patria erit et nova Troia. Ē novā patriā numquam excēdēmus."

Tum Aenēās cum sociō ūnō ex castrīs excessit. Loca explōrāre mātūrāvit. Venus māter eum[2] vīdit et appellāvit. Venus nōmen[3] oppidī, quod[4] appellātur Carthāgō et in Āfricā est, et nōmen rēgīnae, quae[5] est Dīdō, Aenēae[6] nūntiat. Via Aenēae ā deā mōnstrātur; Aenēās prōcessit et magnum oppidum vīdit. In mediō oppidō templum erat. Ad templum rēgīna Dīdō cum paucīs sociīs vēnit. Ibi erant reliquī Troiānī quōs[7] undae ab Aenēā[8] sēparāverant.[9]

Dīdō mala Troiānōrum audit et dīcit:

"Auxiliō meō aut in Italiam aut in Siciliam commodē veniētis, amīcī. Sed sī grātum est in nostrā patriā manēre, oppidum nostrum est vestrum et praesidium habēbitis."

Tum magna cēna et cibī ēgregiī ā rēgīnā parantur. Aenēās nūntium ad fīlium, quī Iūlus appellātur, mittit; nūntius dīcit:

"Properā ad oppidum, Iūle. Pater tē[10] exspectat."

Sed in locō Iūlī Venus deum amōris Amōrem mittit. Sed et Aenēās et reliquī Troiānī deum crēdunt esse Iūlum. Tum Amor rēgīnam afficit, et Dīdō Aenēam amāre incipit.

[1] *us*
[2] *him*
[3] *name*
[4] *which*
[5] *who*
[6] dative
[7] *whom*
[8] ablative
[9] *had separated*
[10] *you*

QUESTIONS

1. How does Aeneas find out where he is?
2. Whom does he see at the temple?
3. What choice does Dido offer the Trojans?

The Metropolitan Museum of Art, Gift of Henry Walters, 1925. (25.41).

At the dinner Dido prepared, Aeneas told the story of the fall of Troy. Can you identify some of the people and events connected with the Trojan War, as shown in this sixteenth-century enamel?

Grammar

Transitive and Intransitive Verbs

A transitive verb is one that can be followed by a direct object:

Puer virum videt.	*The boy sees the man.*
Magister puellās laudat.	*The teacher is praising the girls.*

An intransitive verb is one which cannot have a direct object (accusative). But they are very often used with prepositional phrases.

Puer excēdit.	*The boy departs.*
Mīlitēs in oppidō mansērunt.	*The soldiers remained in the town.*

NOTĀ·BENE

Distinguish carefully between the ablative of agent and the ablative of means, both of which are often translated with by. Remember that "means" refers to a thing, while "agent" refers to a person (or occasionally, an animal). Besides, the ablative of means is never used with a preposition, but the ablative of agent is never used without the preposition **ā/ab**. *This preposition means by only when used before nouns referring to persons and with passive verbs.*

Puella poenā terrētur. *The girl is scared by punishment. (means)*

Puella ā puerīs terrētur. *The girl is scared by the boys. (agent)*

In English, and generally in Latin, transitive verbs are the only verbs that are used in the passive voice. Some verbs that are intransitive in Latin can be used transitively in English:

Anna labōrat.	*Anna is working* (intransitive).
	He works the brakes (transitive).

Ablative of Agent

Let's see what happens when the two sentences containing transitive verbs are turned around and the verb becomes passive:

Aqua ab Annā portātur.	*The water is carried by Anna.*
Vir ā puerō vidētur.	*The man is seen by the boy.*

Notice that in both English and Latin the direct object of the active verb becomes the subject of the passive verb; the subject of the active verb becomes the object of a preposition (**ā/ab**, *by*), indicating the *agent*.

ORAL PRACTICE

A. Tell whether the words in italics require the ablative of means or the ablative of agent construction.

1. I was hit *by a stone.*
2. He was liked *by everybody.*
3. The game will be won *by our team.*
4. This book was bought *by me with my own money.*
5. John will be sent for *by messenger,* Mary *by letter.*
6. The note had been written *by hand* and not *with a word processor.*

B. Change the following from active to passive, or from passive to active, and translate.

1. Vir librum videt.
2. Oppida ā populō reguntur.
3. Puerī verba tua exspectābant.
4. Reliqua pecūnia ab amīcō meō accipiētur.

Present Passive Infinitive

In Latin, the present passive infinitive is formed by changing the final **–e** of the present (active) infinitive to **–ī**. In the third conjugation (both **–o** and **–iō**), the whole **–ere** changes to **–ī**. To translate it, insert the word *be* between the *to* and the past participle form.

ACTIVE	PASSIVE
portāre, *to carry*	portārī, *to be carried*
docēre, *to teach*	docērī, *to be taught*
pōnere, *to put*	pōnī, *to be put*
capere, *to take*	capī, *to be taken*
mūnīre, *to build*	mūnīrī, *to be built*

Līberī portārī amant.	*Children love to be carried.*
Viae novae mūnīrī debent.	*New roads ought to be built.*

ORAL PRACTICE

Form and translate the present passive infinitive of **videō, agō, trahō, suscipiō, ēdūcō, moveō, appellō,** and **inveniō.**

 EXERCISES 

A. Translate the following sentences into good English.

1. Aut puerī aut virī ad agrōs equōs redūcent.
2. Neque servus neque equus in viīs vidēbitur.
3. Equus puerum trahit; puer ab equō trahitur.
4. Mārcus amīcus vērus ā multīs virīs appellābātur.
5. Neque praesidium neque auxilium ā sociīs nostrīs mittitur.
6. Multa praemia ā reliquīs puerīs puellīsque grātē accipientur.
7. Magister puerōs puellāsque docēbat; puerī puellaeque ā magistrō docēbantur.

Scala/Art Resource, NY

The goddess Venus, mother of Aeneas, plays a major role in the stories of the founding of Rome. Portraits of her can be found everywhere.

B. Translate the following sentences into Latin.

1. The letter was written by my friend.
2. At first, the Greeks were conquered by the Trojans.
3. The grain ought to be carried by wagon to the town.
4. The men see few houses; few houses are seen by the men.
5. Neither water nor grain is carried by the rest of the settlers.
6. Children ought to be praised often.

C. You have read about how the Roman gods and goddesses frequently intervened in the lives of mortals. Now let's learn more about Cupid. Work with a partner or in a small group to write a short paragraph about him. The following vocabulary and information will be useful. Use simple sentences and turn the information around to use familiar constructions.

sagitta, -ae, *f. arrow*
virgō, virginis, *f. maiden*
vultus, -ūs, *m. (acc.* **vultum***) face*
invidus, -a, -um, *jealous*
petō, petere; feriō, ferīre, *shoot*
in mātrimonium dūcere, *marry*
Cupīdo, Cupīdinis, *Cupid*
Venus, Veneris, *Venus*
Psȳchē, Psȳchēs, *Psyche (acc.* **Psȳchen***)*
Iuppiter, Iovis, *Jupiter*
nocte, *at night*
dēnique, *finally, at last*

Cupid is the son of Venus. He is also called Amor. He causes love by shooting an arrow. One day, a beautiful maiden named Psyche won Cupid's love. He visited her at night but she never saw his face because he was a god. Once, she saw his face and he went away. Psyche asked Venus for help, but Venus was very jealous of Psyche (because she was beautiful). Venus gave her many things to do. Finally, Jupiter helped and Cupid and Psyche came together. Cupid married Psyche and Jupiter made her a goddess too.

Latin for American Students

Did you know that the Roman ***matrona*** *(matron) enjoyed high respect and influence in the ancient world? Upon marriage, a Roman woman acquired a social position never attained by the women of ancient Greece. A Roman matron was not kept at home in special quarters as were Greek women. She directed the management of the household to include the early education of her children and supervised the tasks of the household slaves.*

Vocabulary

Nouns

amor, amōris, *m. love* (amorous, enamored)
frāter, frātris, *m. brother* (fraternity, fratricide)
māter, mātris, *f. mother* (maternal, maternity)
pāter, pātris, *m. father* (paternal, patriarchy)
soror, sorōris, *f. sister* (sororal, sorority)

Adjectives

ēgregius, -a, -um, *excellent, distinguished* (egregious)
nōtus, -a, -um, *known* (notable, notorious)

Verbs

crēdō, crēdere, crēdidī, crēditus, *believe* (credible, incredible)
explōrō, explōrāre, explōrāvī, explōrātus, *explore* (exploration, exploratory)
nārrō, narrāre, narrāvī, narrātus, *tell, relate* (narrate, narrative)

Word Studies

1. What is meant by taking an *appeal* to a higher court? Why is such a court called an *appellate* court? What is meant by an *appellation*? *Carthage* is a town name in eleven states. Can you name these states?
2. Here are some Latin phrases in English:
   terra firma, *solid earth* (as opposed to water and air)
   In Deo speramus, *In God we trust* (motto of Brown University).
   pauci quos aequus amat Iuppiter, *the few whom fair-minded Jupiter loves*
3. What does **Elizabeth regina** mean?

TERRA NŌN FIRMA

LESSON XXVII

Aenēās et Dīdō

Dīdō ad Annam sorōrem properāvit: "Anna soror," dīxit, "animus meus miser perīculīs terrētur; Aenēam amō. Quid agam?"

Anna respondit: "Aenēās est bonus et amīcus vir. Prō Troiā pugnāvit sed patriam āmīsit; nunc prō nostrā patriā multōs annōs pugnābit. Fīnitimī nōn sunt amīcī. Terminī nostrī ab Aenēā proeliīs dēfendentur."

Aenēās in Āfricā cum rēgīnā pulchrā mānsit. Dīdō Troiānum per medium oppidum dūxit et eī[1] oppidum mōnstrāvit.

Tum Iuppiter Mercurium nūntium ad Aenēam mīsit. "Annum in hōc[2] locō ēgistī," Mercurius dīxit. "Verba deī memoriā nōn tenēs; properā in Italiam cum sociīs tuīs, ubi fīlius tuus reget. Ibi ōtium habēbis."

Aenēās sociōs convocāvit. Sociī frūmentum in nāvēs[3] portāvērunt. Dīdō Aenēam vocāvit:

"Cūr fugis? Dūrus es; iniūriam facis. Magnum est perīculum nostrum. Ā populīs fīnitmīs agrī nostrī occupābuntur, oppidum āmittētur. Praesidium nostrum esse dēbēs. In concordiā perpetuā habitābimus."

Aenēās respondit: "Deum Mercurium vīdī. Officium meum est ad Italiam nāvigāre. Dūrum est, sed deus imperat."

Aenēās tardē excessit et ad nāvēs vēnit. Sociī convēnērunt et nāvēs in aquam trāxērunt. Tum nāvēs undīs ventīsque commīsērunt. Dīdō misera nāvēs vīdit et sē[4] interfēcit.

Troiānī ad Italiam migrāvērunt et patriam novam invēnērunt. Dīdō vītam āmīsit, Aenēās patriam invēnit. Ita in librīs poētārum scrībitur.

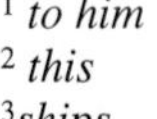

[1] *to him*
[2] *this*
[3] *ships*
[4] *herself*

QUESTIONS

1. What does Mercury tell Aeneas to do?
2. What argument did Dido use to persuade Aeneas to stay in Carthage?

The god Mercury, often shown with a winged hat and sandals, was not only the messenger of the gods but also the god associated with merchants, commerce, science, astronomy, thieves, travelers, and cleverness.

Ronald Sheridan/Ancient Art & Architecture Collection

Grammar

Personal Pronouns

In English, personal pronouns are used to show the person of the verb: ***I** am*, ***you** are*. In Latin, you know that personal endings are used instead. Sometimes, when emphasis or sharp contrast in subjects is desired, the Latin uses the personal pronouns **ego** (*I*) and **tū** (*you*). **Is** and **ea** serve as the personal pronouns of the third person (*he* and *she*). The full declension of these will be given later. For now, memorize the declensions of **ego** and **tū:**

	SINGULAR	PLURAL
Nom.	**ego,** *I*	**nōs,** *we*
Gen.	**meī,** *of me*	**nostrum,** *of us*
Dat.	**mihi,** *to (for) me*	**nōbīs,** *to (for) us*
Acc.	**mē,** *me*	**nōs,** *us*
Abl.	**mē,** *with (from,* etc.) *me*	**nōbīs,** *with (from,* etc.) *us*

	SINGULAR	PLURAL
Nom.	**tū,** *you*	**vōs,** *you*
Gen.	**tuī,** *of you*	**vestrum,** *of you*
Dat.	**tibi,** *to (for) you*	**vōbīs,** *to (for) you*
Acc.	**tē,** *you*	**vōs,** *you*
Abl.	**tē,** *with (from,* etc.) *you*	**vōbīs,** *with (from,* etc.) *you*

NOTĀ·BENE

When you use the ablative of accompaniment with personal pronouns, the **cum** *is attached to the end:* **mēcum, tēcum, nōbīscum, vōbīscum.**

Māter mea mihi dōnum dōnavit. *My mother gave me the gift.*

Nōs in oppidō vīdit. *He saw us in town.*

ORAL PRACTICE

Translate the words in italics into the proper Latin forms.

1. I shall give *you* a present.
2. *I* criticize *you; you* criticize *me.*
3. She showed *us* beautiful flowers.
4. *She* is *my* friend; *he, my* enemy.
5. I shall show *you* (*sing.*) the house.
6. We'll treat *you* (*plur.*) if you'll treat *us.*
7. He came *to us* and showed *us* many pictures.
8. Come *with us* and we shall go *with you* (*plur.*).
9. *He* was mentioned *by me,* but *she* told *me* nothing.
10. *Your* daughter was seen *by us with you* (*sing.*) on the street.

EXERCISES

A. Translate the following sentences into good English.

1. Magna in proeliō fēcit.
2. Nōnne bonum facere dēbēmus?
3. Multa bona ā tē, amīce, accēpī.
4. Puer miser in viā librum āmīsit.
5. Vīta ā multīs in bellō āmittētur.
6. Nostrī prō patriā et familiīs patriae pugnābant.
7. Cupitisne mox vidēre nōs, amīcōs vestrōs?
8. Multōs annōs in perīculō ēgimus; nunc ōtium habēmus.

B. Translate the following sentences into Latin.

1. Were the girls scared by the horses?
2. The people will be called together by the queen.
3. I have entrusted the care of the money to you.
4. The boys saw the danger clearly and fled into the woods.
5. By harsh discipline the master ruled the unhappy slaves.
6. Come with us; we are your friends.

C. Refer to the map of the Roman world on pp. 102-103. Work in small groups, with one student taking the role of the **magister** and the others, the roles of the **discipulī**. The **magister** asks the questions and each **discipulus** answers. As a group, create answers that satisfy the questions, then act out the scene. You may wish to add more questions and answers.

MAGISTER: Spectāte, puerī et puellae.
DISCIPULĪ: Spectāmus, magister.
MAGISTER: Ubi oppida vidētis?
DISCIPULĪ: ______________________
MAGISTER: In mediā terrā aquam vidētis. Illam[1] aquam "Mediterrāneum Mare"[2] appellāmus.
MAGISTER: Ubi est Lūsitānia? Vidētisne?
DISCIPULĪ: ______________________
MAGISTER: Ubi est Hibernia?
DISCIPULĪ: ______________________
MAGISTER: Multī virī multōrum populōrum in Eurōpā habitant. Ubi est Eurōpa?
DISCIPULĪ: ______________________
MAGISTER: Ubi pugnābat Caesar?
DISCIPULĪ: ______________________
MAGISTER: Ubi est Carthagō?
DISCIPULĪ: ______________________
MAGISTER: Quis in Carthagine habitat?
DISCIPULĪ: ______________________

[1] *that*
[2] *Sea*

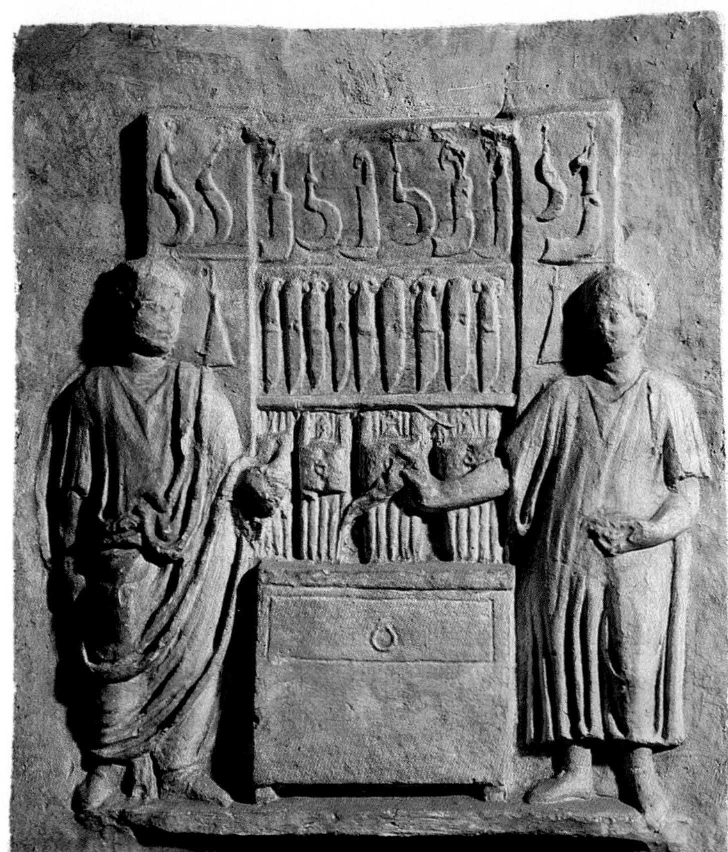

Giraudon/Art Resource, NY

A fine display of carving knives in a cutlery shop. This relief, now in the Vatican Museum, came from the tomb of the shop's owner, Lucius Cornelius Atimetus.

Latin for American Students

Did you know that books were published in ancient Rome by copying each one individually onto rolls of papyrus? If the author was wealthy, his manuscript was distributed for reproduction among his copyists and proofreaders. If the author was a poor man, his patron's copyists did the work. Commercial publishing was essentially similar except that more copyists were employed. After copies went on the market, they could be reproduced by anyone.

Vocabulary

Pronouns

ego, meī, *I* (ego)
tū, tuī, *you* (sing.)
nōs, nostrum, *we* (nostrum)
vōs, vestrum, *you* (pl.)
ea, *she* (nom.)
is, *he* (nom.)

Adjective

integer, -gra, -grum, *untouched, fresh* (integer, integrity)

Verbs

cupiō, cupere, cupīvī, cupītus, *desire, wish, want* (cupidity)

dīmittō, dīmittere, dīmīsī, dīmissus, *let go, send away* (dismiss, dismissal)

interficiō, interficere, interfēcī, interfectus, *kill*

respondeō, respondēre, respondī, respōnsus, *answer* (respond, responsive)

EGOIST

Word Studies

1. As a prefix **prō–** has its prepositional meanings, with the additional one of *forward*. Define the following derivatives of words that you have already studied: *provoke, prospect, produce, proceed.*
2. What is an *annuity?* Tell which of the following are derived from **liber, librī**, and which from **līber, –a, –um:** *liberty, librarian, liberal, liberate.*
3. Here are some Latin phrases in English:
   pro patria, *for (one's) country*
   pro forma, *for (as a matter of) form*
   pro bono publico, *for the public good*

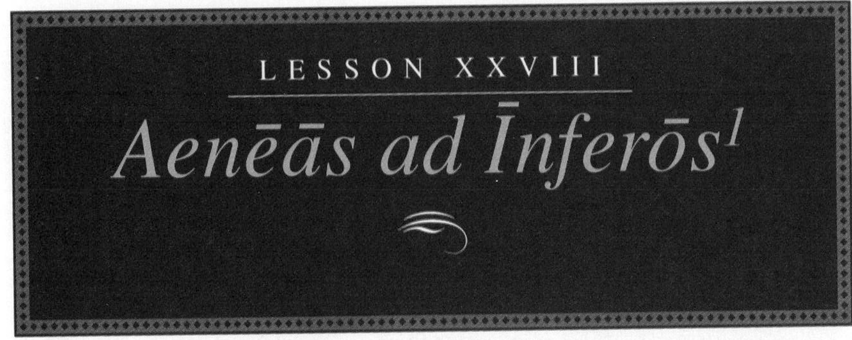

LESSON XXVIII
Aenēās ad Īnferōs[1]

Aenēās fīlius Anchīsae[2] fuit, quī in Siciliā ē vītā excesserat. Tum Anchīsēs in somnō ad fīlium vēnerat et fīlium vocāverat: "Venī, fīlī, ad īnferōs, ubi sum. Sibylla[3] viam nōvit et tē dūcet."

Ita Aenēās in Italiam prōcessit, ubi Sibylla habitābat. Cōnsilium Sibyllae erat: "Sī in silvā rāmum aureum inveniēs, ad īnferōs tē prōdūcam et sine perīculō redūcam, sed sine rāmō numquam tē prōdūcam." Ita Aenēās in silvam properāvit. Auxiliō Veneris rāmum invēnit et cum Sibyllā ad īnferōs dēscendit. Ibi multa nova vīdit et nōvit.

Tum ad magnam silvam vēnērunt. Ibi erat Dīdō. Aenēās rēgīnam vīdit et vocāvit: "Nūntiusne vērum nūntiāvit? Vītamne āmīsistī? Causane fuī? Invītus[4] ex patriā tuā excessī, sed ita deus imperāvit." Sed rēgīna, nunc inimīca, verbīs lacrimīsque Aenēae nōn movētur. Neque Aenēam spectāvit neque respondit sed in silvam fūgit.

Aenēās tardē ex silvā excessit et locum vīdit ubi malī poenā afficiēbantur. Tum Aenēās Sibyllaque in Ēlysium[5] prōcessērunt. Ibi animae[6] bonōrum in concordiā vītam agēbant. Iniūriae et pugnae aberant. Ibi Anchīsēs erat. Grātus fīlium accēpit et nūntiāvit: "Clārōs Rōmānōs quī posteā in terrā erunt et glōriam populī tuī mōnstrābō. Rōmānī malōs superābunt et populōs aequē regent." Aenēās ab Anchīse nōn retinētur et ā Sibyllā in terram redūcitur. Tum loca commoda in Italiā occupāre mātūrāvit.

[1] *The Lower World*
[2] *Anchises*
[3] *the Sibyl* (a prophetess)
[4] *unwillingly*
[5] *Elȳ´sium,* Greek and Roman heaven
[6] *souls*

QUESTIONS

1. What did Aeneas need to go safely into the Lower World?
2. Whom did he see there?

Grammar

The Pluperfect and Future Perfect Tenses

The *pluperfect* tense (sometimes called the past perfect) refers to an action that was completed before a certain time in the past. It is formed by adding the tense sign **–era–** plus the personal endings to the perfect stem. In English, we use the helping verb *had.*

Scala/Art Resource, NY

The epitome of responsibility, Aeneas carries his father, Anchises, and leads his son, Ascanius, from the ruins of Troy to fulfill his destiny as the founder of Rome. He also carries his household gods with him, a critical part of his new home.

Iam excesserat.	*He had already left.*
Puellam laudāveram.	*I had praised the girl.*

The *future perfect* tense refers to an action completed before a certain time in the future. It is formed by adding the tense sign **–eri–** plus the personal endings to the perfect stem. In English, we use the helping verbs *shall have* or *will have*.

Verba fēcerit.	*He will have made the speech.*
Ante crās incēperimus.	*We shall have begun before tomorrow.*

NOTĀ·BENE

Notice that the tense signs and personal endings of the pluperfect together are the same as the imperfect of sum.

ORAL PRACTICE

1. Conjugate in the perfect: **videō, legō, efficiō;** in the pluperfect: **moveō, incipiō;** in the imperfect: **retineō, prōcēdō;** in the future perfect: **laudō, facio.**
2. Give the tense of **āfuimus, prōdūxerat, retinuistī, nōvērunt, prōcesserimus, āmīserātis, docēbās.**

Latin for American Students

Did you know that Roman schools of rhetoric were similar to our colleges and universities? The students were wealthy young men who studied Greek and Latin prose authors, philosophy, and the practice of composition. These studies began with the simple form of narrative and continued with public speaking. Often students would roleplay a famous Roman who had made an important decision and then would discuss his possible courses of action.

EXERCISES

A. Translate the following sentences into good English.

1. Parvī puerī equōs ēdūcere dēbent.
2. Multī puerī aberant. Nōnne valēbant?
3. Carrī ex silvā vēnerant et ad oppidum tardē prōcēdēbant.
4. Fīliī et fīliae agricolārum multa dē agrīs et equīs nōvērunt.
5. Magister puerōs retinuit, quod fōrmās verbōrum nōn nōverant.
6. Paucī labōrābant sed reliquī puerī in castrīs semper manēbant.
7. Fīlius magistrī multa dē librīs nōvit, sed agrī fīlium agricolae docent.

B. Translate the following sentences into Latin.

1. We know much about many lands and peoples.
2. The unfriendly king began battle with the Trojans.
3. Marius had fought in Gaul for (his) native land.
4. We had given the golden branch to the queen.
5. The slave deserved a large reward because he had saved the life of our son.

Scala/Art Resource, NY

*This statue called the **Dying Gaul** is a copy of a lost Greek statue from 230 B.C. by Epigonus of Pergamum. It is part of a monument to commemorate the victory of King Attalus over the Gauls in 241 B.C.*

C. The Sibyl was a prophetess who resided in a cave in Cumae near Naples in Italy. People went to visit her for special requests and to ask for her advice. Sometimes they wrote down their request and had a messenger deliver it to her because she often frightened people while prophesying in a trance. Work with a partner or a small group and write a short note to the Sibyl. Your note might be about Aeneas and the founding of Rome or a more present-day concern.

The sibyls were female prophetesses whose pronouncements were supposed to be inspired by Apollo. This painting, called ***Augustus and the Sibyl****, was done by Antoine Caron in the sixteenth century and now hangs in the Louvre.*

Vocabulary

Nouns

inimīcus, -ī, *m. enemy, (personal enemy)*	(inimical)
rāmus, -ī, *m. branch*	(ramada, ramification)
rēx, rēgis, *m. king*	(regal, regalia)

Scala/Art Resource, NY

Adjectives

aureus, -a, -um, *golden* (aureole, auriferous)
inimīcus, -a, -um, *unfriendly, hostile*

Verbs

absum, abesse, āfuī, āfutūrus, *be away, be absent* (absence, absent)
adsum, adesse, adfuī, adfutūrus, *be near, be present*
ēdūcō, ēdūcere, ēdūxī, ēductus, *lead out* (educe, eductor)
nōscō, nōscere, nōvī, nōtus, *learn;* in perfect tense, *know*
prōcēdō, prōcēdere, prōcessī, prōcessūrus, *go forward, advance* (proceed, procession)
prōdūcō, prōdūcere, prōdūxī, prōductus, *lead out* (produce, productive)
retineō, retinēre, retinuī, retentus, *hold back, keep* (retain, retentive)

Adverb

iam, *already, now*

Word Studies

We have seen that the preposition **in** is used as a prefix. There is another prefix **in–**, used chiefly with adjectives and nouns, which has an entirely different meaning and must be carefully distinguished from the former. It is a *negative* prefix, as in *injustice*. It is assimilated like the other prefix **in–**, as in *il-legal, im-moral, ir-regular.* Identify the Latin roots and define the following derivatives of words that you have already studied: *immemorial, immaterial, inglorious, ingratitude, illiberal, illiteracy, infirm.*

Tell which of the two prefixes (preposition or negative) is used in each of the following words: *inhabit, invalid, invoke, induce, invariable, inequality, inundate, immovable, impecunious.*

The prefix **dis–** in English and Latin means *apart,* but sometimes it is purely negative like **in–.** It is either assimilated or left unchanged, as follows: *dis-inter, dis-locate, dis-arm, dif-fuse, di-vert, di-stant, dis-similar.* Define the first three of these words, derived from words in previous lesson vocabularies.

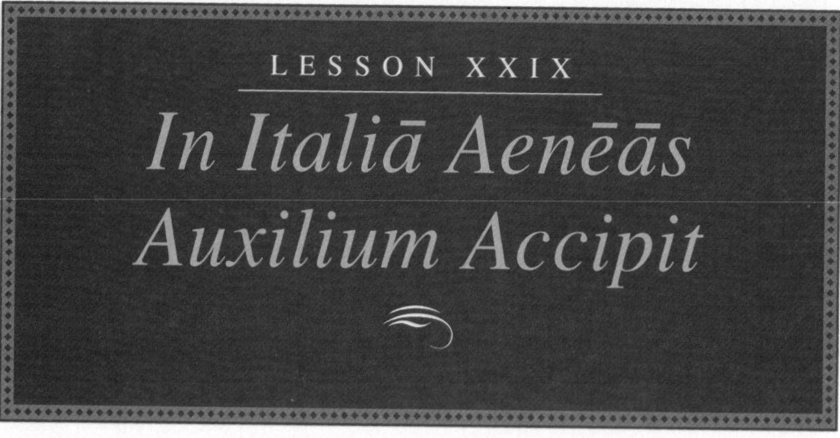
LESSON XXIX
In Italiā Aenēās
Auxilium Accipit

Olim in Latiō erat oppidum appellātum Pallanteum. Rex oppidī, Ēvander, cum multīs colōnīs ab Arcadiā in Graeciā mīgrāverat. In Italiā oppidum mūnīverant in locō ubi posteā Rōmulus Rōmam mūnīvit. Cum fīnitimīs, populīs Latīnīs, bellum semper gerēbant.

Aenēās et colōnī Troiānī etiam in Italiā habitābant et etiam cum Latīnīs pugnābant. Quod sociōs cupiēbant, Aenēās et paucī virī ad Pallanteum accessērunt. Extrā oppidum Troiānī fīlium Ēvandrī et paucōs Arcadiānōs invēnērunt.

PALLAS: Pallas sum, fīlius Ēvandrī. Ego et amīcī meī vōs salūtāmus. Quī[1] estis? Cur tu et virī tuī ad Pallanteum vēnistis?

AENĒĀS: Appellor Aenēās. Ego et virī meī ad Italiam ā deīs ductī sumus. Nunc auxilium vestrum cupimus. Accipite nōs, quaesō, et fābulam nostram audīte.

PALLAS: Vōs nōn dīmittam. Multa dē vōbīs audīvī. Ad oppidum nōbīscum prōcēdite.

(*Rex Ēvander grātē Aenēam accipit.*)

ĒVANDER: Ubi puer eram in Arcadiā, Aenēās, pater tuus ad patriam meam vēnit. Is mihi multa grāta dōnāvit. Virum grātē memoriā teneō. Tu etiam vidēris[2] vir bonus et pius. Tē probō et tibi auxilium dōnābō.

AENĒĀS: Grātiās tibi agō, Ēvander. Firmī sociī erimus.

ĒVANDER: Quod ego nōn iam iuvenis[3] sum, pūgnarē vōbiscum dubītō. Tibi, Aenēās, filium meum mandābō. Is integer est et prō mē pugnābit. Pallas, mī filī, tē cum Troiānīs nunc dīmittam. Tēcum prōdūce multōs virōs.

PALLAS: Valē, pater! Nōs fortiter[4] bellum gerēmus.

Et fortiter pugnāvit Pallas. Sed miser Ēvander numquam fīlium vīvum iterum vīdit.

[1] *who*
[2] *seem to be*
[3] *young*
[4] *bravely*

Scala/Art Resource, NY

In one of the few known depictions of Roman comedy, the lively mimic acting is evident, especially in the roles of servants and old people. Remember that the actors wore masks to indicate their roles and moods.

QUESTIONS

1. What is particularly interesting about the site of Pallanteum?
2. What common enemy did the Trojans and the Arcadians have?
3. Why didn't Evander himself lead his men into battle alongside Aeneas?

Grammar

Possessive Adjectives

The possessive adjectives **meus, noster, tuus,** and **vester** are derived from the bases of their corresponding personal pronouns: **ego (me–), nōs (nostr–), tū (tu–),** and **vōs (vestr–).** The possessive adjective follows its noun except when emphatic.

ORAL PRACTICE

Decline **equus vester** and **familia mea.**

Infinitive Object With Certain Verbs

With certain English verbs such as *order, teach, wish, forbid, force,* etc., the infinitive object is often used with a noun or pronoun in the accusative, which may be regarded as its *subject.* In Latin too, certain verbs of similar meaning have the infinitive with its subject in the accusative case.

Virōs discēdere iussī.	*I ordered the men to go away.*
Mē labōrāre nōn cupīvistī.	*You did not desire me to work.*

In the first sentence above, the phrase **virōs discēdere** is the *object* of **iussī** and the word **virōs** is the *subject* of **discēdere**.

EXERCISES

A. Translate the following sentences into good English.

1. Deus nōs etiam inimīcōs amāre docet.
2. Liber tuus ā mē nōn retinēbitur.
3. Pāter nōs amīcōs ad forum festīnāre iussit.
4. Ego sum amīcus tuus; is est inimīcus.
5. Ego sum miser sine tē; tū misera es quod tēcum nōn maneō.
6. Fīlius meus in perīculum mēcum properāre numquam dubitāverat.

NOTĀ·BENE

To show possession, use the possessive adjectives **meus, tuus, noster,** *and* **vester,** *not the genitives* **meī, tuī, nostrum,** *and* **vestrum: amīcus meus,** *my friend, not* **amīcus meī.** *Remember that an adjective agrees in gender, number, and case with the noun it modifies. A woman referring to a woman friend might comment* **Est amīca mea;** *a woman referring to her husband would say* **Est vir meus.** *In other words, the ending of the possessive adjective does not depend upon the possessor, but upon the person or thing possessed.*

Many specialized craftsmen were memorialized in stone, including this relief of a coppersmith's workshop found in Pompeii.

Ronald Sheridan/Ancient Art & Architecture Collection

B. Translate the following sentences into Latin.

1. We are foreigners; you are Romans.
2. My words are not heard by you.
3. I desire to present the reward to you *(sing.)*.
4. They had not hesitated to free the prisoners.
5. Lucius, order the boy to lead out fresh horses to the gate of the town.

C. Aeneas had help from his mother, the Roman goddess Venus, as well as several other people during his travels, including Dido in Africa (Carthage), the Sibyl in Italy, and now Evander in Pallanteum. Each of them gave him support or advice in some way. Work with a partner to write a thank-you note to one of these individuals for the aid that was given. You may want to review their stories in this unit to recall exactly what each one did for Aeneas.

Vocabulary

Nouns

fābula, -ae, *f. story* (fable, fabulous)
porta, -ae, *f. gate (of a city or a camp)* (portal)

Adjectives

pius, -a, -um, *loyal* (pious)
vīvus, -a, -um, *alive, living* (vivid, vivify)

Verbs

discēdō, discēdere, discessī, discessūrus, *go away, depart*
iubeō, iubēre, iussī, iussus, *order* (jussive)
recipiō, recipere, recēpī, receptus, *take back, recover* (receipt, reception)
redigō, redigere, redēgī, redactus, *drive back, reduce* (redact, redaction)
removeō, removēre, remōvī, remōtus, *remove* (remote, removal)
salūtō, salūtāre, salūtāvī, salūtātus, *greet* (salutation, salute)

Adverbs

nōn iam, *no longer*
ubi, *when* (ubiquity)

Preposition

extrā (+ acc.), *outside, beyond* (extraordinary, extraterrestrial)

Latin for American Students

Did you know that the Roman army had several ways of capturing a gated, fortified city? Their first task was to fill up the ditches around the city walls with ***fascines,*** *small tree branches mixed with soil and then thrown into the ditches. Then the Roman soldiers would make their own trenches, roads, and underground passages. Lastly, they would unleash weapons like the* ***catapulta*** *and* ***ballista*** *upon the beseiged city.*

Word Studies

We have seen that prefixes are so called because they are attached to the beginnings of words. *Suffixes* (**sub,** *under, after;* **fīxus,** *attached*) are attached to the ends of words. Like the Latin prefixes, the Latin suffixes play a very important part in the formation of English words.

The Latin suffix **–ia** usually has the form *–y* in English. Give the English forms of the following words found in the preceding vocabularies: **memoria, glōria, familia, iniūria, victōria, cōpia** (with change of meaning in English).

What are the Latin words from which are derived *elegy, history, industry, infamy, Italy, luxury, misery, perfidy, philosophy, Troy?*

Some **–ia** nouns drop the **–ia** entirely in English: *concord, vigil, matter* (from **māteria**).

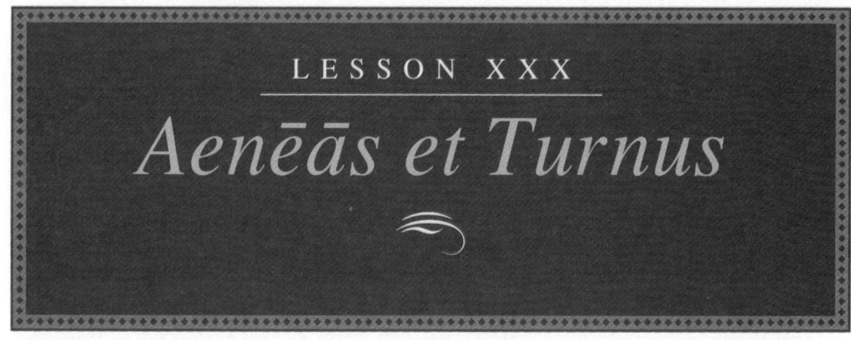

Troia ā Graecīs capta erat et Aenēās cum paucīs Troiānīs ad Italiam vēnerat et per terrās barbarōrum virōs prōdūxerat. Sed Iūnō inimīca mānsit et contrā Aenēam miserum multōs barbarōs populōs Italiae incitāvit. Lāvīnia, fīlia rēgis Latīnī, ā Turnō amābātur sed Aenēae dōnāta est. Turnus bellum gerere nōn dubitāvit. Ab Aenēā bellum nōn grātē susceptum est; ad terminum vītae sub armīs esse nōn cupīvit. Sed causa Troiānōrum ā Fātīs suscepta erat. Aenēās etiam ā Graecīs quī in Italiā habitābant beneficium et auxilium accēpit, quod Turnō inimīcī erant. Per multōs diēs bellum gestum est et multa ēgregia exempla virtūtis in proeliīs clārīs prōposita sunt.

Tandem Turnus sōlus Aenēam sōlum ad pugnam ēvocāvit, quod reliquīs exemplum prōpōnere cupīvit. In locō commodō sub portīs oppidī pugnāvērunt. Nōn longa fuit pugna, quod Venus, māter Aenēae, fīliō ēgregia arma dōnāverat quae deus Vulcānus fēcerat. Fāta iusserant auxilium ad Turnum nōn mittī; itaque Iūnō aberat. Vīta Turnī fūgit et Aenēās ad terminum perīculōrum vēnit et ōtium invēnit.

QUESTIONS

1. Why did Turnus wage war with the Trojans?
2. Why did Aeneas defeat Turnus?

Grammar

The Perfect Passive Tenses

There are three tenses in the perfect passive system: the perfect passive, the pluperfect passive, and the future perfect passive. To form all three tenses, you use the fourth principal part, which you already know is the perfect passive participle, and add an auxiliary verb. All conjugations form these tenses the same way.

The perfect passive tense is formed by using the present tense of **sum** as an auxiliary with the perfect passive participle: **portātus est.** The participle really modifies the subject and therefore agrees with it in gender, number, and case. The English helping verbs are translated as *has/have been* (carried), *were* (carried).

portātus, –a, –um sum	*I have been carried, I was carried*
portātus, –a, –um es	*you have been carried, you were carried*
portātus, –a, –um est	*he/she/it has been carried, he/she/it was carried*
portātī, –ae, –a sumus	*we have been carried, we were carried*
portātī, –ae, –a, estis	*you have been carried, you were carried*
portātī, –ae, –a sunt	*they have been carried, they were carried*
monitī sunt	*they have been, were warned*
petītī sumus	*we have been, were sought*

The pluperfect passive is formed by using the perfect passive participle with the imperfect of **sum**. It is translated by using the helping verb *had been.*

doctus, –a, –um eram	*I had been taught*
doctus, –a, –um erās	*you had been taught*
doctus, –a, –um erat	*he/she/it had been taught*
doctī, –ae, –a erāmus	*we had been taught*
doctī, –ae, –a erātis	*you had been taught*
doctī, –ae, –a erant	*they had been taught*
mūnītum erat	*it had been fortified*
laudāta erās	*you had been praised*

THE GRANGER COLLECTION, New York

Roman gods provided inspiration for many artists through the ages, including this one by Spanish painter Diego Velásquez (1599-1660) entitled "Forge of Vulcan". Remember that Vulcan was the god of fire and volcanoes. Ugly and lame, he married Venus, who was regularly unfaithful.

The future perfect passive is formed by using the perfect passive participle with the future tense of **sum**. It is translated by using the helping verb *shall/will have been.*

captus, –a, –um erō	*I shall have been taken*
captus, –a, –um eris	*you will have been taken*
captus, –a, –um erit	*he/she/it will have been taken*
captī, –ae, –a erimus	*we shall have been taken*
captī, –ae, –a eritis	*you will have been taken*
captī, –ae, –a erunt	*they will have been taken*
tenta erunt	*the things will have been held*
amātus erō	*I shall have been loved*

ORAL PRACTICE

1. Conjugate in the perfect passive: **trahō, –ere, trāxī, trāctus; videō, –ēre, vīdī, vīsus;** in the pluperfect passive: **moveō, –ēre, mōvī, mōtus; agō, –ere, ēgī, āctus;** in the future perfect passive: **prōpōnō, prōpōnere, prōposuī, prōpositus; laudō, laudāre, laudāvī, laudatus.**
2. Translate: *they have been seen, I had been dragged, you have been moved, driven, having been driven, they will have been told.*

EXERCISES

A. Translate the following sentences into good English.

1. Arma carrīs ad castra portāta erant.
2. Causam populī suscipere est officium bonōrum.
3. Equī ab agricolā per silvam ad aquam āctī sunt.
4. Ēgregiumne exemplum amīcitiae memoriā tenētis?
5. Ēgregium exemplum beneficī ā magistrō vestrō prōpositum est.
6. Vir ā puerō sub aquam trāctus erat, sed et vir et puer servātī sunt.
7. Nōnne dūrum est sub aquā remanēre?

B. Translate the following sentences into Latin.

1. He knows much about horses.
2. She was taught by good teachers.
3. The farmer's son had seen few towns.
4. An excellent example was presented to my son.
5. The rest of the books had been removed by the teacher.
6. The boys are absent but the girls are present.
7. The men had been ordered to seize the fortified town.

Ronald Sheridan/Ancient Art & Architecture Collection

The Roman influence spread far in all directions. These remains of a Roman villa from A.D. 250 still stand in Witcombe, England.

C. According to Roman mythology, the Fates, or **Parcae**, were three women who decided everyone's destiny. They were present at the birth of every child and decided how long each person would live. Each of the Fates had a specific job. Clotho spun the thread of life; Lachesis decided the length of each thread; Atropos cut the thread when it was long enough. Work with two other people and create a dialogue that the Parcae might have had. Choose a real or imaginary individual and decide his or her fate. The following vocabulary may be useful.

secō, secāre, secuī, sectus, *cut*
filum, -ī, *n. thread*
neō, nēre, nēvī, nētus, *spin*
longitūdō, longitūdinis, *f. length*
constituō, constituere, constituī, constitūtus, *decide*

Latin for American Students

Did you know that the Romans had a popular agricultural guidebook still held in high regard by farmers today? The ***Georgics*** *was written by the famous poet Vergil who spent nearly seven years composing the most finished poems in the Latin language. The* ***Georgics*** *consist of four books which explain soil management, fruit tree and vine propagation, animal husbandry, and beekeeping.*

Vocabulary

Nouns

beneficium, -ī, *n. kindness, benefit*	(beneficial, benefit)
exemplum, -i, *n. example*	(exemplify, sample)
virtūs, virtūtis, *f. courage*	(virtue, virtuous)
vōx, vōcis, *f. voice*	(vocal, vocalize)

Adjective

prīmus, -a, -um, *first*	(primal, primary)

Verbs

permittō, permittere, permīsī, permissus, *allow, permit*	(permission, permissive)
prōpōnō, prōpōnere, prōposuī, prōpositus, *put forward, offer*	(proposal, propose)
remaneō, remanēre, remānsī, remānsūrus, *remain, stay*	(remain)
suscipiō, suscipere, suscēpī, susceptus, *undertake*	(susceptible, susceptive)

Preposition

per (+ acc.), *through*	(perambulate, percolate)

Word Studies

The preposition **sub**, used as a prefix in Latin and English, means *under, up from under:* **sus-tineō** *hold* ***up***; **suc-cēdō**, *come* ***up***. It is regularly assimilated before certain consonants: *suc-ceed, sus-ceptible, suf-fer, sug-gest, sus-pend, sup-port, sur-rogate, sus-tenance,* but *sub-mit, sub-trahend.* We use it freely in English to form new words: *sub-lease, sub-let, sub-orbital.*

Per usually remains unchanged when used as a prefix.

Explain by derivation the meaning of *permanent, permit, sustain, suspect.* What is meant by being *susceptible* to colds?

Glimpses of Roman Life

EDUCATION

Even before they went to school, some Roman children learned the alphabet by playing with letters cut out of ivory—just as children today do with their blocks. They started school at about the same age as American children. The schools were quite different, however. They were very small private schools, usually run by Greek slaves for small fees and were attended by children of the middle and professional classes and government officials. (The children of the very rich were taught at home by educated slaves.) Schoolwork began early in the morning. The children were taken to and from school by slaves called pedagogues, a Greek word which means "those who lead (take) children." They did no teaching but merely kept their children in order. However, some **paedagōgī** of Greek heritage were able to tutor their charges in Greek.

In the elementary school, called the **lūdus litterārum,** reading, writing, and arithmetic formed the basis of the curriculum, which, like the teaching, was fairly unimaginative. For reading the Romans had to depend at first on the Twelve Tables of the law which were the first set of laws that the Romans put in writing. In the third century B.C. a schoolteacher translated the *Odyssey* from Greek for the use of his pupils. Later, other works of Greek and Roman literature were used. Children learned to read by loudly pronouncing the words and sentences after their teacher. Unlike English, Latin is written phonetically so spelling was not taught as a subject.

The students wrote on wax tablets that consisted of wooden boards covered with a thin layer of wax. They wrote by scratching the wax with a pointed **stilus** made of metal, wood, or bone. The other end of this was flat for erasing, or rather, smoothing over the wax.

Roman students also learned to write with a reed pen and ink on papyrus, a kind of paper made of thin strips of reed that grew in Egypt. Most books were made by hand out of rolls of this material. But papyrus was expensive, and schoolchildren used only the backs of old books and loose sheets for their scratch paper. For tablets, parchment came to be used instead of wax-covered wood. Eventually, a number of these were put together to form a book of the kind familiar to us, and the papyrus roll went out of style.

Arithmetic was complicated by the fact that the Romans did not have the Arabic system of numerals, with its zero, that we use. Multiplication and division were virtually impossible because the system of Roman numerals does not have "place value," like our system. The Romans had two aids in their arithmetic: an elaborate system of finger-counting and the **abacus,** or counting board.

More advanced education prepared boys for the respected profession in ancient Rome, that of law and public life. Hence the secondary school, called the **schola grammaticī** (*school of the grammarian*), specialized in language, composition, rhetoric, and public speaking. But the course was also a broadly cultural one and included both Greek and Latin literature, especially the epics of Homer. Most educated Romans also learned to speak and write Greek fluently.

Physical fitness was also important, especially as a preparation for the army. When academic lessons were over, boys took part in such sports as running, wrestling, and fencing.

The college course in the **schola rhētoricī** (*school of the rhetorician*) was still more technical in preparation for a career in which public speaking, whether in a law court or a legislative body, played a very important role. For graduate work, wealthy students could go to such university centers as Athens or Rhodes and listen to lectures by famous philosophers and professors of rhetoric.

Although the aim of the schools beyond the elementary level was the relatively narrow one of preparing (male) citizens for public service, the practical Romans felt that a liberal training in literature and philosophy was the best educational system.

Scala/Art Resource, NY

Oratory was one of the important subjects of every well-educated young Roman. Wealthy young men even went to Greece to study under the masters there.

QUESTIONS

1. What educational advantages do you have that a Roman boy or girl did not have?
2. Compare books and writing materials then and now.
3. What sort of education should our lawyers and government officials have?

Unit VI Review
LESSONS XXVI-XXX

Vocabulary

Nouns

amor	inimīcus	rēx
beneficium	māter	soror
exemplum	pater	virtūs
fābula	porta	vōx
frāter	rāmus	

Adjectives

aureus	inimīcus	nōtus	prīmus
ēgregius	integer	pius	vīvus

Verbs

absum	interficiō	recipiō
adsum	iubeō	redigō
crēdō	nārrō	remaneō
cupiō	nōscō	removeō
dīmittō	permittō	respondeō
discēdo	prōcēdō	retineō
ēdūcō	prōdūcō	salūtō
explōrō	prōpōnō	suscipiō

Pronouns

ea	is	tū
ego	nōs	vōs

Adverbs

iam	nōn iam	ubi

Prepositions

extrā	per

Grammar Summary

Transitive and Intransitive Verbs

Transitive verbs are those that can (often must) take a direct object. Intransitive verbs are those that do not. Many intransitive verbs are followed by a prepositional phrase. Generally, only transitive verbs are used in the passive voice.

Nōs salūtāvit.	*He greeted us.* (transitive)
Ā Rōma discēdimus.	*We are departing from Rome.* (intransitive)
Ā deā appellātus est.	*He was called by the goddess.* (transitive, passive)

Present Passive Infinitive

The present passive infinitive is formed by changing the final **–e** on the present infinitive to **–i**, except for all third conjugation verbs, where the **–ere** changes to **–i**.

Laudārī amant.	*They love to be praised.*
Capī nōn cupīvērunt.	*They did not desire to be taken.*

Infinitive Object With Certain Verbs

Certain verbs, including *teach, order, wish, forbid,* and *force* are often followed by a complementary infinitive. When this happens, the subject of the infinitive is in the accusative case.

Unit VI Review
LESSONS XXVI-XXX

Inimīcōs accedere iubet.	*He orders the enemies to approach.*
Nōs nārrāre fābulās docuit.	*She taught us to tell stories.*

Pluperfect and Future Perfect Tenses

The pluperfect and future perfect active tenses are formed by adding a tense sign to the perfect stem. The tense sign of the pluperfect is **–era–**; the tense sign of the future perfect is **–eri–**. The regular personal endings are then added. The first person singular in the future perfect is irregular, **–erō**.

Discēdere dūbitāverant.	*They had hesitated to depart.*
Mē salūtāveris.	*You will have greeted me.*

The Perfect Passive Tenses

The perfect passive tenses are all formed by using the fourth principal part which is the perfect passive participle, and a form of **sum** as a helping verb. Because the participle modifies the subject, it must agree in gender, number, and case (which is always nominative).

crēditum est	*it was believed, it has been believed*
retentī erant	*they had been held back*
ductī erimus	*we shall have been led*

Ablative of Agent

The doer of an action in a sentence with a passive verb is expressed by using the preposition **ā/ab** + the ablative case. This construction is called the ablative of agent.

Līberī ā nōbīs appellantur.	*The children are being called by us.*
Equus ā servō ductus est.	*The horse was led by the servant.*

Personal Pronouns

The personal pronouns **ego, nōs, tū,** and **vōs** are used just as they are in English, except that it is not necessary to use them as the subject unless it is for emphasis or clarity.

Tē herī vīdī.	*I saw you yesterday.*
Ea nōbīscum vēnit.	*She came with us.*

Possessive Adjectives

The possessive adjectives **meus, noster, tuus,** and **vester** are derived from the personal pronouns. Like all adjectives, they must agree with the noun they modify in gender, number, and case.

Puellae sunt amīcae meae.	*The girls are my friends.*
Equōs tuōs in agrīs videō.	*I see your horses in the fields.*

Unit VI Review
LESSONS XXVI-XXX

Unit Practice

Oral Form Drill

A. Give the Latin for *I, me, we, us, with me, with us, you* (as sing. subject and object), *you* (as plur. subject and object), *of you* (sing. and plur.), *with you* (sing. and plur.).

B. Give in Latin the singular and plural of *great danger* and *my son* used as subject, used as direct object, and used as indirect object.

C. Give the present passive infinitive of **appellō, āmittō, removeō,** and **audiō**. Translate into Latin: *to undertake, to be undertaken; to order, to be ordered; to lead out, to be led out.*

D. Give in six tenses, translating each tense form: the active first singular of **iubeō**, and the passive third plural of **permittō**.

E. Translate **fuerant, fuistī, iusserāmus, discessit, remōvī, retinuistis, cupīvimus, ēdūxit, prōpositum est, remōtī sunt, dubitāverō**. Provide in Latin: *he had been, she has been seen, it has been presented, he has remained, undertaken, it will be entrusted, they have been, we had been sent away.*

Word Studies

1. Find and use in sentences as many English derivatives as possible from **servō, moveō, dūcō, capiō**. For example: from **servō** is derived *conservation* which could be used as follows: *The* ***conservation*** *of our soil and of our forests is a necessity.*
2. Identify Latin words from which each of the following is derived: *primitive, permission, beneficiary, exemplary, proposition, librarian, inimical, integration, commiserate, retention, reproduce.*

A Latin Play

Post Bellum

Persōnae

Lūcīlia, **Valeria** } *Rōmānae*
Zōē, *serva*
Gāius, *frāter Lūcīliae*
Philippus, *servus*

Locus: *In ātriō Lūcīliōrum.*
(Lūcīlia et Valeria accēdunt.)

VALERIA: Victōria est nostra! Nostrī multa oppida, multa castra occupāvērunt.

LŪCĪLIA: Deī bonī sunt!

VALERIA: Caecilius tuus aderit—et meus vir pactus,[1] Arrius.

LŪCĪLIA: Zōē! Zōē! (*Zōē accēdit.*) Zōē, mea nova ōrnāmenta! (*Exit Zōē.*)

VALERIA: Est nova serva.

LŪCĪLIA: Captīva est. Ea cum praedā praemissa est.

VALERIA: Parva est—et trīstis.[2] Lacrimās in oculīs vīdī. (*Zōē accēdit. Ōrnāmenta et vestēs pulchrās portat. Lūcīlia et Valeria eam nōn vident.*)

LŪCĪLIA: Bellum dūrum est. Zōē patriam et familiam āmīsit. Misera est.

Unit VI Review
LESSONS XXVI-XXX

VALERIA: Serva est.

LŪCĪLIA: Serva nunc est—sed puella misera. Amīca mea erit. Eam amō.

VALERIA: Bah! (*Lūcīlia servam videt.*)

LŪCĪLIA: Ōh, Zōē! (*Zōē Lūcīliae ōrnāmenta et vestēs dat.*) Ecce,[3] Valeria! (*Lūcīlia Valeriae ōrnāmenta et vestēs mōnstrat.*)

VALERIA: Pulcherrima[4] sunt! Et tū es pulcherrima.

LŪCĪLIA: Nōn pulchra sum, Valeria. Ecce, lenticulās[5] habeō, multās lenticulās!

VALERIA: Quod flāva[6] es lenticulae adsunt. Sed tū es pulchra.

LŪCĪLIA: Nōn pulchra, sed misera sum. Caecilius mē nōn amābit.

VALERIA: Nūgae![7] Tē amābit. (*Accēdit Gāius.*)

GĀIUS: Arrius adest, Valeria.

VALERIA: Quid?

GĀIUS: Arrius, vir pactus tuus, domum vēnit.

VALERIA: Quis eum[8] vīdit?

GĀIUS: Ego eum vīdī.

VALERIA: Ōh, valē, Lūcīlia! Valē! (*Exit cum Gāiō.*)

LŪCĪLIA: Beāta est Valeria.

ZŌĒ: Et tū beāta eris, domina.

LŪCĪLIA: Quid dīcis?

ZŌĒ: Serva sum, domina; sed tū amīca mihi es. Lenticulās cūrābō.

LŪCĪLIA: Cūrābisne?

ZŌĒ: Remediō mihi nōtō.

LŪCĪLIA: Vērumne dīcis?

ZŌĒ: Ego multās lenticulās habēbam; nunc absunt.

LŪCĪLIA: Ōh, Zōē! Sī lenticulās cūrābis. Caecilius mē amābit!

ZŌĒ: Tē amābit. (*Accēdit Gāius.*)

GĀIUS: Lūcīlia! Novus servus adest—meus.

LŪCĪLIA: Novusne servus?

GĀIUS: Puer est—captīvus. Is praemissus est. Iam accessit. Appellātur Philippus.

ZŌĒ: Philippus?

GĀIUS: Ecce! (*Ad iānuam[9] properat. Accēdit Philippus.*)

ZŌĒ: Philippus est—frāter meus!

PHILIPPUS: Zōē est—soror mea! (*Lacrimant.*)

ZŌĒ: Ō domina, beāta sum. Deī bonī sunt.

LŪCĪLIA: Familia nostra beātissima Rōmae[10] erit.

[1] *fiancé*
[2] *sad*
[3] *See!*
[4] *very beautiful*
[5] *freckles*
[6] *blonde*
[7] *nonsense*
[8] *him*
[9] *door*
[10] *the happiest in Rome*

Scala/Art Resource, NY

The column of Trajan was erected in A.D. 113 to commemorate Trajan's victories in the Dacian wars. The column is 125 feet high and is decorated with over 2500 sculptured reliefs in a continuous spiral 652 feet long.

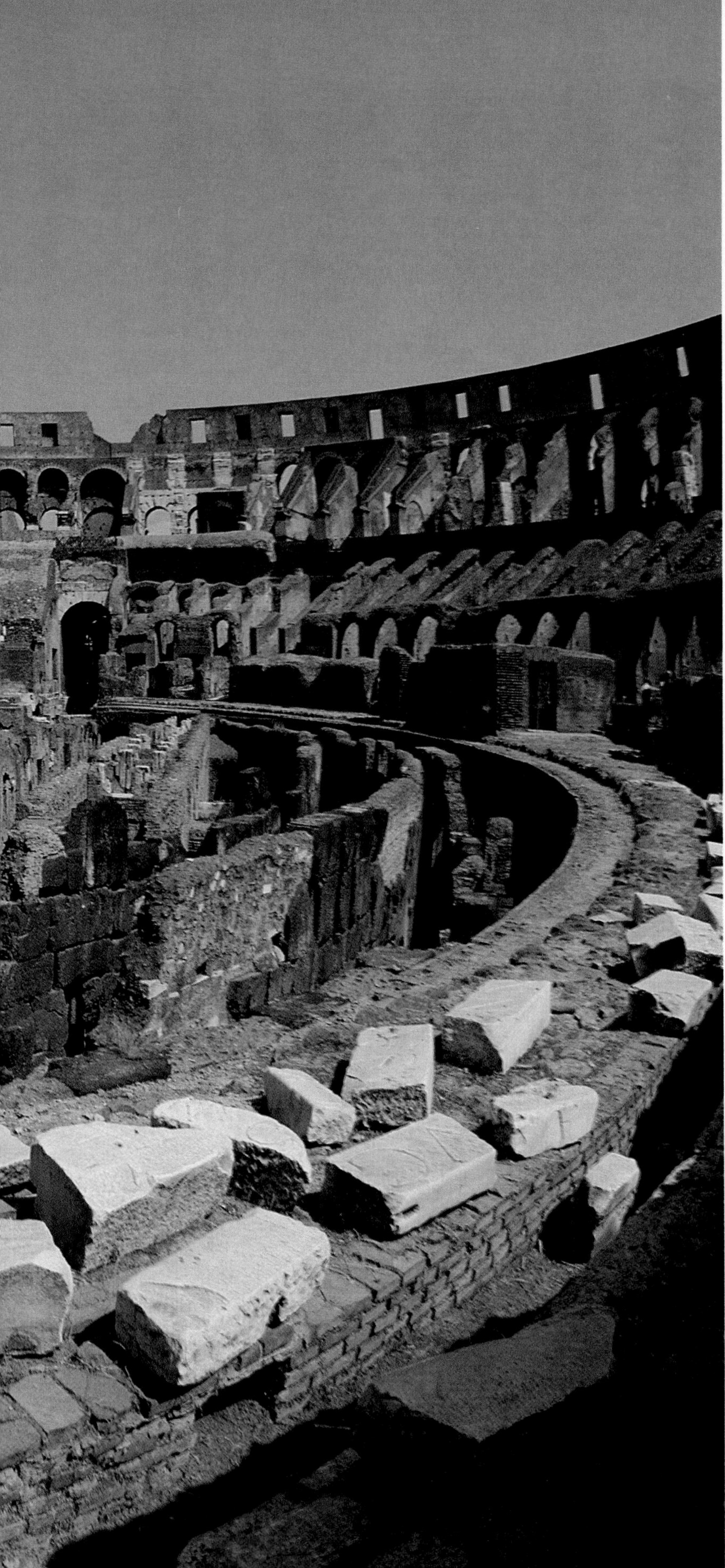

Unit VII

Gods, Goddesses, and Games

The Roman Colosseum, built between A.D. 72-80, is constructed of limestone blocks called travertine. It was built for large-scale gladiatorial combats, fights with wild animals, and naval battles, for which it could be flooded. The seating capacity was 50,000. The seats were divided into three tiers: the lowest tier was for the senators, vestals, and ambassadors; the second tier for the wealthy citizens; and the upper tier for the general public.

Here you can see the subterranean passages that were used for keeping wild animals and through which scenery and props were brought into the arena for the spectacles. Over the centuries, nearly two-thirds of the Colosseum was removed for use in the construction of various other Roman buildings.

S. Vidler/SuperStock

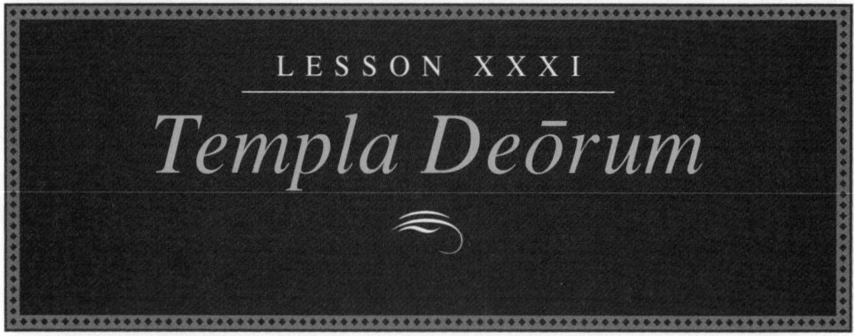

LESSON XXXI
Templa Deōrum

Silvae erant prīma templa deōrum. Prīmō virī in agrīs habitābant et Nātūram colēbant. Posteā virī quī in oppidīs habitābant templa pulchra in altīs locīs ad glōriam deōrum pōnēbant. Templa saepe in locīs altīs posita sunt. Cūr? Quod haec[1] loca caelō fīnitima erant, in quō deī habitābant.

"Nātūra est pulchra," hominēs dīxērunt. "Etiam loca sacra ad quae convenīmus et in quibus beneficia deōrum petimus pulchra esse dēbent. Deī nōbīs fortūnam bonam dedērunt. Deīs grātiam habēmus ob frūmentum quō vītam sustinēmus et ob auxilium perpetuum quod nōbīs submīsērunt."

Itaque Graecī et Rōmānī ob beneficia deōrum magna et pulchra templa faciēbant quae deīs erant grāta. Statua aut deī aut deae semper in templō pōnēbātur.

In Graeciā et in Italiā ruīnae templōrum multōrum et pulchrōrum videntur. Templum clārum Athēnae, appellātum Parthenōn, ob fōrmam pulchram semper laudātum est. Nōnne fuērunt multa templa Rōmāna inter pictūrās quās vīdistī? Cūr pictūrās templōrum et Graecōrum et Rōmānōrum, quae in multīs librīs inveniuntur, nōn spectātis? Etiam in actīs diurnīs[2] pictūrās templōrum antīquōrum inveniētis.

In templīs virī auxilium deōrum petēbant. Virī malī quōrum vīta[3] in perīculō erat saepe ad templa fugiēbant, quod neque ex templīs removēbantur neque ibi poenam sustinēbant.

[1] *these*
[2] *newspapers*
[3] We use the plural in English; **vītae** (plural) means *biographies*.

QUESTIONS

1. Where were the first temples located? Why?
2. How can we find out what these ancient temples looked like?

Explorer/Photo Researchers

Pulchrum templum Bacchi. Baalbek, in Lebanon, was an ancient center of worship of the Phoenician god Baal and an important trading center for spices and luxury goods. It was seized by the Greeks and later became a Roman colony under Augustus in 16 B.C. A Roman temple dedicated to Bacchus still stands on the eastern Mediterranean.

Grammar

Relative Pronouns

Relative pronouns are used to relate to or to refer to some preceding word. This preceding word is called the *antecedent.* A relative pronoun must agree with its antecedent in gender and in number, but it takes its case from the clause in which it is used. The English relative pronouns are expressed by *who, which, what,* and *that.*

Sunt librī quōs cupīvī.	*Those are the books* that *I wanted.*
Est rēgīna quae in Africā habitāvit.	*She is the queen* who *lived in Africa.*

In the first sentence, **quōs** is masculine plural to agree with its antecedent, **librī,** but **quōs** is accusative because it is the direct object of **cupīvī.** In the second sentence, **quae** is feminine singular to agree with its antecedent **rēgīna,** but **quae** is nominative because it is the subject of **habitāvit.** The full declension of the relative pronoun is as follows:

	SINGULAR			PLURAL		
	M	F	N	M	F	N
Nom.	quī	quae	quod	quī	quae	quae
Gen.	cuius	cuius	cuius	quōrum	quārum	quōrum
Dat.	cui	cui	cui	quibus	quibus	quibus
Acc.	quem	quam	quod	quōs	quās	quae
Abl.	quō	quā	quō	quibus	quibus	quibus

NOTĀ·BENE

That and which are used to refer to things, while who refers to a person. The accusative form of who is whom. The genitive is most commonly translated whose.

Puella quam vīdī pulchra est.
The girl whom I saw is beautiful.

Vir cuius vītam servāvī grātus est.
The man whose life I saved is grateful.

When you use the ablative of accompaniment with a relative pronoun, the **cum** is joined to the end of the pronoun.

Vir quōcum ambulābam erat altus.	*The man with whom I was walking was tall.*

ORAL PRACTICE

Identify the gender, number, and case and then give the proper Latin form of the italicized English words.

1. The boy *whom* I visited was my cousin.
2. I saw the horses *that* were on the road.
3. I know the town *in which* the president was born.
4. Have you seen the girl *to whom* I gave the books?
5. The man *by whom* we were robbed has been arrested.
6. The land *from which* our parents came was beautiful.
7. Have you seen the islands *to which* we sailed two years ago?
8. All the men *to whom* we spoke were pleased by your action.
9. All the girls (*whom*) I have invited have accepted, but one girl *whose* mother is sick may not be able to come.

EXERCISES

A. Translate the following sentences into good English.

1. Via quā vēnimus pulchra erat.
2. Librōs quī dē fāmā et fortūna agunt puerī amant.
3. Vir cui pecūniam permīsī amīcus meus vērus erat.
4. Cūr pecūniam puerō vīsō ā tē in Viā Quīntā nōn dedistī?
5. Cūr nōn fortūnam quam Nātūra vōbīs dedit sustinētis?

B. Translate the following sentences into Latin.

1. I saw the boy whose book I had lost.
2. The friendly girl whom I saw in the woods is approaching.
3. You endured constant dangers on account of (your) enemies.
4. I departed from the province on account of the unhappy life that I led there.

C. Working with a partner or in a small group, summarize in Latin what you know about various gods, goddesses, festivals, and sacred rites. You may want to include the Lares and Penates and their relationship to the goddess Vesta, as well as sacrifices, money or gift-giving, the Sibyl, Mercury, Venus, Juno, Jupiter, Ceres, Neptune, or any other gods or goddesses you have studied in previous lessons.

NOTĀ·BENE

The relative pronoun may never be omitted in Latin, although it often is in English.

E. Streichan/SuperStock

The ruins of Hadrian's temple in Ephesus, Turkey, show several of the architectural features that Hadrian, an architect as well as emperor, used in his designs, including curved walls, colonnades, and vaults.

Latin for American Students

Did you know that both Roman men and women were fond of jewelry? Men usually wore an iron or gold ring set with a precious stone and carried a seal ring for indicating ownership of a document, seal, or wooden chest. The poet Martial even told a friend who possessed a large and treasured ring to wear it on his leg! Women wore bracelets, necklaces, earrings, pendants, and rings often set with the precious stones known today, except diamonds.

Vocabulary

Nouns

dīligentia,-ae, *f. diligence*	(diligent)
lapis, lapidis, *m. stone*	(lapidary, lapis lazuli)
lībertās, lībertātis, *f. freedom, liberty*	
lūx, lūcis, *f. light*	(lucid, Lucifer)
pictūra, -ae, *f. picture*	(picturing)
ruīna, -ae, *f. downfall, collapse;* pl. *ruins*	(ruination, ruinous)
statua, -ae, *f. statue*	(statuesque, statuette)

Pronouns

quī, quae, quod, *who, which, that* (quorum)

Verbs

colō, colere, coluī, cultus, *worship, cultivate, till* (cult, culture)

dō, dare, dedī, datus, *give* (data, datum)

submittō, submittere, submīsī, submissus, *let down, furnish* (submission, submit)

Adverb

itaque, *and so, and as a result*

Prepositions

inter (+ acc.), *between, among* (interact, intercede)

ob (+ acc.), *because of, on account of, for* (obese, object)

Word Studies

Most of the Latin prepositions which are used as prefixes in Latin and English may have intensive force, especially **con–, ex–, ob–, per–**. They are then best translated either by an English intensive, as *up* or *out,* or by an adverb, as *completely, thoroughly, deeply.* Thus **commoveō** means to *move greatly;* **permagnus,** *very great;* **obtineō,** to *hold on to;* **concitō,** to *rouse up;* **excipiō,** to *catch, receive;* **cōnservō,** to *save up, preserve;* **complicō,** to *fold up.*

Explain *component, confirmation, evident, elaborate.* What is meant by *conservation* of natural resources? What is a political *conservative?* What is a *contract?*

LESSON XXXII

Colossēum

Lūdōs et pompās populus Rōmānus magnō studiō spectābat. In Italiā, in Āfricā, in Galliā cōnservantur theātra et amphitheātra Rōmānōrum, in quibus lūdī etiam nunc habentur. Nātūra virōrum varia est sed paucī lūdōs nōn amant.

Captīvī et servī malī quōs dominī in amphitheātrum mīserant in mediā arēnā pugnāre cōgēbantur. Populus Rōmānus studium lūdōrum numquam intermīsit. Multī captīvī cum magnō animō pugnābant et lībertātem obtinēbant. Multī malī virī etiam prō vītā pugnābant et poenam in arēnā sustinēbant.

Quondam duo gladiātōrēs in arēnā Rōmānā pugnābant. Tum inter gladiātōrēs vēnit sine armīs vir bonus aequusque, quī petīvit: "Cūr pugnātis? Proelium intermittite, nam amīcī estis. Malum exemplum prōpōnitis." Gladiātōrēs verbīs nōn permōtī sunt sed virum bonum interfēcērunt. Servī virum ex arēnā trahere incipiēbant. Tum populus īrā permōtus est, quod vir erat Tēlemachus, quī amīcus miserīs semper fuerat et magnam fāmam obtinuerat. Numquam posteā gladiātōrēs in Colossēō pugnāvērunt, et Colossēum cum cūrā nōn cōnservātum est.

Scrīptum est:

"Quamdiū[1] stat Colisaeus,[2] stat et[3] Rōma. Quandō[4] cadet Colisaeus, cadet et Rōma. Quandō cadet Rōma, cadet et mundus."

[1] *as long as*
[2] = **Colossēum**
[3] *also*
[4] *when*

QUESTIONS

1. To what use are some ancient theaters put today?
2. What two classes of people fought in the amphitheaters?
3. According to ancient thought, how long will the world last?

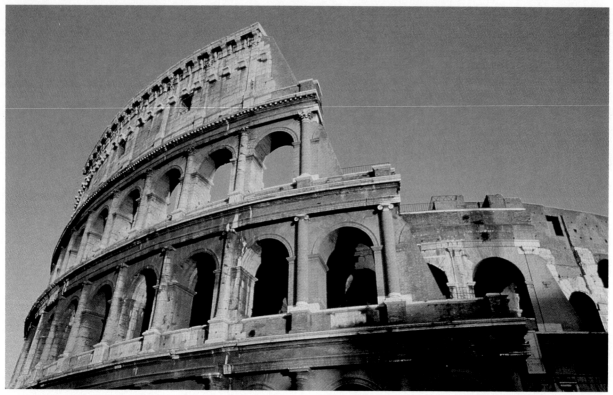

Lawrence Migdale/Photo Researchers

The Flavian amphitheater (the Colosseum) at Rome, one of the largest in the Roman Empire. This close-up of the Colosseum clearly shows the three orders of Greek columns: Doric on the ground level, Ionic on the second level, and Corinthian on the third. The fourth level consisted of Corinthian pilasters that were used to anchor a large canvas cloth that shielded spectators from the sun.

Latin for American Students

Did you know that gladiatorial fights were so enjoyed by the Romans that Augustus had to pass laws which limited their influence? He announced that gladiators could not fight without permission of the senate; that gladiatorial contests were to be limited to two annually; and not more than sixty pairs could be in combat at one time. During his reign, however, he gave eight **munera** *in which no less than ten thousand men fought.*

Grammar

Ablative of Manner

In Latin, the manner of an action is expressed by an adverb or by a phrase answering the question, *how?* When a phrase is used, a preposition such as *with*, introduces it.

Cum studiō labōrat.	*He labors with eagerness (eagerly).*
Magnō (cum) studio labōrat.	*He labors with great eagerness (very eagerly).*

When an adjective is used, **cum** may be omitted. If you use **cum**, the word order is usually adjective + **cum** + noun.

Be careful to distinguish this latest use of *with* from the *with* you studied earlier.

ORAL PRACTICE

Distinguish the three different uses of *with* in the following sentences.

1. *I shall go **with him with the greatest pleasure.***
2. *We can work **with greater success with this equipment.***
3. ***With my car** I can cover the distance **with you with ease.***

Ablative of Time When

The *time when* something happens is expressed in Latin by the ablative case without a preposition. In English, we may use the prepositions *at, in,* or *on,* or no preposition at all.

Aestāte nāvigāre amāmus.	*In the summer, we like to sail.*
Cēnam decimā hōrā ēdimus.	*We ate dinner at the tenth hour.*

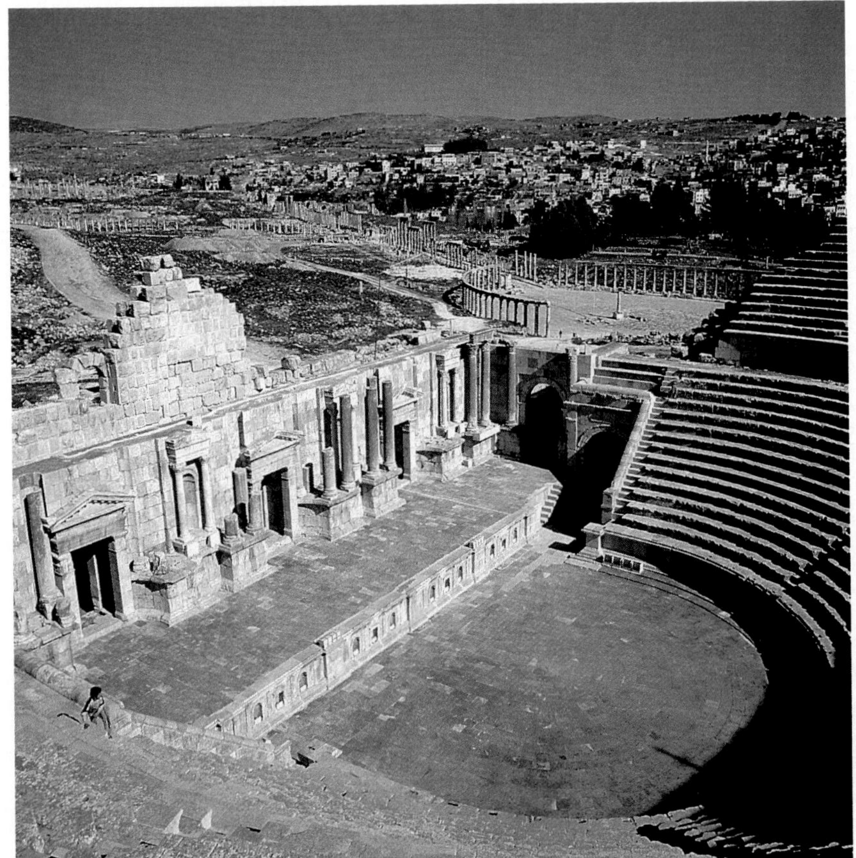

Hubertus Kanus/Photo Researchers

The Roman theater at Jerash (ancient city Gerasa), Jordan. The semicircular area is called the orchestra (originally, "dancing ground"). The actors performed on the raised rectangular platform or stage.

Ablative of Time Within Which

To express the *time* range *within which* something happens is also expressed by the ablative with no preposition. In English, we usually use *in* or *within.*

Tribus horīs frūmentum legētur.	*In three hours the grain will be collected.*
Ūnō annō bellum gerēmus.	*Within a year we shall wage war.*

Accusative of Time How Long

To express *how long* an action will take, you use the accusative case without a preposition. In English, we generally use the preposition *for.*

In Galliā quattuor annōs habitāvī.	*I lived in Gaul for four years.*
Duās hōrās remansit.	*He remained for two hours.*

Accusative of Extent of Space

To express *how far* one thing is from another, use the accusative case without a preposition. Most often, there is no preposition used in English.

Vīgintī pedēs natāvit.	*She swam twenty feet.*
Casa decem pedēs alta est.	*The house is ten feet tall.*

ORAL PRACTICE

Identify the construction and translate the phrase in italics.

1. Caesar captured many towns *in one year.*
2. *In the winter,* we shall pitch camp.
3. Anna carried water *for three hours.*
4. My father is *six feet* tall.
5. We like to eat at the *fifth* hour.
6. My field is *one hundred feet* from your house.

EXERCISES

A. Translate the following sentences into good English.

1. Magnā cum cūrā silvās nostrās cōnservābimus.
2. Cibō et pecūniā colōnōs miserōs līberē sustinuimus.
3. Multī puerī ob bellum duōs annōs studia intermīsērunt.
4. Aqua in silvā vigintī pedēs alta est.
5. Puer quī prīmum locum obtinuerat magnā cum cūrā studiōque labōrāverat.
6. Amīcus noster nōn permōtus est sed firmō animō ad casam nostram prōcēdere mātūrāvit.

B. Translate the following sentences into Latin.

1. He has been deeply moved by my words.
2. The teacher carefully taught the boys to save money.
3. Why did you give a reward to the boy who was absent?
4. The bad boy very carefully removed the teacher's books.
5. In summer, we hasten to the fields.

C. Working with a partner or in a small group, select a famous building or monument anywhere in the Roman world which is still in existence. Do not tell your choice to other groups. Describe the structure by providing its location, size, appearance, color, and best viewing times. One person from the group should read the description aloud and members of the other groups should try to guess what the structure is and where it is located.

Vocabulary

Nouns

aestās, aestātis, *f. summer* (aestival, aestivate)
arēna, -ae, *f. arena, sand, desert, seashore* (arenaceous)
autumnus, -ī, *m. autumn, fall*
gladiātor, gladiātōris, *m. gladiator*
hiems, hiemis, *f. winter* (hiemal)
mundus, -i, *m. world* (mundane)
pompa, -ae, *f. parade, procession* (pomp, pompous)
theātrum, -ī, *n. theater, amphitheater* (theatrical, theatrics)
vēr, vēris, *n. spring* (vernal, vernalize)

Verbs

cōgō, cōgere, coēgī, coactus, *collect, compel* (cogent)

cōnservō, cōnservāre, cōnservāvī, cōnservātus, *save, preserve* (conservation, conservative)

intermittō, intermittere, intermīsī, intermissus, *stop, interrupt* (intermission, intermittent)

obtineō, obtinēre, obtinuī, obtentus, *hold, obtain* (obtainability, obtainable)

permoveō, permovēre, permōvī, permōtus, *move (deeply)*

stō, stāre, stetī, stātūrus, *stand, stand up* (station, stationary)

Conjunction

nam, *for*

Word Studies

As a prefix in Latin and English, **inter–** has its usual meanings. It is rarely assimilated. It is often used in English to form new words: *inter-class, inter-state, inter-scholastic,* etc.

As a prefix **ob–** has the meaning *towards* or *against.* It is regularly assimilated before certain consonants: *oc-cur, of-ficial, o-mission, op-ponent;* but *ob-tain, ob-serve, ob-durate, ob-vious.*

OPPONENTS

Explain by derivation the meaning of *intercede, opponent, intervene, obvious.* What are *data?*

LESSON XXXIII

Niobē

Niobē, rēgīna superba, in Graeciā habitābat. Avus erat Iuppiter, quī deōs virōsque rēxit, et hoc[1] superbiam rēgīnae auxit. Niobē erat superba etiam quod septem fīliōs et septem fīliās habuit.

Apollō deus erat fīlius deae Lātōnae, et Diāna erat fīlia. Aliōs[2] līberōs Lātōna nōn habuit.

Sacra Lātōnae ā populō suscipiēbantur. Superba Niobē adfuit et rogāvit: "Cūr mātrī duōrum līberōrum sacra suscipitis? Hoc nōn permittam. Etiam Niobē dea est; quattuordecim, nōn duōs, līberōs habet. Lātōna glōriam nōn meret—Niobē esse prīma dēbet. Vōbīs līberīsque vestrīs exemplum ēgregium prōpōnō. Sī sententia mea ā vōbīs nōn probata erit, poenā afficiēmini."

Superba verba rēgīnae ā Lātōnā audīta sunt. Novum cōnsilium cēpit: fīlium vocāvit et officium permīsit:

"Tē iubeō septem fīliōs Niobae interficere."

Prīmus fīlius adfuit et interfectus est, tum reliquī. Niobē septem fīliōs nunc per linguam superbam āmīserat, tamen remānsit superba quod fīliae remānsērunt. Itaque Lātōna iussit etiam fīliās septem ēdūcī et ā Diānā interficī. Singulae fīliae ē vitā discessērunt, et Niobē misera in saxum dūrum mūtāta est. Poenā magnā affecta erat. Niobae exemplum memoriā tenēre dēbēmus.

[1] *this*
[2] *other*

Ronald Sheridan/Ancient Art & Architecture Collection

Diana was the goddess of the hunt as well as the protector of women. She is often represented as young, lean, and athletic and accompanied by a deer. She was the twin sister of Apollo.

QUESTIONS

1. Give three reasons for Niobe's pride.
2. Who was Diana's brother?
3. Why were Niobe's children killed?

Grammar

Interrogative Pronouns

Interrogative pronouns are used to ask questions. You are already familiar with the nominative forms **quis** and **quid.** The English equivalent is *who, whose, whom* for people and *what* for things.

Cui dōnum dedistī?	*To whom did you give the gift?*
Quid est in silvā?	*What is in the forest?*

The declension is as follows.

	SINGULAR		PLURAL		
	M AND F	N	M	F	N
Nom.	quis	quid	quī	quae	quae
Gen.	cuius	cuius	quōrum	quārum	quōrum
Dat.	cui	cui	quibus	quibus	quibus
Acc.	quem	quid	quōs	quās	quae
Abl.	quō	quō	quibus	quibus	quibus

NOTĀ·BENE

Lapsūs Linguae *(Slips of the Tongue).* ***Have you ever said,*** *Who did you see?* ***Why is*** *who* ***incorrect? Give the correct form and translate the sentence into Latin.***

Interrogative Adjectives

In Latin, the interrogative adjective is declined just like the relative pronoun **quī, quae, quod.** Because it is an adjective, it must agree with its noun in gender, number, and case. The English equivalent is still *what, whose, which, whom.*

Liber cuius est?	*Whose book is this?*
Quī equus est saucius?	*Which horse is wounded?*

ORAL PRACTICE

Determine whether to use the interrogative adjective or pronoun for the phrases in italics, then translate the phrase into Latin.

1. *Who* said that?
2. *Whose sons* are you?
3. *To which man* did you entrust the money?
4. *To whom* did you say that?
5. *With whom* are you coming?
6. *To what island* are you sailing?

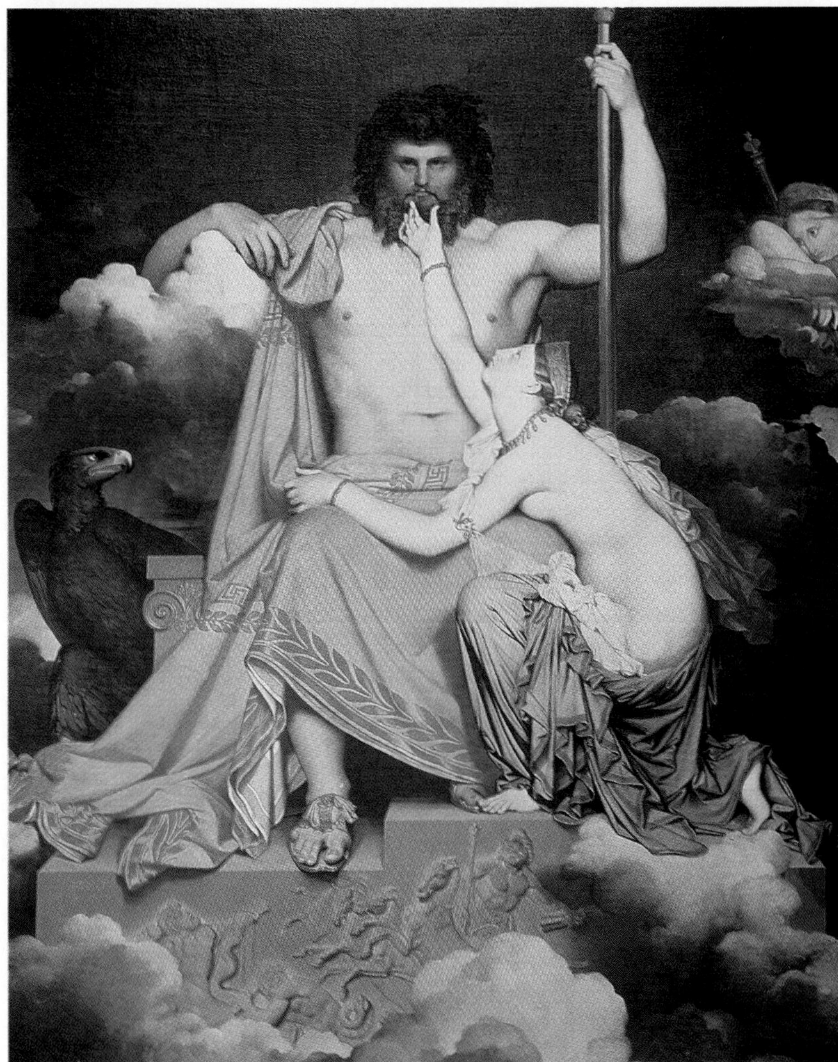

Musee Granet, Aix-En-Provence, France/Bridgeman Art Library/SuperStock

Jupiter, king of the gods, and Thetis in a painting by the French artist Jean Ingres (1780-1867). Thetis was a sea goddess and the mother of Achilles. She was beloved by both Jupiter and Neptune, but neither would marry her because an oracle had prophesied that she would bear a son mightier than his father.

EXERCISES

A. Translate the following sentences into good English.

1. Quis mē petit?
2. Quō modō sociī praedam coēgērunt?
3. Quī puer verbīs bonī virī nōn permōtus est?
4. Cui puerō, cui puellae, Nātūra nōn vītam grātam dedit?
5. Ā quō vōs puerī magnā cūrā dē perīculīs monitī erātis?
6. Quid amīcī tuī fēcērunt atque quod praemium accipient?
7. Quod cōnsilium, puellae, ā magistrō vestrō vōbīs datum est?

B. Translate the following sentences into Latin.

1. Whom did you seek?
2. To whom shall we give the books?
3. By what street did you girls come?
4. In what manner did you obtain the money?
5. In what place is he preparing to make a speech?

C. Niobe was a proud woman who was severely punished for her arrogance by the Roman goddess Latona. Work with a partner to create a dialogue between the two women as each tries to justify her right to be worshipped. You may want to reread the story or you may want to write it from a different point of view.

Latin for American Students

Did you know that sandals were customarily worn only inside the house by the Romans? If a Roman rode to dinner in a litter, he wore sandals; if he walked, he wore shoes while his sandals were carried by a personal slave. Sandals were not worn during meals and were taken by slaves when the guest arrived. Thus, the phrase **soleas poscere** *(to ask for one's sandals) came to mean "to prepare to leave."*

The god Apollo, twin brother of Diana, was born on the island of Delos. His particular areas of concern were prophecy, the arts, archery, medicine, courage, and wisdom. He founded the shrine of the Delphic Oracle in Delphi, Greece.

Scala/Art Resource, NY

Vocabulary

Nouns

avus, -ī, *m. grandfather*
modus, -ī, *m. manner* (modus vivendi)
pēs, pedis, *m. foot* (pedestrian, pedicure)
regnum, -ī, *n. kingdom, royal power* (regnal, regnant)
saxum, -ī, *n. rock* (saxifrage)
superbia, -ae, *f. arrogance, pride*

Adjectives

mutātus, -a, -um, *changed* (mutate, mutation)
superbus, -a, -um, *haughty, proud, snobbish*

Verbs

relinquō, relinquere, relīquī, relictus, *leave behind, abandon* (relinquish, relinquishment)
remaneō, remanēre, remānsī, remānsūrus, *stay behind, remain*

Adverb

tamen, *nevertheless*

Word Studies

1. What is a *cogent* reason for doing something? What is an *intermission* in a play? Explain the meaning of *modal, model, admonition.*
2. Here are some Latin phrases in English:
   inter nos, *between us*
   in absentia, *in absence*
   Pax vobiscum, *Peace* (*be*) *with you!*
   in perpetuum, (*into perpetuity*) *forever*
   sine qua non, *a necessity*
   cui bono? *for whose benefit is it? What good is it?*
   Ilium fuit, *Ilium has been* (i.e., *no longer exists*), said of Troy **(Ilium)** after its destruction; now applied to anything that is past and gone.

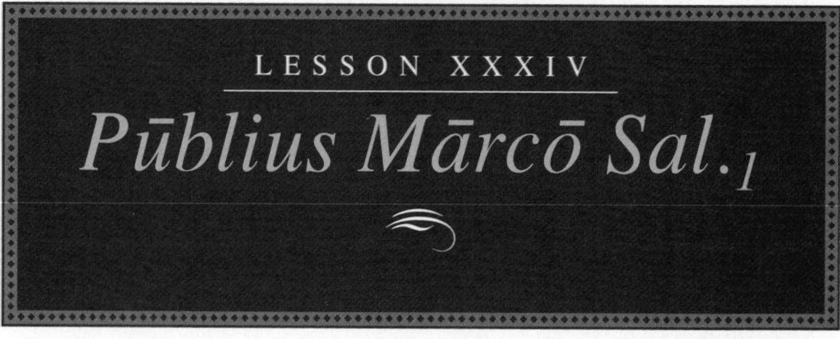

LESSON XXXIV

Pūblius Mārcō Sal.[1]

[A letter that a young Roman with Caesar's forces in Gaul in 55 B.C. might have sent to a friend in Rome.]

Sī valēs, bene est; ego valeō. Magnō studiō litterās tuās lēgī quae cum cūrā scrīptae et plicātae erant.

Dē Galliā rogās ac dē nōbīs cognōscere cupis. Vīta nostra nōn dūra est. In corpore sānī sumus. Magnus numerus captīvōrum in castrīs iam coāctus est. Caesar multās pugnās iam pugnāvit et multa oppida mūnīta cēpit, quae praesidiīs tenet. In paucīs oppidīs, numerō, nōn animō superāmur; et victoria nostra est. Mox Caesar erit dominus Galliae; Gallia in prōvinciam redigētur et viae novae mūnientur. Sed dominus aequus erit. Tum virōs nostrōs trāns Rhēnum flūmen ēdūcet et Germānōs terrēbit. Iam eōs[1] monuit. Modum quō bellum gerit probō. Sententia eius[2] est: "Veniō, videō, vincō." Magnus et ēgregius vir est. Fortasse trāns aquam in Britanniam prōcēdēmus, quae est magna īnsula dē quā nōn ante lēgī aut cognōvī.

Quid Quīntus noster agit? Quae nova officia suscēpit? Cūr nōn ante scrīpsit? Litterās tuās cum studiō exspectābō. Valē.

[1] *them*
[2] *his*

QUESTIONS

1. Did Publius have an easy time in Gaul?
2. Has Publius seen Germany yet? Has he seen Britannia?

[1] This is an abbreviation for **salūtem dīcit:** *Publius pays his respects to Marcus,* the usual form of greeting in a letter.

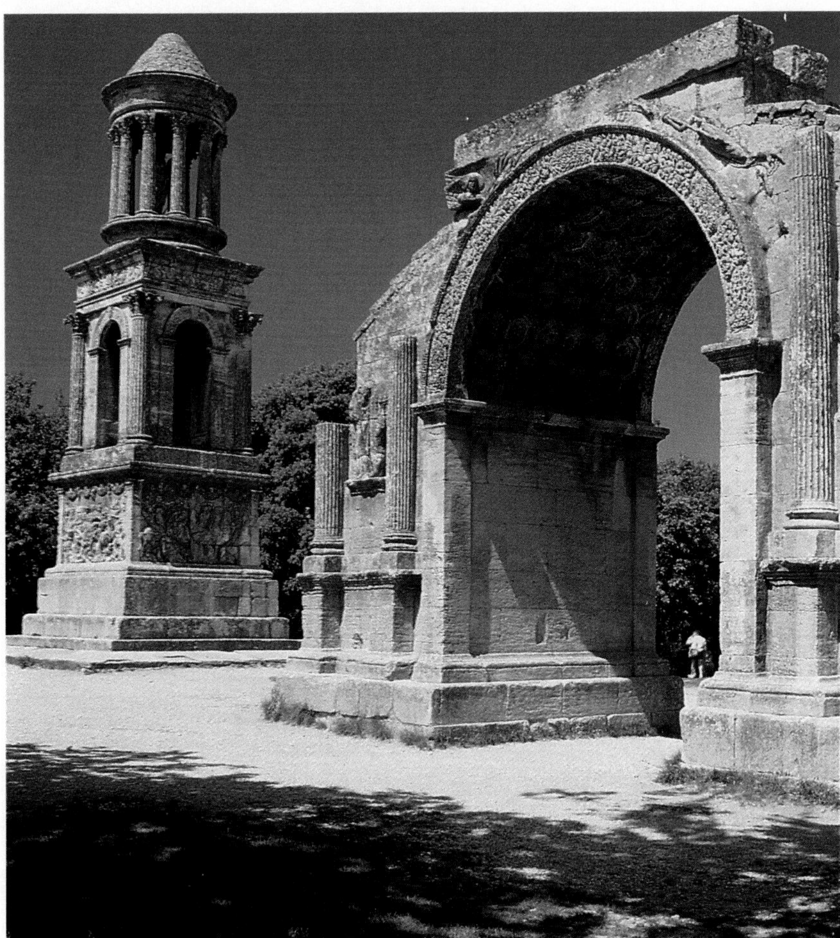

Erich Lessing/PhotoEdit

This Roman arch and tomb near Saint-Rémy in southern France date from the first century A.D. *The top of the tomb has the form of a round Roman temple.*

Latin for American Students

Did you know that although there was no official postal service, slaves called ***tabellarii*** *were employed by the wealthy or important Roman to deliver letters? These slaves could daily cover 26 miles by foot or forty to fifty miles in carts. Letters could be sent to Athens from Rome in twenty-one days and to Britain from Rome in thirty-three days. In colonial America, it took one month for mail to travel from the eastern to the southern states in the winter!*

Grammar

Third Declension Neuter Nouns

You are already familiar with the masculine and feminine nouns of the third declension. The neuter nouns share most of the same endings. Like the masculine and feminine nouns, they tend to have a stem change between the nominative and genitive singular forms. This will affect the accusative singular as well, because, as you recall, neuter nouns have the same form in the nominative and accusative. Also, like other neuter nouns, the nominative and accusative plurals end in **–a**. Neuter nouns are declined like **corpus, corporis** which means *body*.

Nom.	corpus	corpora
Gen.	corporis	corporum
Dat.	corporī	corporibus
Acc.	corpus	corpora
Abl.	corpore	corporibus

Corpora saucia erant in terrā.	*The wounded bodies were on the ground.*
Trāns flūmen natāvimus.	*We swam across the river.*

Multa capita corporaque. In a relief showing a battle between the Romans and the barbarians, you can clearly see the Romans' shields, swords, javelins, and armor.

Scala/Art Resource, NY

ORAL PRACTICE

1. Decline **nōmen clārum**, singular and plural.
2. Give the form(s) of **flūminum, capita, tempus, vulnerī, nōmine**.

Ablative of Respect

The ablative without a preposition is used to express the respect in which an adjective, noun, or verb is true. In English, we generally use the preposition *in*. You can usually insert the words *with respect to* in English as a good test of this construction.

Puer erat vir factīs.	*The boy was a man in (with respect to) deeds.*
Anna celeritāte superat.	*Anna excels in (with respect to) speed.*

EXERCISES

A. Translate the following sentences into good English.

1. Quid corpus tuum sub aquā tenet?
2. Bella trāns multa flūmina cum victōriā gessimus.
3. Litterae ā tē scrīptae cum cūrā plicātae erant.
4. Captīvī, quī ante portam positī erant, līberātī sunt.
5. Litterās quās scrīpsī plicābō et ad familiam meam mittam.
6. Anna Marcum studiīs sed nōn celeritāte superāvit.
7. Linguam Latīnam cum studiō legere incipimus; nova verba iam cognōvimus.

B. Translate the following sentences into Latin.

1. The new words ought always to be learned.
2. Is it Marcus who wrote the letter that you are reading?
3. The poor prisoners had been dragged across the fields.
4. I do not know the small boy who lives across the street.
5. He was king in name; nevertheless he did not have a kingdom.

C. Reread the letter that Publius wrote to Marcus at the beginning of this lesson. Based on what you know about daily life in Rome and her provinces, work with a partner and write him a response. You need not write it from Marcus' point of view, but as simply from a friend.

The meditative and intense expression of the young girl holding wax tablets and a stylus shows the artist's interest in the psychology of his subject. Sometimes called ***Sappho****, the painting from Pompeii dates from the first century* A.D.

Erich Lessing/Art Resource, NY

Vocabulary

Nouns

caput, capitis, *n. head* (capital, decapitate)
celeritās, celeritātis, *f. speed, swiftness* (accelerate, celerity)
corpus, corporis, *n. body* (corporation, corpse)
flūmen, flūminis, *n. river* (flume)
nōmen, nōminis, *n. name* (ignominious, nominate)
tempus, temporis, *n. time* (temporal, temporary)
vulnus, vulneris, *n. wound* (invulnerable, vulnerable)

Adjective

sānus, -a, -um, *sound, sane* (insane, sanitarium)

Verbs

cognōscō, cognōscere, cognōvī, cognitus, *learn,* perf. *know* (cognizance, recognize)
plicō, plicāre, plicāvī, plicātus, *fold* (application, apply)

Adverbs

ante, *before* (antebellum)
bene, *well* (benediction, benevolent)
fortasse, *perhaps*

Preposition

ante (+ acc.), *before (of time or place)* (antediluvian)

Conjunction

ac, *and* (*shortened form of* **atque**)

Word Studies

Ante– has its regular meaning and form when used as a prefix. **Trāns–** (or **trā–**, as in **trā-dūcō**) means *through* or *across.*

The most important part of speech in Latin for English derivation is the verb, and the most important part of the verb is the *perfect participle.* This form is also the most important for Latin word formation. Therefore, you must carefully learn the principal parts of every verb.

By associating Latin word and English derivative, you can make the English help your Latin, and vice versa. You can often tell the conjugation or the perfect participle of a Latin verb with the help of an English derivative. The English word *mandate* shows that **mandō** has **mandātus** as its perfect participle and is therefore of the first conjugation. Similarly *migr**at**e, don**at**ion, spect**at**or,* etc. The word ***vis**ion* helps one remember that the perfect participle of **videō** is **vīsus.** Similarly ***mot**ion* from **mōtus,** ***miss**ive* from **missus,** ***act**ive* from **āctus.**

Give the derivatives from **lēctus, nōtus, ductus.** Explain *election, deposit, complication, domineer.*

In compounds short **–a–** becomes short **–e–** before two consonants: **captus, acceptus.** Give two examples each from compounds of **capiō** and **faciō.**

Glimpses of Roman Life

FOOD AND MEALS

The Romans ate a variety of foods, although some foodstuffs that we take for granted such as corn, potatoes, tropical fruits, and tomatoes were unknown to them. Butter was rarely used, except externally as a sort of salve or cold cream, but dairy products were common foods. Instead of sugar which was also unknown, honey served for sweetening and the extensive use of honey made beekeeping a very important occupation. Fine wheat bread baked in flat, round loaves was the "staff of life." Breads of coarse wheat flour, of flour and bran, or bran alone were also popular. Cabbage, onions, beans, carrots, and peas were among the chief vegetables. Apples, pears, grapes, raisins, figs, plums, and olives were among the chief fruits. The **mālum Persicum** (from which our word *peach* is derived) was, as its name shows, originally brought from Persia.

Canning and freezing were unknown, but salted fish and a fermented fish sauce called **liquamen** were put up in earthenware jars. (**Liquamen** was commercially produced and one of the best brews came from Pompeii.) This practice led to a wider consumption of fish. The lack of refrigeration restricted the importation and preservation of many foods except those that could be preserved by drying, such as grapes and figs. Ice, in the form of snow, was a great luxury available to only a few.

Much use was made of salads of cress and lettuce, as is still true in Italy. This is one reason for the importance of olive oil, which was used also in cooking instead of butter, and was even burned in lamps. It was also used to rub the body after bathing, especially by athletes; it was also a base for perfume.

The favorite meat was pork; beef was less important than mutton. At least six kinds of sausage with pork as a base were popular and one can read of fifty different ways of cooking pork in Roman cookbooks. Various kinds of fowl and birds like chickens, ducks, geese, and pigeons were eaten, even peacocks by the wealthy classes.

Besides milk and water the chief drink of the Romans was wine. There were many grades of native and imported wines. They were usually mixed with water when drunk at meals. **Mērum,** or unmixed wine, was important to the soldiers because it was concentrated, and so less cumbersome to pack. The Romans also made and enjoyed apple cider, mulberry and date wine.

Scala/Art Resource, NY

A bakery in Pompeii. A huge freestanding oven stands at the left, while a row of grain mills to keep the baker well supplied with raw ingredients is to the right.

Poor people primarily ate a porridge of boiled wheat. Meat, fish, and vegetables were often expensive extras for the working class.

Breakfast **(ientaculum)** of even the wealthier Romans was a simple meal, chiefly of bread although raisins, olives, and cheese were sometimes added. In the country, dinner **(cēna)** was at noon, but in the city this was postponed until early evening. Instead there was a luncheon **(prandium)** at midday or somewhat earlier. This consisted of bread, salad, olives, cheese, fruit, nuts, and cold meat from the previous dinner. Dinner consisted of a course of appetizers like lettuce, onions, eggs, oysters, asparagus, etc., called the **gustus** (*taste*), followed by the chief course of meat, fish, or fowl and vegetables, then the dessert, called the **secunda mēnsa** (*second table*), of fruit, nuts, pastry, and sweets. The Latin expression **ab ōvō usque ad māla,** *from eggs to apples,* meaning from beginning to end, shows what the usual relishes and desserts were. Wine with water was served with the meal.

The guests at banquets reclined on couches instead of sitting on chairs. The couches were placed along the three sides of the rectangular table, each with room for three people. As the guests reclined on their left elbows, only their right hands were free. Forks were rarely used; food was eaten with fingers or with spoons. Meat was cut up before being served. Although much use was made of the fingers, we may well imagine that people of culture ate quite as daintily as we do who have forks to help us. They also had finger bowls and napkins, as well as slaves to wipe their hands.

QUESTIONS

1. Where did we originally get some of the important foods that the Romans knew nothing about?
2. Name the order of meals and describe a Roman dinner.
3. How would you arrange a Roman banquet in your Latin club or school?

Alinari/Art Resource, NY

A marble-covered counter or bar, in an inn at ancient Pompeii, near Naples. Here travelers could buy wine, bread, cheese, fruit, and other foods.

Unit VII Review
LESSONS XXXI-XXXIV

Vocabulary

Nouns

aestās	flūmen	mundus	saxum
arēna	gladiātōr	nōmen	statua
autumnus	hiems	pēs	superbia
avus	lapis	pictūra	tempus
caput	lībertās	pompa	theātrum
celeritās	lux	regnum	vēr
corpus	modus	ruīna	vulnus
diligentia			

Pronoun

quī

Adjectives

mutātus sānus superbus

Verbs

cognōscō	dō	permoveō	remaneō
cōgō	intermittō	plicō	stō
colō	obtineō	relinquō	submittō
conservō			

Adverbs

ante fortasse tamen
bene itaque

Prepositions

ante inter ob

Conjunctions

ac nam

Grammar Summary

Third Declension Neuter

The third declension neuter nouns have the same endings as other third declension nouns except for the nominative and accusative plural, which end in **–a.**

In arēnā, quinque corpora erant.	*In the arena there were five bodies.*
Nōmen meum Anna est.	*My name is Anna.*

Relative Pronouns

The relative pronoun **qui, quae, quod** agrees with its antecedent in gender and number but takes its case from the clause in which it is used. The English equivalent can be *who, whom, whose, which, that.*

Est vir cui equum dedī.	*He is the man to whom I gave the horse.*
Librum quem legis amāvī.	*I liked the book that you are reading.*

Interrogative Pronouns

The interrogative pronoun **quis, quid** is used to ask a question.

Cui litterās mandāvistī?	*To whom did you entrust the letter?*
Quid facis?	*What are you doing?*

Unit VII Review
LESSONS XXXI-XXXIV

Interrogative Adjectives

The interrogative adjective **quī, quae, quod** is declined like the relative pronoun but is used to ask a question. It agrees with the noun it modifies in gender, number, and case.

Quae puella tēcum vēnit?	*Which girl came with you?*
Cuius magister in casā est?	*Whose teacher is in the house?*

Ablative of Manner

The manner in which an action is performed is expressed by the ablative with **cum. Cum** may be omitted if an adjective is used.

Magnā cum diligentiā pugnāvērunt.	*They fought with great diligence.*
Cum celeritāte cucurrērunt.	*They ran with speed.*

Ablative of Respect

To show in what respect a noun, adjective, or verb applies, use the ablative without a preposition.

Equus magnus celeritate est.	*The horse is great in speed.*
Firma sententiīs tuīs es.	*You are strong in your opinions.*

Ablative of Time When

The time when an action takes place is expressed by the ablative without a preposition.

Cēnam decimā horā ēdimus.	*We ate dinner at the tenth hour.*
Aestate natāre amō.	*In the summer, I like to swim.*

Ablative of Time Within Which

The time within which an action takes place is expressed by the ablative without a preposition.

Unō annō Gallia provincia erit.	*Within one year, Gaul will be a province.*
Parvō tempore, virī discēdent.	*In a short time, the men will leave.*

Accusative of Time How Long

The length of time that an action takes place is expressed by the accusative without a preposition.

Rex multōs annōs rexit.	*The king ruled for many years.*
Duās hōrās verba ēgit.	*He made a speech for two hours.*

Accusative of Extent of Space

To express how far something is (from something else), use the accusative without a preposition.

Casa tua decem pedēs ā casā meā est.	*Your house is ten feet from my house.*
Flūmen octo pedē altum est.	*The river is eight feet deep.*

Unit VII Review
LESSONS XXXI-XXXIV

Unit Practice

Principal Parts

1. Give the four principal parts of the following verbs: **committō, cēdō, dūcō, agō, efficiō.**
2. Give the principal parts of the following verbs in Latin: *defend, flee, have, be, see, remain, increase, learn.*

Oral Form Drill

1. Give in all tenses the second singular active of **moveō;** the third singular passive of **agō;** the third plural passive of **accipiō.**
2. Decline **quae nātūra, quod signum, quī dominus.**
3. Supply the missing words in the right form and translate these questions.
   a. (*Whom*) petis? b. (*What*) librōs lēgistī? c. (*Who*) litterās scrīpsit? d. (*To whom*) librum dabō? e. (*By whom*) litterae scrīptae sunt?

Working with a partner or a small group, create a dialogue (with at least as many parts as there are people in your group) about a Roman dinner party. Discuss what is going to be served, how many people will be invited, and when it will take place. Then act it out while commenting on the various foods served to the guests.

Word Studies

1. Find and use in sentences as many English derivatives as possible from **vocō, videō, mittō,** and **faciō.** (Remember the importance of the perfect participle.)
2. The first word, printed in boldface type, in each of the following lines is a Latin word. From among the last five words in each line choose the one which is an English derivative of the first word.

dō	dough	dote	do
	dot	dative	
moneō	month	remain	admonition
	moan	remind	
cōgō	cog	incognito	cognate
	cogency	concoct	
petō	pet	compete	petal
	petite	impede	
legō	leg	log	collect
	lag	lick	

Scala/Art Resource, NY

Unit VIII

Ancient Travel and Adventure

*Homer's **Odyssey** was popular among the Romans, either in the original Greek or translated into Latin as a school reader. This epic poem tells the story of Ulysses, King of Ithaca, and his many adventures as he attempts to return to his homeland after the Trojan War. In this painting by Stradano, we see Ulysses descending into the Lower World where he will learn news of his wife, Penelope, and his homeland, from his deceased mother. You may recall a similar episode from Vergil's epic, the **Aeneid**, in which Aeneas goes to the Lower World* *(see p. 197)**. Vergil echoed many other episodes from Homer's **Odyssey**.*

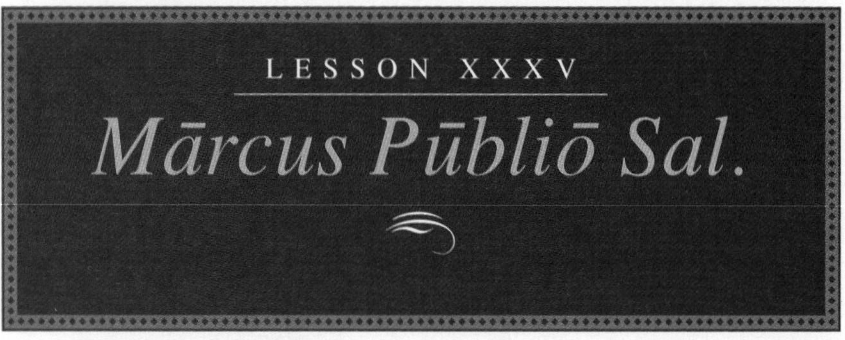

[An answer to the letter in Lesson XXXIV.]

Adductus litterīs ā tē, Pūblī, in Galliā scrīptīs, respondēbō, nam multa rogāvistī. Multa nova sunt. Quid putās? Quīntus noster fīliam tertiam Rūfī in mātrimōnium dūxit! Ego hoc[1] nōn prōvīdī; Quīntus mē nōn cōnsuluit. Tūne hoc prōvīdistī? Tenēsne memoriā puellam, parvam ac timidam? Nōn iam timida est; nunc pulchra est, ā multīs amāta.

Dē Caesaris ducis ēgregiīs victōriīs scrīpsistī. Cum magnō studiō litterās tuās lēgī, nam ultima Gallia semper fuit terra nova et nōn mihi nōta. Paucī nūntiī dē Galliā vēnērunt, quī fugam Gallōrum nūntiāvērunt. Caesar victōriīs suīs[2] glōriam et fāmam armōrum Rōmānōrum auxit et pācem effēcit. Caesarī grātiam habēmus quod prō salūte nostrā pugnāvit. Gallōs in fugam datōs nōn iam timēbimus. Alpēs, quae inter nōs et Gallōs stant, nunc Rōmam ā perīculō dēfendunt, nam Gallī timidī trāns Alpēs mīlitēs nōn trānsportābunt. Mīlitēs trāductōs removēre dūrum erit.

Sī Caesar mē cōnsulit, librum "Dē Bellō Gallicō" scrībere dēbet. Sī liber ab eō[3] scrībētur, ā multīs hominibus legētur; etiam post spatium multōrum annōrum cum cūrā et dīligentiā legētur.

Litterae tuae nōn longae erant. Cūr longās litterās nōn scrībis? Multa nova in terrīs ultimīs vīdistī atque vidēbis. Valē.

[1] *this*
[2] *his*
[3] *him*

QUESTIONS

1. What girl was pretty?
2. Where did Caesar win victories?

Grammar

Perfect Passive Participles Used as Clauses

The participle is not used much in English, but it is very common in Latin. It is often best translated by a subordinate clause, introduced in

THE GRANGER COLLECTION, New York

A nineteenth century engraving depicts Julius Caesar's invasion of Britain in 55 B.C. Note that the Roman soldiers are heavily armed compared to their rivals.

English by *who (whom, whose), when* or *after, since* or *because, although,* and *if*. Sometimes it is translated as a coordinate clause, i.e., one connected with the preceding clause by *and*. The meaning of the Latin sentence as a whole will always show the exact meaning of the participle. Think of the participle's literal meaning before trying to expand it into a clause, then use the English word that makes the most sense. The various translations in the following sentences show the flexibility of the Latin participle.

Pecūniam *amissam* invēnit.	*He found the money* ***which had been lost.***
***Convocātī* puerī verba magistrī audient.**	***After they have been called together,*** *the boys will hear the words of the teacher.*
***Territī* nōn processērunt.**	***Because they were scared,*** *they did not advance.*
Librum *lectum* tibi dabō.	***I shall read*** *the book* ***and*** *give it to you.*

NOTĀ·BENE

Notice that the perfect participle denotes time before that of the main verb, and that it agrees like an adjective with a noun or pronoun (sometimes not expressed) in gender, number, and case.

ORAL PRACTICE

Substitute a participle for the words within parentheses.

1. Quattuor librōs (*after reading them*) accēpī.
2. Liber bonus (*if read*) semper amīcus vērus erit.
3. Numerus librōrum (*which I consulted*) magnus fuit.
4. Multōs librōs lēgī (*because I had been influenced*) ā magistrīs meīs.
5. Nōnne magnum est pretium ultimae casae (*which was shown to me by you*)?

EXERCISES

A. Translate the following sentences into good English.

1. Perīculum prōvīsum nōs nōn terruit.
2. Rōmānī multa oppida occupāta relīquērunt.
3. Vīsī ā puerīs, inimīcī fūgērunt.
4. Pecūnia, ā mē in viā āmissa, ab amīcō meō inventa est.
5. Malus puer, ab amīcīs monitus, līberōs nōn iam terruit.

B. Translate the following sentences into Latin.

1. I have read the letter written by my son.
2. I saw the girl who had been scared by you. (*Express in two ways.*)
3. The boys read the book because they had been influenced by the teacher's words. (*Express in two ways.*)

Scala/Art Resource, NY

A round temple of Hercules Victor from the first century B.C. *stands in the Forum Boarium* **(Bovarium)**, *traditionally called the ancient cattle market of Rome. This is the oldest surviving marble edifice in Rome. The roof is of modern origin.*

C. Marcus and Publius probably corresponded several times during the war. Compare the letter you wrote in the last lesson as a response to the one written by Marcus in this lesson. Now suppose that Publius has just come home from his campaigns with Caesar. Work with a partner to create a dialogue between the two in which they exchange the latest gossip in town, as well as the results of various battles and their encounters with new cultures.

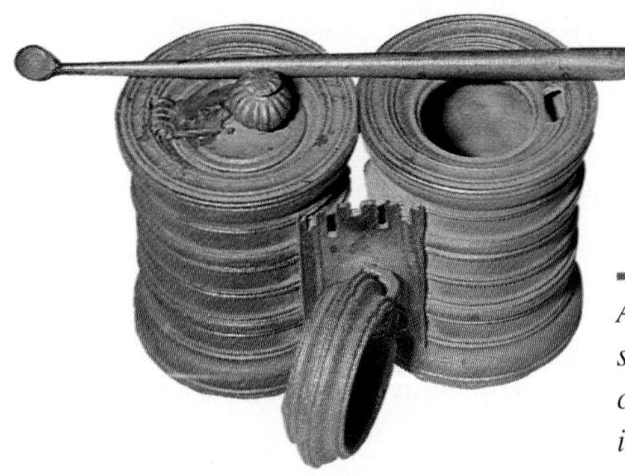

Ronald Sheridan/Ancient Art & Architecture Collection

A Roman inkwell, pen, and stand. The pen, or ***stylus****, could also be used to write in wax on wooden tablets.*

Latin for American Students

Did you know that out of eighty high quality wines known to the Romans, two-thirds of them were produced in Italy? The best grapes were grown south of Rome in Latium, Campania, and on the rich volcanic slopes of Mt. Vesuvius. Much agricultural knowledge was devoted to winemaking and viticulture and Italian wines became famous as far away as India by the first century A.D.

Vocabulary

Nouns

factum, -ī, *n. deed*	(fact, factor)
fuga, -ae, *f. flight;* **in fugam dō,** *put to flight*	(fugitive, fugue)
spatium, spatī, *n. space, time*	(spacious, spatial)

Adjectives

certus, -a, -um, *fixed, sure*	(certain, certainty)
parātus, -a, -um, *ready, prepared*	
timidus, -a, -um, *shy*	(timid, timidity)
ultimus, -a, -um, *farthest*	(ultimate, ultimatum)

Verbs

addūcō, addūcere, addūxī, adductus, *lead to, influence* (adduce, adductor)

antecēdō, antecēdere, antecessī, antecessūrus, *go before* (ancestor, antecedent)

cernō, cernere, crēvī, crētus, *discern, see* (discrete, discretion)

commoveō, commovēre, commōvī, commōtus, *disturb* (commotion)

cōnsulō, cōnsulere, cōnsuluī, cōnsultus, *consult* (consultant, consultation)

prōvideō, prōvidēre, prōvīdī, prōvīsus, *foresee* (provide, provision)

putō, putāre, putāvī, putātus, *think* (putative, reputation)

trādūcō, trādūcere, trādūxī, trāductus, *lead across* (transducer, transduction)

trānsportō, trānsportāre, trānsportāvī, trānsportātus, *transport* (transportation, transporter)

The Latin Influence upon English

Latin words have been coming into English continuously from the beginning of our language to the present. Julius Caesar twice invaded Britain, and a century later the Romans conquered the island. For the next four hundred years the Romans ruled Britain, and the language, at least in the towns, came to be Latin. When the Angles and Saxons invaded Britain in the fifth century and gave their name (*Angle-land, Eng-land*) and language to the island, they adopted a number of Latin words. Even earlier they had come into contact with the Romans in northern Germany and borrowed some Latin words. So you might say that Latin affected English even before English existed as a separate language. Among such early borrowings are *wine* from **vīnum**, *cheese* from **cāseus**, and *pound* from **pondus**.

As the Romans in Britain found it necessary to build many military camps in order to subdue the local peoples, which later developed into towns, the word **castra** can be found in a number of American town names including *Chester, Rochester, Manchester, Worcester,* and *Lancaster.* What other names with these endings can you give?

We have seen a similar evolution in North America where frontier forts, erected originally as defenses against native Americans, became trading posts, out of which have grown such cities as Fort Dodge, Fort Scott, and Fort Worth.

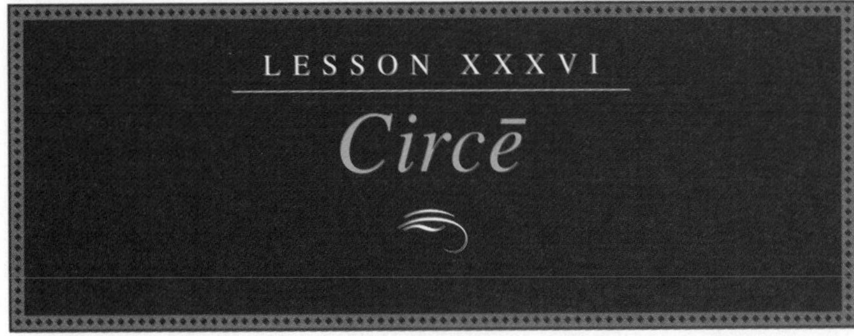

[You may recall that during the Trojan War, Aeneas led the Trojans and Ulysses was one of the Greek leaders. After the war, both left Troy and experienced several adventures. After Ulysses left the land of the Lotus-eaters, he encountered Circe.]

Siciliā relīctā, Ulixēs ad rēgnum Aeolī, rēgis ventōrum, nāvigāvit, quī Ulixī ventōs malōs in saccō ligātōs dedit et dīxit: "Malīs ventīs ligātīs, nōn iam impediēris et in patriā tuā salūtem inveniēs."

Itaque multōs diēs[1] Graecī sine impedīmentō et sine cūrā nāvigāvērunt. Ūnō amīcō ventō āctī sunt, reliquīs ligātīs. Iam Ithacam clārē cernunt. Sed nautae dē saccō cūrā affectī sunt quod dē ventīs quī in saccō erant nihil audīverant. "Praemia et pecūnia in saccō sunt," nauta dīxit. "Rēx Ulixēs nautīs quī mala sustinuērunt pecūniam dare dēbet." Itaque, saccō apertō, ventī expedītī Graecōs ad rēgnum Aeolī redēgērunt. Sed nōn iam Aeolus auxilium dat. Ūnam nāvem[2] Graecī nunc habent, reliquīs āmissīs.

Nunc, impedīmentīs relīctīs, ad īnsulam veniunt quam Circē pulchra regēbat. Vīgintī hominēs, ab Ulixe ad rēgīnam missī, pācem praesidiumque lēgum petīvērunt. Ab Eurylochō[3] duce per silvam ad rēgīnam pedibus ductī sunt, quae eōs[4] in animālia[5] vertit. Eurylochus sōlus[6] in animal nōn versus ad nāvem fūgit et Ulixī omnia[7] dē sociīs impedītīs nūntiāvit. Ulixēs commōtus cum reliquīs auxilium sociīs pressīs dare mātūrāvit. In viā Mercurium deum vīsum cōnsuluit. Mercurius eum[8] monuit et herbam eī[9] dedit. "Hāc[10] herbā," inquit, "vītam tuam servābis et mīlitēs tuōs expediēs." Ulixēs rēgīnam iussit sociōs in hominēs vertere. Circē Ulixis verbīs et factīs territa animālia in hominēs vertit. Rēgīna, quae nōn iam inimīca fuit, magnam cēnam ac cibōs bonōs parāvit; ita concordiam amīcitiamque redūxit. Sociīs expedītīs, annum ibi Ulixēs mānsit et vītam grātam ēgit. Tum, ā sociīs adductus, discessit.

[1] *days*
[2] *ship*
[3] *Eurylochus* (Ūrīl´okus)
[4] *them*
[5] *animals*
[6] *only*
[7] *everything*
[8] *him*
[9] *to him*
[10] *with this*

QUESTIONS

1. What caused the storm that prevented Ulysses from reaching Ithaca?
2. How did Ulysses find out what Circe had done to his men?
3. By what means did he rescue them?

Circe turns some of Ulysses' men into pigs. From an engraving made in 1619. The picture, like many of this period with classical themes, combines details of the time of the artist with some from ancient times.

The Bettmann Archive

Grammar

Ablative Absolute

In English, we sometimes say, *That being the case, there is nothing I can do.* Such phrases as "That being the case" are used loosely and have no direct grammatical connection with either the subject or the predicate of the sentence.

In Latin, this loose construction is very common. This independent use of the participial phrase is called the *ablative absolute*. The perfect participle is most frequently used in this construction, but occasionally a noun, adjective, or another participle is used. As with other participial constructions, it is usually translated with a clause starting with *after, since, when, because,* etc.

Noun plus participle:

Officiō factō, dominus discessit.	*After doing his duty, the master departed.*
Signō datō, dux prōcessit.	*When the signal was given, the leader advanced.*

Noun plus noun:

Caesare duce, Galliam vincēmus.	*Since Caesar is leader, we shall conquer Gaul.*
Numā rēge, pācem habuimus.	*When Numa was king, we had peace.*

Noun plus adjective:

Aquā altā, nōn natābō.	*Since the water is deep, I shall not swim.*
Populō līberō, vīta grāta erit.	*If the people are free, life will be pleasant.*

It is generally better initially to translate using the literal meaning of the words. Often by inserting a *been* or *having been* you can determine the gist of the sentence. Then go back and add an adverb in English that makes sense.

NOTĀ·BENE

It is critical that this construction not be connected grammatically to the rest of the sentence.

Puerō inventō, servus ad casam vēnit.

The boy having been found, the slave came to the house.

ORAL PRACTICE

Identify which of the following are ablative absolutes and which are regular participles, then translate the words in italics.

1. This boy, *sent* to visit his aunt, lost his way.
2. After the boy *was freed,* everyone was happy.
3. *Having read* the books, we returned them to the library.
4. *After putting* the prisoner in jail, the policewoman went home.
5. *After* the money *was given,* the boy was returned to his parents.
6. The boys *having been compelled* to stop fighting, the principal went back to her office.

A cartoon from the fourth century B.C. The sorceress Circe tries to drug the weary Ulysses. Her loom is at the right.

Department of Antiquities, Ashmolean Museum, Oxford

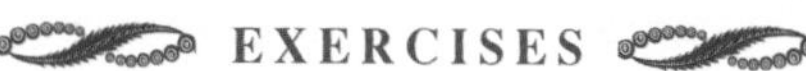

EXERCISES

A. In translating the following sentences, be careful to distinguish the ablative absolute from other uses of the participle.

1. Librō āmissō, puella nōn legit.
2. Dux servōrum, signō datō, equōs ēdūcī iussit.
3. Expedītī ex perīculō, deīs grātias agere dēbēmus.
4. Rōmānī, castrīs positīs, Gallōs in fugam vertērunt.
5. Captīvī miserī, tractī ad pedēs rēgis, pācem timidē petēbant.
6. Impedīmentīs in oppidō relīctīs, mīlitēs salūtem petīvērunt.
7. Librīs lēctīs, discipulī magistrum aequō animō exspectāvērunt.
8. Hominēs, praedā armīsque impedītī, nōn properāvērunt.

B. Translate the following sentences into Latin.

1. Having written good letters, the boys will receive rewards.
2. Hindered on account of bad roads, we did not wish to come on foot.
3. The advice of the teacher having been heard, we shall read the book.
4. After sending a messenger, the king shouted: "My kingdom for (**prō**) a horse!"

C. Ulysses stayed with Circe for a year, forgetting his destiny. Aeneas spent a year with Dido until he was reminded that Carthage was not his final stop. Working in a small group, summarize briefly why you think these two men seemed to forget where they were supposed to be going. What role did the women play? The other men in the group? The gods and goddesses?

Latin for American Students

Did you know that the Romans enjoyed many of the herbs and spices that we enjoy today? Poppy seeds were eaten with honey for dessert or sprinkled over a mushroom-shaped bread before baking. Indian pepper and cinnamon were also important to the Roman haute cuisine. A dish from an existing Roman cookbook lists these herbs for a roast meat sauce: pepper, lovage, parsley, celery seed, dill, asafoetida root, hazelwort, tumeric, caraway, cumin, and ginger.

Vocabulary

Nouns

herba, -ae, *f. herb, plant, grass*	(herbal, herbivore)
impedīmentum, -ī, *n. hindrance;* pl. *baggage*	(impediment)
nihil, *n. nothing* (indeclinable noun)	(nihilist)
saccus, -ī, *m. sack, bag*	(saccate)

*Porta San Sebastiano **(Porta Appia)** marks the beginning of the Appian Way as it leaves Rome going toward southern Italy. In its route near the city, it was thickly lined with tombs on both sides.*

Archivio e Studio Folco Quilici

Verbs

aperiō, aperīre, aperuī, apertus, *open, uncover*	(aperture)
expediō, expedīre, expedīvī, expedītus, *set free*	(expedite, expedition)
impediō, impedīre, impedīvī, impedītus, *hinder*	(impediment)
ligō, ligāre, ligāvī, ligātus, *bind, tie*	(ligament, ligature)
vertō, vertere, vertī, versus, *turn*	(vertigo, versus)
vincō, vincere, vīcī, victus, *conquer*	(invincible, victor)

The Latin Influence upon English (cont.)

In an earlier lesson we saw that a number of Latin words came into English as a result of the Roman occupation of Britain. Other examples are *wall* (from **vāllum**), together with place names like *Walton* (*Walltown*); *port* (from **portus,** *harbor*), together with place names like *Portsmouth; street* (from **strāta**); *Lincoln* (from **colōnia,** *colony*); *Cologne,* the name of a German city which was an ancient Roman colony.

A century and a half after the Angles and Saxons settled in England, Pope Gregory sent missionaries to convert the island to Christianity. Since the missionaries spoke Latin, they introduced a number of new Latin words into English, especially words dealing with the Church, as *temple* **(templum),** *disciple* **(discipulus),** *bishop* **(episcopus).**

Explain *cologne, Stratford, antecedent, relic, providence.*

LESSON XXXVII

Sīrēnēs et Phaeācia

Annō in īnsulā quam Circē rēxit āctō, Ulixēs ad Sīrēnēs[1] vēnit. Sīrēnēs corpora avium[2] et capita puellārum habuērunt. Carmina pulchra canēbant, quibus nautae mōtī nāvēs[3] ad saxa vertēbant. Hōc[4] modō vītam āmittēbant.

Sed Ulixēs dē Sīrēnibus ā Circē[5] monitus erat. Perīculō prōvīsō, aurēs[6] sociōrum cērā clausit, sed nōn suās.[7] Iussit manūs[8] pedēsque suōs ad nāvem ligārī. Hōc modō carmina Sīrēnum clārē audīvit neque vītam āmīsit.

Posteā sociī Ulixis interfectī sunt et Ulixēs sōlus ad īnsulam parvam āctus est in quā habitābat rēgīna pulchra cui[9] nōmen erat Calypsō. Rēgīna Ulixem nōn dīmīsit. Itaque Ulixēs ibi octō annōs—longum temporis spatium—remānsit. Sed tum Iuppiter rēgīnam iussit Ulixī nāvem parāre. Hōc factō, Ulixēs expedītus rēgīnam relīquit.

Sed nāvis undīs frācta est ad īnsulam cui nōmen erat Phaeācia. Vulneribus impedītus, homō miser vix corpus in silvam fīnitimam ad flūmen trahere potuit. Tum somnum cēpit.

Interim Nausicaa, fīlia rēgis Phaeāciae, cum aliīs puellīs carrō ad flūmen prōcēdēbat, quod in flūmine vestēs[10] lavāre cupīvit; nam tempus mātrimōnī Nausicaae aderat. Ubi vestēs in flūmine lāvērunt, labōre intermissō, Nausicaa pilam ad reliquās puellās in ōrdine iaciēbat. Sed puella quaedam[11] in flūmen pilam iēcit. Clāmōribus puellārum ab Ulixe audītīs, Ulixēs nōn dubitāvit sed pilam ex aquā servāvit. Puellae timidae fugere incipiunt, quod is ob mala atque vulnera quae sustinuerat nōn iam pulcher erat. Sed Nausicaa nōn territa ante Ulixem stetit et eī[12] grātiās ēgit. Vestibus plicātīs, ad oppidum in ōrdine prōcessērunt. Ulixēs ab rēge Alcinoō[13] acceptus est, cui factīs clārīs nōtus fuit. Paucōs diēs Ulixēs in Phaeāciā mānsit. Tum Alcinous Ulixem ad patriam Ithacam mīsit. Itaque post vīgintī annōs Ulixēs sōlus sine sociīs ad patriam vēnit.

Ulixe in Ithacā vīsō, Neptūnus nāvem in quā Ulixēs trānsportātus erat ante portum Phaeāciae in saxum vertit. Portus[14] īnsulae hōc[15] impedīmentō clausus est neque posteā Alcinous et hominēs īnsulae nāvigāre potuērunt.

[1] *the Sī´rens*
[2] *of birds*
[3] *ships*
[4] *this* (ablative)
[5] ablative
[6] *ears*
[7] *his own*
[8] *hands*
[9] *whose*
[10] *clothes*
[11] *one girl*
[12] *to him*
[13] *Alcinous* (*Alsin´o-us*)
[14] *harbor*
[15] *this*

QUESTIONS

1. How did Ulysses manage to hear the Sirens without danger?
2. Why did Nausicaa go to the river?
3. With how many comrades did Ulysses return?

Grammar

The Conjugation of Possum

The verb **possum** is a compound of **sum** and shows many of the same irregularities. Its principal parts are **possum, posse, potuī,** (no fourth principal part and no passive). It is translated as *can* or *be able* and is followed by the infinitive. The imperfect can also be translated as *could* or *was able*.

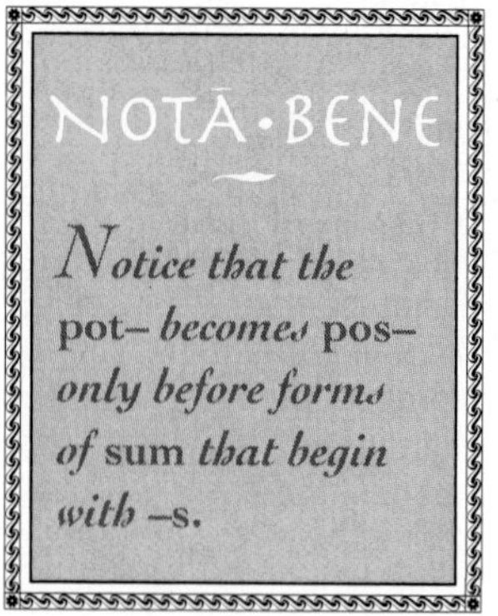
NOTĀ·BENE
Notice that the pot– becomes pos– only before forms of sum that begin with –s.

PRESENT	IMPERFECT	FUTURE
possum	poteram	poterō
potes	poterās	poteris
potest	poterat	poterit
possumus	poterāmus	poterimus
potestis	poterātis	poteritis
possunt	poterant	poterunt

The perfect tenses are formed regularly: **potuī, potueram, potuerō,** etc.

A Roman mosaic from Cherchel, Algeria, showing Ulysses in his ship with the two Sirens (half-women and half-birds) at each end, along with playful dolphins.

Ronald Sheridan/Ancient Art & Architecture Collection

Ronald Sheridan/Ancient Art & Architecture Collection

Puellae timidae fugere incipiunt. The helmeted goddess Minerva watches Ulysses come out of the water. Nausicaa looks ready to run.

ORAL PRACTICE

1. Give the form and meaning of **potuerās, poterātis, potuērunt, possunt, poterit, posse.**
2. Translate into Latin: *you could, they had been able, we shall be able, he can, they could.*

Irregular First and Second Declension Adjectives

There are a few first and second declension adjectives that are irregular in the genitive and dative singular. They are declined like **ūnus**. The plurals are regular.

Nom.	tōtus	tōta	tōtum
Gen.	tōtius	tōtius	tōtius
Dat.	tōtī	tōtī	tōtī
Acc.	tōtum	tōtam	tōtum
Abl.	tōtō	tōtā	tōtō

> **NOTĀ·BENE**
>
> *Distinguish between* alius, *which means* other *of more than two and* alter, *which applies to a group of two.* Alter ... alter *is translated* the one ... the other.

The other adjectives that fit this pattern are:

alius, alia, aliud, *other, another*
alter, altera, alterum, *the other (of two), the second*
neuter, neutra, neutrum, *neither (of two)*
nullus, -a, -um, *not any, no ...*
sōlus, -a, -um, *only, alone*
ullus, -a, -um, *any*
uter, utra, utrum, *which (of two)*

ORAL PRACTICE

Decline **neuter miles, sōla rēgīna, ullum caput.**

> ## Latin for American Students
>
> *Did you know that the Romans had several kinds of bread but did not eat bread with butter? There was suet bread; honey and oil bread; cheese bread; large, grainy Cilician loaves; wafer bread; a soft and salty raised bread called Cappodocian; pancakes; rolls baked on a spit known as* **panis castrensis;** *and* **dice** *which were square loaves flavored with oil, aniseed, and cheese. Roman bakers even made cookies for dogs!*

EXERCISES

A. Translate the following sentences into good English.

1. Quae nōmina flūminum Galliae cognōvistis?
2. Corpore hominis inventō, mīles ducem vocāvit.
3. Rex neutrī fīliō regnum dedit.
4. Ob tempus annī frūmentum trānsportāre nōn poterāmus.
5. Litterae aliae quās scripsistī mittī crās possunt.
6. Rēx, victōriā barbarōrum territus, mīlitēs trāns flūmen trādūxit.

B. Translate the following sentences into Latin.

1. The river that you see is wide.
2. Horses have large bodies but small heads.
3. (There) were many wounds on the farmer's body.
4. Since the river is closed, grain can no longer be transported.
5. They had not been able to come because they were alone.
6. To one sister I shall give money; to the other a book.

C. Another adventure that Ulysses and his crew had on their voyage home was with Scylla and Charybdis. Work with a partner or in a small group to put the following story into Latin. Try not to translate directly, but determine the gist of the story and use familiar structures. You may find the following vocabulary useful.

cave, **spēlunca, -ae,** *f.*
cliff, **scopulus, -ī,** *m.*
monster, **mōnstrum, -ī,** *n.*
neck, **collum, -ī,** *n.*
nymph, **nympha, -ae,** *f.*
side, **latus, lateris,** *n.*
strait, **fretum, -ī,** *n.*
teeth, **dens, dentis,** *m.*
whirlpool, **vertex, verticis,** *m.*
flow, **fluō, fluere, flūxī, fluxus**
swallow, **dēvorō, -āre, -āvī, -ātus**

Once upon a time there was a beautiful nymph named Scylla. A young man named Glaucus loved her, but she did not love him. He went to Circe to ask advice, but Circe became very angry because she wanted Glaucus to love her instead. Then Circe turned Scylla into an evil monster. She lives in a cave in a cliff. She has twelve feet, six long necks each with a horrible head, and three rows of teeth. She looks out of her cave and seizes anything that swims by. On the other side of the strait is Charybdis, the whirlpool. She swallows the water and she lets it flow back. If you sail when she is swallowing, no one can save you. It is good to stay close to Scylla. Ulysses lost six men because of Scylla. Sailors who sail through this strait try to stay in the middle—between Scylla and Charybdis.

Vocabulary

Nouns

carmen, carminis, *n. song*	
cēra, -ae, *f. wax*	(cerate, sincere)
clāmor, clāmōris, *m. noise, shouting*	(clamor, clamorous)
ōrdō, ōrdinis, *n. order, rank, row*	(inordinate, ordinary)
pila, -ae, *f. ball*	(pill, pillar)

Adjectives

alius, alia, aliud, *other, another* (alien, alienate)
alter, altera, alterum, *the other (of two), the second* (alter ego, alteration)
neuter, neutra, neutrum, *neither (of two)* (neutral, neutron)
nullus, -a, -um, *not any, no ...* (null, nullify)
sōlus, -a, -um, *only, alone*
ullus, -a, -um, *any*
uter, utra, utrum, *which (of two)*

Verbs

canō, canere, cecinī, cantus, *sing* (cantor)
claudō, claudere, clausī, clausus, *close* (clause, include)
frangō, frangere, frēgī, fractus, *break, shatter* (fraction, fracture)
iaciō, iacere, iēcī, iactus, *throw, hurl* (project, subject)
lavō, lavāre, lāvī, lautus, *wash, bathe* (lavage, lavatory)

Word Studies

1. Explain *commotion, certificate, notorious, tertiary.*
2. Here are some Latin words and phrases in English:
   erratum (plur. **errata**), *error*
   terra incognita, *an unknown land*
   Te Deum, *Thee, God* (*we praise*); the name of a hymn
   Et tu, Brute, *you too, Brutus* (said by Caesar on receiving the death-blow from his friend, Brutus)
   de facto, *from* or *according to fact, actual;* as a **de facto** government, one which is actually in operation, even if not recognized as legal
   Translate **ante bellum.**
3. Explain *contemporary, invulnerable, decapitate, capitalism, capital punishment.* What is a *corporation?* What is meant by *incorporated?* State two ways in which *siren* is used today.

Ulixēs, nāvī et sociīs āmissīs, corpore vulneribus cōnfectō, in patriam pervēnerat. Ad fīnem itineris sed nōn labōrum perpetuōrum vēnerat. Et cīvēs et hostēs crēdidērunt Ulixem nōn iam vīvum esse.

Prīmus quī Ulixem vīdit sed nōn cognōvit erat pāstor cuius nōmen erat Eumaeus. Ab Eumaeō Ulixēs nōn pauca dē uxōre Pēnelopē et fīliō Tēlemachō audīvit. Tēlemachus ab īnsulā tum aberat, quod Pēnelopē eum[1] trāns mare ad ultima rēgna cīvitātēsque Graeciae mīserat, in quibus locīs itinera faciēbat et Ulixem petēbat. Per multōs annōs nūllam fāmam dē Ulixe Pēnelopē accēperat. Interim multī ducēs rēgēsque, cupiditāte rēgnī Ulixis adductī, dē montibus Ithacae et ē fīnitimīs īnsulīs convēnerant et rēgīnam in mātrimōnium petēbant. Cīvēs hōs[2] hostēs ē fīnibus Ithacae sine auxiliō ad montēs redigere nōn poterant. Itaque Pēnelopē, capite submissō, dīxit:

"Ubi vestem quam faciō cōnfēcerō, nōn iam dubitābō in mātrimōnium darī."

Itaque exspectāvērunt. Sed cōnsilium Pēnelopae fuit tempus trahere. Itaque nocte retexēbat vestem quam multā dīligentiā texuerat. Post trēs annōs hominēs cōnsilium Pēnelopae cognōvērunt, et Pēnelopē vestem cōnficere coācta est.

Hōc[3] tempore Ulixēs nāvī ad īnsulam Ithacam trānsportātus est. Eōdem[4] tempore Tēlemachus, ā Minervā monitus, in patriam properāvit. Ibi ad mare ab Ulixe vīsus atque cognitus est. Ulixēs Tēlemachum ad oppidum antecēdere iussit. Ab Ulixe monitus, Tēlemachus neque mātrī neque aliīs dē patre nūntiāvit.

[1] *him*
[2] *these*
[3] *at this*
[4] *at the same*

QUESTIONS

1. Who was Telemachus' father?
2. Why was Telemachus away when Ulysses arrived in Ithaca?
3. How did Penelope deceive the suitors?

Scala/Art Resource, NY

Penelope weaving, as imagined by the 16th century painter, Giovanni Stradano.

Grammar

Third Declension: I–Stem Nouns

A group of nouns that have **–ium** instead of **–um** in the genitive plural are called ***i****–stem nouns*. In addition to this difference, neuters ending in **–al** or **–e** have **–ī** instead of **–e** in the ablative singular, and **–ia** in the nominative and accusative plural. In order to be an **i**–stem, a noun has to fall into one of the following three categories:

1. Masculine and feminine nouns ending in **–is** and **–ēs** having the same number of syllables in the genitive as in the nominative: **cīvis, cīvis.**
2. Nouns of *one* syllable whose base ends in two consonants: **nox, noctis.**
3. Nouns of one syllable whose nominative ends in **–ns** or **–rs: pars, partis.**

	SINGULAR	PLURAL	SINGULAR	PLURAL
Nom.	cīvis	cīvēs	mare	maria
Gen.	cīvis	cīvium	maris	marium
Dat.	cīvī	cīvibus	marī	maribus
Acc.	cīvem	cīvēs[1]	mare	maria
Abl.	cīve	cīvibus	marī	maribus

[1] Occasionally **–īs** is used in the accusative plural, but not in this textbook.

ORAL PRACTICE

1. Decline **nāvis pulchra, iter longum.**
2. Give the singular and plural in Latin in the case indicated: *high mountain* (gen.), *level sea* (acc.), *small mountains* (dat.), *neighboring enemy* (abl.), *our end* (nom.).

EXERCISES

A. Translate the following sentences into good English.

1. Ad fīnem itineris longī vēnērunt.
2. Altōs montēs et flūmina alta in Eurōpā vīdī.
3. Bonī cīvēs officia pūblica suscipere nōn dubitant.
4. Parvā nāvī colōnī trāns mare lātum ad prōvinciam migrāvērunt.
5. Ob numerum hostium quī in montibus erant cīvēs in castrīs remānsērunt.

B. Translate the following sentences into Latin.

1. By whom was a ship seen on a mountain?
2. We have made a long journey but can now see the end.
3. A large number of citizens was called together by the leader.
4. If [2] the sea is closed, the enemy's ships will not be able to transport soldiers.

Gift of Dr. Lloyd E. Hawes, Courtesy, Museum of Fine Arts, Boston

Like Penelope waiting for Ulysses, this woman carries out her household duties with her maid. A red-figured vase from about 465 B.C.

[2] Use ablative absolute.

C. After twenty long years, Ulysses and Penelope are almost reunited. Working with a partner or in a small group, imagine all the events that have happened and create a dialogue between the two that briefly summarizes their experiences. Then act it out in class.

Vocabulary

Nouns

cīvis, cīvis[3], *m. + f. citizen* (civic, civil)
cīvitās, cīvitātis, *f. citizenship, state*
cupiditās, cupiditātis, *f. desire* (Cupid, cupidity)
fīnis, fīnis, *m. end;* pl. *borders, territory* (final, finite)
hostis, hostis, *m. enemy*[4] *(usually pl.)* (hostile, hostility)
iter, itineris, *n. journey, road, march* (itinerant, itinerary)
labor, labōris, *m. work, hardship* (labor, laborious)
mare, maris, *n. sea* (marine, submarine)
mōns, montis, *m. mountain* (mount)
nāvis, nāvis, *f. ship* (naval, navy)
pāstor, pāstōris, *m. shepherd* (pastor, pastorale)
uxor, uxōris, *f. wife* (uxorial, uxorious)
vestis, vestis, *f. garment, clothes* (vest)

Verbs

cōnficiō, cōnficere, cōnfēcī, cōnfectus, *complete, exhaust* (confect, confection)
texō, texere, texuī, textus, *weave* (text, textile)

Word Studies

1. Many Latin **i**–stem nouns ending in **–is** are preserved in their original form in English. The original plural in **–es** is pronounced like "ease": *axis, axes; basis, bases.*
   Distinguish *axēs* from *axĕs* (plural of *ax*), *basēs* from *basĕs* (plural of *base*).

---

[3] The ablative singular can end in **–ī** or **–e.** A few other masculine and feminine nouns sometimes have this ending.
[4] *national enemy,* differing from **inimīcus** or *personal enemy*

2. Here are some Latin phrases in English:
   Tempus fugit, *Time flies.*
   per capita, *by heads* or *individuals*
   mē iudice, *in my judgment* (lit., *I being judge*)
   Fata viam invenient, *The Fates will find a way.*
   pro tem (pro tempore), *for the time, temporarily*
   de jure, *according to right,* as a **de jure** government

Latin for American Students

Did you know that some of our marriage customs originated in Roman times? The Roman bridegroom carried his bride over their threshold in order to prevent her from slipping on the doorsill which was annointed with oils and fats as symbols of plenty. The groom also gave his bride an iron ring for the third finger of her left hand. It was believed that a vein to the heart was located here and by encircling the finger with iron, the heart was made "captive" and the marriage binding.

Ulixēs, rēx fortis Ithacae, ad portās oppidī quod rēxerat stābat, ā multīs cīvibus vīsus, sed nōn cognitus, quod vestēs sordidās gerēbat. In oppidum facilī itinere prōcessit. Multōs servōs vīdit ā quibus nōn cognitus est. Canis tamen Ulixis dominum cognōvit et gaudiō affectus ē vītā excessit. Ubi Ulixēs ad rēgīnam adductus est, omnēs procī[1] eum[2] hostem appellāvērunt et discēdere iussērunt. Sed tamen Pēnelopē, quae eum nōn cognōverat, vestibus sordidīs permōta eum manēre iussit et eī[3] cibum dedit.

Pēnelopē vestem cōnfēcerat et nunc tempus aderat quō iūs erat marītum dēligere. Magnum arcum ante procōs[1] pōnī iussit quem Ulixēs clārus ante vīgintī annōs tetenderat. Tum nūntiāvit:

"Homō quī arcum Ulixis fortis tendere poterit marītus meus erit; marītus novus pār Ulixī esse dēbet. Ita iūs est."

Itaque singulī in ōrdine arcum cēpērunt sed tendere nōn potuērunt quod Ulixī parēs nōn fuērunt. Tum Ulixēs arcum petīvit. Omnēs rīsērunt, sed Pēnelopē arcum Ulixī darī iussit, nam iūs erat. Id[4] quod reliquī nōn facere poterant—arcum tendere—Ulixī facile erat. Tum in procōs arcum tendit, quōs in fugam dedit. Tēlemachus et Eumaeus auxilium dedērunt. Ulixēs omnēs portās oppidī claudī iusserat, ob quam causam procī ex oppidō ad montēs fugere nōn potuērunt. Salūte petītā, nōn inventā, omnēs interfectī sunt. Hōc[5] modō rēgnum et uxōrem Ulixēs recēpit et in lībertāte pāceque vītam ēgit. Nōn iam nāvibus itinera trāns maria faciēbat.

[1] *suitors*
[2] *him*
[3] *to him*
[4] *that*
[5] *this*

QUESTIONS

1. Why was Ulysses not recognized?
2. Why did everyone laugh when Ulysses asked for the bow?
3. Why did Ulysses not immediately reveal his identity?

Grammar

Third Declension Adjectives

The adjectives studied so far, such as **magnus, –a, –um** and **sacer, –cra, –crum,** have been declined like nouns of the first and second declensions. Many adjectives, however, belong to the third declension. With the exception of one important class, which will be presented in a later lesson, almost all adjectives of the third declension are **i**–stems. They are divided into three categories according to the number of forms that are used in the nominative singular to show gender.

1. **Three endings—**all three genders are different in the nominative: **celer, celeris, celere.**
2. **Two endings—**masculine and feminine in **–is,** neuter in **–e: fortis, forte.**
3. **One ending—**one form for all genders: **pār.**

Adjectives of the third declension have **–ī** in the ablative singular, **–ium** in the genitive plural, and **–ia** in the neuter nominative and accusative plural. Note that the ablative singular, unlike that of most **i**–stem *nouns,* ends in **–ī.**

Penelope is often pictured in an attitude of mourning. This small Greek relief was once a decoration attached to furniture. It shows Ulysses gesturing to Penelope. Behind her is Telemachus.

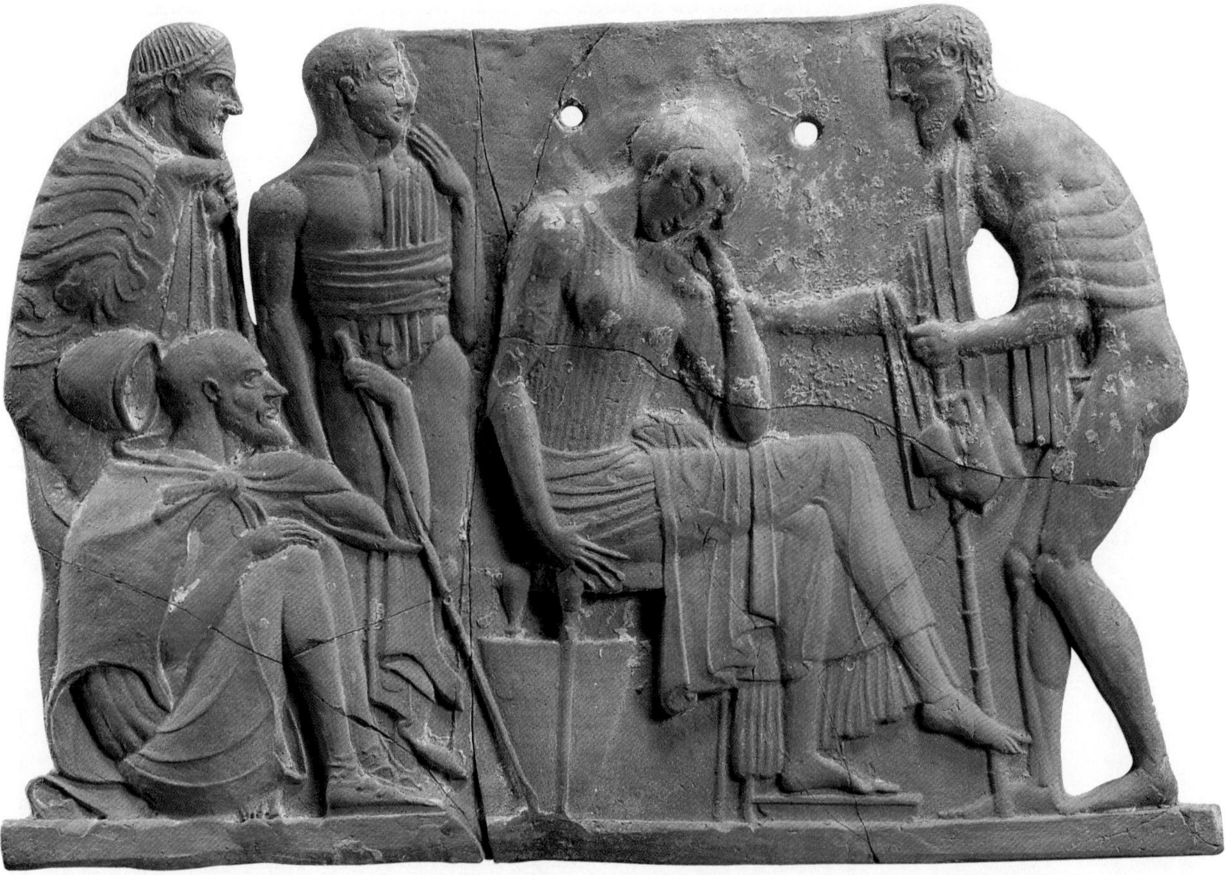

Three-ending adjectives are declined like **celer.**

	SINGULAR			PLURAL		
	M	F	N	M	F	N
Nom.	celer	celeris	celere	celerēs	celēres	celeria
Gen.	celeris	celeris	celeris	celerium	celerium	celerium
Dat.	celerī	celerī	celerī	celeribus	celeribus	celeribus
Acc.	celerem	celerem	celere	celerēs	celerēs	celeria
Abl.	celerī	celerī	celerī	celeribus	celeribus	celeribus

Two-ending adjectives are declined like **fortis**.

	SINGULAR		PLURAL	
	M + F	N	M + F	N
Nom.	fortis	forte	fortēs	fortia
Gen.	fortis	fortis	fortium	fortium
Dat.	fortī	fortī	fortibus	fortibus
Acc.	fortem	forte	fortēs	fortia
Abl.	fortī	fortī	fortibus	fortibus

One-ending adjectives are declined like **pār**.

	SINGULAR		PLURAL	
	M + F	N	M + F	N
Nom.	pār	pār	parēs	paria
Gen.	paris	paris	parium	parium
Dat.	parī	parī	paribus	paribus
Acc.	parem	pār	parēs	paria
Abl.	parī	parī	paribus	paribus

Latin for American Students

Did you know that although the Romans built a variety of ships, they were not very capable sailors? Most Roman ships used oars as well as sails because they could only run before a favorable wind. For reasons of economy, ***naves onerariae*** *(merchant ships) relied on sails.* ***Naves longae*** *(warships) used sail in transit, but as soon as a sea battle started, the masts were lowered and the sails stored. Victory often depended on the artful maneuvering of ships, not on speed.*

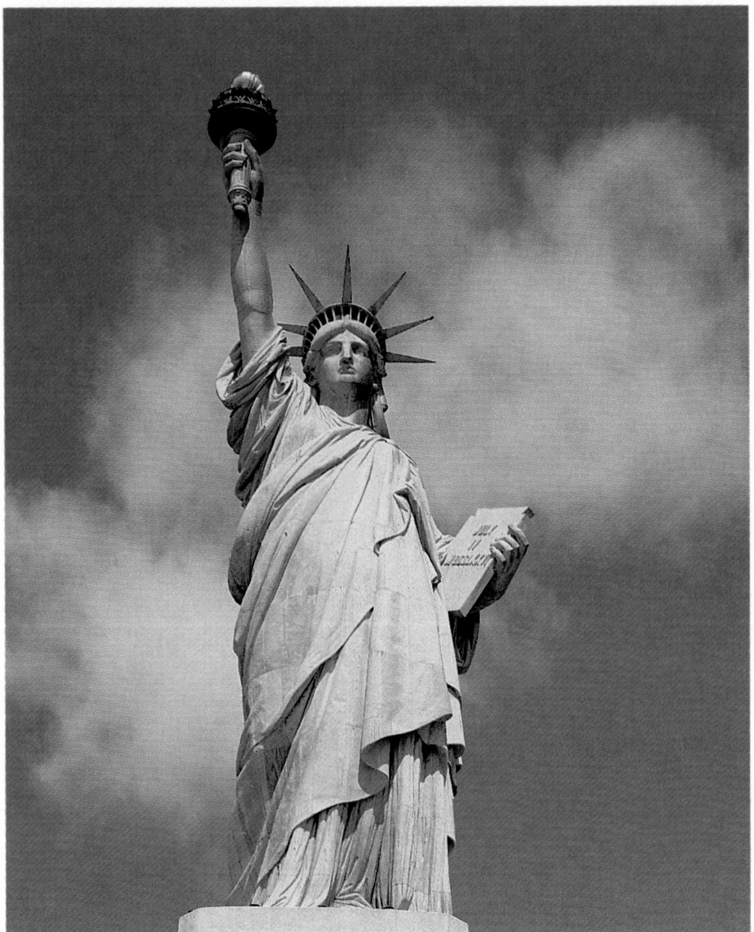

K. Kummels/SuperStock

Libertas. The Statue of Liberty in New York harbor, once used as a lighthouse. She is dressed in Roman garb.

ORAL PRACTICE

1. Decline **lībertās pār, iter facile.**
2. Give in Latin: *swift boys* (acc.), *brave citizen* (abl.), *all towns* (gen.), *equal right* (acc.), *few enemies* (dat.).

EXERCISES

A. Translate the following sentences into good English.

1. Quid est pretium lībertātis?
2. Servus fortibus factīs lībertātem obtinuit.
3. Omnia maria nāvibus hostium clausa erant.
4. In nostrā patriā omnēs cīvēs sunt līberī et parēs.
5. Nōvistīne, amīce bone, hominem quem in nāvī vīdimus?
6. Facilī itinere inventō, dux omnēs mīlitēs dē montibus dūcere mātūrāvit.

B. Translate the following sentences into Latin.

1. All free men love peace.
2. Nature has given us many beautiful (things).
3. We ought not to undertake a long journey now.
4. It will not be easy to defend the freedom of our country on the sea.

C. After ten long years of war and ten more years of travel, Aeneas founded Lavinium and Ulysses arrived home to Ithaca. Work with a partner or a small group and write a brief paragraph explaining which one of our heroes, in your opinion, had the most difficult time. Do not forget that both suffered mental as well as physical hardships. Both endured, for better or for worse, the interference of one or more gods, and both were responsible for the people traveling with them.

Vocabulary

Nouns

canis, canis, *m. + f. dog*	(canine, canicular)
gaudium, gaudī, *n. joy, gladness*	(gaudery, gaudy)
iūs, iūris, *n. right*	(jury, justice)
lībertās, lībertātis, *f. freedom, liberty*	(liberty, liberation)
marītus, -ī, *m. husband*	(marital)

Adjectives

celer, celeris, celere, *swift*	(accelerate, celerity)
facilis, facile, *easy*	(facilitate, facility)
fortis, forte, *strong, brave*	(fort, fortitude)
omnis, omne, *all, every*	(omnipotent, omniscient)
pār (gen.) **paris,** *equal*	(parity, peer)
sordidus, -a, -um, *dirty*	(sordid, sordidness)

THE GRANGER COLLECTION, New York

Ulysses' dog, the only one who recognized him after twenty years' absence, shows the loyalty that people have always felt toward canines. Dogs were frequently kept as household pets in the ancient world. "Cave canem" can be seen in mosaics in many Roman homes. The dog in this relief was obviously very important to its owner.

Ronald Sheridan/Ancient Art & Architecture Collection

In Portchester, England, substantial remains of a Roman fortification still stand.

Verbs

rīdeō, rīdēre, rīsi, rīsus, *laugh (at)* (ridiculous, risible)

tendō, tendere, tetendī, tentus, *stretch* (intent, tendon)

Word Studies

The first word in each of the following lines is a Latin word. From among the last five words in each line choose the one that is an English derivative of the first word.

stāre	status	stair	stare	star	stay
hominī	homely	home	hominy	homicide	hum
mīles	mile	militant	mill	millinery	million
premō	supreme	premises	premonition	express	prime
clāmō	clam	clamp	clammy	inclement	exclaim
pāx	pace	packs	Pacific	impact	pass

Glimpses of Roman Life

AMUSEMENTS AND SPORTS

Roman children enjoyed playing games just as children do today. Babies had their rattles; girls had their dolls; and boys played various kinds of marble games with nuts. The phrase **relinquere nucēs** (*to give up nuts*) meant to grow up, but adult men, even the Emperor Augustus, sometimes played such games. Vacation was the time for marble games. The poet Martial says: "Sadly the boy leaves his marbles and is called back to school by the teacher—the Saturnalia vacation is all over."

Other amusements for children included spinning tops, walking on stilts, flying kites, rolling hoops, playing with toy wagons and toy soldiers. Among Roman children's games were also blindman's buff, hide and seek, leapfrog, and jacks. Ball games, some like today's tennis and handball, were favorites, especially for men who played them at the large public baths.

For indoor amusement the Romans had a board game which was something like chess and checkers, and another like the many games we have in which the throwing of dice controls the number of moves made on a board called **capita dicis an navem?** A game called knucklebones, **tali,** was played with knucklebones and dice-like pieces, **tesserae,** that had numbers on each side.

Erich Lessing/Art Resource, NY

This stone relief shows Roman children playing a game. One game they liked to play was similar to bowling, but they rolled a walnut at walnut "castles" built up on the ground.

Giraudon/Art Resource, NY

The Arena and Amphitheater in Arles, France. The arena was used by the Romans for various athletic contests and games. The amphitheater was for plays and public readings.

Roman boys and men had their sports: swimming, fishing, hunting, as well as athletic contests: running, jumping, throwing the discus and javelin, boxing, wrestling, and fencing. Most of these activities were useful training for a soldier.

The chief amusements for the Roman people as a whole were the circus, the gladiatorial shows, and the theater. The oldest and most popular was the circus with its races. Although the races were the main event, gradually various side shows and acrobatic exhibitions were added to entertain between races. The modern circus is a revival of the ancient circus, but the chariot races no longer have the same prominence. Even the circus parade that precedes the performance today is borrowed from the Romans, who called it a **pompa.**

The circus games were held at public expense on holidays. They took place in the valley between the Palatine and Aventine hills. Originally the people sat on the hillsides; later, magnificent stands seating as many as 200,000 people were built. Other circuses were built in Rome and elsewhere, but the original Circus Maximus remained the chief one.

The games created as much interest as our professional baseball, football, tennis, and hockey. There were various racing companies, distinguished by their colors, like those in modern schools and colleges and professional teams. Successful drivers were slaves or freedmen who became popular heroes and often won their freedom and became rich. Their records and those of the horses were carefully kept. One man, Pompeius Muscosus, is said to have won 3559 races. This attention is much like that we give to the number of home runs made by famous major league baseball players today.

The theater was another important place for outdoor amusement. In imitation of Greek custom, Roman theaters were semicircular. The actors usually wore masks that indicated what part each actor was playing. As in Shakespeare's time women's parts were played by men. Comedies, tragedies, farces, and pantomimes were given. The most famous Roman writers of comedies were Plautus and Terence, whose plays are not only still being performed but have been turned into former Broadway hits—*The Boys from Syracuse* and *A Funny Thing Happened on the Way to the Forum.*

The gladiatorial contests were rather late importations from Etruria, the region to the north of Rome. At first they consisted of sword fights at funerals between two men who were often slaves. Later on they became very popular, and fights between men and animals (like Spanish bullfights) were added, as well as fights between animals. Sometimes very elaborate shows were staged in open-air amphitheaters. The most famous amphitheater was the Colosseum at Rome which had room for 50,000 spectators. It was not built until A.D. 80 and was large enough and durable enough to forgo the need for another amphitheater in the city.

QUESTIONS

1. What modern sports compare with the circus games of the Romans in popular appeal?
2. In what ways did the Roman theater differ from ours?
3. What were the good and bad features of the gladiatorial contests?

Unit VIII Review
LESSONS XXXV-XXXIX

Vocabulary

Nouns

canis
carmen
cēra
cīvis
cīvitās
clāmor
cupiditās
factum
fīnis
fuga
gaudium
herba
hostis
impedīmentum
iter
iūs
labor
lībertās
mare
marītus
mōns
nāvis
nihil
ōrdō
pāstor
pīla
saccus
spatium
uxor
vestis

Adjectives

alius
alter
celer
certus
facilis
fortis
omnis
neuter
nullus
pār
parātus
sōlus
sordidus
timidus
ullus
ultimus
uter

Verbs

addūcō
antecēdō
aperiō
canō
cernō
claudō
commoveō
cōnficiō
cōnsulō
expediō
frangō
iaciō
impediō
lavō
ligō
prōvideō
putō
rīdeō
tendō
texō
trādūcō
trānsportō
vertō
vincō

Grammar Summary

Participles Used as Clauses

The perfect passive participle is often used to stand in for a whole clause in Latin. The English equivalent uses a clause beginning with *when, after, because, since, if, although*—whatever adverb makes the best sense. Remember that it agrees with the noun that it is describing in gender, number, and case.

Adductī ā ventīs, nautae herī nāvigāvērunt.	*Since they were influenced by the winds, the sailors sailed yesterday.*
Iacta ā puellā, pīla caput puerī ferīvit.	*After it was thrown by the girl, the ball hit the boy's head.*

Ablative Absolute

The ablative absolute construction most often consists of two words: a noun and a noun, a noun and an adjective, or a noun and a participle (usually a perfect passive participle). All words are in the ablative case, set off from the rest of the sentence by commas, and grammatically unconnected with it.

Portā clausā, hostēs fugere nōn potuērunt.	*After the gate was closed, the enemies were unable to flee.*
Nāvibus amissīs, Ulixēs miser erat.	*Since the ships were lost, Ulysses was unhappy.*

Unit VIII Review
LESSONS XXXV-XXXIX

The Conjugation of *Possum*

The verb **possum,** a compound of **sum,** is somewhat irregular in the present, imperfect, and future. The perfect tenses are regular. The principal parts are **possum, posse, potuī.**

Ad casam tuam venīre nōn possum.	*I am not able to come to your house.*
Anna multa carmina canere poterat.	*Anna could sing many songs.*

Third Declension I–Stem Nouns

A group of third declension nouns, called **i**–stems, have **–ium** in the genitive plural. Additionally, neuter nouns ending in **–al** or**–e** have **–ī** in the ablative singular and **–ia** in the nominative and accusative plural. To determine if a masculine or feminine noun is an **i**–stem, it must pass one of three tests: if it ends in **–is** or**–es** in the nominative singular and has the same number of syllables in the genitive singular; if it is a monosyllable whose base ends in two consonants; or if the nominative singular ends in **–ns** or **–rs.**

Dux multārum nāvium est.	*He is the leader of many ships.*
Trāns mare Britannia est.	*Britain is across the sea.*

Irregular First and Second Declension Adjectives

There are several adjectives that are declined in most respects like regular first and second declension adjectives, except that they have **–īus** in the genitive singular and **–ī** in the dative singular.

Pīla puerī alterīus sordida est.	*The ball of the other boy is dirty.*
Amīco neutrī pecūniam dedī.	*To neither friend did I give money.*

Third Declension Adjectives

Third declension adjectives are declined like third declension **i**–stem nouns except that they have an **–ī** in the ablative singular. Adjectives that have two or three nominative forms provide the stem in the nominative; for those that have only one nominative form, you must also learn the genitive.

Equus celer trāns agrōs cucurrit.	*The swift horse ran across the fields.*
Nautae pāres agricolīs civitāte sunt.	*The sailors are equal to the farmers in citizenship.*

Unit Practice

Oral Participle Drill

A. Substitute a Latin participle in the right gender, number, and case for the italicized words.

1. Perīcula (*if foreseen*) mē nōn terrent.
2. Librum (*after I had read it*) amīcō dōnāvī.
3. Puerī (*although they were called*) nōn vēnērunt.
4. Puellae (*because they had been scared*) fūgērunt.

5. Auxilium (*which had been furnished*) ā sociīs nostrīs patriam cōnservāvit.

B. Translate the ablative absolute in each of the following sentences into good English.

1. **Litterīs scrīptīs,** I took a walk.
2. **Rēgnō āmissō,** he was still king.
3. **Auxiliō missō,** they can still win.
4. **Agrīs occupātīs,** the people were starving.

Oral Form Drill

1. Decline **rēx fortis, lēx bona, mare lātum.**
2. What is the case of **ducum, hominī, mīlitibus, disciplīnae, pācem?**
3. Give in all tenses the third plural of **possum,** translating each tense form.
4. Give the principal parts of **commoveō, dō, expediō, submittō, absum, prōpōnō, premō.**

Exercise

Myths, legends, and heroes are all important to a culture. One of the most important legends for the Romans concerned the twin brothers Romulus and Remus. Work with a partner or in a small group to translate the following story. Then compare it with the story of Aeneas and his arrival in Italy. Which one do you like better? Why?

Rōmulus et Remus

Silvius Proca, rēx fortis Albānōrum, Numitōrem et Amūlium fīliōs habuit. Numitōrī rēgnum relīquit. Sed Amūlius, Numitōre ē cīvitāte pulsō, rēxit. Rhēa Silvia, fīlia Numitōris, geminōs Rōmulum et Remum habuit. Pater geminōrum deus Mārs erat; itaque Mārs auctor populī Rōmānī appellābātur. Amūlius puerōs in Tiberī flūmine pōnī iussit. Sed aqua geminōs in sicco relīquit. Lupa accessit et puerōs aluit. Posteā Faustulus, pāstor rēgis, puerōs invēnit. Post multōs annōs Rōmulō et Remō dīxit: "Numitor est avus vester." Verbīs pāstōris adductī, geminī Amūlium interfēcērunt. Numitōrī, quem Amūlius ē cīvitāte pepulerat, rēgnum mandāvērunt.

Posteā oppidum mūnīvērunt in locō in quō inventī erant, quod dē nōmine Rōmulī Rōmam appellāvērunt.

Rōmulus Remusque parēs erant, sed tamen Remō cēdere Rōmulō nōn facile erat. Remō interfectō, Rōmulus sōlus Rōmānōs rēxit et omnibus iūra dedit.

THE GRANGER COLLECTION, New York

Artists throughout the ages have offered their own interpretations of the story of Romulus and Remus.

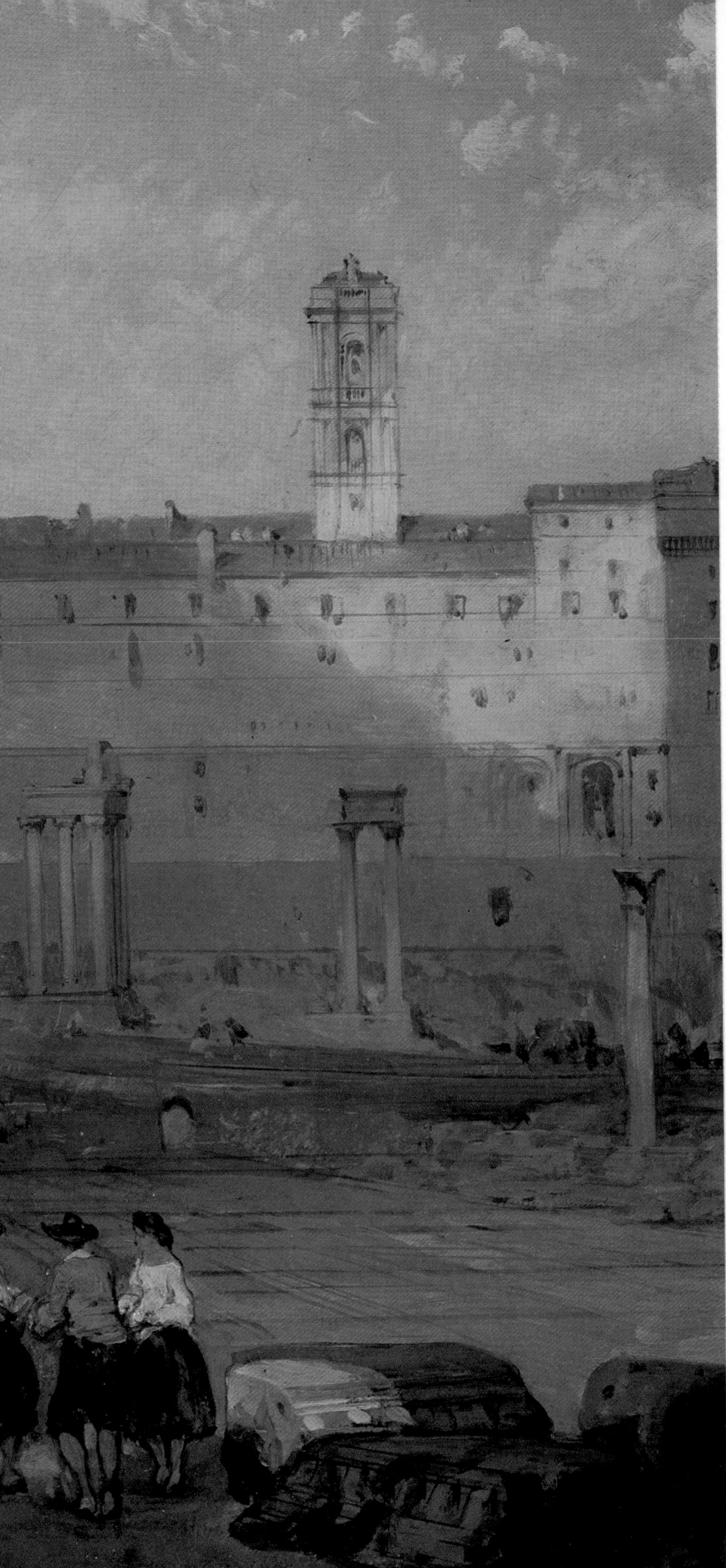

Bridgeman/Art Resource, NY

Unit IX

Gods, Goddesses, and History

The area of the Roman Forum was originally a marsh. At the peak of the Roman Republic, this same location was the center of Roman political, religious, and social life. By the time of Julius Caesar (100-44 B.C.), Rome had grown so large that much of the political and social activity had expanded to other areas of the city. After the fall of the Roman Empire, the Forum gradually became covered with earth; by the Middle Ages, it was not much more than a cattle pasture. This is the condition of the Roman Forum approximately 150 years ago, as seen in this painting by David Roberts (1796-1864).

LESSON XL

Deī

Rōmānī multōs deōs quōrum officia erant varia habuērunt. Deōs in omnibus locīs vīdērunt—in terrā, in agrīs, in frūmentō, in montibus, in silvīs, in fluctibus maris, in aquā flūminum, in omnī nātūrā. Nōn omnēs parēs auctōritāte erant, nam magnī deī erant et parvī deī, deī deaeque. Inter magnōs deōs prīmus auctōritāte erat Iuppiter, rēx atque pater deōrum hominumque, quī in caelō habitābat et fulmine tentō in manū malōs terrēbat. Iūnō erat uxor Iovis[1] et rēgīna deōrum. Venus erat pulchra dea amōris. Mārs, deus bellī, arma et pugnās et exercitūs amābat. Auctor populī Rōmānī vocābātur, et fortasse ob hanc[2] causam Rōmānī semper bella gerēbant. Mercurius, celer nūntius deōrum, omnēs celeritāte superābat. Neptūnus erat deus maris, quī equōs in undīs regēbat. Reliquī magnī deī erant Cerēs, dea frūmentī, Minerva, dea sapientiae, Diāna, dea silvārum, Vulcānus, deus ignis, Apollō, quī omnia prōvidēbat et quem hominēs cōnsulēbant, Bacchus, deus vīnī. Rōmānī nōmina omnium magnōrum deōrum et multōrum parvōrum cognōverant—quod nōn facile erat, nam magnus erat numerus deōrum deārumque. Etiam "terminus agrōrum" deus erat.

[1] genitive singular of **Iuppiter**
[2] *this*

QUESTIONS

1. What did Jupiter throw?
2. Who was the goddess of wisdom?
3. Who was "Terminus"?

Iuppiter, rex deorum.

Ronald Sheridan/Ancient Art & Architecture Collection

Grammar

The Fourth Declension

The fourth declension has far fewer nouns than any of the first three declensions. It is characterized by the vowel **u.** Fourth declension nouns are declined like **cāsus.**

	SINGULAR	PLURAL
Nom.	cāsus	cāsūs
Gen.	cāsūs	cāsuum
Dat.	cāsuī	cāsibus
Acc.	cāsum	cāsūs
Abl.	cāsū	cāsibus

NOTĀ·BENE

Most nouns of the fourth declension are masculine. The only feminine nouns used in this book are **manus** *(hand) and* **domus** *(home).*

ORAL PRACTICE

1. Decline **exercitus noster, manus fortis**.
2. Name the case(s) of each of the following: **senatū, impetum, manibus, exercituī**.

EXERCISES

A. Translate the following sentences into good English.

1. Quid manū tuā tenēs?
2. Exercitus noster impetum in ōrdinēs Gallōrum fēcit.
3. Cāsū dūcis nūntiātō, militēs fūgērunt.
4. Omnēs colōnī manibus hostium interfectī sunt.

B. Translate the following sentences into Latin.

1. In the summer, we shall attack the army of the enemy.
2. Which god held the sky with (his) hands?
3. The leader of the citizens will call together the senate soon.
4. I wrote a book about the ships on the waves of the sea; I am an author.

C. As you continue your study of Latin, you have learned much about the Roman gods and goddesses. You know that they can grant favors to those whom they care about. Work with a partner and write a letter to one of the gods (or goddesses), describing a situation for which you need his (or her) particular expertise and guidance. Ask for his or her advice and help. Perhaps you need wisdom to pass a certain test, or speed to win a race, or a little help from Cupid's arrow for a date!

Scala/Art Resource, NY

From the Pantheon, which comes from the Greek meaning "all the gods," we can see Jupiter rising above the Titans, having defeated them. How many of these gods and goddesses can you identify?

Latin for American Students

Did you know that the word ***senatus*** *(senate) originally meant "council of the old men"? The first Roman senates consisted of 300 members who were heads of ancient clans. In 82 B.C., the number of senators was increased to 600. The main function of the* ***senatus*** *was to examine each proposal submitted by an assembly of citizens* ***(comitia)*** *in relation to the constitution, treaty, or rights of any citizen.*

Vocabulary

Nouns

auctor, auctōris, *m. author, writer* (authorize, authorship)
auctōritās, auctōritātis, *f. authority, influence*
cāsus, -ūs, *m. fall, chance* (case)
exercitus, -ūs, *m. (trained) army* (exercise)
fluctus, -ūs, *m. wave* (fluctuate, fluctuation)
fulmen, fulminis, *n. lightning* (fulminate)
impetus, -ūs, *m. attack;* (impetuous, impetus)
  impetum facio in + acc., *make an attack against*
manus, -ūs, *f. hand* (manual, manufacture)
senātus, -ūs, *m. senate* (senatorial, senatorship)
virtūs, virtūtis, *f. manliness, courage* (virtue, virtuoso)

Adjective

familiāris, -e, *of the family, friendly;* as a noun, *m., friend* (familiar)

Verbs

cōnfirmō, cōnfirmāre, cōnfirmāvī, cōnfirmātus, *make firm, encourage, establish* (confirm, confirmation)

pellō, pellere, pepulī, pulsus, *drive, defeat* (expulsion, repel)

respondeō, respondēre, respondī, respōnsus, *answer* (respondent, response)

Word Studies

1. The suffix **–tās** is usually found in nouns formed from adjectives. Its English form is *–ty.* What are the Latin words from which are derived *commodity, integrity, liberty, publicity, timidity, variety?* Note that the letter preceding the ending is usually *–i–.*
2. Here are some Latin phrases in English:
   ad fin. (ad finem), *near the end* (of the page)
   P.S. (post scriptum), *written after* (at the end of a letter)

   What is the sense behind the motto of the University of Texas: **Disciplina praesidium civitatis?** The motto **in libris libertas** of the Los Angeles Public Library?

LESSON XLI

Sāturnus et Iuppiter

Auctor et prīmus rēx deōrum Ūranus erat. Hunc fīlius Sāturnus ex rēgnō expulit. Ūranus hīs verbīs Sāturnum monuit: "Tempus auctōritātis tuae nōn longum erit; nam tū ā fīliō tuō expellēris." Hīs verbīs territus Sāturnus omnēs fīliōs in ōrdine dēvorābat. Sed māter illum quem ante[1] reliquōs amābat servāvit. Hic fuit Iuppiter, ad īnsulam Crētam ā mātre missus. Post paucōs annōs hic patrem expulit et rēgnum illīus occupāvit. Sāturnus reliquōs fīliōs reddere coāctus est. Rēgiam in monte Olympō Iuppiter posuit, ex quō in omnēs partēs spectāre poterat. Frātrēs convocāvit. Neptūnō maris rēgnum, Plūtōnī rēgnum īnferōrum permīsit.

Sed posteā Gigantēs,[2] fīliī Terrae, cum deīs bellum gessērunt. Illī ad Olympum praecipitēs cucurrērunt sed, ā deīs proeliō superātī, poenīs dūrīs affectī sunt. Posteā multa templa in terrā deīs ab hominibus posita sunt.

[1] *more than*
[2] *the Giants*

QUESTIONS

1. Who was the father of Saturn?
2. Who was the father of Jupiter?
3. Who were the sons of Saturn?

Grammar

The Demonstratives *Hic* and *Ille*

In Latin, **hic** means *this* (near the speaker in place or thought), while **ille** means *that* (more distant from the speaker). As in English, *this* (plur., *these*) and *that* (plur., *those*) are called *demonstratives* because they demonstrate or point out persons or objects. They may be used as either adjectives or pronouns.

Hic vir illud nōn scrīpsit.	*This man did not write that.*
Illud ab hīs puerīs nōn factum est.	*That was not done by these boys.*

	SINGULAR			PLURAL		
	M	F	N	M	F	N
Nom.	**hic**	**haec**	**hoc**	**hī**	**hae**	**haec**
Gen.	**huius**	**huius**	**huius**	**hōrum**	**hārum**	**hōrum**
Dat.	**huic**	**huic**	**huic**	**hīs**	**hīs**	**hīs**
Acc.	**hunc**	**hanc**	**hoc**	**hōs**	**hās**	**haec**
Abl.	**hōc**	**hāc**	**hōc**	**hīs**	**hīs**	**hīs**

	SINGULAR			PLURAL		
	M	F	N	M	F	N
Nom.	**ille**	**illa**	**illud**	**illī**	**illae**	**illa**
Gen.	**illīus**	**illīus**	**illīus**	**illōrum**	**illārum**	**illōrum**
Dat.	**illī**	**illī**	**illī**	**illīs**	**illīs**	**illīs**
Acc.	**illum**	**illam**	**illud**	**illōs**	**illās**	**illa**
Abl.	**illō**	**illā**	**illō**	**illīs**	**illīs**	**illīs**

NOTĀ·BENE

From such expressions as this man, that woman, *etc., the demonstrative adjectives* **hic** *and* **ille** *came to be used occasionally as a third person pronoun* he, she, it. *As you already know, however, the personal pronoun is usually not required in Latin.*

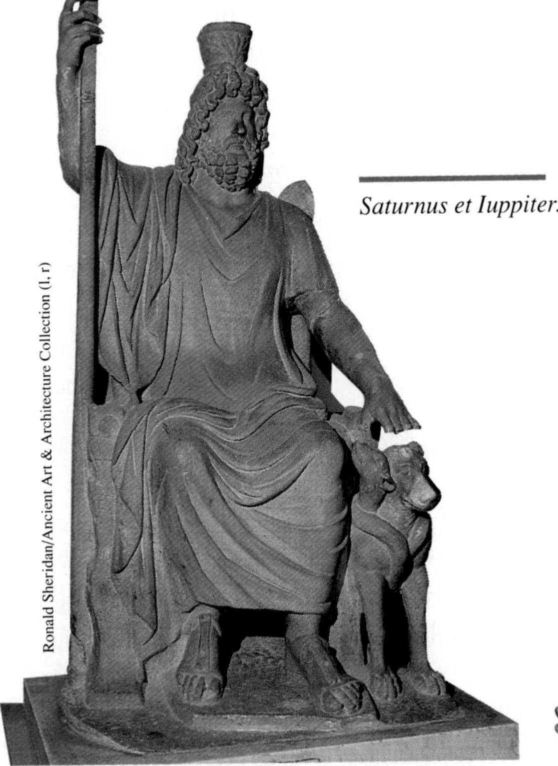

Ronald Sheridan/Ancient Art & Architecture Collection (l, r)

Saturnus et Iuppiter. Iuppiter erat filius Saturni.

Both **hic** and **ille** are declined regularly in the plural, like **bonus,** with the exception of the nominative and accusative plural neuter of **hic,** i.e., **haec**.

Demonstrative adjectives regularly precede their nouns in both English and Latin: *these boys,* **hī puerī;** *that girl,* **illa puella.** In English, when *that* precedes its noun, it is the demonstrative adjective **(ille);** when it follows, it is the relative pronoun **(quī).**

Vir *quem* (not **illum**) **vīdī clārus erat.**	*The man* ***that*** *I saw was famous.*
Ille **vir clārus erat.**	***That*** *man was famous.*

ORAL PRACTICE

Supply the right forms of **hic** and **ille** and translate the following sentences.

1. (*This*) flūmen altum est, (*that*) nōn altum est.
2. (*These*) hominēs laudō, (*those*) numquam probābō.
3. (*This*) puerī patrem et (*that*) puellae mātrem vīdī.
4. Studia ab (*this*) puellā intermissa sunt, nōn ab (*that*).

EXERCISES

A. Translate the following sentences into good English.

1. Ille erat dux ducum.
2. Hunc cognōvī sed illum ante hoc tempus nōn vīdī.
3. Hī hominēs sunt patris meī amīcī; illī sunt inimīcī.
4. Haec est mea patria; nam ego cīvis in hōc locō sum.
5. Praeceps in fluctūs illīus flūminis cucurrī, quod illōs nōn vīdī.
6. Māter mea huic servō grātiam habet, quod hic patrem meum cāsū conservāvit.

B. Translate the following sentences into Latin.

1. This is my money; that is yours.
2. This girl excels that (one) in discipline.
3. What names did the mother give to the children?
4. When this prisoner has been bound,[1] I shall bind that (one).

C. There were twelve major gods and goddesses in the Roman pantheon: Jupiter, Juno, Mercury, Venus, Neptune, Vulcan, Apollo, Ceres, Diana, Minerva, Vesta, and Mars. Each one held particular responsibilities. Work with a partner or in a small group and create a dialogue between two or more of these deities as they receive their assigned areas of expertise from Jupiter. Perhaps there is an argument—one wants to have duties that were given to someone else. You know by now that they tended to play favorites with individuals—perhaps Jupiter had his favorites, too!

[1] Use the ablative absolute.

Christie's/SuperStock

This painting of the Roman Pantheon was done around 1800 by the artist Francesco Tironi. The twin bell towers were removed in the 1840s.

Latin for American Students

Did you know that there was a building in ancient Rome called the ***Regia*** *or* ***Atrium Vestae****? It was located on the Via Sacra near the Temple of Vesta and was surrounded by columns. A sacred grove separated the* ***Regia*** *from the temple which housed the Vestal Virgins. The* ***Regia*** *was the home of the Pontifex Maximus and also the assembly area where the pontifices gathered.*

Vocabulary

Nouns

cor, cordis, *n. heart* (accord, cordial)
focus, -ī, *m. hearth* (focus)
īnferī, -ōrum, *m. inhabitants of the Lower World* (inferior)
mors, mortis, *f. death* (mortal, mortuary)
rēgia, -ae, *f. palace*

Adjectives

hic, haec, hoc, *this*
ille, illa, illud, *that*
praeceps, (gen.) **praecipitis,** *headlong, steep* (precipice, precipitate)

Verbs

dēvorō, dēvorāre, dēvorāvī, dēvorātus, *swallow* (devour)
expellō, expellere, expulī, expulsus, *drive out* (expel)
timeō, timēre, timuī, —, *fear, be afraid* (timid, timorous)

Word Studies

More English words are derived from nouns and adjectives of the third declension than from any other. The English word is usually derived from the stem, not from the nominative. It is therefore doubly important to memorize the genitive, from which the stem is obtained. It would be difficult to see that *itinerary* is derived from **iter** if you did not know that the genitive is **itineris.** See how many of the third declension words you have studied have derivatives from the base. Note the help given for English spelling: *temporal, corporal, military, nominal,* etc.

On the other hand, the English derivative will help you remember the genitive. In the following list of words, a derivative is placed after each. Give the genitive: **religiō** (*religion*), **sermō** (*sermon*), **latus** (*lateral*), **rādīx** (*radical*), **orīgō** (*original*), **ēruptiō** (*eruption*), **custōs** (*custody*), **dēns** (*dental*), **mōs** (*moral*).

Erich Lessing/Art Resource, NY

The ships in this pavement mosaic remind us that the city of Ostia was the main seaport for ancient Rome. It served as the base for Roman overseas expeditions and later developed into a major commercial trading center.

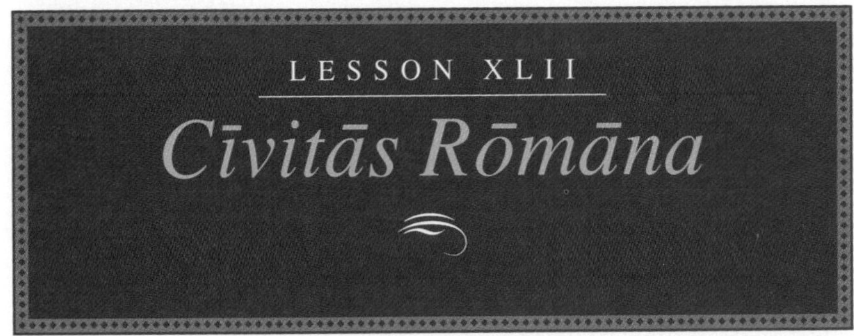

Duae partēs cīvitātis Rōmānae, Troiānī et Latīnī, contrā perīcula commūnia pugnāvērunt. Ubi cīvitās nova concordiā aucta est, rēgēs populīque fīnitimī, cupiditāte praedae adductī, partem agrōrum Rōmānōrum occupābant. Paucī ex amīcīs auxilium Rōmānīs submittēbant quod perīculīs territī sunt. Sed Rōmānī properābant, parābant, cum hostibus proelia committēbant, lībertātem patriamque commūnem armīs dēfendēbant, mortem nōn timēbant. Dum pāx incerta est, dum eī nē spīrāre quidem[1] sine perīculō possunt, cūram perpetuam nōn remittēbant.

Dum haec geruntur, eī Rōmānī quōrum corpora ob annōs nōn iam firma erant sed quī bonō cōnsiliō valēbant dē rē pūblica[2] cōnsulēbantur; ob aetātem patrēs aut senātōrēs appellābantur. In senātū convēnērunt.

Prīmō rēgēs erant, quī lībertātem cōnservābant et rem pūblicam augēbant, sed posteā, quod duo eōrum rēgum ex Etrūriā superbī fuērunt, Rōmānī rēgēs pepulērunt et duo cōnsulēs fēcērunt. Eī cōnsulēs appellābantur quod senātōrēs dē rē pūblicā cōnsulēbant.

Eō tempore corda omnium Rōmānōrum glōriam spērāvērunt. Virī fortēs bella amābant, in castrīs aestāte atque hieme labōrābant, nihil timēbant: virtūs vēra eōrum omnia superāverat. Itaque populus Rōmānus magnum numerum hostium paucīs mīlitibus in fugam dabat, oppida nātūrā mūnīta pugnīs capiēbat. Hostibus superātīs et perīculō remōtō, Rōmānī aequē regēbant. Iūra bellī pācisque cōnservābant; hōc modō auctōritās eōrum cōnfirmāta est. In ultimās partēs mīlitēs colōnīque eōrum missī sunt. Lingua Latīna in omnibus terrīs docēbātur. Post tertium Pūnicum bellum Rōmānī fuērunt dominī omnium terrārum mariumque. Nunc sine cūrā spīrāre et animōs remittere potuērunt.

Sed tum fortūna, semper incerta, eōs superāvit. Hī pecūniam imperiumque, nōn iam glōriam spērāvērunt. Superbī, nōn iam aequī, fuērunt; iūra lēgēsque nōn iam cōnservāvērunt.

[1] **nē . . . quidem,** *not even*
[2] *republic*

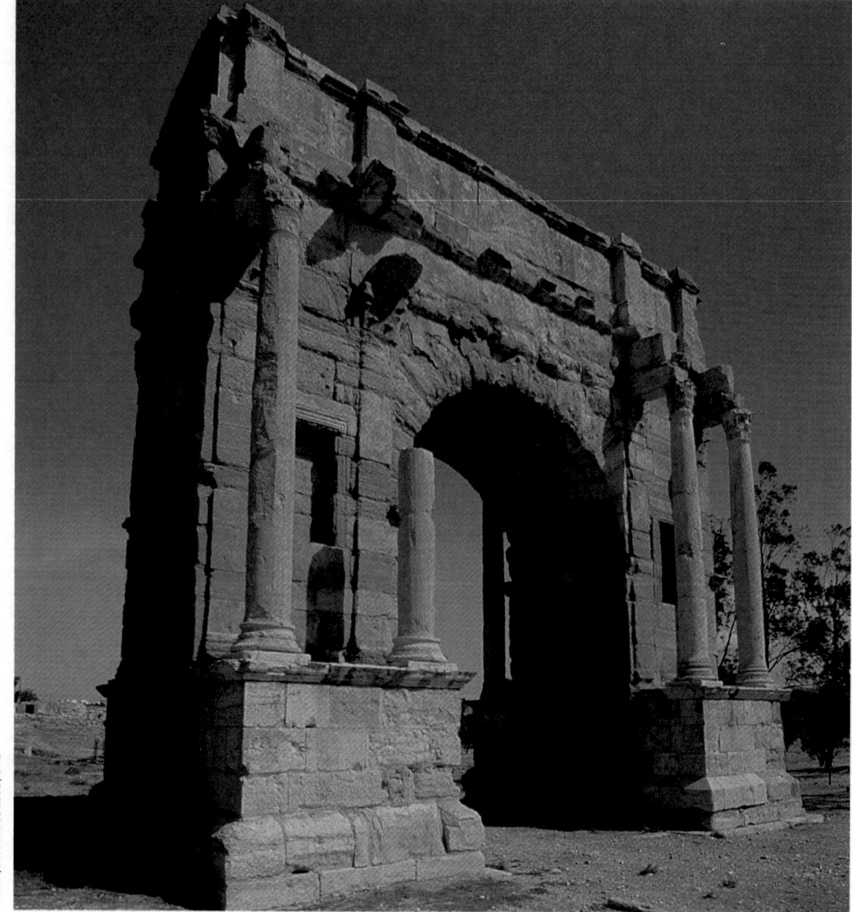
Vanni/Art Resource, NY

The Arch of Diocletian at now-deserted Sbeitla in northern Africa. After the destruction of Carthage in 146 B.C., Africa became a Roman province. Roman colonists later built a new Carthage, which became a flourishing provincial capital and educational center. Sbeitla, about 30 miles away, was in a fertile area important for the production of grain and olive oil.

QUESTIONS

1. How did the old men serve the state?
2. After the expulsion of the kings, how was the power shared?
3. What caused the decay of Rome?

Grammar

The Demonstrative *Is*

Instead of pointing out a particular person or thing, as **hic** and **ille** do, **is** usually refers less emphatically to somebody or something just mentioned. When used without a noun, it is usually translated as a personal pronoun, *he, she,* or *it;* therefore, the genitive **eius** may be translated *his, her, its,* while **eōrum** and **eārum** mean *their.* **Is** often serves as the antecedent of a relative clause.

Is quī videt probat.	*He who sees approves.*

	SINGULAR			PLURAL		
	M	F	N	M	F	N
Nom.	**is**	**ea**	**id**	**eī**	**eae**	**ea**
Gen.	**eius**	**eius**	**eius**	**eōrum**	**eārum**	**eōrum**
Dat.	**eī**	**eī**	**eī**	**eīs**	**eīs**	**eīs**
Acc.	**eum**	**eam**	**id**	**eōs**	**eās**	**ea**
Abl.	**eō**	**eā**	**eō**	**eīs**	**eīs**	**eīs**

ORAL PRACTICE

Decline **ea pars, id longum iter, is vir.**

The Declension and Use of *Mille*

Mille is an indeclinable adjective in the singular, when it means *one thousand,* but it is declined like a third declension neuter **i**–stem in the plural, when it means two or more *thousands*. The noun that follows the *thousands* must be in the genitive. When used with **passus,** it means mile.

mille hominēs	*one thousand men*
duo milia hominum	*two thousand men*
mille passūs	*one mile (a thousand paces)*
milia passuum	*miles*

ORAL PRACTICE

Give in Latin: *2 boys, 100 children, 1000 women, 2000 citizens, 3000 sailors, 3 miles.*

EXERCISES

A. Translate the following sentences into good English.

1. Dum spīrō spērō. (*The state motto of South Carolina.*)
2. Is cui librōs dedī eōs nōn remīsit.
3. Certa āmittimus dum incerta petimus.
4. Puellās et mātrem eārum in lūdō vīdī.
5. Mille nautās cum tribus ducibus in maria ultima mīsimus.
6. Eī puerī quōs aestāte vīdimus erant fīliī eius.
7. Hostibus pulsīs, tamen disciplīnam nostram nōn remittēmus.

Vanni/Art Resource, NY

The Roman ruins at Dougga, Tunisia, are among the best-preserved in all Roman Africa. The Temple of Jupiter shown here dates from the second century A.D. *The high platform is characteristic of Roman temples.*

B. Translate the following sentences into Latin.

1. Her father and mine are away.
2. Give him a part of the money.
3. We shall see him and his mother this summer.
4. This man is my teacher; that man is her father.
5. A thousand soldiers were killed; three thousand were wounded.

C. The Punic Wars were a very important part of the history of the Roman Empire. Work with a partner to briefly summarize what these wars meant to the Romans. You may wish to follow the model at the top of p. 299 or add some other details that you know. You may find the following vocabulary helpful.

condō, condere, condidī, conditus, *found, establish*
destruō, destruere, destruxī, destructus, *destroy*
Poēnus, -a, -um, *Punic, Carthaginian*
Hispania, -ae, *f. Spain*
Carthāgo, Carthāginis, *f. Carthage*

The Punic Wars were three wars between Rome and Carthage in ancient times. They are called the Punic Wars because Punic is the Latin word for Phoenician, and these were the people who founded Carthage. The First Punic War was fought from 264 B.C. to 241 B.C., the Second from 218 B.C. to 201 B.C., and the Third from 149 B.C. to 146 B.C. Rome was victorious in all three wars. Rome won Sicily in the first war and Spain in the second. The Roman army destroyed Carthage in the Third Punic War. The Carthaginian territory then became a Roman province and its name was changed to Africa.

Latin for American Students

Did you know that all public lands within fifty miles of Rome were mortgaged after the Second Punic War? In order to finance wars in an emergency, Rome often needed to borrow money from both wealthy landowners and capitalists. Sometimes, when their patriotism wore thin and the lenders demanded repayment, the government was obliged to mortgage public lands to them.

Vocabulary

Nouns

pars, partis, *f. part* (partition, party)
passus, -ūs, *m. pace* (pass, passable)
senātor, senātōris, *m. senator* (senatorial)

Pronoun

is, ea, id, *this, that; he, she, it*

Adjectives

commūnis, -e, *common* (commune, communism)
incertus, -a, -um, *uncertain*
mille, *thousand* (millenial, millipede)

Verbs

remittō, remittere, remīsī, remissus, *relax, send back* (remission, remit)
spērō, spērāre, spērāvī, spērātus, *hope (for)* (despair)
spīrō, spīrāre, spīrāvī, spīrātus, *breathe* (inspiration, spirit)

Conjunction

dum,[1] *while*

Word Studies

1. Give the Latin noun suggested by each of the following: *civil, finish, submarine, navigate, corpulent, legislate, nominal, decapitate.*

2. Give the Latin verb suggested by each of the following: *expedite, press, verse, attention, repellent.*
3. Give the Latin adjective suggested by each of the following: *omnipresent, celerity, facilitate, disparity, fortitude.*
4. Find and use in sentences as many English derivatives as possible from **parō, teneō, agō,** and **scrībō.**

[1] **Dum** is generally followed by the present tense, although English often calls for a past tense.

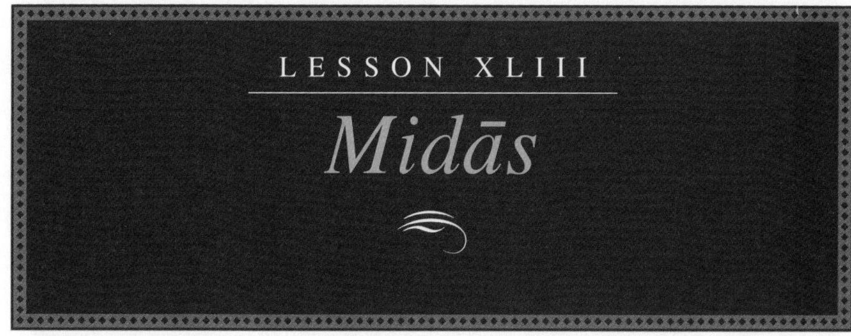

LESSON XLIII
Midās

Midās, nōbilis genere, rēx Phrygiae, multīs oppidīs expugnātīs, magnam auctōritātem habuit. Quondam Sīlēnus, magister deī Bacchī, in agrīs Phrygiae interceptus, ad eum rēgem ductus est. Quod Sīlēnus ab eōdem rēge multa beneficia accēpit, Bacchus parātus fuit rēgī dare id quod spērāvit. Midās dīxit: "Sī omnia quae parte corporis meī tetigerō in aurum vertentur, mihi grātum erit."

Hōc praemiō datō, omnia commūnia quae rēx tangēbat in aurum vertēbantur. Terram tangit: nōn iam terra est sed aurum. Aquam tangit: eōdem modō in aurum vertitur. Tum grātiās Bacchō prō magnō praemiō ēgit.

Tum rēx magnam cēnam parārī iussit et omnia genera cibōrum in mēnsā pōnī. Haec mēnsa ab eōdem tācta in aurum versa est. Dum magnā celeritāte servī cēnam parant, Midās familiārēs nōbilēs convocāvit. Grātō animō cēnam bonam quae parāta erat spectāvit. Dum cibum capit, cibus in aurum versus est. Vīnum in mēnsā pōnī iussit. Hoc tangit et nōn iam idem est sed in aurum vertitur. Omnibus amīcīs ēgregia cēna grāta fuit sed nōn rēgī. Inter multōs cibōs Midās tamen edere nōn potuit.

Tandem ad Bacchum, auctōrem malōrum, rēx miser prōcēdere mātūrāvit et fīnem supplicī petīvit—nam supplicium et impedīmentum, nōn iam praemium erat id quod ā deō accēperat. Bacchus iussit eum in mediō flūmine Pactōlo sē[1] lavāre. Praeceps rēx ad flūmen cucurrit, ubi sē lāvit, sē remīsit, sine cūrā spīrāvit, nam aurum remōtum erat. Arēna flūminis in aurum versa est, et etiam nunc in hōc eōdem flūmine aurum est.

[1] *himself*

QUESTIONS

1. Why did Bacchus reward Midas? How?
2. What is meant by the expression "the Midas touch"?
3. What is meant by comparing the gold buried at Fort Knox to that acquired by Midas?

Bacchus watches while Midas bathes in the River Pactolus to get rid of the "golden touch." A seventeenth-century painting by the French artist Nicolas Poussin (1594-1665).

Latin for American Students

Did you know that the Romans valued gold so highly that they banned the burial of any gold with the corpse, except for gold cavity fillings? Cavities were also filled with silver by barbers who often practiced as dentists. Gold wire was used to attach wooden false teeth to the jaws of wealthy Romans. Some well-to-do Romans even had a decayed tooth replaced by a healthy tooth from a slave's mouth, which was then hammered into the jaw and kept in place by a gold wire.

Grammar 

The Demonstrative *Īdem*

The demonstrative **īdem,** meaning *same,* is a compound of **is** and **–dem,** with slight changes for ease of pronunciation.

	SINGULAR		
	M	F	N
Nom.	**īdem**	**eădem**	**ĭdem**
Gen.	**eiusdem**	**eiusdem**	**eiusdem**
Dat.	**eīdem**	**eīdem**	**eīdem**
Acc.	**eundem**	**eandem**	**ĭdem**
Abl.	**eōdem**	**eādem**	**eōdem**

	PLURAL		
	M	F	N
Nom.	**eīdem**	**eaedem**	**eădem**
Gen.	**eōrundem**	**eārundem**	**eōrundem**
Dat.	**eīsdem**	**eīsdem**	**eīsdem**
Acc.	**eōsdem**	**eāsdem**	**eădem**
Abl.	**eīsdem**	**eīsdem**	**eīsdem**

ORAL PRACTICE

Give the Latin in the singular and plural for *the same body* in the accusative, *the same summer* in the ablative, *the same year* in the genitive, *the same punishment* in the nominative, *the same part* in the dative.

EXERCISES

A. Translate the following sentences into good English.

1. Eōdem annō lībertās captīvīs data est.
2. Dux eum ad idem supplicium trahī iussit.
3. Dum omnia timēmus, glōriam spērāre nōn possumus.
4. Oppidō expugnātō, Caesar impedīmenta hostium intercēpit.
5. Hic homō nōbilī genere sed nōn magnīs factīs illum superat.
6. Hominēs līberī parēsque esse dēbent, quod eadem iūra habent.

A harmless looking Vesuvius in the background provides rich soil for the grapes of Bacchus. The snake was a Roman good luck symbol, which in this case did not seem to work for this house in Pompeii.

Erich Lessing/Art Resource, NY

B. Translate the following sentences into Latin.

1. His punishment scared the rest.
2. He will not send back the same book.
3. When I saw the same boy,[1] I was no longer afraid.
4. Their towns were captured one at a time the same year.

C. Bacchus was not one of the twelve major Olympian gods of the Roman pantheon but was, nonetheless, important. Imagine the conversation he must have had with King Midas. Work with a partner to create a dialogue wherein Bacchus offers Midas anything he wants because he had done many kindnesses for people and the king then decides on his reward (punishment). You may want to make up some examples.

Vocabulary

Nouns

aurum, -ī, *n. gold* (aurous)
genus, generis, *n. birth, kind* (generation, genus)
supplicium, supplicī, *n. punishment* (supplication)

[1] Use ablative absolute.

Adjectives

īdem, eadem, idem, *same* (identify, identity)
nōbilis, -e, *noble* (nobility, noblewoman)

Verbs

edō, edere, ēdī, ēsus, *eat* (edible)
expugnō, expugnāre, expugnāvī, expugnātus, *capture by assault*
intercipiō, intercipere, intercēpī, interceptus, *intercept, cut off, steal* (intercept, interception)
tangō, tangere, tetigī, tactus, *touch* (tactile, tangent)

Adverb

tandem, *finally*

Word Studies

1. Explain the word *community.* **Supplicium** literally means *folding* (or *bending*) *down* for punishment. Explain *supplication.*
2. Here are some Latin phrases in English:
   ibid. (ibidem), *in the same place*
   id. (idem), *the same* (i.e., as mentioned above)
   quid pro quo, *something for something*
   Homo proponit, sed Deus disponit, *Man proposes, but God disposes.*

   Explain **semper idem, genus homo.**

Erich Lessing/Art Resource, NY (l, r)

This gold ring and armband from Pompeii are fine examples of Roman workmanship and show their love of jewelry.

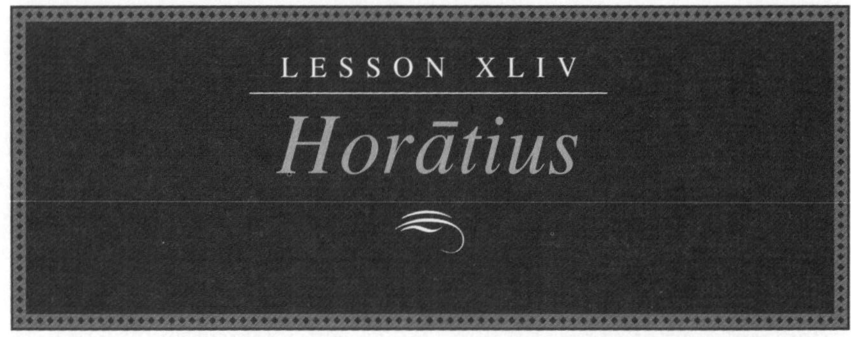

Nunc in locīs commodīs sedēbimus et legēmus dē Horātiō, virō fortī nōbilīque genere. Sī haec fābula, nōn tibi nōta, tē dēlectābit, tū ipse lege eandem sorōribus frātribusque tuīs parvīs (sī frātrēs sorōrēsque habēs), quī circum tē sedēbunt et magnō cum studiō audient.

Tarquiniī,[1] ā Rōmānīs pulsī, auxilium petīvērunt ā Porsenā, rēge Etrūscōrum. Itaque Porsena ipse cum multīs mīlitibus Rōmam[2] vēnit. Rōmānī, dē salūte commūnī incertī, territī sunt, quod magna erat potestās Etrūscōrum magnumque Porsenae nōmen. Rōmānī quī agrōs colēbant in oppidum migrāvērunt; portās clausērunt et oppidum ipsum praesidiīs dēfendērunt. Pars urbis Tiberī flūmine mūnīta est. Pōns sublicius[3] iter hostibus dabat, sed ēgregius vir prohibuit, Horātius Coclēs,[4] illō cognōmine appellātus quod in proeliō oculum āmīserat. Is, extrēmā pontis parte occupātā, sōlus sine auxiliō mīlitēs hostium intercēpit et sustinuit et Rōmānōs quī fugiēbant pontem frangere iussit. Ipsa audācia hostēs terruit. Ponte frāctō, Horātius nōn dubitāvit sed armīs impedītus praeceps in Tiberim dēsiluit et per multa tēla integer ad Rōmānōs natavit. Eius virtūte oppidum nōn expugnātum est et potestās Porsenae frācta est. Grāta ob factum clārum eius cīvitās fuit. Multī agrī eī pūblicē datī sunt, quōs ad terminum vītae coluit. Exemplum virtūtis ab eō prōpositum Rōmānī semper memoriā retinuērunt.

[1] *the Tar´quins,* Etruscan rulers of Rome in the sixth century B.C.
[2] *to Rome*
[3] *bridge made of wooden pilings*
[4] *Cō´clēs* ("One-Eye")

QUESTIONS

1. Why did Porsena come to Rome?
2. How was he prevented from entering the city?
3. How did Cocles get his name?

J. P. Stevens/Ancient Art & Architecture Collection

The single arch on the left is all that remains of the Pons Aemilius (second century B.C.), the first stone bridge built within the city of Rome. Many think that the wooden Pons Sublicius (Horatius' Bridge) stood nearby. This ancient bridge stood almost intact until the sixteenth century, when floods destroyed most of it.

Latin for American Students

Did you know that Roman engineers are considered to be the greatest builders of bridges? The first bridge (referred to in this lesson's reading) was constructed of wood with a semi-circular arch across the Tiber River in the seventh century B.C. This and other early bridges served as models for the later stone structures. Julius Caesar had two bridges erected across the Rhine and the Emperor Trajan built a five thousand foot long bridge across the Danube.

Grammar

The Intensive Adjective/Pronoun *Ipse*

In Latin, the intensive adjective/pronoun **ipse** is a compound of **is** and the intensive ending **–pse**. It is translated by joining *–self* or *–selves* to the pronoun. **Ipse** may also be used alone in the nominative to emphasize an omitted subject. It is declined like **ille**, except in the neuter nominative and accusative singular. The plural is regular: **ipsī, ipsae, ipsa**.

Ipse hominem vīdī.	*I saw the man myself.*
Hominem ipsum vīdī.	*I saw the man himself.*

	SINGULAR		
	M	F	N
Nom.	**ipse**	**ipsa**	**ipsum**
Gen.	**ipsīus**	**ipsīus**	**ipsīus**
Dat.	**ipsī**	**ipsī**	**ipsī**
Acc.	**ipsum**	**ipsam**	**ipsum**
Abl.	**ipsō**	**ipsā**	**ipsō**

ORAL PRACTICE

Translate: **frātris ipsīus, suppliciō ipsō, partēs ipsae, hic cīvis ipse, illārum nāvium ipsārum, sorōrī meae ipsī, eiusdem generis, eōrundem auctōrum.**

Words Often Confused

1. **alius** = *another,* one of a group of *three or more*
   alter = *the other,* i.e., *of two* and no more
2. **tōtus** = *whole,* i.e., no part missing, not capable of being divided
   omnis (singular) = *every*
   omnēs (plural) = *all,* i.e., a complete collection of units or parts
3. **nūllus** = *not any, no*—an adjective
   nihil = *not a thing, nothing*—a noun
   nēmō = *no man, no one*—a noun

EXERCISES

A. Translate the following sentences into good English.

1. Nōnne idem ipsī cernitis, puerī?
2. Quae officia soror vestra ipsa suscipiet?
3. Deī quōs Rōmānī colēbant multī erant.
4. Quis est ille puer quī cum sorōre meā sedet?
5. Ille homō agricola appellātur quod agrōs colit.
6. Frātrēs et sorōrēs eiusdem familiae paria iūra habēre dēbent.

B. Translate the following sentences into Latin.

1. These (men) are standing; those are sitting.
2. These letters were written by the king himself.
3. We ourselves shall get much money in a few years.
4. The same winter they saw and heard him themselves.

C. Horatius was greatly rewarded for his heroism and bravery. To inspire other citizens to go above and beyond for the good of the society, the news of courageous acts was carried by messengers throughout the Roman Empire. Work with a partner to summarize the exploits of Horatius so that a messenger can deliver the news quickly to the people in the provinces.

Vocabulary

Nouns

cognōmen, cognōminis, *n. nickname, surname*
oculus, -ī, *m. eye* (ocular, oculist)
pons, pontis, *m. bridge* (pontifex, pontoon)
potestās, potestātis, *f. power* (potent, potential)

Adjectives

ipse, ipsa, ipsum, *-self, very* (ipsilateral)

Verbs

dēlecto, dēlectāre, dēlectāvī, dēlectātus, *please* (delectable, delectation)
dēsiliō, dēsilīre, dēsiluī, dēsultūrus, *jump down, dismount* (desultory)
sedeō, sedēre, sēdī, sessūrus, *sit* (preside, session)

Word Studies

1. An *excursion* is a little *run out of* town. What is a *current* of water? *Cursive* writing? A *recurrent* illness? *Concurrent* powers of the federal government and the states? *Discord* is *hearts apart; concord, hearts together.* What is a *cordial* welcome? An apple *core?*
2. Here are some Latin phrases in English:
   primus inter pares, *first among (his) equals*
   A.D. (anno Domini), *in the year of the Lord*
   aut Caesar aut nihil, *either Caesar or nothing*
   Alma Mater, *kindly mother* (applied to a school or college)
   iustitia omnibus, *justice for all* (motto of the District of Columbia)
   Pater Noster, *Our Father,* (the beginning of the Lord's Prayer)

Glimpses of Roman Life

RELIGION

The earliest Romans believed that for almost every object and activity—the sky, the flow of rivers, the ripening of crops, even the hinges of a door—there was a mysterious and protecting spirit or power **(anima)**. This is the *animism* common in primitive agricultural societies, filled with what we would call superstitions, magic, and taboos. Gradually these spirits began to take on clearer form and personality as Roman gods and goddesses. Worship was centered in the family around various household gods: the **Lar Familiaris** (plural, **Larēs Familiarēs**), originally a field spirit who had been domesticated to protect the entire homestead; **Vesta**, goddess of the hearth; the **Penatēs**, gods of the food supply; and the **Genius**, the guardian spirit of the household head. The family's simple offerings and prayers to these deities long remained the most vital part of Roman religion. Offerings were most often made to the household deities before dessert was served at dinner, although devout Romans prayed every morning.

A household shrine in the house of the Venii in Pompeii. Beneath the Lares is the Genius of the head of the house, wearing a toga drawn over his head. The snake, too, represents the Genius, or guardian spirit.

Bill Roberts/PhotoEdit

As Rome grew as a political community, public religious activity became an integral part of state affairs, and rapidly assimilated other gods, goddesses, and forms of worship from people throughout the Empire. From the Etruscans the Romans learned a style of building temples and foretelling the future. The first temple in Rome was built by the Etruscans and was dedicated to Jupiter, Juno, and Minerva. When Greek influence on Rome increased, the Romans identified their native gods with the chief Greek deities: the sky god Jupiter with Zeus, the war god Mars with Ares, the love goddess Venus with Aphrodite, the grain goddess Ceres with Demeter, and so on. Still later, as all the world flocked to Rome, new religions were introduced from Egypt, Asia Minor, and even Persia, while the official state cult turned more towards emperor worship. Mystery religions also became popular such as the worship of the Egyptian goddess Isis, and Mithraism from the East which became the cult of the Roman army.

The generally tolerant and *polytheistic* (belief in many gods) Romans found *monotheism* (belief in a single god) strange. For nearly three centuries they persecuted the Christians because they scorned the pagan gods of the state and would not admit the divinity of the emperor (which began with the deification of Julius Caesar). Christianity itself was officially recognized by Emperor Constantine in A.D. 313. As Christianity grew in strength, the great pagan gods and goddesses faded from the ceremonies of the state, and the simple family rituals retreated to the peasant folk from whom they had originally sprung.

Just as remarkable as the variety and ability of the Roman religion to borrow other forms of worship was the closeness of its tie with politics. Originally the chief priest **(pontifex maximus)** had been the king himself; later the chief priest was elected, and he and all other priests or **pontificēs** were government officials. The duties of the **pontifex maximus** included inaugurating **pontificēs**, caring for public records, and overseeing sacred rites of Vesta. The state had charge of the building and restoration of temples, which in addition to being centers of worship were public treasuries, record offices, museums, and meeting places.

A statuette (about ten inches tall) of a Lar Familiaris, or family god. He dances and pours wine from a goat-shaped drinking horn onto the dish in his left hand, symbolizing the blessings of a happy and abundant household.

Metropolitan Museum of Art, Rogers Fund, 1919. (19.192.3).

Giraudon/Art Resource, NY

Oftentimes, a frieze is done to record important rituals, not just celebrations. This one is the taking of the census, which was done every five years. A census not only counted individuals, but assigned them to classes, so it was seen not only as a political institution but as a religious one as well.

Another political feature of the ancient religion was the attempt to determine the will of the gods in various ways. The duty of priests who were called **augurēs** (augurs) was to determine whether a certain important act (such as a military expedition) would be successful. They did this by observing the flight of birds. Certain movements were supposed to indicate success; others, failure. Another practice borrowed from the Etruscans was to sacrifice animals and examine their entrails in order to discover the will of the gods. These two methods were official and were used before important public matters were undertaken. Such acts of interpretation were called the "taking of the auspices." Eventually, many educated Romans lost faith in these practices, but they kept them up in order to influence the more ignorant classes. Private persons also resorted to numerous unofficial fortunetellers, such as astrologers, as some people do today.

With so many gods to worship, the Romans naturally had many holidays. Some of these were celebrated with amusements as well as with religious observances, as is true of our holidays today. For example, the festival called Consualia was celebrated on August 18 and was given in honor of Consus who presided over counsels and secret plans. The Palilia festival occurred on April 21 and was in honor of Pales, the goddess of flocks. This was also the official day honoring the founding of Rome.

QUESTIONS

1. What part did family worship play in Roman life?
2. To what extent is astrology practiced today?
3. In what countries today is religion directly connected with the state?

Unit IX Review
LESSONS XL-XLIV

Vocabulary

Nouns

auctor
auctōritās
aurum
cāsus
cognōmen
cor
exercitus
fluctus
focus
fulmen
genus
impetus
inferī
manus
mors
oculus
pars
passus
pōns
potestās
rēgia
senātor
senātus
supplicium
virtūs

Adjectives

commūnis
familiāris
hic
idem
ille
incertus
ipse
is
mille
nōbilis
praeceps

Verbs

cōnfīrmō
dēlectō
dēsiliō
dēvorō
edō
expellō
expugnō
intercipiō
pellō
remittō
respondeō
sedeō
spērō
spīrō
tango
timeō

Adverb

tandem

Conjunction

dum

Grammar Summary

The Fourth Declension

The fourth declension nouns are characterized by the vowel **–u**. Almost all of them are masculine.

In manū vulnerāta est.	*She was wounded in the hand.*
Dūx exercituum omnium est.	*He is the leader of all the armies.*

The Demonstratives *Hic, Ille, Is, Idem*

Demonstratives are used to point out things. They are generally translated by *this* or *that*. **Idem** means *the same*. They agree with the noun they modify—even if it is not expressed—in gender, number, and case.

Haec fēmina in agrō labōrat.	*This woman is working in the field.*
Illa aquam portat.	*That one (woman) is carrying water.*
Eum et eam in forō vīdīmus.	*We saw him and her in the Forum.*
Eundem equum herī vīdī.	*I saw the same horse yesterday.*

The Intensive *Ipse*

The intensive is used to emphasize any noun or pronoun in the sentence. It is translated as *–self* or *very*.

Unit IX Review
LESSONS XL-XLIV

Ea ipsa ad flumen cucurrit.	*She herself ran to the river.*
Ea ad flumen ipsum cucurrit.	*She ran to the river itself.*

The Declension and Use of *Mille*

The word **mille,** *thousand,* is indeclinable in the singular. In the plural, however, it is declined like a neuter **i**–stem. When used in the plural, the noun following *thousands* is in the genitive.

Mille militēs in campō erant.	*A thousand soldiers were on the plain.*
Duo milia militum in campō erant.	*Two thousand soldiers were on the plain.*

Unit Practice

Oral Form Drill

A. Make **hic, ille,** and **īdem** agree as demonstrative adjectives with the following nouns in the case required, as follows:
māteriae (gen.): **huius, illīus, eiusdem māteriae**

aestāte	**frātrēs** (nom.)	**patris**
capita (nom.)	**mortium**	**pretium** (acc.)
cor (acc.)	**partī**	**sorōrem**

B. Supply the correct form of **is** and translate the following sentences.

1. (*Him, her, it*) vīdī.
2. (*By him, by her*) ēvocātus sum.
3. Fīlium (*his, her*) docēbō.
4. Nōvistīne (*their*) patrem?
5. Hunc librum (*to him, to her, to them*) mandābō.

C. Decline **nūlla māter, alius auctor**.

Fortuna was the Roman goddess of luck, fortune, and chance. She could raise the humble and smite the mighty. In art, she is often represented with a ship's rudder and a cornucopia.

Ronald Sheridan/Ancient Art & Architecture Collection

D. You have read much about the Olympian gods and goddesses as well as some of the secondary deities. The following paragraph is a summary of some others. Work with a partner to translate it into good English.

Dē magnīs deīs iam lēgimus. Nunc dē multīs parvīs deīs legēmus. Concordiam, Victōriam, Salūtem, Pācem, Fortūnam, Virtūtem Rōmānī deās vocāvērunt, quod sacrae erant et ā Rōmānīs amābantur. Etiam pecūnia ā Rōmānīs amābātur et dea erat, sed tamen nōn in templō habitāvit.

Aliī deī erant deī familiārēs. Lār familiāris erat is deus quī familiam cōnservābat. Penātēs erant eī deī quī cibum servābant. Vesta erat dea focī, in quō cibus parābātur. Ad focum erant parvae fōrmae deōrum. Ibi, omnibus līberīs et familiāribus convocātīs, pater ipse deīs grātiās agēbat et cibum dōnābat. Saepe nōn multus cibus erat, sed tamen pater deīs partem cibī dōnābat.

Word Studies

1. Give the Latin words suggested by the derivatives: *cordial, partial, sedentary, fraternity, inspiration, cult, generation, sorority, cursive, remiss, maternal, intercept, infinite, sediment.*
2. Find and use in sentences as many derivatives as possible from **trahō, audiō,** and **premō.**

INTERCEPT

Scala/Art Resource, NY

Unit X

Famous Romans

Ara Pacis Augustae. The Altar of Augustan Peace was dedicated in 9 B.C. *to commemorate Augustus' pacification of Spain and Gaul, through diplomatic means. The repeated pattern of the togas and the reverent but aloof expressions on the faces underscore the overall feeling of pomp and ceremony. The altar was restored in the nineteenth century from pieces found in the Forum Romanum.*

LESSON XLV

Cicerō et Tīrō

Cicerō et Tīrō fuērunt Rōmānī clārī, alter maximus ōrātor tōtīus Italiae, alter servus fīdus. Quod Tīrō dīligentiā sapientiāque Cicerōnī magnum auxilium dabat, Cicerō eum tōtō corde amābat et posteā līberāvit. Neutrī grātum erat sine alterō ūllum iter facere.

Cicerō cum Tīrōne in Graeciā fuerat. Ubi ille in Italiam revertit, Tīrō sōlus in Graeciā relīctus est quod aeger fuit. Cicerō ad eum trēs litterās in itinere ūnō diē scrīpsit. Inter alia haec ipsa scrīpsit:

"Variē litterīs tuīs affectus sum, prīmā parte territus, alterā cōnfirmātus. Hōc tempore tē neque marī neque itinerī committere dēbēs. Medicus tuus bonus est, ut[1] scrībis et ego audiō; sed eum nōn probō; nam iūs[2] nōn dēbet stomachō[3] aegrō darī. Sed tamen et ad illum et ad Lysōnem[4] scrīpsī. Lysōnis nostrī neglegentiam nōn probō, quī, litterīs ā mē acceptīs, ipse nūllās remīsit; respondēre dēbet. Sed Lysō Graecus est et omnium Graecōrum magna est neglegentia. In nūllā rē properāre dēbēs.

"Curium[5] iussī omnem pecūniam tibi dare quam cupis. Sī medicō pecūniam dabis, dīligentia eius augēbitur. Magna sunt tua in mē officia; omnia superāveris, sī, ut spērō, salūtem tuam cōnfirmātam vīderō. Ante, dum magnā dīligentiā mihi auxilium dās, nōn salūtem tuam cōnfirmāre potuistī; nunc tē nihil impedit. Omnia dēpōne; salūs sōla in animō tuō esse dēbet."

Nōnne Cicerō dominus aequus amīcusque erat? Aliī dominī erant bonī, aliī malī. Omnī aetāte et in omnibus terrīs bonī et malī hominēs fuērunt et sunt et fortasse semper erunt.

[1] *as*
[2] *soup*
[3] *stomach*
[4] Tiro was staying at Lyso's house.
[5] *Cu´rius,* a banker

QUESTIONS

1. What was Tiro's relation to Cicero?
2. To whom did Cicero write about Tiro's illness?

Scala/Art Resource, NY

The Acropolis in Athens, sitting atop the highest point in the city (which is what acropolis *means in Greek) at 500 feet above sea level. The Doric style Parthenon, dedicated to Athena, is the largest of the group of temples located there. It is made entirely of white marble.*

Latin for American Students

Did you know that doctors, doctors' assistants, and nurses in Rome were often Greek slaves or freedmen? Such medical personnel had been imported from Greece since the second century B.C. *Although Greek physicians were not generally well regarded by the Romans because they were foreigners and/or slaves, Julius Caesar made citizens of Greek physicians who practiced in Rome and Augustus later granted them additional privileges.*

Grammar

The Fifth Declension

Like the fourth declension, the fifth declension has relatively few nouns, but they are important. The fifth declension can be characterized by the letter **–e,** which occurs in most of the endings. Fifth declension nouns are declined like **diēs,** *day.*

	SINGULAR	PLURAL
Nom.	diēs	diēs
Gen.	diēī	diērum
Dat.	diēī	diēbus
Acc.	diem	diēs
Abl.	diē	diēbus

ORAL PRACTICE

1. Decline **rēs fortis** and **ūna spēs.**
2. Give each of the following in the form indicated: **diēs ultimus** *(abl. pl.),* **lex nostra** *(acc. sing.),* **speciēs nova** *(dat. sing.),* **exercitus magnus** *(acc. pl.),* **manus pulchra** *(gen. pl.),* **alter puer** *(gen. sing.).*

The Third Person Reflexive Adjective

You are already familiar with four reflexive adjectives: **meus, tuus, noster,** and **vester,** which are derived from the personal (as well as reflexive) pronouns: **ego, tū, nōs,** and **vōs.** These adjectives correspond to first (I, we) and second (you) persons. There is also a third person reflexive adjective: **suus, –a, um.** Like all reflexives, it refers back to the subject only, and may be translated as *his, her, its,* or *their,* depending on the person and number of the subject. Because **suus** is an adjective, it agrees in gender, number, and case with the noun it modifies.

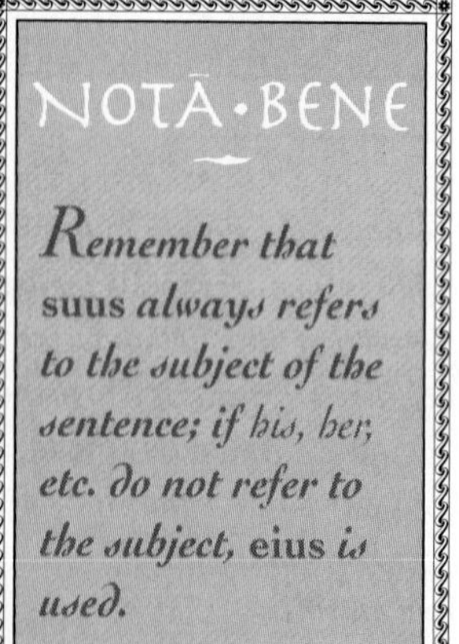
NOTĀ·BENE
Remember that suus always refers to the subject of the sentence; if his, her, etc. do not refer to the subject, eius is used.

Anna cum patre suō ambulābat.	*Anna was walking with her father.*
Marcus cum patre suō ambulābat.	*Marcus was walking with his father.*
Cum suīs patribus ambulābant.	*They were walking with their fathers.*

ORAL PRACTICE

Translate the words in italics.

1. We saw *his* joy.
2. You will see *their* friends.
3. The girl loved *her* horse.
4. He carried *his* baggage and *theirs.*
5. They will defend *their* families and *ours.*
6. She gave it to *her* mother.

North Wind Picture Archives

Educated Roman slaves were often an important part of the master's entourage, frequently acting as personal secretaries.

EXERCISES

A. Translate the following sentences into good English.

1. Dūx exercitum suum trāns montēs dūxit.
2. Eius librum amīsit quod eum nōn servāvit.
3. Amīcus certus in rē incertā cernitur.
4. Speciēs illōrum barbarōrum mē puerum terrēbat.

B. Translate the following sentences into Latin.

1. Many people are deceived by the appearance of things.
2. Show him his new books.
3. He ordered his four brothers to leave the town.
4. She saw her servant but not his in the Forum.

C. Work with a partner and write a letter from Tiro as a response to the letter that was just received from Cicero. Thank him for his concern, tell him how you are feeling, that you are getting better, and plan to return to Rome soon. Include as much detail as possible—how you will travel home and when, how long it might take, with whom you will be traveling, etc.

Scala/Art Resource, NY

Marcus Tullius Cicero was Rome's most outstanding orator. Born in 106 B.C. in Arpinum, he held all the positions in the ***cursus honorum****, including consul. His letters, some 800 of which exist, tell us much about life in the first century B.C.*

Vocabulary

Nouns

aetās, aetātis, *f. age*
diēs, diēī, *m. day* (diary, diurnal)
neglegentia, -ae, *f. negligence* (negligent, negligible)
rēs, reī, *f. thing, matter, affair* (real)
sapientia, -ae, *f. wisdom* (sapient, savant)
speciēs, speciēī, *f. appearance* (special, species)
spēs, speī, *f. hope*

Adjectives

aeger, aegra, aegrum, *sick, ill*
fīdus, -a, -um, *faithful, reliable, loyal* (fidelity)
maximus, -a, -um, *greatest* (maxim, maximize)

Verbs

dēpōnō, dēpōnere, dēposuī, dēpositus, *put down, lay aside* (deposit, deposition)
fallō, fallere, fefellī, falsus, *deceive, disappoint* (fallacy, falsify)

Word Studies

Here are some Latin phrases used in English:
in omnia paratus, *prepared for all things*
Dominus providebit, *The Lord will provide.*
Fortes Fortuna adiuvat, *Fortune aids the brave.*
extempore, *without preparation* (lit., *from the moment*)
Arma non servant modum, *Armies do not show* (preserve) *restraint.*
Virtute et armis, *By courage and by arms* (motto of the state of Mississippi).
Vanitas vanitatum et omnia vanitas, *Vanity of vanities, and all (is) vanity* (from the Vulgate or Latin translation of the Bible, *Ecclesiastes, I,* 2).
Ense petit placidam sub libertate quietem, *With the sword she seeks quiet peace under liberty* (motto of the state of Massachusetts).

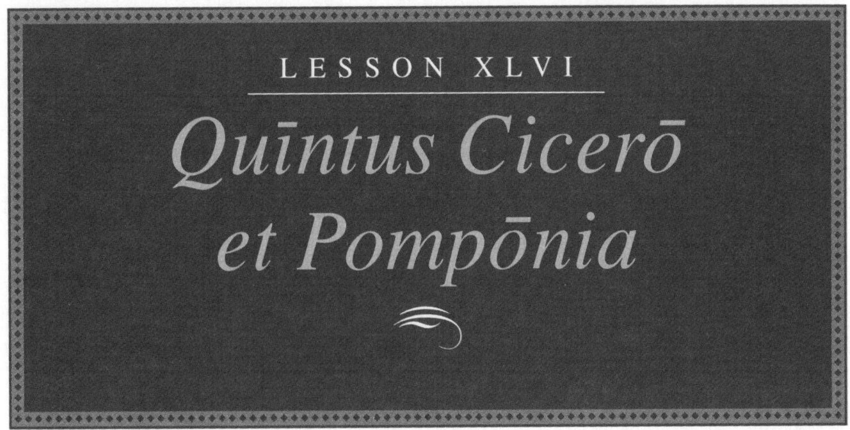

Pompōnius Atticus erat firmus amīcus M. Cicerōnis. Pompōnia, soror Atticī, erat uxor Quīntī, frātris M. Cicerōnis. Sed inter Pompōniam Quīntumque nōn semper concordia erat. Ūna gravis causa inter aliās erat haec, quod apud[1] Quīntum auctōritās Stātī[2] valēbat, quem Pompōnia domō expellere nūllō modō potuit; aliēnae auctōritātī cēdere nōn cupīvit. Neuter alterī cēdere potuit; neuter alterum movēre potuit. Cicerō Pompōniam accūsāvit, Atticus Quīntum. Cicerō ad Atticum hōc modō scrīpsit:

"Frātrem meum vīdī. Tōtus sermō inter nōs dē tē et sorōre tuā fuit. Verba Quīntī nōn inimīca fuērunt. Tum ad Pompōniam contendimus. Quīntus eī amīcā vōce dīxit: 'Pompōnia, tū rogā mulierēs ad cēnam, ego puerōs rogātūrus sum.' (Hī puerī erant fīliī Cicerōnis et frātris eius.) Sed illa, audientibus nōbīs, 'Ego ipsa sum,' respondit, 'in hōc locō hospita.' Hoc dīxit quod īdem Stātius cēnam parārī iusserat. Tum Quīntus, 'Audīsne?' inquit mihi, 'haec semper sustinēre cōgor.' Dīcēs: 'Haec vōx nihil est.' Sed magnum est; vōce dūrā atque animō aliēnō eius oppressus et commōtus sum. Ad cēnam illa nōn adfuit; Quīntus tamen ad eam sedentem sōlam cibum mīsit; illa remīsit. Grave vulnus Quīntus accēpit neque ipse ūllam iniūriam fēcit. Cupiēns eam plācāre nōn potuit. Gravibus cūrīs opprimor. Quid factūrī sumus? Contendere dēbēmus inter sorōrem tuam et frātrem meum pācem efficere."

[1] *with*
[2] *Statius* (*Stā´shus*), a freedman of Quintus
[3] *from the house*

QUESTIONS

1. Who was Atticus' brother-in-law?
2. Of whom was Pomponia jealous?

Scala/Art Resource, NY

This portrait of the magistrate Terentius Neo and his wife was part of the wall decoration in the Pompeiian house that is supposed to have belonged to the baker Terentius Troculus, brother of the magistrate. Note the symbols of learning—the scroll, the wax tablets, and the stylus.

Grammar

The Present Participle

In English, the *present active participle* ends in *–ing: I saw your brother reading a book.* In Latin, it is formed by adding **–ns** to the present stem. It is declined like a third declension adjective of one ending with the stem ending in **–nt–: portāns, portantis.** In verbs of the fourth conjugation, and **–iō** verbs of the third, **–ie–** appears throughout, forming the base **–ient–**, as **audiēns, audientis; capiēns, capientis. Sum** has no present participle in common use; that of **possum** is **potēns.**

Līberōs ambulantes in viā vīdī.	*I saw the children walking in the street.*
Me sciēns, hoc crēdis?	*Knowing me, do you believe this?*

The present participle modifies a noun or pronoun. Like the present infinitive, it represents an act that is happening at the same time as the main verb.

ORAL PRACTICE

Form and translate the present active participles of **vocō, moneō, dicō, faciō, mūniō.**

The Future Active Participle

Unlike English, Latin has a future active participle. In most verbs it is formed by dropping the **–us** of the perfect passive participle and adding **–ūrus: portātūrus,** *going to (about to) carry;* **factūrus,** *going to (about to) make.* It is declined like **magnus.** Note that in English we have to use a phrase to translate it. It is often used with the verb **sum.**

Lectūrus sum illum librum.	*I am going to read that book.*
Nōs pugnātūrī te salūtāmus.	*We who are about to fight salute you.*

ORAL PRACTICE

Form and translate the future active participle of **nāvigō, obtineō,** and **prōdūco.**

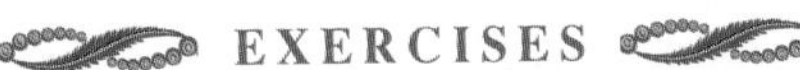

EXERCISES

A. Translate the following sentences into good English.

1. Duo puerī pugnantēs ā magistrō captī sunt.
2. Rōmānīs tardē prōcēdentibus, barbarī fūgērunt.
3. Hieme nūllōs agricolās in agrīs labōrantēs vidēbimus.
4. Cūr in hōc locō sine frātribus tuīs remānsūrus es?
5. Hī puerī, suppliciō gravī affectī, ā magistrō dīmissī sunt.
6. Vōcēs amīcōrum rogantium auxilium ā nōbīs numquam audītae sunt.
7. Oppressī in aliēnō locō, hostēs cum impedīmentīs ad montēs contentūrī erant.

Erich Lessing/Art Resource, NY

A deluxe Roman butcher shop. The cleaver and chopping block look very modern. From a relief on a sarcophagus, 2nd-3rd century, Ostia.

B. Instead of clauses, use participles wherever possible to translate the following sentences.

1. The arms given to the other soldiers are heavy.
2. The number of (those) approaching was not large.
3. He is going to fold the letter which he has written.
4. He was dragged to death by you (while he was) defending the public cause.

C. You have learned about the strained personal relationships among Quintus, Cicero, Statius, and Pomponia in this lesson's reading. Statius was a freedman who was the best friend of Quintus. Pomponia was Quintus' wife and was jealous of the men's relationship as well as unsure of her position in the group. You probably know how difficult it is for three people to get along well together. Work with a partner to take the side of one of the three main characters in the reading and defend his or her behavior. Did he or she have a right to feel a certain way? What could be done to ease the tension? Is anyone more at fault than any other? Feel free to create details about how you feel that the other two are not being reasonable. Present your side to the class and then listen to the defenses from other groups.

Latin for American Students

*Did you know that **hospita** often meant both "guest" and "host" to the Romans? This relationship was strictly reciprocal, and each individual was bound to provide food and shelter, legal protection, medical assistance, and personal contacts when visiting the other. The **hospites** exchanged tokens, which were passed on to descendants, as a means of identification. It was considered an honor to continue the **hospitum** tradition in a Roman family.*

Vocabulary

Nouns

hospita, -ae, *f. guest* (hospitable, hospitality)
mulier, mulieris, *f. woman*
sermō, sermōnis, *m. talk, conversation* (sermon, sermonize)
urbs, urbis, *f. city* (suburb, urban)

Adjectives

aliēnus, -a, -um, *another's, unfavorable* (alien, alienate)

gravis, -e, *heavy, severe* (gravitation, gravity)

Verbs

ascendō, ascendere, ascendī, ascensus, *climb (up), ascend* (ascendant, ascension)

contendō, contendere, contendī, contentūrus, *struggle, hasten* (contend, contention)

opprimō, opprimere, oppressī, oppressus, *overcome, surprise* (oppress, oppressive)

plācō, plācāre, plācāvī, plācātus, *please, calm* (placate, placater)

Preposition

apud (+ acc.), *among, with*

A Roman matron and child. Note that the woman is wearing the full-length dress called a ***stola*** *beneath her outer shawl, or* ***palla****. She may also have a knee-length* ***tunica*** *under the* ***stola****.*

Word Studies

1. What is a *neutral*? An *alien*? What is meant by the statement in the Declaration of Independence "that all men ... are endowed by their Creator with certain *unalienable* [usually misquoted *inalienable*] rights; that among these are life, liberty, and the pursuit of happiness"?
2. Here are some Latin phrases in English:
   inter alia, *among other things*
   ipso facto, *by the fact itself, thereby*
   in loco parentis, *in place of a parent*
   una voce, *with one voice, unanimously*
   Vox populi vox Dei, *The voice of the people (is) the voice of God.*
   obiter dictum, (*something*) *said by the way* **(ob iter),** *incidentally*
   Timeo Danaos et dona ferentes, *I fear the Greeks even when they bring gifts* (Vergil).
   Explain **in toto, vox humana.**

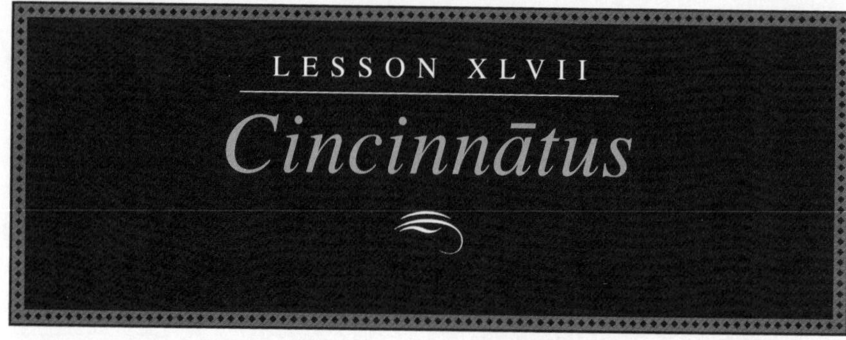

LESSON XLVII
Cincinnātus

Hostēs Minucium,[1] ducem Rōmānum, et mīlitēs eius in locō aliēnō magnā vī premēbant. Ubi id nūntiātum est, omnēs Rōmānī timentēs vim hostium cupīvērunt Cincinnātum[2] dictātōrem facere, quod is sōlus Rōmam ā perīculō nōn levī prohibēre et cīvitātem servāre poterat. Ille trāns Tiberim eō tempore agrum parvum colēbat. Nūntiī ā senātū missī eum in agrō labōrantem invēnērunt et cōnstitērunt. Salūte datā acceptāque, Cincinnātus uxōrem parāre togam iussisse dīcitur; nam nōn oportēbat sine togā nūntiōs audīre.

Hī nūntiī eum dictātōrem appellant et dīcunt: "Mīlitēs nostrī ab hostibus premuntur et cīvēs terrentur. Perīculum nostrum nōn leve est. Hostēs nōn cōnsistent sed mox ad portās nostrās ipsās venient. Auxilium tuum rogāmus." Itaque Cincinnātus, vōcibus eōrum adductus, contrā hostēs contendit. Rōmānī, tēlīs iactīs, hostēs opprimunt et castra expugnant. Minuciō servātō, Cincinnātus dīcitur hostēs sub iugum[3] mīsisse. Tum, nūllīs hostibus prohibentibus, mīlitēs ad urbem redūxit et triumphāvit. Vīs hostium frācta erat. Ductī sunt in pompā ante eum ducēs hostium, capta arma ostenta sunt; post eum mīlitēs vēnērunt praedam gravem ostendentēs. Et haec omnia Cincinnātus magnā celeritāte gessit: potestāte dictātōris sex mēnsēs acceptā, sextō decimō diē ad agrōs discessit, nōn iam dictātor sed triumphāns agricola. Eōdem mēnse agricola et dictātor et iterum agricola fuit.

[1] *Minucius* (*Minū´shus*)
[2] *Cincinnatus* (*Sinsinā´tus*)
[3] *under the yoke,* i.e., an arch of spears. This act signified surrender.

QUESTIONS

1. Where was Cincinnatus' farm?
2. Who was with him when the messengers came?
3. How long did he stay away from his farm?

Kaveler/Art Resource, NY

Cincinnatus was a Roman patriot who lived in the fifth century B.C. Called to help defend Rome against the Aequi and the Volscians, he left his farm, was named dictator, drove out the enemy, and returned to his farm after 16 days.

Grammar

The Perfect Active Infinitive

The *perfect active infinitive* is formed by adding **–isse** to the perfect stem.

portāvisse	*to have carried*	**posuisse**	*to have put*
docuisse	*to have taught*	**mūnīvisse**	*to have built*

The perfect active infinitive is used to indicate an action that took place *before* the time of the main verb.

Rēgīna terram occupāvisse putātur.	*The queen is thought to have seized the land.*
Dūx hostēs vīcisse dicitur.	*The general is said to have conquered the enemy.*

ORAL PRACTICE

Form the perfect active infinitive of **dīmittō, intercipiō, videō, expediō, laudō.**

EXERCISES

A. Translate the following sentences into good English.

1. Ostendite omnibus bonum exemplum.
2. Vim prohibēre et pācem cōnservāre est nōbile.
3. Rēgis fīlia librum scrīpsisse sine auxiliō dīcitur.
4. Quis dīxit: "Dā mihi lībertātem aut dā mihi mortem"?
5. Rōmānī paucās nāvēs ad Britanniam mīsisse dīcuntur.
6. Mīlitēs cōnsistentēs tēla levia cum magnā vī iēcisse dīcuntur.
7. Homō malus mē cōnsistere iussit et omnem meam pecūniam dare.

B. Translate the following sentences into Latin.

1. We cannot breathe under water.
2. I saw your mother folding a letter.
3. That king is said to have tilled the fields himself.
4. Those men are said to have come together in a strange land.

C. The leading citizens of Rome sought out Cincinnatus at his home because they had such respect for him and his ability to be a leader. Work with a partner to create the dialogue that you imagine took place that day, in which the citizens persuaded Cincinnatus to lead the troops against the enemy and save Minucius, despite the fact that the former consul was now a farmer.

An ostrich and its keeper, from Piazza Amerina, Sicily. Mosaic was an important part of interior decoration and was found even in modest Roman homes. Ostriches were occasionally used in warfare by the military in Egyptian and Nubian campaigns.

Tomas D.W. Friedmann/Photo Researchers

Latin for American Students

Did you know that Julius Caesar was responsible for the calendar system that we follow today? He modified the Egyptian calendar in 46 B.C. by discontinuing the Egyptian thirty-day months and distributing the five extra days of a 365-day year. He gave every other month one of these days and took one day from February, except in every fourth or leap year. The Julian Calendar also made January the first month. In his honor, his successor Augustus named the seventh month July.

Vocabulary

Nouns

mensis, mensis, *m. month* (semester)
princeps, principis, *m. leader* (prince, principal)
tēlum, -ī, *n. weapon*
vīs, vīs,[1] *f. force, violence;* pl. *strength* (vim)

Adjective

levis, -e, *light (in weight)* (levitate, levity)

Verbs

cōnsistō, cōnsistere, cōnstitī, cōnstitūrus, *stop, stand still* (consist, consistent)
oportet, oportēre, oportuit,[2] *it is fitting, it is necessary* (*with* acc. *of person* + inf.)
ostendō, ostendere, ostendī, ostentus, *show, stretch out* (ostensible, ostentatious)
prohibeō, prohibēre, prohibuī, prohibitus, *prevent, keep from* (prohibit, prohibition)

Adverbs

bene, *well* (benefit, nota bene)
iterum, *again, a second time* (iterate, reiterate)

---

[1] This is an irregular noun. It is declined *(sing.)* **vīs, vīs, vī, vim, vī;** *(pl.)* **vīrēs, vīrium, vīribus, vīrēs, viribus.**
[2] This is an impersonal verb; it only is used in the third person singular.

Preposition

contrā (+ acc.), *against, opposite* (contradict)

Word Studies

1. The suffix **–or** is added to the stem of the past participle and therefore is preceded by **t** or **s**. It indicates the doer of an action: **monitor** *(one who warns)*, **scrīptor** *(one who writes)*, **inventor** *(one who finds)*. It is used in English in the same way.

EJECT

A different suffix **–or** is added to the present base of a verb; it usually indicates a state of being or condition: **timor, amor, terror**. It is used in English.

Find five English words which are formed by adding one of these **–or** suffixes to the stems of verbs that you have studied. Explain *eject, injection, reject, ostentation, prohibition.*

2. The city of *Cincinnati,* Ohio, was named from the Society of the Cincinnati, formed by army officers at the end of the Revolutionary War. Why do you suppose the society took that name? What does its motto **Omnia reliquit servare rem publicam** mean?

LESSON XLVIII
Bella

Quae sunt causae bellī? Variī auctōrēs ostendērunt multās esse causās. Multa bella aut ob iniūriās aut prō lībertāte gesta esse vidēmus. In aliīs bellīs lībertās sociōrum dēfēnsa est. Haec bella iūsta fuērunt. Multī populī pugnant quod putant potestātem imperiumque vī bellōque augērī posse. Hī cupiunt patriam esse nūllī secundam. Sī superantur, omnia saepe āmittunt; sī superant, aliēnās terrās occupant, quās in fōrmam prōvinciārum redigunt. Putāsne bella huius generis iūsta esse? Multī dīcunt omnia bella iūsta esse, aliī putant nūlla esse iūsta. Quid dē hōc putās? Nōvimus aliōs prō lībertāte, aliōs prō glōriā bella gessisse. Quae fuērunt causae bellōrum nostrōrum? Audīvistīne dē bellō frīgidō?

Horātius, poēta Rōmānus, scrībit dulce esse prō patriā vītam āmittere. Sī patria in perīculō est, nōnne putās mūnus nostrum esse eam dēfendere? Scīmus nōn levēs esse labōrēs mīlitum, gravia eōs accipere vulnera, multōs ad mortem mittī; etiam scīmus eōs tamen nōn dubitāre omnēs labōrēs prō patriā grātō animō suscipere et sustinēre. Prō hīs mūneribus praemia aequa eīs solvere nōn possumus. Sed nec praemia nec beneficia exspectant; spērant cīvēs facta sua memoriā tentūrōs esse et aliōs semper parātōs futūrōs esse patriam dēfendere. Hōc modō praemia solvere possumus.

Bellane ūllō tempore cōnstitūra sunt? Possuntne bella prohibērī? Quis scit? Sed spērāmus parvō spatiō temporis nōn iam bella futūra esse; spērāmus omnēs hominēs aliōrum iūra cōnservātūrōs esse.

QUESTIONS

1. Which wars were just?
2. What do soldiers hope for?
3. What are your answers to the questions asked in the Latin reading?

Roman soldiers used different instruments of war, depending on the situation. Here, a battering ram is used to weaken or break into the walls of the fortification.

Mary Evans/Photo Researchers

Grammar

The Perfect Passive and Future Active Infinitives

The *perfect passive infinitive* is formed by using the perfect passive participle plus **esse.**

laudātus, -a, -um esse	*to have been praised*
monitus, -a, -um esse	*to have been warned*

The *future active infinitive* is formed by using the future active participle plus **esse**.

captūrus, -a, -um esse	*to be going to take*
mūnītus, -a, -um esse	*to be about to build*

Because both infinitives are formed from a participle, they must agree with the subject of the infinitive.

Spērō eam haec factūram esse.	*I hope that she will do these things.*
Putāvī haec facta esse.	*I thought that these things had been done.*

ORAL PRACTICE

1. Form and translate the perfect passive and future active infinitives of **iaciō, solvō,** and **prohibeō.**
2. Form and translate all five infinitives of **putō, veniō, mittō, terreō.**

Direct and Indirect Statement

In English, after verbs of *thinking, knowing, hearing, perceiving,* etc., if words are not quoted directly (direct statement), a clause is often introduced by *that* (indirect statement). In Latin, an infinitive, with an accusative subject, is used instead of a *that* clause to express an indirect statement.

Dicit, "Pueri labōrant."	*He says, "The boys are working."*
Dicit puerōs labōrāre.	*He says (that) the boys are working.*

Note that **puerōs** is accusative because it is the subject of an infinitive. The subject of an infinitive is in the accusative in English, too, as you can see from the following sentences. Perhaps this will make it easier for you to use *who* and *whom* correctly in English.

Marcus est homō quem esse iustum crēdō.	*Marcus is a man whom I believe to be fair.*
Marcus est homō quī, crēdō, iustus est.	*Marcus is a man who, I believe, is fair.*

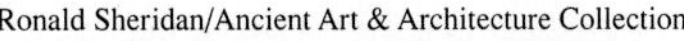
Ronald Sheridan/Ancient Art & Architecture Collection

Captives were also an integral part of war. This relief shows two chained captives in Trajan's triumphal procession in A.D. *107.*

ORAL PRACTICE

Translate the words in italics into Latin.

1. I know *him to be* wise.
2. I know the *signal was given.*
3. They say the *wagon was drawn* by mules.
4. I hear that your *sister will live* in town.
5. I believe the *men have been led across* the river.

EXERCISES

A. Translate the following sentences into good English.

1. Dīcunt, "Cīvis iūstus lībertātem amat."
2. Cīvis iūstus lībertātem amāre dīcitur.
3. Dīcunt cīvem iūstum lībertātem amāre.
4. Putāmus nostra mūnera futūra esse levia.
5. Nōs omnēs scīmus in spatiō vītae esse cūrās et labōrēs.
6. Putāsne hunc pecūniam dēbitam solvisse aut solūtūrum esse?
7. Sciō et dīcō pecūniam ab illō homine dēbitam nōn solūtam esse.
8. Putō, Mārce, illam fēminam numquam futūram esse prīmam aut secundam ōrdine.

B. Translate the following sentences into Latin.

1. Galba said, "My father is a soldier."
2. We all know that his father is a soldier.
3. I think that Galba himself will be a soldier.
4. I hear that Galba's brother was a sailor and was not scared by the sea.
5. He himself said, "I am going to be a soldier, for my father is a soldier."

Nimatallah/Art Resource, NY

This fresco from Pompeii shows a scene from the Trojan War. In the foreground, you can see four Trojan soldiers pulling the horse into the city.

C. You have read about some of the causes of war and the adventures of Aeneas and Ulysses. But how did the war begin? The following is a brief summary of the events leading up to that war. Work with a partner to put it into Latin using familiar constructions. It should not necessarily be a direct translation. The following vocabulary may be helpful to you.

Helena, -ae, *f. Helen*
Menelaus, -i, *m. Menelaus*
Paris, Paridis, *m. Paris*
Priamus, -i, *m. Priam*
Troia, -ae, *f. Troy*
infeliciter, *unfortunately*
condiciō, -ciōnis, *f. offer*
dēlectus, -us, *m. choice*
disputātiō, -tiōnis, *f. argument*
continuō, -āre, -āvī, -ātus, *continue*
dēligō, dēligere, dēlēgī, dēlectus, *choose*
pulcherrimus, -a, -um, *most beautiful, fairest*

There was an argument among three goddesses—Juno, Minerva, and Venus—about who was the fairest. Paris, the son of Priam who was king of Troy, was picked to make the choice. Juno promised him wealth; Minerva promised him wisdom; and Venus promised him the most beautiful woman in the world for a wife. Selecting Venus' offer, she gave him his reward. Unfortunately, the beautiful woman was Helen, who was already married to Menelaus, king of Sparta. Paris took Helen and fled with her to Troy. The Greeks then sent an army to Troy, they began battle, and the war continued for ten years.

Latin for American Students

*Did you know that a cold room in a Roman public bath was called a **frigidarium?** Going to the baths was a very important daily social event in the lives of most Romans. Here one could also spend time in a room for a warm bath called a **tepidarium,** a room for a hot bath called a **calidarium,** a dressing room called a **apodyterium,** and a **paelestra** or room for athletic exercise.*

Vocabulary

Nouns

gēns, gentis, *f. nation, family, class*	(gentile, gentle)
labor, labōris, *m. work, hardship*	(laboratory, laborious)
mūnus, mūneris, *n. duty, service, gift*	(munificient)

Adjectives

frīgidus, -a, -um, *cold*	(frigid)
iūstus, -a, -um, *just*	(justice, justify)

Verbs

intellegō, intellegere, intellexī, intellectus, *understand*	(intellect, intellectual)
nesciō, nescīre, nescīvī, nescītus, *not know*	(nescience)
sentiō, sentīre, sensī, sensus, *feel, realize*	(sense, sensual)
solvō, solvere, solvī, solūtus, *loosen, pay*	(solution, solvable)

Conjunction

sī, *if*

Word Studies

The base of the Latin present participle is **–ant, –ent,** or **–ient,** according to the conjugation. This is used as a suffix in English, with the same meaning as the participial ending *–ing.*

A common mistake in the spelling of English words is due to the confusion of *–ant* and *–ent.* Reference to the Latin can help:

1. Almost all English words derived from the first conjugation follow the Latin spelling with an *–a–: expectant, emigrant.*
2. Most English words that are derived from the other conjugations follow the Latin spelling with an *–e–: regent, agent, efficient, expedient.*
3. But some words in the latter group have an *–a–: tenant, defendant.*

Give eight English words with suffix *–ant* or *–ent* derived from Latin words previously studied. Explain *laboratory, omniscient, solvent, absolve, remunerate.*

Mārcius, nōbilis Rōmānus, Coriolōs,[1] oppidum Volscōrum,[2] expugnāverat. Ob hoc mūnus "Coriolānus" appellātus est.

Post bellum ob variās causās plēbs īrā ācrī permōta clāmāvit Coriolānum esse hostem. Is sentiēns, perīculum īnstāre, fūgit ad Volscōs quōs ipse superāverat. Volscī dīcuntur eum benigne accēpisse, nam sēnsērunt eum esse ducem fortem ac iūstum et Rōmam nōn iam amāre. Etiam spērāvērunt eum contrā Rōmānōs pugnātūrum esse.

Mox Coriolānus, dux ā Volscīs lēctus, ad urbem Rōmam contendit, omnēs in itinere superāns. Rōmānī, castrīs eius ad urbem positīs, bellō īnstantī territī sunt. Lēgātī dē pāce ad Coriolānum missī sunt sed ubi pervēnērunt ab eō remissī sunt.

"Mātrem eius ad eum mittēmus," putāvērunt Rōmānī; "sī cūra urbis cor eius nōn tanget, ille amōre mātris certē tangētur et īra eius frangētur; tum fīnem labōrum nostrōrum inveniēmus." Itaque māter et uxor Coriolānī cum duōbus parvīs fīliīs ad castra hostium pervēnērunt.

Coriolānus, verbīs ācribus mātris permōtus et lacrimīs omnium tāctus, dīcitur clāmāvisse: "Quid fēcistī, māter? Tū sōla Rōmam servāvistī sed mē vīcistī." Tum iussit Volscōs discēdere. Rōma lacrimīs, nōn armīs servāta erat. Coriolānī facta semper in memoriā omnium haerēbunt.

[1] *Corī´olī*
[2] *Volsci* (*Vol´sī*)

QUESTIONS

1. How did Coriolanus get his name?
2. Where did he go when exiled?
3. Why did he spare Rome?

Roman coins often had the faces of important individuals on them. In this case, the Emperor Nero and his mother, Agrippina, appear on the coin. If you look closely around the edge, you can make out the word "Nero" just over his head.

Ronald Sheridan/Ancient Art & Architecture Collection

Grammar

How the Indicative and the Infinitive Differ in Tense

The tenses of the indicative are determined by their relation to present time, that is, something is happening now (present tense), has already happened (perfect tense), or has not yet happened but will (future tense).

Ad īnsulam nāvigat.	*He is sailing to the island.*
Ad īnsulam nāvigāvit.	*He sailed to the island.*
Ad īnsulam nāvigābit.	*He will sail to the island.*

The tenses of the infinitive—since an infinitive cannot stand alone in a sentence—are determined by their relation to the verbs on which they depend. If the action of the infinitive is going on *at the same time* as that of the main verb, you use a present infinitive, even if the main verb is not in the present tense.

Dīcit eam legere.	*He says that she is reading.*
Dīxit eam legere.	*He said that she was reading.*

To indicate that the action of the infinitive happened *before* that of the main verb, you use the perfect infinitive.

Putō tē hoc sensisse.	*I think that you realized this.*
Putāvī tē hoc sensisse.	*I thought that you had realized this.*

To indicate that the action of the infinitive has not yet happened, or will happen *after* the time of the main verb, you use the future infinitive.

Audiō eum tē vocātūrum esse.	*I hear that he will call you.*
Audīvī eum tē vocātūrum esse.	*I heard that he would call you.*

NOTĀ · BENE

When you translate from Latin to English, take careful note of the tense of the main verb and the infinitive to determine before you translate whether the action is going on at the same time, at a time before, or at a time after.

ORAL PRACTICE

Translate the words in italics into Latin.

1. She knew *me to be* her friend.
2. He knew that *I was working* hard.
3. We saw that *we would* not *answer* in time.
4. He said that his *son was being taught* by new methods.
5. We hear that your *father has been sent* to Europe on a secret mission.

NOTĀ · BENE

Remember that the participle in the compound forms of the infinitive must agree with its subject.

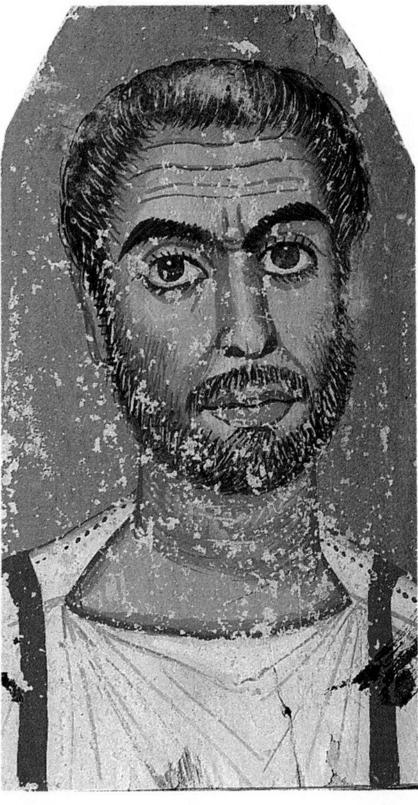

Another type of Roman art comes from Egypt—the mummy portrait. Painted on a wood panel with colors mixed with melted wax, the portrait was fastened to the person's mummy after death. Thanks to the dry climate of Egypt, about 600 of these portraits have been preserved.

Erich Lessing/Art Resource, NY (l, r)

EXERCISES

A. Translate the following sentences into good English.

1. Omnēs sēnsimus perīculum īnstāre.
2. Puer nōn clāmāre potuit, quod vōx haesit.
3. Quis dīxit socium meum sine frātre suō pervēnisse?
4. Servī spērāvērunt labōrem futūrum esse facilem.
5. Omnēs līberī certē sciunt Columbum ad Americam pervēnisse.
6. Rōmānī dīcēbant Caesarem esse fortem ducem nec numquam superātum esse.

B. Translate the following sentences into Latin.

1. We can prove that our cause is just.
2. Who said that we would not arrive?
3. My mother wrote that the city was beautiful.
4. The boy thought that his father had been saved.
5. The envoy says that the soldiers of the provinces were brave.

C. Coriolanus was deterred from his actions against Rome because of his mother's words. His wife and two small children were also present. Work with a partner or in a small group to create a dialogue that might have taken place on the battlefield that day. What do you suppose his family could have said that persuaded him to give up the fight?

Latin for American Students

Did you know that the Roman plebian class, which made up the majority of the Roman population, did not possess full citizenship rights? Among the privileges enjoyed by the patricians, or those who had full citizenship, were: they could not be bound or imprisoned without a formal trial; they could not be whipped; they could enter into inheritances; they could appeal from a provincial tribunal to the emperor of Rome; they had the right to vote.

Vocabulary

Nouns

cōnsul, cōnsulis, *m. consul* (consular, consulate)
lēgātus, -ī, *m. envoy* (legate)
plēbs, plēbis, *f. common people, plebeians* (plebiscite)

Verbs

dēserō, dēsere, dēseruī, dēsertus, *desert* (deserter, desertion)
haereō, haerēre, haesī, haesus, *stick, cling* (adhere, adhesive)
instō, instāre, institī, —, *threaten*
reddō, reddere, reddidī, redditus, *give back*

Adjectives

ācer, ācris, ācre, *sharp, keen, fierce* (acrid)
audax, (gen.) **audācis,** *bold, daring* (audacious, audacity)
difficilis, -e, *difficult, hard* (difficulty)
potēns, (gen.) **potentis,** *powerful* (potent, potential)
similis, -e, *like, similar* (dissimilarity, simile)

Word Studies

By adding the suffix **–ia** to the base of the present participle, a suffix **–antia** or **–entia** is formed that becomes *–ance, –ence, –ancy,* or *–ency* in English. Give eight English nouns with this suffix derived from Latin words previously studied. Explain *coherence, sensitive, consensus, intangible, dissension, inherent.* What is the difference between *adhesion* and *cohesion?*

In this statue of a Roman consul during the Republic, you can easily see the extensive length of the draped toga. Togas for this social class were made out of white wool and were quite heavy.

Michael Holford

Glimpses of Roman Life

AGRICULTURE AND COMMERCE

In the early days of Rome nearly every individual was a farmer; even later, farming remained the chief occupation of the Romans, as it once was in most countries. It is not surprising, therefore, that Cincinnatus left his plow to lead the Romans in war and on its successful completion returned to his farm. In the early days many wars were won by the "embattled farmers." Nor is it surprising that agriculture was considered the foundation of Roman life, and that the sturdy Roman character was largely shaped by the hard work on the farm.

At first farms were small and were worked by the owner and his family and perhaps, one or two slaves. The work in the fields was done with the use of simple tools and intensive hand labor. The increased use of slaves on the farm led to the decline of free labor, and the destruction of land by war in southern Italy led to larger farms and a change in the attitude toward farming. Managing a farm now often became the domain of wealthy landowners who could afford large tracts of land and the slaves to work them.

Pastoral scene of a sheepherder in a Roman mosaic from Antioch, Turkey, an important city during the Roman Empire.

Department of Art & Archeology, Princeton University

Industry was not so highly developed among the Romans as it is today. There were no large factories. Much of the work was done by hand either at home or in small shops which were often part of the home. The spinning of thread and its weaving into cloth were often done at home by women. Even the Emperor Augustus wore clothing made by his household slaves under the direction of his wife, Livia. There were carpenters, metalworkers, masons and bricklayers, toolmakers, wagonmakers, brickmakers, and so on employed in ancient Rome. The making of bricks, red-glazed pottery, copper and bronze utensils, and ironwork throughout Italy came nearest to being industry in the modern sense.

Erich Lessing/Art Resource, NY

A shopkeeper selling fresh vegetables supplied an important part of the family meal. Here you can plainly see that he has squashes, leeks, and several other varieties for sale.

The shops were very small, usually a room at the front of a private residence was used as a shop for goods made in the back rooms. The wares were often displayed outside the shops. Sometimes the shopkeepers cluttered up the sidewalks and streets so much that traffic was interfered with until some strict official prevented this practice—even as today.

The free workers of certain industries like potters, dyers, gold and coppersmiths, carpenters, and tanners were members of guilds or unions, whose chief purposes were to bring the members together for good fellowship and to provide burials for the members who died. Many slaves, too, were employed in industry.

Such were the occupations of the poorer classes. Rich men invested their money in wholesale trade, real estate, loans, government contracts, and foreign trade. Great profits could be made by buying from the government the right to collect the taxes in a province—everything collected over and above the cost of the contract went to the **publicanus** (tax collector). The professions, with the exception of law, the army, architecture, and public life, were not well developed. Doctors and teachers of all levels were usually slaves or poorly paid freedmen, i.e., former slaves. Law and politics were reserved largely for the upper classes, although both lawyers and politicians could not legally accept payment for their services.

QUESTIONS

1. What professions are highly respected today?
2. What percentage of people today are engaged in farming?
3. How does mass production better the life of the worker?

Unit X Review
LESSONS XLV-XLIX

Vocabulary

Nouns

aetās	mensis	sapientia
cōnsul	mulier	sermō
diēs	mūnus	speciēs
gēns	neglegentia	spēs
hospita	plēbs	tēlum
labor	prīnceps	urbs
lēgātus	rēs	vīs

Adjectives

ācer	difficilis	gravis	maximus
aeger	fīdus	iūstus	potēns
aliēnus	frīgidus	levis	similis
audax			

Verbs

ascendō	fallō	oportet	prohibeō
cōnsistō	haereō	opprimō	reddō
contendō	instō	ostendō	sentiō
dēpōnō	intellegō	placō	solvō
dēserō	nesciō		

Adverbs

bene iterum

Conjunction

sī

Prepositions

apud contrā

Grammar Summary

The Fifth Declension

Fifth declension nouns are relatively few but fairly important. They are characterized by the letter **e**.

Decimō diē hostēs vicimus.	*On the tenth day, we conquered the enemy.*
Est spēs nobīs in provinciīs.	*There is hope for us in the provinces.*

The Third Person Reflexive Adjective

The third person reflexive adjective is **suus, –a, –um.** It is translated as *his, her, its, their* (own). Because it is a reflexive, it must refer to the subject. If it does not, use **eius**.

Matrem suam in forō vīdit.	*She saw her (own) mother in the Forum.*
Matrem eius in forō vīdit.	*She saw her (someone else's) mother in the Forum.*

The Present Participle

The present participle is formed, for first and second conjugations, by adding **–ns** to the present stem; for third and fourth conjugations by adding **–ens** and for third conjugation **–iō** by adding **–iens** to the present stem. It is declined like a one-ending third declension adjective with **–ntis** as the genitive.

Unit X Review
LESSONS XLV-XLIX

Audiēns hoc, excēdere cupīvī.	*Hearing this, I wanted to leave.*
Līberōs ludentes in viā vīdī.	*I saw the children playing in the street.*

The Future Active Participle

The future active participle is formed by adding **–ūrus, –ūra, –ūrum** to the stem of the fourth principal part. Like all participles, it agrees with the noun it modifies in gender, number, and case.

Rex verba actūrus est.	*The king is about to make a speech.*
Ad hanc urbem perventūrī sunt.	*They are going to arrive at this city.*

The Perfect Active Infinitive

The perfect active infinitive is formed by adding **–isse** to the perfect stem.

dedisse	*to have given*
iēcisse	*to have thrown*

The Perfect Passive Infinitive

The perfect passive infinitive is the fourth principal part plus **esse**.

fractus, –a,–um esse	*to have been broken*
prohibitus, –a, –um esse	*to have been prevented*

The Future Active Infinitive

The future active infinitive is formed by adding **–urus, –ura, –urum** to the stem of the fourth principal part, plus **esse**.

captūrus, –a, –um esse	*to be going to take*
laudātūrus, –a, –um esse	*to be about to praise*

Direct and Indirect Statement

A direct statement quotes a person's words directly. An indirect statement is a report of someone's words. In English, after verbs of thinking, saying, knowing, perceiving, etc., a clause often introduced by *that* is used. In Latin, an infinitive phrase is used instead of a clause. The subject of the infinitive is in the accusative.

Dicit, "Amīcus meus tē vocat."	*He says, "My friend is calling you."*
Dicit amīcum meum tē vocāre.	*He says that my friend is calling you.*

How the Indicative and Infinitive Differ in Tense

Indicative tenses are determined by their relation to present time: something is happening, has happened, or is going to happen. Infinitive tenses are determined by the main verb, and whether the infinitive action is going on at the same time, time before, or time after that main verb.

Unit X Review
LESSONS XLV-XLIX

Intellegō Annam adesse.	*I understand that Anna is here.*
Intellēgī Annam adfuisse.	*I understood that Anna had been here.*
Intellegō Annam adfuturam esse.	*I understand that Anna will be here.*
Intellēgī Annam adesse.	*I understood that Anna was here.*

Unit Practice

Oral Form Drill

1. Decline **vōx ipsa, nūllus pēs, hic mēnsis**.
2. Give in all tenses the third plural active of **timeō;** the third singular passive of **opprimō.**
3. Form the participles, active and passive, of **regō, iaciō, sciō,** and **respondeō.**
4. Form the infinitives, active and passive, of **sentiō, intercipiō, ostendō,** and **mōnstrō.**

Ancient Roman fresco of a funeral dance of women, now in a museum in Naples. Such rhythmic movements can still be seen in the communal folk dancing of the Mediterranean world.

Scala/Art Resource, NY

Unit X Review

LESSONS XLV-XLIX

Exercises

A. Translate the words in italics into Latin. Be careful to make the participle agree with its noun in gender, number, and case.

1. *Running* water is usually fresh.
2. We saw the boys *dragging* a big sled.
3. They heard the sound of men *approaching*.
4. Are they *going to remain* in this country?
5. She was *going to say* something to her friend.
6. He forgot to mail the letter *after he had folded* it.
7. *When he had heard these words,* he felt encouraged.

B. Complete in Latin these indirect statements and then translate the sentences into English.

1. Sciō (*the boys are reading*) librōs.
2. Spērō (*the boys will read*) librōs.
3. Putō (*the boys have read*) librōs.
4. Dīxit (*the books were being read*) ā puerīs.
5. Dīxit (*the books had been read*) ā puerīs.

C. What occupation would you like to have when you graduate from high school or college? Write a short paragraph stating what you want to be, what you will do in that occupation, and why. Some occupations you might like to choose and discuss are **magister, medicus, iurisconsultus** (lawyer), **vir/fēmina reīpūblicae perītus** (politician), **physicus** (scientist), **auctor, poēta, negōtiator** (business person), **artifex** (artist), **pictor** (painter), **agricola, nauta, miles,** etc.

Word Studies

1. Explain the following and give the Latin words from which they are derived: *omnipotent, alienate, vocal, expulsive, oppressive, diction, ostensible, prohibit.*
2. Find and use in sentences as many English derivatives as possible from **dīcō** and **putō.**
3. The first word in each of the following lines is a Latin word. From among the last five words in each line pick the one which is an English derivative of the first word.

scit	*skit*	*sky*	*sigh*
	scientific	*sit*	
tangō	*tangerine*	*tang*	*intangible*
	tango	*tactics*	
putātus	*putty*	*put*	*repute*
	potato	*pot*	
dīcere	*contradict*	*dixie*	*dice*
	decree	*decent*	
gravia	*graft*	*graveyard*	*gravity*
	engrave	*gray*	

Alinari/Art Resource, NY

Unit XI

Greek Myths and Roman History

Although the Romans had their own stories and traditions surrounding their gods, many stories were also borrowed or adapted from the Greek. In this scene, Perseus is seen slaying the dragon that threatens Andromeda, an Ethiopian princess whose mother had boasted that Andromeda was more beautiful than the Nereids. This enraged Neptune, who sent a sea monster to ravage Ethiopia. The only recourse was to sacrifice Andromeda, so she was chained to a cliff. Perseus saw her, rescued her, and killed the monster, who was then turned into the world's first coral.

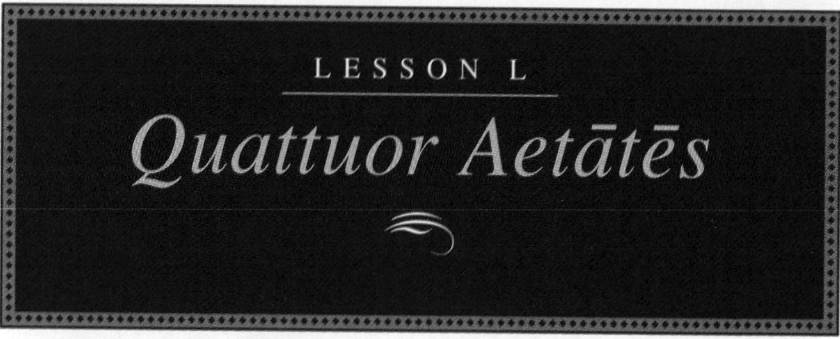

Antīquī dīxērunt prīmam aetātem esse auream. Sāturnus erat rēx deōrum hominumque. Illō tempore poenae lēgēsque aberant, quod omnēs hominēs iūstī erant. Nūllae nāvēs in marī erant, nec trāns mare lātum hominēs nāvigābant. Bellum numquam erat nec mīlitēs et arma. In ōtiō vītam hominēs agēbant, nam omnēs terrae concordiā et pāce ligātae sunt. Hominēs in agrīs nōn labōrābant; terra nōn culta ipsa frūmentum et omnia ūtilia dabat. Urbēs nōn erant. Neque hiems neque aestās erat: semper erat vēr. Flūmina lactis et vīnī erant. Quod omnēs agrī commūnēs erant, terminī agrōrum nōn erant. Aliēnōs agrōs hominēs nōn cupiēbant.

Sāturnō expulsō, Iuppiter rēx erat. Nunc incipit secunda aetās, quae ex argentō est, dūrior quam prīma, grātior tamen quam tertia. Tum aestās et hiems esse incipiunt; quattuor sunt tempora annī. Tum prīmum in agrīs labōrāre hominēs incipiunt.

Tertia aetās ex aere est. Dūrior est quam secunda.

Quārta aetās, quae ex ferrō est, dūrissima omnium est. Poenae gravissimae statuuntur, sed hominēs interficiunt et rapiunt. Nautae in omnī marī ad ultima loca nāvigant et ūtilia petunt quae in variīs terrīs continentur. Bellīs numquam intermissīs, hominēs terrās aliēnās vincere mātūrant. Nihil sacrum est; omnia rapiuntur. Hominēs in agrīs labōrant; nam labor omnia vincit.

Haec dīcunt auctōrēs clārissimī Graecī dē quattuor aetātibus. Vergilius,[1] poēta Rōmānus, putābat iterum aetātem auream futūram esse. Etiam nunc multī putant vītam semper grātiōrem futūram esse. Putātisne fortasse condiciōnem fortūnamque populōrum antīquōrum meliōrem[2] fuisse quam condiciōnem nostram? Quō modō statuistis hanc sententiam vēriōrem esse? Quae erit condiciō hominum post mīlle annōs? Aliī dīcunt: "Tempora mūtantur, et nōs mūtāmur in illīs." Aliī respondent hominēs semper eōsdem fuisse et futūrōs esse. Quae est sententia vestra? Possuntne fortasse ambae sententiae vērae esse?

[1] *Vergil*
[2] *better*

QUESTIONS

1. Why didn't men work in the Golden Age?
2. When did they begin?
3. When did crime begin?

Grammar

Comparison of Adjectives

Adjectives change form to show *degree*. This is called *comparison*. There are three degrees: *positive, comparative, superlative*. The positive is the simple form of the adjective; the others indicate a greater degree. To *compare* an adjective is to give the three degrees.

In Latin, the comparative is formed by adding **–ior** (*m.* and *f.*), **–ius** (*n.*) to the base of the positive. The superlative is formed by adding **–issimus, –a, –um.**

POSITIVE	COMPARATIVE	SUPERLATIVE
altus, –a, –um, *high*	**altior, altius,** *higher*	**altissimus, –a,–um,** *highest*
fortis, –e, *brave*	**fortior, fortius,** *braver*	**fortissimus, –a, –um,** *bravest*

In this woodcut from an edition of Ovid in 1501, Prometheus creates man out of clay and sends him fire. Thus the Golden Age was born. The Silver Age is shown by men working in the fields and building homes. Fighting started in the Bronze Age but became worse in the Iron Age, when ships began putting to sea.

Metropolitan Museum of Art, Rogers Fund, 1922 (22.16).

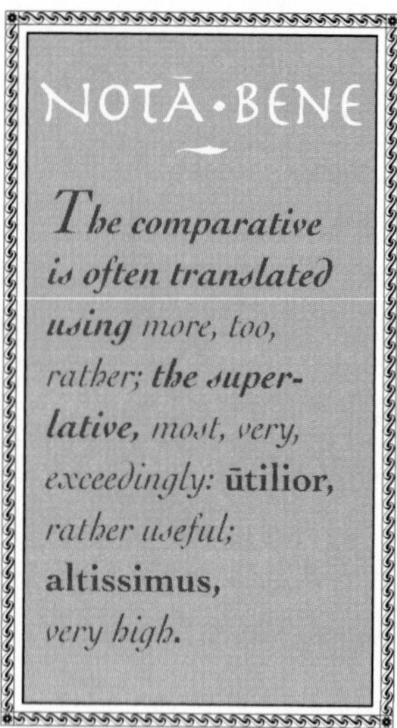

NOTĀ·BENE

The comparative is often translated using more, too, rather; the superlative, most, very, exceedingly: **ūtilior,** *rather useful;* **altissimus,** *very high.*

The Art Museum, Princeton University. Bequest of Dan Fellows Platt.

This sketch of the Age of Iron by Pietro da Cortona shows how far man has fallen from the height of the Golden Age.

Adjectives are declined as follows in the comparative. Note that although comparatives are declined like adjectives of the third declension, they do not have **–ī** in the abl. sing., **–ium** in the gen. plur., or **–ia** in the nom. and acc. plur. neuter; thus, comparatives are *not* **i**–stems.

	SINGULAR		PLURAL	
	M, F	N	M, F	N
Nom.	altior	altius	altiōrēs	altiōra
Gen.	altiōris	altiōris	altiōrum	altiōrum
Dat.	altiōrī	altiōrī	altiōribus	altiōribus
Acc.	altiōrem	altius	altiōrēs	altiōra
Abl.	altiōre	altiōre	altiōribus	altiōribus

In Latin, when two things are compared, you use **quam** *(than),* and put both things in the same case.

Fortiōrem virum quam illum nōn vīdī.	*I have not seen a braver man than he* (*is*).
Hic mons est altior quam ille.	*This mountain is higher than that.*

ORAL PRACTICE

1. Compare **grātus, nōbilis, clārus, levis, longus.**
2. Decline **tardus** in the comparative.
3. Decline **supplicium iūstius.**

EXERCISES

A. Translate the following sentences into good English.

1. Novissimum librum ad frātrem meum mittere constituī.
2. Quid est ūtilius grātiusque quam librōs bonōs semper legere?
3. Gallī vīribus corporis Rōmānōs superābant sed nōn erant fortiōrēs virī.
4. Condiciōnēs pācis ab hostibus victīs semper dūrissimae esse habentur.
5. Homō dē viīs mē rogāvit; ego respondī hanc esse plāniōrem quam illam.
6. Eī duo itinera ostendimus—alterum facile, alterum longius et incertius.

B. Translate the following sentences into Latin.

1. Nothing is more useful than water.
2. Why are not the rivers of Italy very long?
3. Does peace have nobler victories than war?
4. I know that that river is swift but not very wide.
5. More severe terms of peace than these will be determined.

C. The ancients described four ages: gold, silver, bronze, and iron. How would you describe the age you are living in now? Do your parents work? Do you work? Do you and your family eat well? Do you enjoy sufficient leisure? Work with a partner to write a short paragraph describing the age you feel you are living in and why. Then compare your description with the evaluations of other groups.

Latin for American Students

*Did you know that the Romans knew of only eight metals: copper, gold, iron, lead, mercury, silver, tin, and zinc? Gold was as highly valued by the Romans as it is today and was used for jewelry and coins (**aureus** and **solidus**); iron was used to make axes, chains, scissors, razors, knives, javelins, darts, stakes, nails, styli, and swords; lead was used in the construction of water pipes and bullets; silver was used to make jewelry, serving dishes, and coins (**denarius** and **sestertius**).*

Scala/Art Resource, NY

*During the Empire, gold coins (the **aureus**) were used which usually carried the head of the emperor on the obverse. Military conquests, political events, and the great monuments were often depicted on the reverse.*

Vocabulary

Nouns

aes, aeris, *n. copper, bronze*
argentum, -ī, *n. silver* (argent)
condiciō, condiciōnis, *f. condition, terms* (conditional, conditioned)
ferrum, -i, *n. iron* (ferrous)
lac, lactis, *n. milk* (lactic, lactose)

Adjectives

ambo, -ae, -o,[1] *both* (ambidextrous, ambivalent)
quartus, -a, -um, *fourth* (quarter, quartile)
ūtilis, -e, *useful* (utilitarian, utility)

Verbs

constituō, constituere, constituī, constitūtus, *determine, decide* (constitute, reconstitute)
rapiō, rapere, rapuī, raptus, *carry off, steal* (rapacious, rapacity)
statuō, statuere, statuī, statūtus, *establish, determine, arrange*

Conjunction

quam, *than*

Word Studies

1. Give the Latin words suggested by the following English derivatives: *accident, appropriate, conditional, conspicuous, credible, fallacious, instructive, opera, proximity, rapture, regional, redemptive, repulsive, centipede, millipede.*
2. From your knowledge of Latin rearrange these French numerals in the proper sequence: *trois, sept, un, cinq, quatre, dix, huit, neuf, deux, six.*
3. Find and use in sentences as many English derivatives as possible from **nāvigō, doceō, vincō, sūmō.**
4. Complete each of the following analogies as in this example: **Perficiō** is to *perfection* as **incipiō** is to *inception.*
   a. **Emō** is to *redemption* as __?__ is to *repulsion.*
   b. *Creditor* is to **crēdō** as *instructor* is to __?__.
   c. **Ūtilis** is to *utility* as __?__ is to *humility.*
   d. *Statute* is to **statuō** as *institute* is to __?__.
   e. *Consistency* is to **cōnsistō** as __?__ is to **currō.**

[1] declined like **duo, duae, duo**

Iuppiter et Mercurius per Phrygiam, quae in Asiā est, iter fēcērunt, sed nēmō in tōtā illā gente eōs cognōvit. Omnēs iūdicāvērunt eōs esse hominēs humilēs quod vestēs miserās gerēbant. Ad mīlle casās accessērunt; nam locum somnō aptum petīvērunt. Sed omnēs, hīs vīsīs, casās celeriter clausērunt. In tōtā regiōne ācriter repulsī sunt. Tamen ūna casa, parva et humilis, eōs nōn reppulit. Ibi Baucis et Philēmōn[1] multōs annōs ēgerant. Condiciōne humilī nōn affectī, paupertātem leviter ac fortiter sustinuērunt. Duo tōta domus fuērunt, et dominī et servī ipsī; nam nūllōs servōs habuērunt.

[1] *Baucis* (*Bau´sis*), *Philē´mon*

Cēnam humilem Baucis magnā dīligentiā celeritāteque parāvit; numquam celerius labōrāverat. Tum, omnibus īnstrūctīs, deōs ad cēnam vocāvit. Mēnsa, nōn pulchra sed ūtilis, paucīs sed bonīs cibīs īnstrūcta erat. Vīnum sumēbant, sed semper crāter vīnum continēbat. Tum Philēmōn et Baucis, ad mēnsam sedentēs, clārē sēnsērunt deōs adesse. Tum Iuppiter, "Deī sumus," inquit. "Tōtam hanc gentem poenam solūtūram esse statuimus, quod nēmō nōbīs auxilium dedit, sed vōs vīvētis. Ad montem prōcēdēmus." Itaque Baucis et Philēmōn, hāc ōrātiōne permōtī, ad montem tardē prōcessērunt. Ibi cōnstitērunt et vīdērunt tōtam regiōnem sub aquā esse, casam suam sōlam manēre. Dum spectant, casa eōrum in pulchrum templum vertitur.

Tum Iuppiter, "Quid cupitis?" inquit; "id quod petitis dōnābō." Philēmōn, uxōre cōnsultā, respondit: "Iūdicāmus nūllum mūnus nōbīs grātius aptiusque esse quam esse sacerdōtēs illīus templī et ē vītā eōdem tempore excēdere, quod in concordiā multōs annōs ēgimus." Post hanc ōrātiōnem hoc mūnus Iuppiter eīs permīsit.

Post multōs annōs, Philēmōn et uxor, aetāte gravēs, ante sacrum templum stābant. Corpora eōrum in arborēs tardē vertī incipiunt; vōcēs haerent; nōn iam spīrant nec vīvunt. Neuter ante alterum ē vītā excessit. Multōs annōs hae duae arborēs ante templum stābant.

QUESTIONS

1. What was Jupiter looking for?
2. Why did it take so long to find it?
3. How did Philemon find out that his guests were gods?

NOTĀ·BENE

Note that in the comparative degree the adverb always has the same form as the neuter accusative singular of the comparative adjective.

Casa humilis deos non reppulit. Philemon and Baucis recognize their visitor as Jupiter. Mercury looks on.

Grammar

Formation and Comparison of Adverbs

You may recall that adverbs formed from adjectives of the first and second declensions add **–e** to the base. Adverbs formed from adjectives of the third declension generally add **–iter** to the base.

fortis	*brave*	**fortiter**	*bravely*
acer	*sharp*	**acriter**	*sharply*

The comparison of adverbs is very similar to that of adjectives:

POSITIVE	COMPARATIVE	SUPERLATIVE
altē	**altius**	**altissimē**
fortiter	**fortius**	**fortissimē**

Giraudon/Art Resource, NY

ORAL PRACTICE

Form and compare adverbs from the following adjectives: **longus, ūtilis, levis, clārus, firmus, gravis, vērus.**

EXERCISES

A. Translate the following sentences into good English.

1. Sciō hoc flūmen esse longius quam illud.
2. Pater meus omnia iūstē et celeriter iūdicat.
3. Praemiō acceptō, magister ōrātiōne aptā respondit.
4. Hī mīlitēs, ē castrīs ēductī, ad pugnam ā duce īnstruuntur.
5. Tardius pervēnimus quod reliquī puerī celerius cucurrērunt.
6. Hī hominēs, ab hostibus repulsī, in pāce vīvere statuērunt.

B. Translate the following sentences into Latin.

1. We shall breathe more easily.
2. No one approves a very long speech.
3. The battle was sharply fought, but few men received severe wounds.
4. We certainly hope that all nations will live in peace, (now that it has been) established.

C. There are several parallels between the ancient story of Baucis and Philemon and the modern story, *Beauty and the Beast*. Work with a partner or in a small group to retell the latter fairy tale in Latin. Use familiar vocabulary and structures, even if it means somewhat manipulating the words. You may find the following words helpful.

bēlua, -ae, *f. beast*
mendica, -ae, *f. beggar (woman)*
rosa, -ae, *f. rose*
timor, ōris, *m. fear*
horribilis, -e, *horrible*
tristis, -e, *sad*

Vocabulary

Nouns

arbor, arboris, *m. tree*	(arboreal, arboretum)
crātēr, crātēris, *m. large bowl*	(crater)
nēmo, (dat.) **nēminī,** (acc.) **nēminem** (no other forms), *no one*	
ōrātiō, ōrātiōnis, *f. speech*	(oration, oratory)
paupertās, paupertātis, *f. poverty, humble circumstances*	(pauper)
regiō, regiōnis, *f. region*	(regional, regionalism)
sacerdōs, sacerdōtis, *m. + f. priest, priestess*	(sacerdotal)

Philemon et Baucis, aetate graves, ante sacrum templum stabant. Corpora eorum in arbores vertuntur. A woodcut from an edition of Ovid, 1563.

Getty Center, Resource Collections

Adjectives

aptus, -a, -um, *fit, suitable* (+ dat.) (adapt, adept)
humilis, -e, *low, humble* (humiliate, humility)

Verbs

instruō, instruere, instruxī, instructus, *arrange, provide* (instruction, instructor)
iūdicō, iūdicāre, iūdicāvī, iūdicātus, *judge* (adjudicate, judicial)
repellō, repellere, reppulī, repulsus, *drive back, repulse* (repel, repulsive)
vīvō, vīvere, vīxī, vīctus, *be alive, live* (victuals, vivid)

Latin for American Students

Did you know that the rose was among the favorite flowers of the Romans? Other popular garden flowers included lilies and violets. The conventional garden features of Roman villas were terraces; bordered walks; colonnades and hedges of scented shrubs like rosemary, myrtle and laurel; rows of statues; aviaries and fish ponds. Grapevines were trained to grow over trellises or arbors while ivy hid foundations and retaining walls.

Word Studies

Ne– is sometimes used as a negative prefix in Latin: **nēmō (ne–homō), negōtium (ne–ōtium), neuter (ne–uter), nūllus (ne–ūlus)**. We do the same thing in English with *no: nothing, none (no-one), neither (no-either).*

Circum, contrā, prae, and **super** have their usual meanings when used as prefixes in Latin and English. In English **prae** becomes *pre–*, as *pre–pare, pre–fix;* **contrā** sometimes retains its form, sometimes becomes *counter–,* as *contra-dict, counter-act.* **Super** sometimes becomes *sur–* in English, in which form it must be distinguished from assimilated **sub:** *surplus, surmount* **(super),** but *surreptitious* **(sub).**

Find ten English words with these prefixes, compounded with Latin words which you have studied. Explain *intelligence, supervisor, surplus, precedent;* also *treason* and *tradition,* which are doublets derived from **trādō.**

TREASON

LESSON LII

Daedalus et Īcarus

In īnsulā magnā Crētā Mīnōs[1] fuit rēx. Daedalus[2] cum fīliō parvō Īcarō[2] ibi captīvus fuit. Fugere nōn potuit quod mare prohibuit. “Neque per terram,” inquit, “neque per mare fugere possum, sed caelum certē nōn clauditur. Illā viā difficillimā prōcēdēmus.” Itaque ālās parāvit, simillimās ālīs vērīs avium. Partēs ālārum cērā ligāvit. Īcarus ad patrem stābat, ālās levissimās tangēbat, opus patris impediēbat. Tandem fīnis labōris difficilis aderat; ālae parātae erant. Daedalus tempus aptum esse iūdicāvit. Tum ālās corporī fīlī iūnxit et eum hīs verbīs ācriter monuit:

“In mediō caelō prōcēdēmus; nam, sī humilius volābimus, undae ālās graviōrēs facient; sī altius volābimus, ignis ālās ūret et in mare cadēs. Omnia nunc tibi explicābō.”

Tum omnēs partēs ālārum fīliō ostendit et omnia in ōrdine explicāvit. Perīculum esse sēnsit et fīliō timuit, quī patrī dissimillimus erat. Ālīs propriīs īnstrūctus antecessit et fīlium post volāre iussit.

Agricolae territī ex agrīs eōs vīdērunt; multī putāvērunt eōs deōs aut deīs similēs esse. Celerrimē pater fīliusque āera ālīs pepulērunt.

Multās regiōnēs multāsque gentēs relīquērunt. Tum puer nōn iam timidus patrem ducem relīquit. Ōrātiōnem patris memoriā nōn tenuit et altius volāvit quod iūdicāvit nihil accidere posse. Sed multa accidērunt: celeriter sōl cēram solvit; nōn iam ālae haesērunt. Praeceps puer miser in mare cecidit; nōn iam vīvit. Ab illō posteā hoc mare nōmen proprium “Īcarium” accēpit.

Interim pater, nōn iam pater, in omnibus regiōnibus fīlium petīvit, nōmen fīlī clāmāvit. Tandem ālās Īcarī in undīs vīdit sed corpus eius numquam invēnit.

Tum ipse ad Siciliam facile pervēnit et ibi multōs annōs ēgit. Sed fābula ab aliīs dicta huic dissimilis est: scrībunt eum in Italiam volāvisse et ibi in templō ālās posuisse. Hōc modō deīs prō salūte grātiās ēgit.

Prīmus omnium hominum Daedalus, Nātūrā victā, per caelum lātum volāvit, sī auctōrēs Graecī et Rōmānī vērum dīxērunt. Nunc multī hominēs facile volant, etiam per immēnsum,[3] sed nēmō ālīs propriīs. Quid hominibus difficilius est?

[1] *Mī´nos* (nom. sing.)
[2] *Daedalus (Dĕd´alus), Ic´arus*
[3] *the immeasurable*, i.e., *space*

Ronald Sheridan/Ancient Art & Architecture Collection

The boy Icarus watches confidently as his father Daedalus anxiously stitches the feathers to his arm. A statue in Venice by the Italian sculptor Antonio Canova (1757-1822).

QUESTIONS

1. In what way did Icarus disobey his father?
2. Where did Daedalus land?

Grammar

Comparison of –er Adjectives and Their Adverbs

The superlative of all adjectives ending in **–er** is formed by adding **–rimus, –a, –um** to the nominative singular masculine of the positive:

POSITIVE	COMPARATIVE	SUPERLATIVE
līber, lībera, līberum	**līberior, līberius**	**līberrimus, –a, –um**
ācer, ācris, ācre	**ācrior, ācrius**	**ācerrimus, –a, –um**
celer, celeris, celere	**celerior, celerius**	**celerrimus, –a, –um**

The corresponding adverbs are compared as follows:

POSITIVE	COMPARATIVE	SUPERLATIVE
līberē	**līberius**	**līberrimē**
ācriter	**ācrius**	**ācerrimē**
celeriter	**celerius**	**celerrimē**

NOTĀ·BENE

The superlative of other –lis *adjectives, such as* nōbilis, –e, ūtilis, –e, *etc., is formed regularly—i.e., by adding* –issimus *to the base of the positive:* nōbil–issimus, –a, –um.

The adverbs formed from these adjectives are generally formed regularly, but the adverb from facilis *is* facile. *In the superlative, the corresponding adverbs end in* –ē: facillimē.

Quam is used with the superlative adverb to express *as ... as possible.*

quam celerrime	*as quickly as possible*
quam audacissimē	*as boldly as possible*

ORAL PRACTICE

1. Compare the adjectives **miser, pulcher, altus.** Form and compare the corresponding adverbs.
2. Decline **illa līberior patria.**

Adjectives with Superlative in –limus

The superlative of five adjectives ending in **–lis** is formed by adding **–limus, –a, –um** to the base of the positive. The comparatives are regular.

POSITIVE	COMPARATIVE	SUPERLATIVE
facilis, –e	**facilior, facilius**	**facillimus, –a, –um**
difficilis, –e	**difficilior, difficilius**	**difficillimus, –a, –um**
similis, –e	**similior, similius**	**simillimus, –a, –um**
dissimilis, –e	**dissimilior, dissimilius**	**dissimillimus, –a, –um**
humilis, –e	**humilior, humilius**	**humillimus, –a, –um**

Dative with Adjectives

The dative case is often used with Latin adjectives whose English equivalents are followed by *to.* You are already familiar with many of them: **amīcus, inimīcus, similis, dissimilis, aptus, grātus.**

Hic liber est similis illī.	*This book is similar to that.*
Ille homō est frātrī meo inimīcus.	*That man is unfriendly to my brother.*

EXERCISES

A. Translate the following sentences into good English.

1. Hic equus similior meō est quam ille.
2. Rōmānōrum deī dissimillimī aliīs deīs erant.
3. Ille liber difficillimus est, nam pauca clārē explicat.
4. Humilis homō nec altē cadere nec graviter potest.
5. Nihil est nōbīs ūtilius quam bonus liber; nam est nōbilissimus amīcōrum.

B. Translate the following sentences into Latin.

1. This region is fit for some settlers, but not for others.
2. As the bad men approached, the boys ran more quickly.
3. The places in which our soldiers fell are most sacred.
4. The teacher, in a very beautiful speech, unfolded the life of Caesar.

C. Many of the Greek and Roman myths are meant to explain a practice, belief, phenomenon, or a world view of a culture. Work with a partner to write a short paragraph explaining the moral behind the Daedalus and Icarus story. Why is it important? Why do you think it became part of historical legend?

Ray Matthews

Praeceps puer miser in mare cecidit. Icarus on the door of the Wright brothers' memorial at Kitty Hawk, N.C., honoring their first airplane flight in 1903.

Vocabulary

Nouns

āēr, āeris, *m. air*	(aerate, aerial)
āla, -ae, *f. wing*	(aisle, alate)
avis, avis, *f. bird*	(avian, aviary)
ignis, ignis, *m. fire*	(igneous, ignite)
opus, operis, *n. work, labor*	(cooperate, operation)

Adjectives

dissimilis, -e, *unlike*	(dissimilar, dissimilate)
proprius, -a, -um, *(one's) own*	(appropriate, proprietary)

Verbs

accidō, accidere, accidī, —, *fall to, befall, happen* (+ dat.) (accident, accidental)

cadō, cadere, cecidī, cāsūrus, *fall* (cadence, casualty)

explicō, explicāre, explicāvī, explicātus, *unfold, explain* (explicate, explicit)

iungō, iungere, iunxī, iunctus, *join (to)* (joint, junction)

ūro, ūrere, ussī, ustus, *burn*

volō, volāre, volāvī, volātus, *fly* (volatile, volley)

Latin for American Students

Did you know that most Romans memorized the Twelve Tables of the Law as students? This important law code was inscribed on bronze tablets which were displayed in the Roman Forum. Only a few of the tablets have been preserved and no fragments of the ninth and tenth tablets have been discovered. Each tablet contained a number of laws regulating the punishment of debtors, the gathering of fallen fruit, the power of a father over his sons, and the establishment of the interest rate, etc.

Word Studies

Lawyers use so many Latin phrases daily that they must be familiar with Latin. A few such phrases are:

subpoena, a summons to court *under penalty* for failure to attend

in propria persona, *in one's own person* (not through someone else)

ex post facto, *resulting after the fact;* as a law which makes punishable acts committed before its passage

in forma pauperis, *in the form* (or *manner*) *of a poor man;* to sue as a poor man and so avoid the costs of the suit

Look through the court records and legal items in the newspapers for other Latin phrases.

Rōmānī, quī erant optimī mīlitēs, gentēs quae proximae urbī erant vīcerant et in ulteriōrēs partēs Italiae pervēnerant. Summā virtūte contrā maiōrem numerum hostium in extrēmīs ac difficillimīs regiōnibus Italiae bene pugnāverant. Posteā bellum novī generis, dissimile aliīs, cum Pyrrhō, duce summō et rēge maximō Ēpīrī, gessērunt.

Pyrrhus in Italiam īnferiōrem ā Tarentīnīs, gente pessimā, vocātus erat, quī eō tempore cum Rōmānīs pugnābant. Is in Italiam mīlitēs trānsportāvit et elephantōrum auxiliō Rōmānōs fortiter pugnantēs reppulit, quod Rōmānī elephantōs maximōs nōn ante vīsōs timuērunt. Peius tamen Pyrrhō victōrī quam victīs Rōmānīs accidit, nam plūrimī mīlitēs Pyrrhī cecidērunt. Pyrrhus, ubi plūrima corpora Rōmānōrum interfectōrum in fronte vulnera habēre vīdit, haec verba fēcit: "Bene Rōmānī pugnāvērunt. Cum tālibus[1] mīlitibus tōtus orbis facillimē ā mē vincī potest!" Familiāribus dē victōriā agentibus dīxit: "Sī iterum eōdem modō vīcerō, nūllōs mīlitēs ex Italiā īnferiōre in Ēpīrum redūcam." Nam hanc victōriam nōn ūtilem esse iūdicāvit quod plūrēs mīlitēs āmīserat.

[1] *such*

QUESTIONS

1. What was the cause of Pyrrhus' victories?
2. What is a Pyrrhic victory?

Latin for American Students

Did you know that the Romans had many customs involving the celebration of victory and peace? The ***laurea*** *was a wreath of laurel which was worn by victorious Roman generals. The victorious Roman admiral was often presented with a* ***corona classica*** *or crown of victory for his naval successes. To the Roman sailor who first boarded a captured enemy ship, a* ***corona navalis*** *was presented. Then, as now, the olive branch was a symbol of peace.*

Grammar

The Comparison of Irregular Adjectives

In Latin, the following adjectives are compared irregularly and should be memorized:

POSITIVE	COMPARATIVE	SUPERLATIVE
bonus, –a, –um	**melior, melius**	**optimus, –a, –um**
(*good*)	(*better*)	(*best*)
malus, –a, –um	**peior, peius**	**pessimus, –a, –um**
(*bad*)	(*worse*)	(*worst*)
magnus, –a, –um	**maior, maius**	**maximus, –a, –um**
(*large*)	(*larger*)	(*largest*)
parvus, –a, –um	**minor, minus**	**minimus, –a, –um**
(*small*)	(*smaller*)	(*smallest*)
multus, –a, –um	**—, plūs**[1]	**plūrimus, –a, –um**
(*much*)	(*more*)	(*most*)

Even elephants were used in battle. How many different weapons do you see depicted here? Notice the strips of metal attached to the chariot axles to prevent anyone from coming too close.

The adverbs formed from the preceding adjectives are compared, in general, according to this rule: Comparative adverbs are the same as the neuter comparative adjectives; the superlatives change the **–us** to **–ē.** Exceptions, such as **bene,** are noted in the vocabularies.

North Wind Picture Archives

[1] Gen. **plūris;** neuter sing. only; no dative singular at all. The plural is **plūrēs, plūra,** *gen.* **plūrium,** etc.

A few adjectives are lacking one of the three degrees.

POSITIVE	COMPARATIVE	SUPERLATIVE
—	**exterior, exterius** *(outer)*	**extrēmus, –a, –um** *(outermost, end of)*
—	**interior, interius** *(inner)*	**intimus, –a, –um** *(inmost)*
—	**superior, superius** *(higher)*	**summus, –a, –um** *(highest, top of)*
—	**īnferior, īnferius** *(lower)*	**īnfimus, –a, –um** *(lowest, bottom of)*
—	**propior, propius** *(nearer)*	**proximus, –a, –um** *(nearest, next)*
—	**ulterior, ulterius** *(farther)*	**ultimus, –a, –um** *(farthest)*
multus, –a, –um *(much)*	—	**plurimus, –a, –um** *(most)*
senex, *(gen.)* **senis** *(old)*	**senior, —**[2] *(older)*	—

ORAL PRACTICE

Give the Latin for: *more horses, the oldest city, more water, the farthest land, the end of the speech, the highest mountain, the lower field.*

EXERCISES

A. Translate the following sentences into good English.

1. Puerī puellaeque ad īnferiōrem partem flūminis quam celerrimē ambulant.
2. Optimī cīvēs patriam semper optimē dēfendent.
3. Summus mōns ā nōbīs facillime occupātus est.
4. Pessimī hominēs in ultimās regiōnēs mittī dēbent.
5. Hī septem puerī territī sunt quod perīculum maximum esse sēnsērunt.
6. Agricolae quī meliōrēs agrōs habent maiōrem cōpiam frūmentī habēbunt.
7. Nōnne spērās proximum mēnsem nōn futūrum esse dūriōrem quam hunc?

B. Translate the following sentences into Latin.

1. The smallest dog is not the worst.
2. Can a horse run more swiftly than a man?
3. The smaller man fought more bravely than the larger.
4. We shall do this as well as possible and as quickly as possible without your aid.

[2] **Senex** is masculine only. It is not an **i**–stem.

Soldiers wore helmets and carried a shield with one hand while gripping their ***gladius*** *in the other for hand-to-hand combat.*

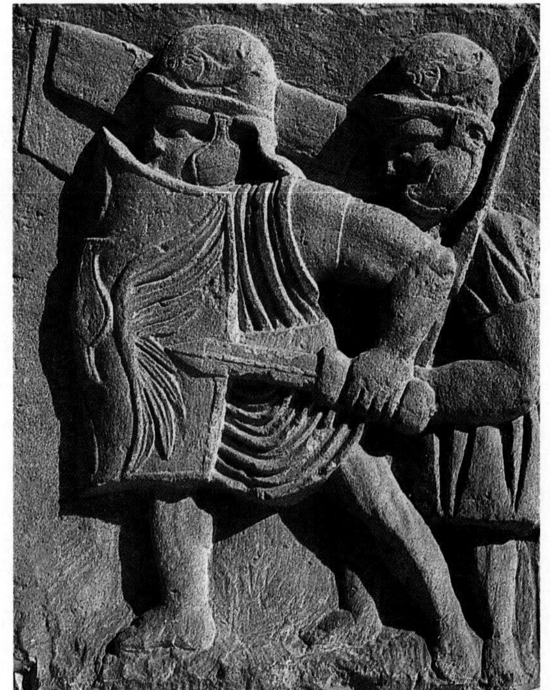

Erich Lessing/Art Resource, NY

C. A Pyrrhic victory is a victory won at extreme personal, financial, and/or social costs. Work with a partner and think of a scenario that might be an example of a Pyrrhic victory and briefly summarize it, or write a short dialogue about it. The following are some ideas, but feel free to invent from your own experiences.

1. You wanted to go away for a weekend but you first had to finish some school projects. As a result, you were so tired that you just wanted to sleep.
2. You wanted to buy a fashionable article of clothing but by the time you had earned enough money, it was no longer in fashion.
3. You wanted to spend a weekend away with your friend and his or her family; your parents did not want you to go for some reason. Finally they agree, after you make many promises, but then your friend gets sick and the trip has to be canceled.

Vocabulary

In addition to the following words, you should learn the comparisons and meanings of the irregular adjectives given in this lesson.

Nouns

frons, frontis, *f. front, forehead* (frontal)
orbis, orbis, *m. world, circle, ring* (orb, orbicular)
victor, victōris, *m. conqueror, victor* (victorious)

Word Studies

1. A number of English words preserve the forms of the comparative and superlative of Latin irregular adjectives: *major* (cf. *mayor*), *maximum, minor, minus, minimum, plus, inferior, superior, ulterior, prior, anterior, posterior, interior, exterior, junior, senior.*
   What is the difference between a *majority* and a *plurality* vote? Between a *majority* and a *minority* report?
2. Here are some Latin phrases in English:
   excelsior, *higher* (motto of the state of New York)
   esse quam videri, *to be rather than to seem* (*to be*) (motto of the state of North Carolina)
   e pluribus unum, *one* (*country*) *out of many* (*states*) (motto of the United States, found on its coins)
   Translate the motto of Oklahoma (also of the University of Illinois and the American Federation of Labor) into English: **Labor omnia vincit.**

Erich Lessing/Art Resource, NY

This relief shows various pieces of armor worn by Roman soldiers, as well as a few of the weapons and equipment they carried.

LESSON LIV

Pyrrhus et Fabricius

Fabricius, quī erat īnferior genere quam aliī Rōmānī, tamen ab omnibus amātus est quod optimus fortissimusque mīles erat. Neque amīcōs neque inimīcōs suōs fallēbat. Praemia numquam sūmēbat. Itaque Rōmānī cīvitātis suae salūtem eī crēdidērunt et eum inter aliōs lēgātōs ad Pyrrhum mīsērunt.

Multa quae dē Fabriciō et eius summā honestāte Pyrrhus audīverat vēra esse crēdidit. Itaque hunc lēgātum in castrīs suīs cōnspectum bene accēpit. Ad extrēmum eī dīxit: "Cūr nōn in Ēpīrum mēcum venīs et ibi manēs? Tibi quārtam rēgnī meī partem tribuam." Sed Fabricius respondit sē neque partem rēgnī sibi tribuī cupere neque sūmptūrum esse.

Proximō annō Fabricius contrā Pyrrhum pugnāvit. Medicus rēgis mediā nocte ad eum vēnit et dīxit sē prō praemiō Pyrrhum interfectūrum esse. Fabricius, quī nēminem fefellerat, respondit sē nūllum praemium prōpōnere et iussit hunc ligātum ad dominum redūcī et Pyrrhō omnia dīcī. Ubi rēx medicum ligātum cōnspexit, maximē mōtus dīxit: "Ille est Fabricius quī nōn facilius ab honestāte quam sōl ā cursū suō āvertī potest!"

QUESTIONS

1. Why did the Romans have so much confidence in Fabricius?
2. What offer did Pyrrhus make to Fabricius?
3. What reason did Pyrrhus have for being grateful to Fabricius?

Grammar

Reflexive Pronouns

In Latin, the personal pronouns of the first and second persons (**ego, tū, nōs, vōs**) may be used reflexively, but in the third person Latin has a special reflexive pronoun, **suī**, declined alike in the singular and plural:

Vanni/Art Resource, NY

These theater ruins in Epirus, Greece again underscore the importance of public entertainment to the ancients.

Gen.	**suī**	*of himself, herself, itself, themselves*
Dat.	**sibi**	*to himself, herself, itself, themselves*
Acc.	**sē**	*himself, herself, itself, themselves*
Abl.	**sē**	*with/from himself, herself, itself, themselves*

Why do reflexive pronouns have no nominative?

Use of Reflexive Pronouns

(ego) mē rogo *I ask myself*	**(nōs) nōs rogāmus** *we ask ourselves*
(tu) tē rogās *you ask yourself*	**(vōs) vōs rogātis** *you ask yourselves*
(is) sē rogat *he asks himself*	**(eī) sē rogant** *they ask themselves*

Nōs contrā hostēs dēfendimus.	*We defended ourselves against the enemies.*
Sē ob victoriam laudāvit.	*He praised himself on account of the victory.*

ORAL PRACTICE

Give in all tenses the first singular of **līberō;** the second plural of **fallō;** the third singular of **interficiō,** using the correct reflexive pronoun with each.

Words Often Confused

The words in the following groups closely resemble one another in form or sound and must be carefully distinguished. Use each word in a sentence that shows you know its meaning.

accēdō, accidō | **cīvis, cīvitās** | **ob, ab**
aetās, aestās | **gēns, genus** | **pars, pār**
alius, alter, altus | **ibi, ubi** | **pōnō (posuī), possum**
cadō, cēdō | **liber, līber, līberī** | **vīs, vir**

EXERCISES

A. Translate the following sentences into good English.

1. Frāter eius mātrem suam fefellit et posteā sē in mare iēcit.
2. Tū tē ipsum fallere semper potuistī sed mē numquam fefellistī.
3. Mūnera pūblica optimīs, nōn pessimīs, civibus tribuī dēbent.
4. Arma sūmēmus et nōs fortiter dēfendēmus contrā pessimōs hostēs.
5. Puerum currentem cōnspexī, sed ille crēdidit sē ā mē nōn vīsum esse.

The Bettmann Archive

In this painting of a fully armored Roman soldier, you can see the heavy knob with a sharp point in the middle of his shield. Also notice that his armor is made of segmented metal plates.

B. Translate the following sentences into Latin.

1. He says that he himself has four brothers.
2. We always praise ourselves and say the worst (things) about others.
3. Entrust yourselves and all your (possessions) to us.
4. The leader of the enemy, having seen us, killed himself.

C. Work with a partner or in a small group to write a letter to Fabricius on behalf of Rome. Explain your appreciation for his deeds and honesty, and give him a suitable reward, one that fits both his personality and temperament.

Vocabulary

Nouns

cursus, -ūs, *m. running, course, voyaging* (cursive, cursory)
genus, generis, *n. kind, class, sort* (gender, general)
honestās, honestātis, *f. honesty*
negōtium, negōtī, *n. business* (negotiate, negotiation)

Verbs

avertō, avertere, avertī, aversus, *turn away, turn off, remove* (aversion, avert)
cōnspiciō, cōnspicere, cōnspexī, cōnspectus, *catch sight of, see* (conspicuous)
exerceō, exercēre, exercuī, exercitus, *train, keep busy* (exercise)
praemittō, praemittere, praemīsī, praemissus, *send ahead* (permit, premise)
sūmō, sūmere, sūmpsī, sūmptus, *take* (resume, sumptuous)
supersum, superesse, superfuī, superfutūrus, *be left (over), survive*
tribuō, tribuere, tribuī, tribūtus, *grant* (contribute, tribute)

Conjunction

autem, *however (never first word)*

Prepositions

prae (+ abl.), *before, in front of* (preamble, precede)
super (+ acc.), *over, above* (superstar, supervene)

Giraudon/Art Resource, NY

*The **Iliad** is an epic poem that takes place during the last year of the Trojan War. Achilles is the main character. When his slave girl is taken away by Agamemnon, the Greek commander, Achilles goes to his tent and sulks. He rejoins the battle, however, when Hector, prince of Troy, kills Achilles' best friend, Patroclus. Here, Achilles contemplates the body of Patroclus.*

Latin for American Students

Did you know that the **eques** *or knight of the Roman social class was the businessman of his day? Equites financed the public works of Rome by successfully bidding for government contracts. Knights also found the provinces to be a source of wealth by collecting taxes and financing provincial business operations. Grain, manufactured articles, ores, and wool could often only be transported throughout the Roman Empire with the money this class advanced.*

Word Studies

The suffixes **–ilis** and **–bilis** are added to verb stems to form adjectives. They indicate what *can be done:* **facilis** is "doable," *easy.* The suffix **–ilis** usually becomes *–ile* in English: *facile, fertile.* The more common suffix **–bilis** becomes, *–ble, –able, –ible* in English: *amiable, comparable, credible, divisible, noble, visible.*

Several suffixes meaning *pertaining to* are added to nouns and adjectives to form adjectives: **–āris** (English *–ar*), **–ārius** (*–ary*), **–ānus** (*–an, –ane*), **–icus** (*–ic*). Examples of their use in Latin and English are: **familiāris, frūmentārius, Rōmānus, pūblicus;** *singular, ordinary, human, humane, generic.*

The suffix **–tūdō** (English *–tude*) is added to adjective stems to form nouns and means *state of being;* **magnitūdō,** *magnitude.*

Find fifteen other examples of these suffixes in English words derived from Latin words already studied.

Glimpses of Roman Life

THE EMPERORS

Perhaps nothing calls to mind the grandeur of ancient Rome better than its Caesars or emperors. In the last years of the Roman republic, powerful military leaders struggled for control of the state. Consulships, in which power was shared by two men, and triumvirates, in which it was shared by three men, were just two of the forms of early Roman government. Because someone was always trying to get the upper hand, these arrangements often collapsed. Julius Caesar, as a member of the first triumvirate, held the title of dictator. After his assassination, there was civil war for several years. Eventually, Caesar's grand-nephew (and adopted son), Octavian, rose to supreme power. In 27 B.C., the Senate awarded him the title Augustus, meaning "highly-venerated" or "majestic." This title, like the name Caesar itself, became an imperial title. Octavian thus became Rome's first emperor.

Julius Caesar (who never was an emperor himself) and the eleven emperors who ruled after him have been immortalized by the Roman biographer and historian Suetonius. His work, *Lives of the Twelve Caesars,* tells us much about the palace intrigue and corruption of power that was prevalent. He describes, for example, how the emperor Claudius was poisoned by his wife, Agrippina, and how Agrippina was, in turn, executed by her son, Nero. Suetonius also reports about the activities of the emperor Gaius, better known as Caligula ("Little Boot"), who, he alleges, actually wanted to make his horse, Incitatus, a consul!

Despite the peculiarities of some of the rulers, the Roman world enjoyed much prosperity and unparalleled stability under the early emperors. In fact, beginning with Augustus, there was almost 200 years of relative peace in the Roman Empire. This period of time is called the **pax Romana**. All in all, the Roman emperors probably exhibited as wide a spectrum of abilities as we see in many of our political leaders. Some of the later emperors, like Marcus Aurelius and Julian, were philosophers, whose works can still be studied. Others, such as Aurelian, who built the walls of Rome (which still stand), were superb military leaders.

The period of the "adoptive emperors" from 96 to 180 saw Rome at its majestic height and the empire at its largest. Some historians call this period one of the premier "golden ages" of human history. During this time, the Roman Empire extended from Britain to the Persian Gulf.

The triumph of Caesar in a fifteenth-century painting by the Italian artist Andrea Mantegna (1431-1506). The inscription reads, "To Gen. Julius Caesar for conquering Gaul by military power, a triumph was decreed, (all) malice (against him) having been removed and overcome." ***Devict*** *is for* ***devictam, potencia*** *for* ***potentia****.*

Some time during the third century, the Roman Empire began to decline in spite of the Edict of Caracalla in 212 that granted citizenship to all male freeborn inhabitants. Coups and assassinations of emperors by the army, barbarian invasions, and in-fighting for the throne did serious damage to the fabric of imperial government. Finally, the very capable emperors Diocletian and Constantine were able to provide direction, administrative innovations, and reforms to the empire and to salvage it from this chaotic period. Among their reforms were the enhancement of a central imperial power and the division of the empire into two parts, making it more efficient to administer.

One emperor ruled in the west at Milan, Ravenna, or elsewhere, with the emphasis clearly placed on military strategy; the other ruled in the east, generally at Constantinople.

In the fifth century, the emperors of the west had to contend with increasing pressures from Germanic tribes, who were, themselves, being invaded by the Huns. Although their generals were actually quite successful, the western provinces lacked the resources and the manpower of the east, and gradually the real power of the western emperors declined. The eastern part of the empire lasted until 1453; the western part of the empire finally ended in 476 when the German ruler, Odoacer, deposed the child-emperor, Romulus Augustulus.

QUESTIONS

1. How do we know so much about the early Roman emperors?
2. When was the Golden Age of Rome?
3. If, as legend has it, Romulus and Remus founded Rome in 753 B.C., how long did the Roman Empire last?

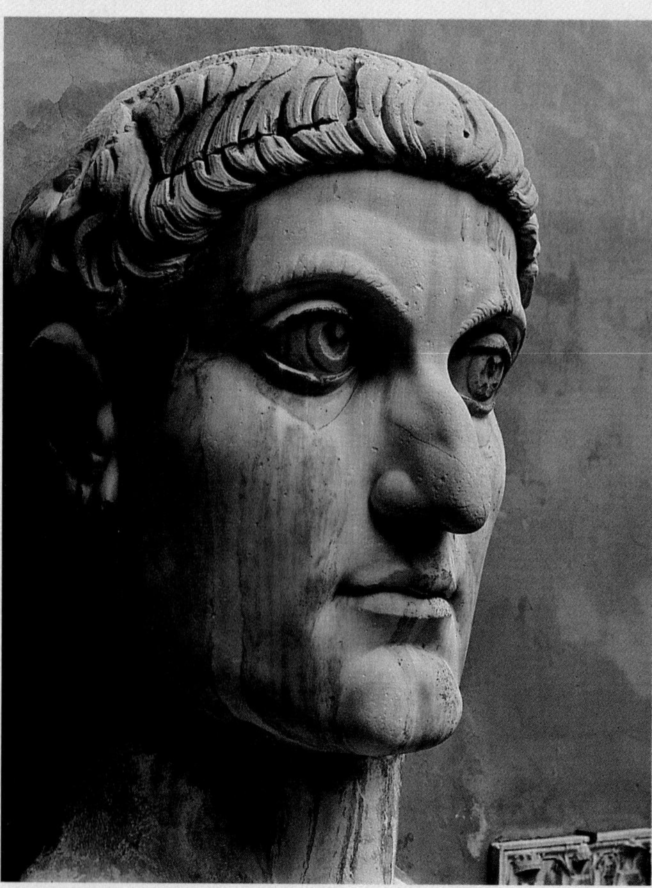

Monumental head of Constantine the Great, emperor from 306 to 337 A.D. Only parts of this huge marble statue have survived. Constantine (280-337) was the first Roman emperor to adopt Christianity. In 325 he gathered together in Nicaea the bishops who would produce the Nicene Creed, the statement of doctrine of the Christian faith.

Erich Lessing/Art Resource, NY

Unit XI Review
LESSONS L-LIV

Vocabulary

Nouns

āēr	condiciō	honestās	ōrātiō
aes	crāter	ignis	orbis
āla	cursus	lac	paupertās
arbor	ferrum	negōtium	rēgiō
argentum	frōns	nēmō	sacerdōs
avis	genus	opus	victōr

Adjectives

ambō	interior	pessimus	senex
aptus	intimus	plūrimus	senior
dissimilis	maior	plūs	summus
exterior	maximus	propior	superior
extrēmus	melior	proprius	ulterior
humilis	minimus	proximus	ultimus
inferior	optimus	quartus	utilis
īnfimus	peior		

Verbs

accidō	exerceō	praemittō	supersum
avertō	explicō	rapiō	tribuō
cadō	instruō	repellō	ūrō
cōnspiciō	iūdicō	statuō	vīvō
cōnstituō	iungō	sūmō	volō

Adverb

autem

Prepositions

prae super

Conjunction

quam

Grammar Summary

Regular Comparison of Adjectives

The comparative of regular adjectives is formed by adding **–ior, –ius** to the base. The superlative is formed by adding **–issimus, –a, –um** to the base. The comparatives are declined like a regular third declension. **Quam** is used to say *than.*

Hoc flumen est altius quam illud.	*This river is deeper than that (one).*
Rēgīna nostra iustissima est.	*Our queen is most just.*

Adjectives whose base ends in **–r** add **–rimus, –a, –um** to the base to form the superlative. Some adjectives that end in **–ilis** add **–limus** to the base to form the superlative.

Illa mulier pulcherrima est.	*That woman is very beautiful.*
Captīvī humillimī sunt.	*The captives are most humble.*

Irregular Comparison of Adjectives

Some adjectives have irregular comparative and superlative forms and must simply be memorized.

Unit XI Review
LESSONS L-LIV

Hic liber melior quam ille est.	*This book is better than that.*
Equus meus maior quam tuus est.	*My horse is bigger than yours.*

Formation and Comparison of Adverbs

Adverbs formed from third declension adjectives generally add **–iter** to the base to form the positive. The comparative is formed by adding **–ius** to the base and the superlative adds **–e** to the base of the superlative adjective.

Mīlitēs fortiter pugnāvērunt.	*The soldiers fought bravely.*
Haec gravius illa vulnerātur.	*This woman is wounded more seriously than that one.*
Omnēs celerrimē cucurrērunt.	*They all ran very quickly.*

Quam is used with the superlative adverb to say *as ... as possible*.

Quam celerrime labōrāvimus.	*We worked as quickly as possible.*

The Dative with Adjectives

The dative is used with certain adjectives that often contain the word *to* in English.

Hic similis illī est.	*This is similar to that.*
Amīca mihi est.	*She is friendly to me.*

The Reflexive Third Person Pronoun

The third person singular and plural reflexive pronouns **sui, sibi, sē, sē** are used when the object refers back to the subject.

Dixit sē laborāre.	*He said that he was working.*
Pūtavērunt sē eam vidēre.	*They thought that they saw her.*

Unit Practice

Oral Form Drill

1. Decline **senātus noster, diēs longior**.
2. Give the genitive and accusative singular and the genitive plural of: **id negōtium, haec potestās, impetus fortis, īdem prīnceps, quae ratiō, rēs ipsa, cāsus peior, domus ūlla.**
3. Give in all tenses the third singular active of **noceō**; the third plural passive of **dēserō;** the first plural active of **imperō**; the third plural passive of **dēspiciō;** the second singular active of **audiō.**

Unit XI Review
LESSONS L-LIV

4. Identify by giving voice, tense, and when possible, mood, person, and number: **praemīsit, incoluisse, exercērī, interclūdēns, dēserunt, redde, dēmōnstrāte, explōrārī, dīvidī, imperāns, superestis, praeerimus, praeficiēmus, ascendam, vīvite, dīvīsus, interclūdentur, intellēctum est, permissūrus.**

Word Studies

1. Give the Latin words and prefixes suggested by the following English derivatives: *ascendancy, casualty, circumnavigate, demonstration, familiarity, indivisible, innocuous, intellectual, lucid, opponent, preview, subjunctive, superscription, transcend, virtue.*
2. Find and use in sentences as many English derivatives as possible from **pōnō, veniō,** and **pellō.**

IN BRITANNIĀ—A Play in Latin

Persōnae

Dīvicus	**Brigida,** *fīlia Dīvicī*
Cocurō	**Sulpicius Rūfus,** *Rōmānus*
Osbus	**Antōnia,** *uxor Rūfī*
Caractō	**Medicus**
Aliī Britannī	**Servī et Servae**

Britannī

LOCUS: In tabernā Dīvicī, in Britanniā. (*Aliī Britannī dormiunt, aliī bibunt.*)

COCURŌ: Brigida! Vīnum!

BRIGIDA: Ecce! (*Vīnum Cocurōnī dat.*)

COCURŌ: Vīnum Rōmānum est. Vīnum Rōmānum amō—nōn autem Rōmānōs.

OSBUS: Rōmānōs nōn ōdī.[1] Per Rōmānōs in Britanniā nunc sunt viae bonae, castra mūnīta, multī mercātōrēs, melior cibus.

COCURŌ: Rōmānī autem nōn sunt Britannī. Sī hīc[2] manēbunt, Britannia erit Rōmāna.

DĪVICUS: Rōmāna erat mulier quae quondam Brigidam meam servāvit.

[1] *I do not hate*
[2] *here*

Unit XI Review
LESSONS L-LIV

BRIGIDA: Bene dīcit. Graviter aegra eram. Mulier Rōmāna servum suum, medicum doctum, ad mē mīsit. Ille mē cūrāvit.

OSBUS: Quis erat illa mulier?

BRIGIDA: Antōnia.

DĪVICUS: Uxor Sulpicī Rūfī est, cuius vīlla est proxima.

BRIGIDA: Benignī sunt.

COCURŌ: Rōmānīs nōn cōnfīdō. Medicīs nōn cōnfīdō.

OSBUS: Nōn paucī Rōmānī puellās nostrās in mātrimōnium dūcunt. Cavē, Brigida!

DĪVICUS: Brigida Caractōnī spōnsa est.

COCURŌ: Vir fortis est—et Britannus.

OSBUS: Etiam Rōmānī fortēs sunt. Mīlitēs Rōmānī Britannōs ab hostibus dēfendunt.

COCURŌ: Britannī sē dēfendere possunt. (*Clāmōrēs audiuntur.*)

BRIGIDA: Pater! Clāmōrem audiō! Quid est?

(Accēdit Caractō cum aliīs Britannīs. In tabernam dūcunt Sulpicium Rūfum et Antōniam, cum servīs eōrum.)

CARACTŌ: Ecce, Dīvice! Nōnne clārī sunt captīvī?

DĪVICUS: Caractō! Quid ēgistī?

CARACTŌ: Hī Rōmānī in viā iter faciēbant. Magnam pecūniam habent. Itaque nōs illōs cēpimus.

BRIGIDA: Caractō! Latrō es!

CARACTŌ: Latrō? Minimē! Rōmānī fīnēs Britannōrum occupāvērunt. Omnia quae habent sunt nostra.

SULPICIUS: Latrō pessime, quid cupis?

ANTŌNIA: Ecce ōrnāmenta mea! Omnia tua erunt, sī nōs dīmittēs.

CARACTŌ: Ōrnāmenta nōn cupiō; plūs cupiō.

SULPICIUS: Plūs? Quid dīcis?

CARACTŌ: Pecūniam habēs. Ubi nūntiābitur familiae tuae amīcīsque tuīs vōs captōs esse, illī prō vōbīs magnum praemium dabunt.

BRIGIDA: Caractō! Hī Rōmānī sunt fīnitimī nostrī et amīcī. Hic vir est Sulpicius Rūfus. Haec mulier, Antōnia, mē quondam servāvit. Ecce—ille servus est medicus quī mē cūrāvit!

CARACTŌ: Omnēs Rōmānī hostēs Britannōrum sunt.

ALIĪ BRITANNĪ: Hostēs sunt!

OSBUS: Caractō! Mīlitēs Rōmānī venient. Vōs capient.

Unit XI Review
LESSONS L-LIV

DĪVICUS: Caractō! Nisi[3] hōs Rōmānōs līberābis, Brigida uxor tua nōn erit.

CARACTŌ: Quid? Brigida mihi spōnsa est.

DĪVICUS: Nōn iam tibi spōnsa est.

BRIGIDA: Uxor latrōnis nōn erō.

BRITANNĪ: Caractō! Praeda magna erit!

ALIĪ BRITANNĪ: Caractō! Mīlitēs Rōmānī mox aderunt!

SULPICIUS: Mīlitēs Rōmānī latrōnēs interficiunt.

ANTŌNIA: Vōbīs nōn nocuimus. Nōs dīmitte!

BRIGIDA: Eōs dīmitte!

CARACTŌ: Prō tē, Brigida—illōs dīmittō. Discēdite omnēs!

ANTŌNIA: Tibi grātiās agimus, Brigida!

(*Discēdunt Rōmānī et Britannī et servī et servae.*)

DĪVICUS: Fortis vir es, Caractō—nimis[4] autem audāx.

CARACTŌ: Brigida mē retinēbit, mē docēbit, magistra mea erit.

[3] *unless*
[4] *too* (with **audāx**)

John P. Stevens/Ancient Art & Architecture Collection

Even in the farthest northeastern borders of the Roman Empire—Wheeldale Moor in Yorkshire, England—Roman roads are still in existence.

Grammar Appendix

Basic Grammatical Terms

The material here given may be reviewed in connection with the lessons. For the use of those who prefer to review basic grammar before taking up the lessons, a number of explanations are given here that are also in the body of the textbook. Teachers can easily devise English exercises for drill with classes that need it, or the sentences on these pages may be used for that purpose.

The Sentence: Subject and Predicate

A *sentence* is a group of words that completely expresses a thought. Every sentence consists of two parts—the *subject*, about which something is said, and the *predicate*, which says something about the subject.

The sailor (subject) *saved the girl* (predicate). **Nauta puellam servāvit.**

A subject or predicate is said to be *modified* by those words that affect or limit its meaning.

Parts of Speech

The words of most languages are divided, according to their use, into eight classes called *parts of speech*. These are: nouns, adjectives, adverbs, conjunctions, pronouns, verbs, prepositions, and interjections.

Nouns

A *noun* (from Latin **nōmen**, *name*) is a word that names a person, place, or thing: *Anna,* **Anna**; *island,* **īnsula**; *letter,* **littera**.

Nouns may be classified as:

1. *Common* (applied to any one of a group): *city,* **urbs**; *girl,* **puella**.
2. *Proper* (applied to a particular one of a group and always begin with a capital letter): *Rome,* **Rōma**; *Julia,* **Iūlia**.

Pronouns

A *pronoun* (Latin **prō,** *for;* **nōmen,** *name*) is a word used instead of a noun. The noun whose place is taken by a pronoun is called an *antecedent* (Latin **ante,** *before;* **cēdō,** *go*).

1. *Personal* pronouns distinguish the three persons: the person speaking (*I,* **ego**; *we,* **nōs**–first person), the person spoken to (*you,* **tū**, **vōs**–second person), the person or thing spoken of (*he,* **is**; *she,* **ea**; *it,* **id**; *they,* **eī**–third person).
2. *Interrogative* pronouns are used to ask questions: *who,* **quis**; *which, what,* **quid**.
3. *Relative* pronouns relate to a preceding (antecedent) word and join to it a dependent clause: *who,* **quī**; *which, what, that,* **quod**.

4. *Demonstrative* pronouns point out persons or objects definitely—often accompanied with a gesture: *this,* **hic;** *that,* **ille;** *these,* **hī;** *those,* **illī.**

Adjectives

An *adjective* is used to describe a noun or pronoun or to limit its meaning.

1. *Descriptive* adjectives are either *common* or *proper: good,* **bonus;** *Roman,* **Rōmānus.** Proper adjectives begin with a capital letter.
2. *Limiting* adjectives can be divided into six groups.
   a. *Article—definite* (*the*), *indefinite* (*a, an*). There is no definite or indefinite article in Latin.
   b. *Numerals—cardinals* (*one, two, three, etc.,* **ūnus, duo, trēs,** etc.), *ordinals* (*first, second, third,* etc., **prīmus, secundus, tertius,** etc.).
   c. *Possessive* adjectives (formed from personal pronouns): *my, mine,* **meus;** *our, ours,* **noster;** *your, yours,* **tuus, vester;** *his, her, its,* **eius;** *their, theirs,* **eōrum.**

When interrogative, relative, and demonstrative pronouns are used as adjectives, they are called respectively:

d. *Interrogative* adjectives: ***What*** *street?* ***Quae*** **via?**
e. *Relative* adjectives: *He spent a year in Italy, in* ***which*** *country he saw many beautiful things,* **Annum in Italiā ēgit, in *quā* terrā multa pulchra vīdit.**
f. *Demonstrative* adjectives: ***that*** *road,* ***illa*** **via.**

In English, the demonstrative adjectives are the only ones that have different forms in the singular and plural: *this, these; that, those.*

Verbs

A *verb* tells what a subject does or is.

*He **fought.***	***Pugnāvit.***
*He **is** good.*	**Bonus *est.***

1. According to use, verbs are either *transitive* or *intransitive.*
   a. A *transitive* verb tells what a person or thing does to another person or thing.
   *Anna **is carrying** water.* — **Anna aquam *portat.***
   b. An *intransitive* verb is one whose action is limited to the subject.
   *Anna **is working.*** — **Anna *labōrat.***
2. Intransitive verbs are either *complete* or *linking.*
   a. A *complete* verb is complete in meaning without an object or other word.
   *He **sails.*** — ***Nāvigat.***
   b. A *linking* verb links a noun or adjective to the subject.
   *They **are** good.* — **Bonī *sunt.***

The chief linking verbs in English are *be, appear, seem, become, feel, look, taste, smell.*

3. An *auxiliary* verb (Latin **auxilium,** *help*) is one used in the conjugation of other verbs: *I **am** learning; **Did** you see? They **have** given.*

Adverbs

An *adverb* is used to modify the meaning of a verb, adjective, or other adverb.

*He is working **now.*** **Nunc labōrat.**

Prepositions

A *preposition* is used to show the relation of a noun or pronoun, called its *object*, to some word (usually the verb) in the sentence.

He sails **to** *the island.* ***Ad* īnsulam nāvigat.**

Conjunctions

A *conjunction* is used to join words, phrases, and clauses. Conjunctions are classified according to their use as:

1. *Coordinate,* connecting words or sentences of equal rank (*and,* **et;** *but,* **sed;** *or,* **aut;** *nor,* **neque**).
2. *Subordinate,* connecting a subordinate clause of a sentence with the principal clause (*if,* **sī;** *while,* **dum;** *because,* **quod,** etc.).
3. *Correlative,* used in pairs (*both . . . and,* **et . . . et;** *neither . . . nor,* **neque . . . neque,** etc.).

Interjections

An *interjection* is used to show emotion. It has no direct relation to any other word in the sentence: *O! Alas! Ah! Oh!*

Inflection

The change of form that words undergo to indicate differences in their use is called *inflection: boy—boys,* **puer—puerī;** *see, saw, seen,* **videō, vīdī, vīsus.** The inflection of nouns, pronouns, and adjectives is called *declension.* They are *declined* to indicate change in number and case, and sometimes gender. Personal pronouns also indicate person.

Number

A noun or pronoun is *singular* when it refers to one person or thing: *girl,* **puella;** *house,* **casa;** *mouse,* **mūs;** *tooth,* **dēns.** It is *plural* when it refers to more than one: *girls,* **puellae;** *houses,* **casae;** *mice,* **mūrēs;** *teeth,* **dentēs.**

Gender

Gender is a distinction in the form of words corresponding to a distinction of sex. It is shown by change of word, by change of ending, or by use of a prefix: *father—mother,* **pater—māter,** *master—mistress,* **dominus—domina;** *he-goat—she-goat.* The first words given in each group are *masculine,* the second are *feminine.* Most nouns in English have no gender and are therefore *neuter* ("neither" masculine nor feminine). In Latin, however, many such nouns are masculine or feminine. The gender of the noun must be memorized as part of the basic form.

Case

Case is a change in the form of a noun, pronoun, or adjective to show its use in the sentence:

She (subject) *is here.*	***Ea* adest.**
I saw *her* (object).	***Eam vīdī.***

Subject and Object

1. The *subject* of a verb is that about which something is said.
2. The *direct object* is that which is directly affected by the action indicated in the transitive active verb.

Anna carries ***water.***	**Anna *aquam* portat.**

   The term *object* is also applied to a word dependent upon a preposition.
3. The *indirect object* indicates that which is indirectly affected by the action of the verb.

She gave the gift ***to me.***	**Ea *mihi* dōnum dedit.**

Names and Uses of the Cases

1. *Nominative.* A noun or pronoun used as the subject of a verb is in the *nominative* case.

The ***farmer*** *calls.*	***Agricola* vocat.**

2. *Genitive* (*Possessive*). Possession is expressed by the *genitive* (or *possessive*) case: *the* ***boy's*** *book,* ***puerī* liber.**
3. *Dative.* The noun or pronoun that indicates to or for whom the direct object is given, shown, or told is called the *indirect object* and is put in the *dative* case.

I gave ***him*** *a book.*	***Eī* librum dedī.**

4. *Accusative* (*Objective*). A noun or pronoun used as the object of a verb or preposition is in the *accusative* (or *objective*) case:

I sent a ***book*** *to* ***him.***	**Ad *eum librum* mīsī.**

5. *Ablative.* The *ablative* case is used for a variety of special reasons in Latin.
6. *Vocative.* The *vocative* case is used to address someone directly.

Marcus, *are you coming?*	**Venisne, *Marce?***

Conjugation

The inflection of verbs is called *conjugation.* Verbs are *conjugated* by putting together the various parts that indicate *person, number, tense, voice,* and *mood.*

Person and Number

A verb must agree with its subject in person and number.

The girl ***is*** *good.*	**Puella *est* bona.**
The girls ***are*** *good.*	**Puellae *sunt* bonae.**

Tense

Tense means time. There are six tenses in Latin.

1. The *present* represents an act as taking place now: *He* ***goes.***

2. The *imperfect* represents an act as having already taken place: *He* ***went*** *yesterday.* Also, an action complete in the past: *He* ***has gone.***
3. The *future* represents an act that will occur later: *He* ***will go*** *tomorrow.*
4. The *imperfect* represents an act in the past as incomplete or repeated: *He* ***was going;*** *He* ***used to go.***
5. The *pluperfect* represents an act as completed at some definite time in the past (before something else occurred): *He* ***had gone.***
6. The *future perfect* represents an act as completed at or before some definite time in the future: *He* ***will have gone*** (before something else will occur).

Interrogative, Negative, and Emphatic Verb Forms

Interrogative, negative, and *emphatic* (with some form of the auxiliary "do," used only in the present and past):

1. Used in questions: ***Do*** (***did***) *you* ***know*** *this?*
2. Negative: ***I do*** (***did***) *not* ***know*** *it.*
3. Emphatic: ***I do*** (***did***) ***believe*** *it.*

Voice

A transitive verb is in the *active voice* when it represents the subject as the doer or agent.

Anna ***loves*** *Clara.*	**Anna Clāram** ***amat.***

A transitive verb is in the *passive voice* when it represents the subject as the receiver of the action.

Clara ***is loved.***	**Clāra** ***amātur.***

Intransitive verbs are used only in the active voice in English.

Mood

1. The *indicative mood* is used to state a fact or to ask a question.

Rome ***is*** *a great city.*	**Rōma** ***est*** **magna urbs.**
Where ***is*** *Anna?*	**Ubi** ***est*** **Anna?**

2. The *imperative mood* is used to express commands.

Look *at the waves.*	***Spectā*** **undās.**

Infinitive

The *infinitive* is a verbal noun. It is a form of the verb to which *to* is usually prefixed in English: ***to*** *go,* ***to*** *sing.* It has tense and voice, but not person, number, or mood.

Participle

The participle is a verbal adjective. As an adjective it modifies a noun or pronoun: *a* ***losing*** *fight.* As a verb it may have an object or adverbial modifiers: *Suddenly* ***losing*** *his balance, he fell off.* It has three forms in Latin:

Present Active:	*seeing*
Perfect Passive:	*seen, having been seen*
Future Active:	*about to see, going to see*

Phrases

A *phrase* is a group of words without subject and predicate. One important kind of phrase is the *prepositional phrase,* that is, a preposition together with its object: *in great danger,* ***in magnō perīculō.***

Clauses

A *clause,* like a phrase, is a part of a sentence but differs from a phrase in having a subject and a predicate.

Clauses are classified as:

1. *Main,* the leading or independent statement in a sentence:

   The girl *whom you saw on the street* ***is my sister.*** — ***Puella*** **quam in viā vīdistī** ***soror mea est.***

2. *Subordinate,* a dependent statement modifying the main clause:

   The girl ***whom you saw on the street*** *is my sister.* — **Puella** ***quam in viā vīdistī*** **soror mea est.**

Sentences

1. A *simple sentence* contains one main clause.

   My friend, the farmer, has many horses. — **Amīcus meus, agricola, multōs equōs habet.**

2. A *compound sentence* contains two or more main clauses connected by a coordinate conjunction, such as "and," "but," etc.

   My friend, the farmer, has many horses, but I have not seen them. — **Amīcus meus, agricola, multōs equōs habet, sed eōs nōn vīdī.**

3. A *complex sentence* contains one main clause to which one or more subordinate clauses are joined by subordinate conjunctions or by relative or interrogative pronouns.

   My friend, the farmer, has many horses which I have not seen. — **Amīcus meus, agricola, multōs equōs habet quōs nōn vīdī.**

Basic Forms

Nouns

First Declension

via, viae, *f. road*

	SINGULAR	PLURAL
NOM.	via	viae
GEN.	viae	viārum
DAT.	viae	viīs
ACC.	viam	viās
ABL.	viā	viīs
(VOC.)		

Second Declension

servus, servī, *m. slave*

	SINGULAR	PLURAL
NOM.	servus	servī
GEN.	servī	servōrum
DAT.	servō	servīs
ACC.	servum	servōs
ABL.	servō	servīs
(VOC.)	(serve)	

Second Declension

	ager, agrī, *m. field*		**puer, puerī,** *m. boy*		**signum, signī,** *n. sign*	
	SING.	PLUR.	SING.	PLUR.	SING.	PLUR.
NOM.	ager	agrī	puer	puerī	signum	signa
GEN.	agrī	agrōrum	puerī	puerōrum	signī	signōrum
DAT.	agrō	agrīs	puerō	puerīs	signō	signīs
ACC.	agrum	agrōs	puerum	puerōs	signum	signa
ABL.	agrō	agrīs	puerō	puerīs	signō	signīs

Third Declension

	mīles, mīlitis, *m. soldier*		**lēx, lēgis,** *f. law*		**corpus, corporis,** *n. body*	
	SING.	PLUR.	SING.	PLUR.	SING.	PLUR.
NOM.	mīles	mīlitēs	lēx	lēgēs	corpus	corpora
GEN.	mīlitis	mīlitum	lēgis	lēgum	corporis	corporum
DAT.	mīlitī	mīlitibus	lēgī	lēgibus	corporī	corporibus
ACC.	mīlitem	mīlitēs	lēgem	lēgēs	corpus	corpora
ABL.	mīlite	mīlitibus	lēge	lēgibus	corpore	corporibus

Third Declension I–Stems

	cīvis, cīvis, *m. and f. citizen*		**mare, maris,** *n. sea*	
	SINGULAR	PLURAL	SINGULAR	PLURAL
NOM.	cīvis	cīvēs	mare	maria
GEN.	cīvis	cīvium	maris	marium
DAT.	cīvī	cīvibus	marī	maribus
ACC.	cīvem	cīvēs	mare	maria
ABL.	cīve	cīvibus	marī	maribus

Fourth Declension

	cāsus, cāsūs, *m. chance*	
	SING.	PLUR.
NOM.	cās**us**	cās**ūs**
GEN.	cās**ūs**	cās**uum**
DAT.	cās**uī**	cās**ibus**
ACC.	cās**um**	cās**ūs**
ABL.	cās**ū**	cās**ibus**

Fifth Declension

	diēs, diēī, *m. day*		**rēs, reī,** *f. thing*	
	SING.	PLUR.	SING.	PLUR.
NOM.	di**ēs**	di**ēs**	r**ēs**	r**ēs**
GEN.	di**ēī**	di**ērum**	r**eī**	r**ērum**
DAT.	di**ēī**	di**ēbus**	r**eī**	r**ēbus**
ACC.	di**em**	di**ēs**	r**em**	r**ēs**
ABL.	di**ē**	di**ēbus**	r**ē**	r**ēbus**

Irregular Nouns

	SING.	PLUR.	SING.	SING.	PLUR.
NOM.	v**ī**s	vīr**ēs**	nēm**ō**	dom**us**	dom**ūs**
GEN.	———	vīr**ium**	(nūll**īus**)	dom**ūs**	dom**uum**
DAT.	———	vīr**ibus**	nēmin**ī**	dom**uī**	dom**ibus**
ACC.	v**im**	vīr**ēs**	nēmin**em**	dom**um**	dom**ōs**
ABL.	v**ī**	vīr**ibus**	(nūll**ō**)	dom**ō**	dom**ibus**
(LOC.)				(dom**ī**)	

Adjectives

First and Second Declensions

	SINGULAR			PLURAL		
	M	F	N	M	F	N
NOM.	magn**us**	magn**a**	magn**um**	magn**ī**	magn**ae**	magn**a**
GEN.	magn**ī**	magn**ae**	magn**ī**	magn**ōrum**	magn**ārum**	magn**ōrum**
DAT.	magn**ō**	magn**ae**	magn**ō**	magn**īs**	magn**īs**	magn**īs**
ACC.	magn**um**	magn**am**	magn**um**	magn**ōs**	magn**ās**	magn**a**
ABL.	magn**ō**	magn**ā**	magn**ō**	magn**īs**	magn**īs**	magn**īs**
(VOC.)	(magn**e**)					

	SINGULAR			SINGULAR		
NOM.	līber	līber**a**	līber**um**	noster	nostr**a**	nostr**um**
GEN.	līber**ī**	līber**ae**	līber**ī**	nostr**ī**	nostr**ae**	nostr**ī**
DAT.	līber**ō**	līber**ae**	līber**ō**	nostr**ō**	nostr**ae**	nostr**ō**
ACC.	līber**um**	līber**am**	līber**um**	nostr**um**	nostr**am**	nostr**um**
ABL.	līber**ō**	līber**ā**	līber**ō**	nostr**ō**	nostr**ā**	nostr**ō**

Plural, **līberī, līberae, lībera,** etc.   Plural, **nostrī, –ae, –a,** etc.

Alius has **aliud** in the nom. and acc. sing. neuter; plural regular.

Third Declension

THREE ENDINGS

	SINGULAR			PLURAL		
	M	F	N	M	F	N
NOM.	ācer	ācris	ācre	ācrēs	ācrēs	ācria
GEN.	ācris	ācris	ācris	ācrium	ācrium	ācrium
DAT.	ācrī	ācrī	ācrī	ācribus	ācribus	ācribus
ACC.	ācrem	ācrem	ācre	ācrēs (–īs)	ācrēs (–īs)	ācria
ABL.	ācrī	ācrī	ācrī	ācribus	ācribus	ācribus

	TWO ENDINGS				ONE ENDING			
	SINGULAR		PLURAL		SINGULAR		PLURAL	
	M F	N	M F	N	M F	N	M F	N
NOM.	fortis	forte	fortēs	fortia	pār	pār	parēs	paria
GEN.	fortis	fortis	fortium	fortium	paris	paris	parium	parium
DAT.	fortī	fortī	fortibus	fortibus	parī	parī	paribus	paribus
ACC.	fortem	forte	fortēs	fortia	parem	pār	parēs	paria
ABL.	fortī	fortī	fortibus	fortibus	parī	parī	paribus	paribus

Present Participle

	SINGULAR		PLURAL	
	M F	N	M F	N
NOM.	portāns	portāns	portantēs	portantia
GEN.	portantis	portantis	portantium	portanium
DAT.	portantī	portantī	portantibus	portantibus
ACC.	portantem	portāns	portantēs	portantia
ABL.	portante	portante	portantibus	portantibus

Comparison of Regular Adjectives and Adverbs

POSITIVE		COMPARATIVE		SUPERLATIVE	
ADJ.	ADV.	ADJ.	ADV.	ADJ.	ADV.
altus	altē	altior	altius	altissimus	altissimē
fortis	fortiter	fortior	fortius	fortissimus	fortissimē
līber	līberē	līberior	līberius	līberrimus	līberrimē
ācer	ācriter	ācrior	ācrius	ācerrimus	ācerrimē
facilis	facile	facilior	facilius	facillimus	facillimē

Comparison of Irregular Adjectives

POSITIVE	COMPARATIVE	SUPERLATIVE
bonus, –a, –um	melior, –ius	optimus, –a, –um
malus, –a, –um	peior, –ius	pessimus, –a, –um
magnus, –a, –um	maior, –ius	maximus, –a, –um
parvus, –a, –um	minor, –us	minimus, –a, –um
multus, –a, –um	—, plūs	plūrimus, –a, –um

Declension of Comparatives

	SINGULAR		PLURAL		SINGULAR	PLURAL	
	M F	N	M F	N	N	M F	N
NOM.	altior	altius	altiō**res**	altiō**ra**	plūs	plūr**ēs**	plūr**a**
GEN.	altiōr**is**	altiōr**is**	altiō**rum**	altiō**rum**	plūr**is**	plūr**ium**	plūr**ium**
DAT.	altiōr**ī**	altiōr**ī**	altiōr**ibus**	altiōr**ibus**	——	plūr**ibus**	plūr**ibus**
ACC.	altiōr**em**	altius	altiōr**ēs**	altiōr**a**	plūs	plūr**ēs**	plūr**a**
ABL.	altiōr**e**	altiōr**e**	altiōr**ibus**	altiōr**ibus**	plūr**e**	plūr**ibus**	plūr**ibus**

Declension of Numerals

	M	F	N	M	F	N
NOM.	ūn**us**	ūn**a**	ūn**um**	du**o**	du**ae**	du**o**
GEN.	ūn**īus**	ūn**īus**	un**ius**	du**ōrum**	du**ārum**	du**ōrum**
DAT.	ūn**ī**	ūn**ī**	ūn**ī**	du**ōbus**	du**ābus**	du**ōbus**
ACC.	ūn**ūm**	ūn**am**	ūn**um**	du**ōs**	du**ās**	du**o**
ABL.	ūn**ō**	ūn**ā**	ūn**ō**	du**ōbus**	du**ābus**	du**ōbus**

	M F	N	M F N *(adj.)*	N *(noun)*
NOM.	tr**ēs**	tr**ia**	mīlle	mīl**ia**
GEN.	tr**ium**	tr**ium**	mīlle	mīl**ium**
DAT.	tri**bus**	tri**bus**	mīlle	mīl**ibus**
ACC.	tr**ēs**	tr**ia**	mīlle	mīl**ia**
ABL.	tri**bus**	tri**bus**	mīlle	mīl**ibus**

Numerals

	ROMAN NUMERALS	CARDINALS	ORDINALS
1.	I.	ūnus, –a, –um	prīmus, –a, –um
2.	II.	duo, duae, duo	secundus (alter)
3.	III.	trēs, tria	tertius
4.	IIII *or* IV.	quattuor	quārtus
5.	V.	quīnque	quīntus
6.	VI.	sex	sextus
7.	VII.	septem	septimus
8.	VIII.	octō	octāvus
9.	VIIII *or* IX.	novem	nōnus
10.	X.	decem	decimus
11.	XI.	ūndecim	ūndecimus
12.	XII.	duodecim	duodecimus
13.	XIII.	tredecim	tertius decimus
14.	XIIII *or* XIV.	quattuordecim	quārtus decimus
15.	XV.	quīndecim	quīntus decimus
16.	XVI.	sēdecim	sextus decimus
17.	XVII.	septendecim	septimus decimus
18.	XVIII.	duodēvīgintī	duodēvīcēsimus
19.	XVIIII *or* XIX.	ūndēvīgintī	ūndēvīcēsimus
20.	XX.	vīgintī	vīcēsimus
21.	XXI.	vīgintī ūnus *or* ūnus et vīgintī	vīcēsimus prīmus *or* ūnus et vīcēsimus
30.	XXX.	trīgintā	trīcēsimus
40.	XXXX *or* XL.	quadrāgintā	quadrāgēsimus
50.	L.	quīnquāgintā	quīnquāgēsimus
60.	LX.	sexāgintā	sexāgēsimus
70.	LXX.	septuāgintā	septuāgēsimus
80.	LXXX.	octōgintā	octōgēsimus
90.	LXXXX *or* XC.	nōnāgintā	nōnāgēsimus
100.	C.	centum	centēsimus
101.	CI.	centum (et) ūnus	centēsimus (et) prīmus
200.	CC.	ducentī, –ae, –a	ducentēsimus
300.	CCC.	trecentī, –ae, –a	trecentēsimus
400.	CCCC.	quadringentī, –ae, –a	quadringentēsimus
500.	D.	quīngentī, –ae, –a	quīngentēsimus
600.	DC.	sescentī, –ae, –a	sescentēsimus
700.	DCC.	septingentī, –ae, –a	septingentēsimus
800.	DCCC.	octingentī, –ae, –a	octingentēsimus
900.	DCCCC.	nōngentī, –ae, –a	nōngentēsimus
1000.	M.	mīlle	mīllēsimus
2000.	MM.	duo mīlia	bis mīllēsimus

Pronouns

Personal

	SING.	PLUR.	SING.	PLUR.	M	F	N
NOM.	**ego**	**nōs**	**tū**	**vōs**	**is**	**ea**	**id**
					Plural, **eī, eae, ea,** etc.		
GEN.	**meī**	**nostrum (nostrī)**	**tuī**	**vestrum (–trī)**	**eius**	**eius**	**eius**
DAT.	**mihi**	**nōbīs**	**tibi**	**vōbīs**	**eī**	**eī**	**eī**
ACC.	**mē**	**nōs**	**tē**	**vōs**	**eum**	**eam**	**id**
ABL.	**mē**	**nōbīs**	**tē**	**vōbīs**	**eō**	**eā**	**eō**

Reflexive

	FIRST PERSON	SECOND PERSON	THIRD PERSON SING. AND PLUR.
GEN.	**meī**	**tuī**	**suī**
DAT.	**mihi**	**tibi**	**sibi**
ACC.	**mē**	**tē**	**sē (sēsē)**
ABL.	**mē**	**tē**	**sē (sēsē)**

Reflexives are not used in the nominative and therefore have no nominative form.

Demonstrative

	SINGULAR			PLURAL		
	M	F	N	M	F	N
NOM.	**hic**	**haec**	**hoc**	**hī**	**hae**	**haec**
GEN.	**huius**	**huius**	**huius**	**hōrum**	**hārum**	**hōrum**
DAT.	**huic**	**huic**	**huic**	**hīs**	**hīs**	**hīs**
ACC.	**hunc**	**hanc**	**hoc**	**hōs**	**hās**	**haec**
ABL.	**hōc**	**hāc**	**hōc**	**hīs**	**hīs**	**hīs**
NOM.	**is**	**ea**	**id**	**eī (iī)**	**eae**	**ea**
GEN.	**eius**	**eius**	**eius**	**eōrum**	**eārum**	**eōrum**
DAT.	**eī**	**eī**	**eī**	**eīs (iīs)**	**eīs (iīs)**	**eīs (iīs)**
ACC.	**eum**	**eam**	**id**	**eōs**	**eās**	**ea**
ABL.	**eō**	**eā**	**eō**	**eīs (iīs)**	**eīs (iīs)**	**eīs (iīs)**

	SINGULAR			PLURAL		
	M	F	N	M	F	N
NOM.	**īdem**	**eadem**	**idem**	**eīdem**	**eaedem**	**eadem**
GEN.	**eiusdem**	**eiusdem**	**eiusdem**	**eōrundem**	**eārundem**	**eōrundem**
DAT.	**eīdem**	**eīdem**	**eīdem**	**eīsdem**	**eīsdem**	**eīsdem**
ACC.	**eundem**	**eandem**	**idem**	**eōsdem**	**eāsdem**	**eadem**
ABL.	**eōdem**	**eādem**	**eōdem**	**eīsdem**	**eīsdem**	**eīsdem**

	SINGULAR			PLURAL		
	M	F	N	M	F	N
NOM.	**ille**	**illa**	**illud**	**illī**	**illae**	**illa**
GEN.	**illīus**	**illīus**	**illīus**	**illōrum**	**illārum**	**illōrum**
DAT.	**illī**	**illī**	**illī**	**illīs**	**illīs**	**illīs**
ACC.	**illum**	**illam**	**illud**	**illōs**	**illās**	**illa**
ABL.	**illō**	**illā**	**illō**	**illīs**	**illīs**	**illīs**

	SINGULAR			PLURAL		
	M	F	N	M	F	N
	ipse	**ipsa**	**ipsum**	**ipsī**	**ipsae**	**ipsa**
	ipsīus	**ipsīus**	**ipsīus**	**ipsōrum**	**ipsārum**	**ipsōrum**
	ipsī	**ipsī**	**ipsī**	**ipsīs**	**ipsīs**	**ipsīs**
	ipsum	**ipsam**	**ipsum**	**ipsōs**	**ipsās**	**ipsa**
	ipsō	**ipsā**	**ipsō**	**ipsīs**	**ipsīs**	**ipsīs**

Relative

	SINGULAR			PLURAL		
	M	F	N	M	F	N
NOM.	**quī**	**quae**	**quod**	**quī**	**quae**	**quae**
GEN.	**cuius**	**cuius**	**cuius**	**quōrum**	**quārum**	**quōrum**
DAT.	**cui**	**cui**	**cui**	**quibus**	**quibus**	**quibus**
ACC.	**quem**	**quam**	**quod**	**quōs**	**quās**	**quae**
ABL.	**quō**	**quā**	**quō**	**quibus**	**quibus**	**quibus**

Interrogative

	SINGULAR		PLURAL		
	M F	N	M	F	N
NOM.	**quis**	**quid**	**quī**	**quae**	**quae**
GEN.	**cuius**	**cuius**	**quōrum**	**quārum**	**quōrum**
DAT.	**cui**	**cui**	**quibus**	**quibus**	**quibus**
ACC.	**quem**	**quid**	**quōs**	**quās**	**quae**
ABL.	**quō**	**quō**	**quibus**	**quibus**	**quibus**

Verbs

First Conjugation

PRINCIPAL PARTS: **portō, portāre, portāvī, portātus**

	ACTIVE		PASSIVE	
		INDICATIVE		
PRESENT	*I carry,* etc.		*I am carried,* etc.	
	portō	portāmus	portor	portāmur
	portās	portātis	portāris	portāminī
	portat	portant	portātur	portantur
IMPERFECT	*I was carrying,* etc.		*I was (being) carried,* etc.	
	portābam	portābāmus	portābar	portābāmur
	portābās	portābātis	portābāris	portābāminī
	portābat	portābant	portābātur	portābantur
FUTURE	*I shall carry,* etc.		*I shall be carried,* etc.	
	portābō	portābimus	portābor	portābimur
	portābis	portābitis	portāberis	portābiminī
	portābit	portābunt	portābitur	portābuntur
PERFECT	*I carried, have carried,* etc.		*I was carried, have been carried,* etc.	
	portāvī	portāvimus	portātus (–a, –um) { sum	portātī (–ae, –a) { sumus
	portāvistī	portāvistis	es	estis
	portāvit	portāvērunt	est	sunt
PLUPERFECT	*I had carried,* etc.		*I had been carried,* etc.	
	portāveram	portāverāmus	portātus (–a, –um) { eram	portātī (–ae, –a) { erāmus
	portāverās	portāverātis	erās	erātis
	portāverat	portāverant	erat	erant
FUTURE PERFECT	*I shall have carried,* etc.		*I shall have been carried,* etc.	
	portāverō	portāverimus	portātus (–a, –um) { erō	portātī (–ae, –a) { erimus
	portāveris	portāveritis	eris	eritis
	portāverit	portāverint	erit	erunt

INFINITIVE

	ACTIVE	PASSIVE
PRESENT	**portāre,** *to carry*	**portārī,** *to be carried*
PERFECT	**portāvisse,** *to have carried*	**portātus esse,** *to have been carried*
FUTURE	**portātūrus esse,** *to be going to carry*	

PARTICIPLE

	ACTIVE	PASSIVE
PRESENT	**portāns,** *carrying*	
PERFECT		**portātus** *(having been) carried*
FUTURE	**portātūrus,** *going to carry*	

IMPERATIVE

PRESENT *carry*

portā portāte

	ACTIVE		PASSIVE	

Second Conjugation

PRINCIPAL PARTS: **doceō, docēre, docuī, doctus**

INDICATIVE

	Active		Passive	
PRESENT	*I teach,* etc.		*I am taught,* etc.	
	doce**ō**	docē**mus**	doce**or**	docē**mur**
	docē**s**	docē**tis**	docē**ris**	docē**minī**
	doce**t**	doce**nt**	docē**tur**	doce**ntur**
IMPERFECT	*I was teaching,* etc.		*I was (being) taught,* etc.	
	docē**bam**	docē**bāmus**	docē**bar**	docē**bāmur**
	docē**bās**	docē**bātis**	docē**bāris**	docē**bāminī**
	docē**bat**	docē**bant**	docē**bātur**	docē**bantur**
FUTURE	*I shall teach,* etc.		*I shall be taught,* etc.	
	docē**bō**	docē**bimus**	docē**bor**	docē**bimur**
	docē**bis**	docē**bitis**	docē**beris**	docē**biminī**
	docē**bit**	docē**bunt**	docē**bitur**	docē**buntur**
PERFECT	*I taught, have taught,* etc.		*I have been taught,* etc.	
	docu**ī**	docu**imus**	doct**us** (–a, –um) { **sum**, **es**, **est**	doct**ī** (–ae, –a) { **sumus**, **estis**, **sunt**
	docu**istī**	docu**istis**		
	docu**it**	docu**ērunt**		
PLUPERFECT	*I had taught,* etc.		*I had been taught,* etc.	
	docu**eram**	docu**erāmus**	doct**us** (–a, –um) { **eram**, **erās**, **erat**	doct**ī** (–ae, –a) { **erāmus**, **erātis**, **erant**
	docu**erās**	docu**erātis**		
	docu**erat**	docu**erant**		
FUTURE PERFECT	*I shall have taught,* etc.		*I shall have been carried,* etc.	
	docu**erō**	docu**erimus**	doct**us** (–a, –um) { **erō**, **eris**, **erit**	doct**ī** (–ae, –a) { **erimus**, **eritis**, **erunt**
	docu**eris**	docu**eritis**		
	docu**erit**	docu**erint**		

INFINITIVE

	Active	Passive
PRESENT	docē**re,** *to teach*	docē**rī,** *to be taught*
PERFECT	docu**isse,** *to have taught*	doct**us esse,** *to have been taught*
FUTURE	doct**ūrus esse,** *to be going to teach*	

PARTICIPLE

	Active	Passive
PRESENT	docē**ns,** *teaching*	
PERFECT		doct**us,** *(having been) taught*
FUTURE	doct**ūrus,** *going to teach*	

IMPERATIVE

PRESENT	*teach*	
	docē	docē**te**

	ACTIVE		PASSIVE	

Third Conjugation

PRINCIPAL PARTS: **pōnō, pōnĕre, posuī, positus**

INDICATIVE

	ACTIVE		PASSIVE	
PRESENT	*I put, place,* etc.		*I am placed,* etc.	
	pōn**ō**	pōn**imus**	pōn**or**	pōn**imur**
	pōn**is**	pōn**itis**	pōn**eris**	pōn**iminī**
	pōn**it**	pōn**unt**	pōn**itur**	pōn**untur**
IMPERFECT	*I was placing,* etc.		*I was (being) placed,* etc.	
	pōnē**bam**	pōnē**bāmus**	pōnē**bar**	pōnē**bāmur**
	pōnē**bās**	pōnē**bātis**	pōnē**bāris**	pōnē**bāminī**
	pōnē**bat**	pōnē**bant**	pōnē**bātur**	pōnē**bantur**
FUTURE	*I shall place,* etc.		*I shall be placed,* etc.	
	pon**am**	pōn**ēmus**	pōn**ar**	pōn**ēmur**
	pōn**ēs**	pōn**ētis**	pōn**ēris**	pōn**ēminī**
	pōn**et**	pōn**ent**	pōn**ētur**	pōn**entur**
PERFECT	*I placed, have placed,* etc.		*I have been placed,* etc.	
	posu**ī**	posu**imus**	posit**us** (**–a, –um**) **sum**	posit**ī** (**–ae, –a**) **sumus**
	posu**istī**	posu**istis**	**es**	**estis**
	posu**it**	posu**ērunt**	**est**	**sunt**
PLUPERFECT	*I had placed,* etc.		*I had been placed,* etc.	
	posu**eram**	posu**erāmus**	posit**us** (**–a, –um**) **eram**	posit**ī** (**–ae, –a**) **erāmus**
	posu**erās**	posu**erātis**	**erās**	**erātis**
	posu**erat**	posu**erant**	**erat**	**erant**
FUTURE PERFECT	*I shall have placed,* etc.		*I shall have been carried,* etc.	
	posu**erō**	posu**erimus**	posit**us** (**–a, –um**) **erō**	posit**ī** (**–ae, –a**) **erimus**
	posu**eris**	posu**eritis**	**eris**	**eritis**
	posu**erit**	posu**erint**	**erit**	**erunt**

INFINITIVE

	ACTIVE	PASSIVE
PRESENT	pōn**ere,** *to put, place*	pōn**ī,** *to be placed*
PERFECT	posu**isse,** *to have placed*	posit**us esse,** *to have been placed*
FUTURE	posit**ūrus esse,** *to be going to place*	

PARTICIPLE

	ACTIVE	PASSIVE
PRESENT	pōn**ēns,** *placing*	
PERFECT		posit**us,** *(having been) placed*
FUTURE	posit**ūrus,** *going to place*	

IMPERATIVE

	ACTIVE	
PRESENT	*place*	
	pōne	pōn**ite**

	ACTIVE		PASSIVE	

Third Conjugation –iō Verbs

PRINCIPAL PARTS: **capiō, capĕre, cēpī, captus**

INDICATIVE

PRESENT	*I take,* etc.		*I am taken,* etc.	
	capi**ō**	capi**mus**	capi**or**	capi**mur**
	capi**s**	capi**tis**	cape**ris**	capi**minī**
	capi**t**	capi**unt**	capi**tur**	capi**untur**
IMPERFECT	*I was taking,* etc.		*I was (being) taken,* etc.	
	capi**ēbam**	capi**ēbāmus**	capi**ēbar**	capi**ēbāmur**
	capi**ēbās**	capi**ēbātis**	capi**ēbāris**	capi**ēbāminī**
	capi**ēbat**	capi**ēbant**	capi**ēbātur**	capi**ēbantur**
FUTURE	*I shall take,* etc.		*I shall be taken,* etc.	
	capi**am**	capi**ēmus**	capi**ar**	capi**ēmur**
	capi**ēs**	capi**ētis**	capi**ēris**	capi**ēminī**
	capi**et**	capi**ent**	capi**ētur**	capi**entur**
PERFECT	*I took, have taken,* etc.		*I have been taken,* etc.	
	cēp**ī**	cēp**imus**	capt**us sum**	capt**ī sumus**
	cēp**istī**	cēp**istis**	capt**us es**	capt**ī estis**
	cēp**it**	cēp**ērunt**	capt**us est**	capt**ī sunt**
PLUPERFECT	*I had taken,* etc.		*I had been taken,* etc.	
	cēp**eram**	cēp**erāmus**	capt**us eram**	capt**i erāmus**
	cēp**erās**	cēp**erātis**	capt**us eras**	capt**i erātis**
	cēp**erat**	cēp**erant**	capt**us erat**	capt**i erant**
FUTURE PERFECT	*I shall have taken,* etc.		*I will have been taken,* etc.	
	cēp**erō**	cēp**erimus**	capt**us erō**	capt**i erimus**
	cēp**eris**	cēp**eritis**	capt**us eris**	capt**i eritis**
	cēp**erit**	cēp**erint**	capt**us erit**	capt**i erunt**

INFINITIVE

PRESENT	cap**ere,** *to take*	cap**ī,** *to be taken*
PERFECT	cēp**isse,** *to have taken*	capt**us esse,** *to have been taken*
FUTURE	capt**ūrus esse,** *to be going to take*	

PARTICIPLE

PRESENT	capi**ēns,** *taking*	
PERFECT		capt**us,** *(having been) taken*
FUTURE	capt**ūrus,** *going to take*	

IMPERATIVE

PRESENT	*take*	
	cape	capite

	ACTIVE		PASSIVE	

Fourth Conjugation

PRINCIPAL PARTS: **mūniō, mūnīre, mūnīvī, mūnītus**

INDICATIVE

PRESENT	*I fortify,* etc.		*I am fortified,* etc.	
	mūniō	mūnī**mus**	mūni**or**	mūnī**mur**
	mūnīs	mūnī**tis**	mūnī**ris**	mūnī**minī**
	mūnit	mūni**unt**	mūnī**tur**	mūni**untur**
IMPERFECT	*I was fortified,* etc.		*I was (being) fortified,* etc.	
	mūni**ēbam**	mūni**ēbāmus**	mūni**ēbar**	mūni**ēbāmur**
	mūni**ēbās**	mūni**ēbātis**	mūni**ēbāris**	mūni**ēbāminī**
	mūni**ēbat**	mūni**ēbant**	mūni**ēbātur**	mūni**ēbantur**
FUTURE	*I shall fortify,* etc.		*I shall be fortified,* etc.	
	mūni**am**	mūni**ēmus**	mūni**ar**	mūni**ēmur**
	mūni**ēs**	mūni**ētis**	mūni**ēris**	mūni**ēminī**
	mūni**et**	mūni**ent**	mūni**ētur**	mūni**entur**
PERFECT	*I fortified, have fortified,* etc.		*I was fortified, have been fortified,* etc.	
	mūnīvī	mūnīv**imus**	mūnītus (–a, –um) **sum**	mūnītī (–ae, –a) **sumus**
	mūnīv**istī**	mūnīv**istis**	mūnītus (–a, –um) **es**	mūnītī (–ae, –a) **estis**
	mūnīv**it**	mūnīv**ērunt**	mūnītus (–a, –um) **est**	mūnītī (–ae, –a) **sunt**
PLUPERFECT	*I had fortified,* etc.		*I had been fortified,* etc.	
	mūnīv**eram**	mūnīv**erāmus**	mūnītus (–a, –um) **eram**	mūnītī (–ae, –a) **erāmus**
	mūnīv**erās**	mūnīv**erātis**	mūnītus (–a, –um) **erās**	mūnītī (–ae, –a) **erātis**
	mūnīv**erat**	mūnīv**erant**	mūnītus (–a, –um) **erat**	mūnītī (–ae, –a) **erant**
FUTURE PERFECT	*I shall have fortified,* etc.		*I will have been fortified,* etc.	
	mūnīv**erō**	mūnīv**erimus**	mūnītus (–a, –um) **erō**	mūnītī (–ae, –a) **erimus**
	mūnīv**eris**	mūnīv**eritis**	mūnītus (–a, –um) **eris**	mūnītī (–ae, –a) **eritis**
	mūnīv**erit**	mūnīv**erint**	mūnītus (–a, –um) **erit**	mūnītī (–ae, –a) **erunt**

INFINITIVE

	ACTIVE	PASSIVE
PRESENT	mūnī**re**, *to fortify*	mūnī**rī**, *to be fortified*
PERFECT	mūnīv**isse**, *to have fortified*	mūnīt**us esse**, *to have been fortified*
FUTURE	mūnīt**ūrus esse**, *to be going to fortify*	

PARTICIPLE

	ACTIVE	PASSIVE
PRESENT	mūni**ēns**, *fortifying*	
PERFECT		mūnīt**us**, *(having been) fortified*
FUTURE	mūnīt**ūrus**, *going to fortify*	

IMPERATIVE

PRESENT	*fortify*	
	mūnī	mūnī**te**

Irregular Verbs

PRINCIPAL PARTS: **sum, esse, fuī, futūrus**

INDICATIVE

PRESENT	*I am, you are,* etc.	
	sum	sumus
	es	estis
	est	sunt
IMPERFECT	*I was,* etc.	
	eram	erāmus
	erās	erātis
	erat	erant
FUTURE	*I shall be,* etc.	
	erō	erimus
	eris	eritis
	erit	erunt
PERFECT	*I was,* etc.	
	fuī	fuimus
	fuistī	fuistis
	fuit	fuērunt
PLUPERFECT	*I had been,* etc.	
	fueram	fuerāmus
	fuerās	fuerātis
	fuerat	fuerant
FUTURE PERFECT	*I shall have been,* etc.	
	fuerō	fuerimus
	fueris	fueritis
	fuerit	fuerint

INFINITIVE

PRESENT	esse, *to be*
PERFECT	fuisse, *to have been*
FUTURE	futūrus esse, *to be going to be*

PARTICIPLE

FUTURE	futūrus, *going to be*

IMPERATIVE

PRESENT	*be*	
	es	este

PRINCIPAL PARTS: **possum, posse, potuī, ——**

INDICATIVE

PRESENT	*I am able, I can,* etc.	
	possum	possumus
	potes	potestis
	potest	possunt
IMPERFECT	*I was able, I could,* etc.	
	poteram	poterāmus
	poterās	poterātis
	poterat	poterant
FUTURE	*I shall be able,* etc.	
	poterō	poterimus
	poteris	poteritis
	poterit	poterunt
PERFECT	*I was able, I could,* etc.	
	potuī	potuimus
	potuistī	potuistis
	potuit	potuērunt
PLUPERFECT	*I had been able,* etc.	
	potueram	potuerāmus
	potuerās	potuerātis
	potuerat	potuerant
FUTURE PERFECT	*I shall have been able,* etc.	
	potuerō	potuerimus
	potueris	potueritis
	potuerit	potuerint

INFINITIVE

PRESENT	posse, *to be able*
PERFECT	potuisse, *to have been able*
FUTURE	——

PARTICIPLE

PRESENT	potēns (*adj.*), *powerful*

Basic Syntax

Agreement

1. *Adjectives.* Adjectives and participles agree in number, gender, and case with the nouns they modify.
2. *Adjectives as Nouns.* Adjectives are often used as nouns.
3. *Verbs.* Verbs agree in person and number with their subjects. When two subjects are connected by **aut, aut... aut, neque... neque,** the verb agrees with the nearer subject.
4. *Relative Pronoun.* The relative pronoun agrees in gender and number with its antecedent, but its case depends upon its use in its own clause.
5. *Appositives.* Appositives regularly agree in case with the nouns or pronouns they describe and usually follow them.

Noun Syntax

Nominative

1. *Subject.* The subject of a verb is in the nominative.
2. *Predicate.* A noun or adjective used in the predicate after a linking verb (*is, are, seem,* etc.) to complete its meaning is in the nominative.

Genitive

1. *Possession.* Possession is expressed by the genitive.
2. *Description.* The genitive, if modified by an adjective, may be used to describe a person or thing.

Dative

1. *Indirect Object.* The indirect object of a verb is in the dative. It is used with verbs of *giving, reporting, telling,* etc.
2. *With Special Verbs.* The dative is used with a few intransitive verbs, such as **noceō.**
3. *With Adjectives.* The dative is used with certain adjectives, as **amīcus, pār, similis,** and their opposites.

Accusative

1. *Direct Object.* The direct object of a transitive verb is in the accusative.
2. *Extent.* Extent of time or space is expressed by the accusative.
3. *Place to Which.* The accusative with **ad** (*to*) or **in** (*into*) expresses *place to which.*
4. *Subject of Infinitive.* The subject of an infinitive is in the accusative.
5. *With Prepositions.* The accusative is used with the prepositions **ad, ante, apud, circum, contrā, inter, ob, per, post, super,** and **trāns;** also with **in** and **sub** when they show the direction toward which a thing moves.

Ablative

1. *Place From Which.* The ablative with **ab, dē,** or **ex** expresses *place from which.*
2. *Agent.* The ablative with **ā** or **ab** is used with a passive verb to show the person (or animal) by whom something is done.

3. *Accompaniment.* The ablative with **cum** expresses accompaniment.
4. *Manner.* The ablative of manner with **cum** describes how something is done. **Cum** may be omitted if an adjective is used with the noun.
5. *Means.* The means by which a thing is done is expressed by the ablative without a preposition.
6. *Description.* The ablative without a preposition is used (like the genitive) to describe a person or thing.
7. *Place Where.* The ablative with **in** expresses *place where.*
8. *Time When. Time when* is expressed by the ablative without a preposition.
9. *Respect.* The ablative without a preposition is used to tell in what respect the statement applies.
10. *Absolute.* A noun in the ablative used with a participle, adjective, or other noun in the same case and having no grammatical connection with any other word in its clause is called an ablative absolute.
11. *With Prepositions.* The ablative is used with the prepositions **ab, cum, dē, ex, prae, prō, sine;** also with **in** and **sub** when they indicate *place where.*

Vocative

The *vocative* is used in addressing a person.

Verb Syntax

Tenses

1. *Imperfect.* Repeated, customary, or continuous action in the past is expressed by the imperfect.
2. *Perfect.* An action completed in the past is expressed by the perfect. It is translated by the English past.

Participles

1. The tenses of the participle (present, perfect, future) indicate time *present, past,* or *future* from the standpoint of the main verb.
2. Perfect participles are often used as simple adjectives and, like adjectives, may be used as nouns.
3. The Latin participle is often a one-word substitute for a subordinate clause in English introduced by *who* or *which, when* or *after, since* or *because, although,* and *if.*

Infinitive

1. The infinitive is a verbal indeclinable neuter noun, and as such it may be used as the subject of a verb.
2. With many verbs the infinitive, like other nouns, may be used as a direct object.
3. The infinitive object of some verbs such as **iubeō** and **doceō** often has a noun or pronoun subject in the accusative.
4. Statements that convey indirectly the thoughts or words of another, used as the objects of verbs of *saying, thinking, knowing, hearing, perceiving,* etc., require verbs in the infinitive with subjects in the accusative.

Vocabulary 

Latin–English

Proper names are not included unless they are spelled differently in English or are difficult to pronounce in English. Their English pronunciation is indicated by a simple system. The vowels are as follows: ā as in *hate,* ă as in *hat,* ē as in *feed,* ĕ as in *fed,* ī as in *bite,* ĭ as in *bit,* ō as in *hope,* ŏ as in *hop,* ū as in *cute,* ŭ as in *cut*. In the ending *ēs* the *s* is soft as in *rose*. When the accented syllable ends in a consonant, the vowel is short; otherwise it is long.

A

ā, ab *prep. w. abl.,* from, away from, by
absum, abesse, āfuī, āfutūrus, be away, be absent
ac, *see* **atque**
accēdō, –ere, accessī, accessūrus, approach
accidō, –ere, accidī, —, fall to, befall, happen (*w. dat.*)
accipiō, –ere, accēpī, acceptus, receive
accūsō, –āre, –āvī, –ātus, blame, accuse
ācer, ācris, ācre, sharp, keen, fierce
ācriter, *adv.,* sharply
ad, *prep. w. acc.,* to, toward, for, near
addūcō, –ere, addūxī, adductus, lead to, influence
adiuvo, –āre, –āvī, –ātus, help
adōrō, –āre, –āvī, –ātus, worship
adsum, –esse, adfuī, adfutūrus, be near, be present
adulēscentulus, –ī, *m.,* young man
aeger, aegra, aegrum, sick, ill
Aegyptiī, –ōrum, *m. pl.,* the Egyptians
Aegyptus, –ī, *f.,* Egypt
Aenēās, –ae, *m.,* Aeneas (Enē´as)
Aeolus, –ī, *m.,* Aeolus (E´olus)
aequē, *adv.,* justly
aequus, –a, –um, even, just, calm
āēr, āeris, *m.* air
aes, aeris, *n.,* copper, bronze
aestās, –tātis, *f.,* summer
aetās, –tātis, *f.,* age
Aetna, –ae, *f.,* (Mt.) Etna
afficiō, –ere, affēcī, affectus, affect, afflict with
Āfricānus –ī, *m.,* Africā´nus
ager, agrī, *m.,* field, farm, country
agō, –ere, ēgī, āctus, do, drive, treat, discuss, live, spend (*time*); **grātiās agō,** thank; **vītam agō,** lead a life
agricola, –ae, *m.,* farmer
āla, –ae, *f.,* wing
albus, –a, –um, white
aliēnus, –a, –um, another's, unfavorable
alius, alia, aliud, other, another; **alius . . . alius,** one . . . another; **aliī . . . aliī,** some . . . others
Alpēs, –ium, *f. pl.,* the Alps
altē, *adv.,* high, far
alter, altera, alterum, the other (*of two*), the second; **alter . . . alter,** the one . . . the other
altus, –a, –um, high, tall, deep
ambō, –ae, –ō, both
ambulō, –āre, –āvī, –ātus, walk
Americānus, –a, –um, American; **Americānus, –ī,** *m.,* an American
amīcitia, –ae, *f.,* friendship
amīcus, –a, –um, friendly; **amīcus, –ī,** *m.,* **amīca, –ae,** *f.,* friend
āmittō, –ere, āmīsī, āmissus, lose, let go, send away
amō, –āre, –āvī, –ātus, love, like
amor, –ōris, *m.,* love
amphitheātrum, –ī, *n.,* amphitheater
Anglicus, –a, –um, English
animus, –ī, *m.,* soul, spirit, mind, courage
annus, –ī, *m.,* year
ante, *adv. and prep. w. acc.,* before (*of time or place*)
antecēdō, –ere, –cessī, –cessūrus, go before, take the lead
antīquus, –a, –um, old, ancient
aperiō, –īre, –uī, –tus, open, uncover
appellō, –āre, –āvī, –ātus, call, name, address

Appius, –a, –um, *adj.,* of Appius, Appian; **Appius, –pī,** *m.,* Appius
aptus, –a, –um, fit, suitable (*w. dat.*)
apud, *prep. w. acc.,* among, with
aqua, –ae, *f.,* water
aquaeductus, –ūs, *m.,* aqueduct
Aquītānus, –ī, *m.,* an Aquitā´nian
arbor, –is, *m.* tree
arcus, –ūs, *m.,* arch, bow
arēna, –ae, *f.,* arena, sand, desert, seashore
argentum, –ī, *n.,* silver
arma, –ōrum, *n. pl.,* arms, weapons
ascendō, –ere, ascendī, ascēnsus, climb (up), ascend
Athēna, –ae, *f., a Greek goddess* = Minerva
atque (ac), *conj.,* and
ātrium, ātrī, *n.,* atrium, entry hall
auctor, –ōris, *m.,* maker, author, writer
auctōritās, –tātis, *f.,* authority, influence
audācia, –ae, *f.,* boldness
audāx, *gen.* **audācis,** bold, daring
audiō, –īre, –īvī, –ītus, hear
augeō, –ēre, auxī, auctus, increase
aureus, –a, –um, golden
aurīga, –ae, *m.,* charioteer
aurum, –ī, *n.,* gold
aut, or; **aut . . . aut,** either . . . or
autem, *conj.* however (*never first word*),
autumus, –ī, *m.* autumn, fall
auxilium, –lī, *n.,* aid, help; *pl.* reinforcements
āvertō, –ere, āvertī, āversus, turn from, turn away, turn off, remove
avis, avis, *f.* bird
avus, –ī, *m.,* grandfather
axis, –is, *m.,* axle

B

barbarus, –a, –um, foreign, barbarous; **barbarus, –ī,** *m.,* foreigner, barbarian
beātus, –a, –um, happy, blessed
Belgae, –ārum, *m. pl.,* the Belgians; the Belgian people
bellum, –ī, *n.,* war
bene, *adv.,* well, well done; *comp.* **melius,** better; *superl.* **optimē,** best, very good
beneficium, –ī, *n.,* kindness, benefit
benignē, thank you
benignus, –a, –um, kind
bibō, –ere, bibī, —, drink
bonus, –a, –um, good; *comp.* **melior, melius,** better; *superl.* **optimus, –a, –um,** best
Britannia, –ae, *f.,* Britain
Britannus, –ī, *m.,* a Briton

C

C., *abbreviation for* **Gāius**
cadō, –ere, cecidī, cāsūrus, fall
Caecilius, lī, *m.,* Caecilius (Sēsil´ius)
caelum, –ī, *n.,* sky
Caesar, –aris, *m.,* Caesar
campus, –ī, *m.,* field
canis, –is, *m. & f.,* dog
canō, –ere, cecinī, cantus, sing
caper, caprī, *m.,* goat
capiō, –ere, cēpī, captus, take, seize, capture; **cōnsilium capiō,** adopt a plan
Capitōlium, –lī, *n.,* the Capitol, *temple of Jupiter at Rome;* the Capitoline Hill
captīvus, –ī, *m.;* **captīva, –ae,** *f.,* prisoner
caput, capitis, *n.,* head
carmen, –minis, *n.,* song
carrus, –ī, *m.,* cart, wagon
Carthāginiēnsēs, –ium, *m. pl.,* the Carthaginians (Carthajin´ians)
Carthāgō, –ginis, *f.,* Carthage, *a city in Africa;* **Carthāgō Nova,** New Carthage, *in Spain*
casa, –ae, *f.,* house
castra, –ōrum, *n. pl.,* camp
cāsus, –ūs, *m.,* fall, chance, accident
Catilīna, –ae, *m.,* Catiline
causa, –ae, *f.,* cause, reason, case
cēdō, –ere, cessī, cessūrus, move, retreat, yield
celebrō, –āre, –āvī, –ātus, celebrate, honor
celer, celeris, celere, swift
celeritās, –tātis, *f.,* speed, swiftness
celeriter, *adv.,* quickly, swiftly
Celtae, –ārum, *m. pl.,* Celts, *a people of Gaul*
cēna, –ae, *f.,* dinner
centum, hundred

cēra, –ae, *f.* wax
Cerēs, –eris, *f.,* Ceres (Sē´rēs), *goddess of agriculture*
cernō, –ere, crēvī, crētus, separate, discern, see
certē, *adv.,* certainly
certus, –a, –um, fixed, sure
cibus, –ī, *m.,* food
Cicerō, –ōnis, *m.,* Cicero (Sis´ero)
Circē, –ae, *f.,* Circe (Sir´sē), *a sorceress*
circum, *prep. w. acc.,* around
circus, –ī, *m.,* circle, circus, *esp. the Circus Maximus at Rome*
cīvis, cīvis, *m. & f.,* citizen
cīvitās, –tātis, *f.,* citizenship, state
clam, *adv.,* secretly
clāmō, –āre, –āvī, –ātus, noise, shout, cry out
clāmor, –ōris, *m.,* shout(ing), noise
clārē, *adv.,* clearly
clārus, –a, –um, clear, famous
claudō, –ere, clausī, clausus, close
cognōmen, –minis, *n.,* nickname, surname
cognōscō, –ere, –nōvī, –nitus, learn, recognize; *perf.,* know, understand
cōgō, –ere, coēgī, coactus, drive together, collect, compel
colō, –ere, coluī, cultus, worship, cultivate, till, inhabit
colōnus, –ī, *m.,* settler
Colossēum, –ī, *n.,* the Colossē´um, *an amphitheater at Rome*
committō, –ere, –mīsī, –missus, join together, commit, entrust; **proelium committō,** begin battle
commodē, *adv.,* suitably
commodus, –a, –um, suitable, convenient
commoveō, –ēre, mōvī, –mōtus, disturb
commūnis, –e, common
comprehendō, –ere, –hendī, –hēnsus, understand
concordia, –ae, *f.,* harmony
condiciō, –ōnis, *f.,* condition, terms
cōnficiō, –ere, –fēcī, –fectus, do up, complete, exhaust
cōnfīdō, –ere, cōnfīsus, have confidence (in)
cōnfirmō, –āre, –āvī, –ātus, make firm, encourage, establish
cōnservō, –āre, –āvī, –ātus, save, preserve
cōnsilium, –lī, *n.,* plan, advice
consistō, –ere, constitī, constitūrus, stop, stand still
cōnspiciō, –ere, –spexī, –spectus, catch sight of, see
cōnstituō, –ere, –uī, –ūtus, determine, decide
cōnsul, –ulis, *m.,* consul, *the highest Roman official*
cōnsulō, –ere, –suluī, –sultus, consult
contendō, –ere, –tendī, –tentūrus, struggle, hasten
contineō, –ēre, –uī, –tentus, hold (together), contain
contrā, *prep. w. acc.,* against, opposite
conveniō, –īre, –vēnī, –ventūrus, come together
convocō, –āre, –āvī, –ātus, call together
cōpia, –ae, *f.,* supply, abundance
cor, cordis, *n.,* heart
corium, corī, *n.* skin, leather
corōna, –ae, *f.,* crown
corpus, –poris, *n.,* body
crās, *adv.,* tomorrow
crātēr, –is, *m.* large bowl
crēdō, –ere, –didī, –ditus, believe, entrust (*w. dat.*)
Crēta, –ae, *f.,* Crete
cum, *prep. w. abl.,* with
cupiditās, –tātis, *f.,* desire
cupiō, –ere, cupīvī, cupītus, desire, wish, want
cūr, *adv.,* why
cūra, –ae, *f.,* care, concern; **(cum) magnā cūrā,** very carefully
cūrō, –āre, –āvī, –ātus, care for, cure
currō, –ere, cucurrī, cursūrus, run
currus, –ūs, *m.,* chariot
cursus, –ūs, *m.* running, course, voyaging

D

dē, *prep. w. abl.,* from, down from, about
dea, –ae, *f.,* goddess
dēbeō, –ēre, dēbuī, dēbitus, ought, owe
decem, ten
decimus, –a, –um, tenth
dēfendō, –ere, dēfendī, dēfēnsus, defend
dēlecto, –āre, –āvī, –ātus, please

dēligō, –ere, dēlēgī, dēlēctus, select

dēmōnstrō, –āre, –āvī, –ātus, show

dēpōnō, –ere, dēposuī, dēpositus, put down, lay aside

dēscendō, –ere, dēscendī, dēscēnsus, descend

dēserō, –ere, dēseruī, dēsertus, desert

dēsiliō, –īre, dēsiluī, dēsultūrus, jump down, dismount

dēspiciō, –ere, dēspexī, dēspectus, look down on, despise

deus, –ī, *m.,* god

dēvorō, –āre, –āvī, –ātus, swallow

dīcō, –ere, dīxī, dictus, say, tell

dictātor, –ōris, *m.,* dictator

dictum, –ī, *n.,* word

diēs, diēī, *m.,* day

difficilis, –e, difficult, hard

digitus, –ī, *m.,* finger

dīligentia, –ae, *f.,* diligence

dīmittō, –ere, dīmīsī, dīmissus, let go, send away, dismiss

discēdō, –ere, –cessī, –cessūrus, go away, depart

disciplīna, –ae, *f.,* training, instruction, discipline

discipulus, –ī, *m.,* **discipula, –ae,** *f.,* student learner, pupil

dissimilis, –e, unlike

dīvidō, –ere, dīvīsī, dīvīsus, divide

dō, dare, dedī, datus, give, put; **poenam dō,** pay the penalty

doceō, –ēre, docuī, doctus, teach

dominus, –ī, *m.,* master; **domina, –ae,** *f.,* mistress

domus, –ūs, *f.,* house, home

dōnō, –āre, –āvī, –ātus, give, present

dormiō, –īre, –īvī, –ītus, sleep

dubitō, –āre, –āvī, –ātus, hesitate, doubt

dūcō, –ere, dūxī, ductus, lead, draw

dulcis, –e, sweet

dum, *conj.,* while

duo, –ae, –o, two

duodecim, twelve

durē, *adv.,* harshly

dūrus, –a, –um, hard, harsh

dux, ducis, *m.,* leader, general

E

ē, ex, *prep. w. abl.,* from, out of, out from

ea, she *(nom.)*

ecce, *interj.,* look, here!

edo, ēsse, ēdī, ēsus, eat

ēdūcō, –ere, ēdūxī, ēductus, lead out

efficiō, –ere, effēcī, effectus, make (out), bring about, complete

ego, meī, I

ēgregius, –a, –um, excellent, distinguished

eius, his, her

elephantus, –ī, *m.,* elephant

emō, –ere, ēmī, ēmptus, take, buy

Ēpīrus, –ī, *f.,* Ēpī´rus, *a province in Greece*

equus, –ī, *m.,* horse

ērumpō, –ere, ērūpī, ēruptus, burst forth

et, *conj.,* and, even; **et . . . et,** both . . . and

etiam, *adv.,* even, also, too

Etrūscī, –ōrum, *m. pl.,* the Etruscans

Eumaeus, –ī, *m.,* Eumaeus (Ūmē´us)

Eurōpa, –ae, *f.,* Europe

ēvādō, –ere, ēvāsī, ēvāsūrus, go out, escape

ēvocō, –āre, –āvī, –ātus, summon, call out

excēdō, –ere, excessī, excessūrus, depart

exclāmo, –āre, –āvī, –ātus, shout

exemplum, –ī, *n.,* example

exerceō, –ēre, exercuī, exercitus, train, keep busy

exercitus, –ūs, *m.,* (trained) army

exit, he goes out

expediō, –īre, –īvī, –ītus, set free

expellō, –ere, expulī, expulsus, drive out

explicō, –āre, –āvī, –ātus, unfold, explain

explōrō, –āre, –āvī, –ātus, investigate, explore

expugnō, –āre, –āvī, –ātus, capture by assault

exspectō, –āre, –āvī, –ātus, look out for, await, wait

exstinguō, –ere, exstīnxī, exstīnctus, extinguish

extrā, *(prep. w. acc.),* outside, beyond

extrēmus, –a, –um, farthest, last, end of

F

fābula, –ae, *f.,* story
facile, *adv.,* easily
facilis, –e, easy
faciō, –ere, fēcī, factus, do, make; **verba faciō,** speak, make a speech
factum, –ī, *n.,* deed
fallō, –ere, fefellī, falsus, deceive, disappoint
fāma, –ae, *f.,* report, fame
familia, –ae, *f.,* family
familiāris, –e, of the family, friendly; *as noun, m.,* friend *(familiar)*
fāmōsus, –a, –um, famous, notorious
fātum, –ī, *n.,* fate; *often personified,* the Fates
fēmina, –ae, *f.,* woman, wife
fēriae, –ārum, *f. pl.,* holiday
ferio, –īre, –īvī, –ītus, hit, strike
ferrum, –ī, *n.,* iron
festīno, –āre, –āvī, –ātus, hurry
fīdus, –a, –um, faithful, reliable, loyal
fīlius, –lī, *m.,* son; **fīlia, –ae,** *f.,* daughter
fīnis, fīnis, *m.,* end; *pl.,* borders, territory
fīnitimus, –a, –um, neighboring, near; *as noun,* neighbor
firmus, –a, –um, strong, firm
flagellum, –ī, *n.,* whip
fluctus, –ūs, *m.,* wave
flūmen, flūminis, *n.,* river
fluō, –ere, flūxī, fluxuss, flow
focus, –ī, *m.,* hearth
fōrma, –ae, *f.,* shape, image, form
fortasse, *adv.,* perhaps
fortis, –e, strong, brave
fortiter, *adv.,* bravely
fortūna, –ae, *f.,* fortune, luck
forum, –ī, *n.,* market place; Forum (*at Rome*)
frangō, –ere, frēgī, fractus, break, shatter
frāter, frātris, *m.,* brother
frīgidus, –a, –um, cold
frōns, frontis, *f.,* front, forehead
frūmentum, –ī, *n.,* grain
fuga, –ae, *f.,* flight; **in fugam dō,** put to flight
fugiō, –ere, fūgī, fugitūrus, run away, flee
fulmen, –minis, *n.,* lightning
futūrus, *see* **sum**

G

Gāius, –ī, *m.,* Gā´ius
Gallia, –ae, *f.,* Gaul, *ancient France*
Gallicus, –a, –um, Gallic
Gallus, –a, –um, Gallic *(from Gaul); as noun, m.,* a Gaul
gaudium, –ī, *n.,* joy, gladness
gēns, gentis, *f.,* people, nation, family, class
genus, generis, *n.,* birth, kind, class, sort
Germānia, –ae, *f.,* Germany
Germānus, –ī, *m.,* a German
gerō, –ere, gessī, gestus, carry on, wear
gladiātor, –ōris, *m.,* gladiator
gladius, –ī, *m.,* sword
glōria, –ae, *f.,* glory
glōriōsus, –a, –um, glorious
Graecia, –ae, *f.,* Greece
Graecus, –a, –um, Greek; **Graecus, –ī,** *m.,* a Greek
grammaticus, –ī, *m.,* school teacher
grātē, *adv.,* gratefully
grātia, –ae, *f.,* gratitude, influence; **grātiam habeō,** feel grateful; **grātiās agō,** thank *(w. dat.)*
grātus, –a, –um, pleasing, grateful
gravis, –e, heavy, severe
graviter, *adv.,* heavily, seriously

H

habeō, –ēre, habuī, habitus, have, hold, consider; **grātiam habeō,** feel grateful (*w. dat.*); **ōrātiōnem habeō,** deliver an oration
habitō, –āre, –āvī, –ātus, live, dwell
haereō, –ēre, haesī, haesus, stick, cling
Hannibal, –alis, *m.,* Hannibal, *a Carthaginian general*
herba, –ae, *f.,* herb, plant, grass
Hibernia, –ae, *f.,* Ireland
hic, haec, hoc, this; *as pron.,* he, she, it
hiems, hiemis, *f.,* winter
Hispānia, –ae, *f.,* Spain
Hispānus, –a, –um, Spanish
hodiē, *adv.,* today
homō, hominis, *m.,* man, human being
honestās, –tātis, *f.,* honor, honesty

honor, –ōris, *m.,* honor, office
hōra, –ae, *f.,* hour
hospita, –ae, *f.,* guest
hostis, hostis, *m.,* enemy (*usually pl.*)
humilis, –e, low, humble

I

iaciō, –ere, iēcī, iactus, throw, hurl
iam, *adv.,* already, now; **nōn iam,** no longer
ibi, *adv.,* there
īdem, eadem, idem, same
ignāvus, –a, –um, lazy
ignis, –is, *m.,* fire
ille, illa, illud, that; *as pron.,* he, she, it
impedīmentum, –ī, *n.,* hindrance; *pl.,* baggage
impediō, –īre, –īvī, –ītus, hinder
imperātor, –ōris, *m.,* commander, general
imperium, –rī, *n.,* command, power
imperō, –āre, –āvī, –ātus, command (*w. dat.*)
impetus, –ūs, *m.,* attack; **impetum facio in** *(w. acc.),* make an attack against
in, *prep. w. acc.,* into, to, against; *w. abl.,* in, on, upon
incertus, –a, –um, uncertain
incipiō, –ere, incēpī, inceptus, take to, begin
incitō, –āre, –āvī, –ātus, urge on, arouse
incolō, –ere, incoluī, incultus, live, inhabit
īnferī, –ōrum, *m.* inhabitants of the Underworld
īnferior, īnferius, lower
inimīcus, –a, –um, unfriendly, hostile; *as noun, m.,* enemy
iniūria, –ae, *f.,* injustice, wrong, injury
iniūriōsus, –a, –um, harmful
inquit, he, she said
īnsānus, –a, –um, insane
īnstō, –āre, institī, —, threaten
īnstruō, –ere, instruxī, instructus, arrange, provide, draw up
īnsula, –ae, *f.,* island
integer, –gra, –grum, untouched, fresh
intellegō, –ere, –lēxī, –lēctus, understand
inter, *prep. w. acc.,* between, among
intercipiō, –ere, –cēpī, –ceptus, intercept, cut off, steal
interclūdō, –ere, –clūsī, –clūsus, cut off
interficiō, –ere, –fēcī, –fectus, kill
interim, *adv.,* meanwhile
intermittō, –ere, –mīsī, –missus, let go, stop, interrupt
inveniō, –īre, invēnī, inventus, find, come upon
iō, *interj.,* hurrah!
ipse, ipsa, ipsum, –self, very
īra, –ae, *f.,* anger
is, ea, id, this, that; *as pron.,* he, she, it
ita, *adv.,* so
Italia, –ae, *f.,* Italy
itaque, *adv.,* and so, therefore, and as a result
iter, itineris, *n.,* journey, road, march
iterum, *adv.,* again, a second time
iubeō, –ēre, iussī, iussus, order
iūdicō, –āre, –āvī, –ātus, judge
Iūlius, –lī, *m.,* Julius; **Iūlia, –ae,** *f.,* Julia
iungō, –ere, iūnxī, iūnctus, join (to)
Iūnō, –ōnis, *f.,* Juno, *a goddess, wife of Jupiter*
Iuppiter, Iovis, *m.,* Jupiter, *king of the gods*
iūs, iūris, *n.,* right
iūstē, *adv.,* justly
iūstus, –a, –um, just

L

labor, –ōris, *m.,* work, hardship
labōrō, –āre, –āvī, –ātus, work
lac, lactis, *n.,* milk
lacrima, –ae, *f.,* tear
lacrimō, –āre, –āvī, –ātus, weep
lanterna, –ae, *f.,* lantern
lapis, lapidis, *m.,* stone
Lār, Laris, *m.,* Lar, *a household god*
lassitūdō, –tūdinis, *f.,* weariness
lātē, *adv.,* widely
Latīnus, –a, –um, Latin, belonging to Latium; **Latīnī, –ōrum,** *m.,* the Latins
Latīnus, –ī, *m.,* Latī´nus
latrō, –ōnis, *m.,* bandit
lātus, –a, –um, wide
laudō, –āre, –āvī, –ātus, praise
lavō, –āre, lāvī, lautus, wash, bathe
lēgātus, –ī, *m.,* envoy

legō, –ere, lēgī, lēctus, collect, gather, choose pick, read
levis, –e, light (*in weight*)
leviter, *adv.,* lightly
lēx, lēgis, *f.,* law
liber, librī, *m.,* book
līber, –era, –erum, free
līberē, *adv.,* freely
līberī, –ōrum, *m. pl.,* children
līberō, –āre, –āvī, –ātus, free
lībertās, –tātis, *f.,* freedom, liberty
ligō, –āre, –āvī, –ātus, bind, tie
lingua, –ae, *f.,* tongue, language
littera, –ae, *f.,* letter (*of the alphabet*), *pl.,* a letter (*epistle*) (*literal, literary*), letters (*if modified by an adjective such as* **multae**), literature
locus, –ī, *m.,* (*pl.* **loca, locōrum,** *n.*), place
longus, –a, –um, long
Lūcīlius, –lī, *m.,* Lucilius (Lūsil´ius)
lūdō, –ere, lūsī, lūsus, play
lūdus, –ī, *m.,* school, game, play
Lūsitānia, –ae, *f.,* Portugal
lūx, lūcis, *f.,* light, daylight

M

M., *abbreviation for* **Mārcus**
mactē, *interj.,* well done!
magister, –trī, *m.,* teacher
magistra, –2e, *f.,* teacher
magnus, –a, –um, large, great; *comp.* **maior, maius,** greater; *superl.* **maximus, –a, –um,** greatest, very great
maior, *see* **magnus**
malus, –a, –um, bad; *comp.* **peior, peius,** worse; *superl.* **pessimus, –a, –um,** very bad, worst; **malum, –ī,** *n.,* trouble
mandō, –āre, –āvī, –ātus, entrust
maneō, –ēre, mānsī, mānsūrus, remain
manus, –ūs, *f.,* hand
Mārcius, –cī, *m.,* Marcius (Mar´shus)
mare, maris, *n.,* sea
marītus, –ī, *m.,* husband
Mārs, Mārtis, *m.,* Mars, *god of war*
māter, mātris, *f.,* mother
māteria, –ae, *f.,* matter, timber
mātrimōnium, –nī, *n.,* marriage
mātūrō, –āre, –āvī, –ātus, hasten
maximē, *adv.,* very greatly, especially
maximus, *see* **magnus**
medicus, –ī, *m.,* doctor
Mediterrāneum (Mare), Mediterranean Sea
medius, –a, –um, middle (of)
mel, mellis, *n.,* honey
melior, *see* **bonus**
memoria, –ae, *f.,* memory; **memoriā teneō,** remember
mēnsa, –ae, *f.,* table
mēnsis, –is, *m.,* month
mercātor, –ōris, *m.,* merchant
Mercurius, –rī, *m.,* Mercury
mereō, –ēre, meruī, meritus, deserve, earn
mēta, –ae, *f.,* goal, turning post (*in the Circus*)
meus, –a, –um, my, mine
migrō, –āre, –āvī, –ātūrus, depart
mīles, mīlitis, *m.,* soldier
mille, *pl.,* **milia,** thousand
Minerva, –ae, *f., a goddess*
minimē, *adv.,* not at all; *interj.,* no
minimus, minor, *see* **parvus**
miser, –era, –erum, unhappy, poor, wretched
mittō, –ere, mīsī, missus, let go, send
modus, –ī, *m.,* manner
moneō, –ēre, –uī, –itus, remind, warn, advise
mōns, montis, *m.,* mountain
mōnstrō, –āre, –āvī, –ātus, point out, show
mors, mortis, *f.,* death
mōs, mōris, *m.,* custom
moveō, –ēre, mōvī, mōtus, move
mox, *adv.,* soon
mulier, mulieris, *f.,* woman
multus, –a, –um, much; *pl.,* many; *comp.* **plūrēs, plūra,** more; *superl.* **plūrimus, –a, –um,** most
mundus, –ī, *m.,* world
mūniō, –īre, –īvī, –ītus, fortify; **viam mūniō,** build a road
mūnus, mūneris, *n.,* duty, service, gift
mutātus, –a, –um, changed
mūtō, –āre, –āvī, –ātus, change

N

nam *conj.*, for
nārrō, –āre, –āvī, –ātus, tell, relate
nātō, –āre, –āvī, –ātus, swim
nātūra, –ae, *f.*, nature
nātūrālis, –e, natural
nauta, –ae, *m.*, sailor
nāvigō, –āre, –āvī, –ātus, sail
nāvis, nāvis, *f.*, ship
–ne, *introduces questions*
nec, *see* **neque**
neglegentia, –ae, *f.*, negligence
negōtium, –tī, *n.*, business
nēmo, *dat.* **nēminī,** *acc.* **nēminem** (*no other forms*), no one
Neptūnus, –ī, *m.*, Neptune, *god of the sea*
neque (*or* **nec**), and not, nor; **neque . . . neque,** neither . . . nor
nesciō, –īre, –īvī, –ītus, not know
neuter, –tra, –trum, neither (*of two*)
nihil, *n.*, nothing *(indecl. noun)*
nōbilis, –e, noble
nōbīscum = cum nōbīs
noceō, –ēre, nocuī, nocitūrus, do harm to (*w. dat.*)
nōmen, nōminis, *n.*, name
nōn, *adv.*, not; **nōn iam,** no longer
nōs, nostrum, we, *pl. of* **ego**
nōscō, –ere, nōvī, nōtus, learn; *perf.*, have learned, know
noster, –tra, –trum, our
nōtus, –a, –um, known, familiar
novem, nine
novus, –a, –um, new, strange
nox, noctis, *f.*, night
nullus, –a, –um, no . . . , not any, none
numerus, –ī, *m.*, number
numquam, *adv.*, never
nunc, *adv.*, now
nūntiō, –āre, –āvī, –ātus, announce, report
nūntius, –tī, *m.*, messenger

O

ob, *prep. w. acc.*, toward, because of, on account of, for
obtineō, –ēre, obtinuī, obtentus, hold, obtain
occultus, –a, –um, secret
occupō, –āre, –āvī, –ātus, seize
Ōceanus, –ī, *m.*, ocean
octō, eight
oculus, –ī, *m.*, eye
officium, –cī, *n.*, duty, office
ōlim, once, formerly, sometime
omnis, omne, all, every
oportet, –ēre, –tuit, it is fitting, it is necessary *(w. acc. of person + inf.)*
oppidum, –ī, *n.*, town
opprimō, –ere, oppressī, oppressus, overcome, surprise
optimē, *see* **bene**
optimus, *see* **bonus**
opus, operis, *n.*, work, labor
ōrātiō, –ōnis, *f.*, speech
ōrātor, –ōris, *m.*, orator
orbis, –is, *m.*, world, circle, ring
ōrdō, ōrdinis, *m.*, order, rank, row
ōrnāmentum, –ī, *n.*, jewel, costume
ostendō, –ere, ostendī, ostentus, show, stretch out
ōtiōsus, –a, –um, leisurely, idle
ōtium, ōtī, *n.*, leisure, peace

P

P., *abbreviation for* **Pūblius**
paene, *adv.*, almost
pār, *gen.* **paris,** equal
parātus, –a, –um, ready, prepared
parō, –āre, –āvī, –ātus, get, get ready, prepare
pars, partis, *f.*, part, side
parvus, –a, –um, small, little; *comp.* **minor, minus,** less; *superl.* **minimus, –a, –um,** least
passus, –ūs, *m.*, pace
pāstor, –ōris, *m.*, shepherd
pater, patris, *m.*, father
patria, –ae, *f.*, fatherland, country
paucī, –ae, –a, a few, few
Paulus, –ī, *m.*, Paul
paupertās, –tātis, *f.*, poverty, humble circumstances
pāx, pācis, *f.*, peace

pecūnia, –ae, *f.,* sum of money, money
peior, *see* **malus**
pellō, –ere, pepulī, pulsus, drive, drive out, defeat
Penātēs, –ium, *m.,* the Penā´tēs, *household gods*
Pēnelopē, –ae, *f.,* Penĕl´ope, *wife of Ulysses*
per, *prep. w. acc.,* through, by
perficiō, –ere, –fēcī, –fectus, finish
perīculum, –ī, *n.,* danger
permittō, –ere, –mīsī, –missus, let go through, allow, permit, entrust (*w. dat.*)
permoveō, –ēre, –mōvī, –mōtus, move (deeply)
permūtātiō, –ōnis, *f.,* exchange
perpetuus, –a, –um, constant
persōna, –ae, *f.,* character
perveniō, –īre, –vēnī, –ventūrus, come through, arrive
pēs, pedis, *m.,* foot; **pedibus,** on foot
pessimus, *see* **malus**
petō, –ere, petīvī, petītus, seek, attack, aim at, ask (for)
Philippus, –ī *m.,* Philip
philosophia, –ae, *f.,* philosophy
Phrygia, –ae, *f.,* Phrygia (Frij´ia), *a country of Asia Minor*
pictūra, –ae, *f.,* picture
pila, –ae, *f.,* ball
pius, –a, –um, loyal
plācō, –āre, –āvī, –ātus, please, calm
plāgōsus, –a, –um, fond of whipping
plānus, –a, –um, level
plēbs, plēbis, *f.,* common people, plebians
plicō, –āre, –āvī, –ātus, fold
plūrēs, plūra, more, *see* **multus**
plūrimus, *see* **multus**
plūs, *see* **multus**
Plūtō, –ōnis, *m.,* Plū´tō
poena, –ae, *f.,* punishment, penalty
poēta, –ae, *m.,* poet
Polyphēmus, –ī, *m.,* Polyphē´mus, *a man-eating giant*
pompa, –ae, *f.,* parade, procession
pōnō, –ere, posuī, positus, put, place; **castra pōnō,** pitch camp
pōns, pontis, *m.,* bridge
pontifex, –ficis, *m.,* priest
Pontus, –ī, *m., a country in Asia Minor*
populus, –ī, *m.,* people; *pl.,* peoples, nations
porta, –ae, *f.,* gate *(of a city or a camp)*
portō, –āre, –āvī, –ātus, carry
portus, –ūs, *m.,* harbor
possum, posse, potuī, —, can, be able
post, *adv. and prep. w. acc.,* behind (*of place*); after (*of time*)
posteā, *adv.,* afterwards
postquam, *conj.,* after
potēns, *(gen.)* **potentis,** powerful
potestās, –tātis, *f.,* power
prae, *prep. w. abl.,* before, in front of
praeceps, *gen.* **praecipitis,** headlong, steep
praeda, –ae, *f.,* loot, booty
praeficiō, –ere, –fēcī, –fectus, put in charge of
praemittō, –ere, –mīsī, –missus, send ahead
praemium, –ī, *n.,* reward
praesidium, –dī, *n.,* guard, protection
praesum, –esse, –fuī, –futūrus, be in charge of
praetextus, –a, –um, (woven in front), bordered; **toga praetexta,** crimson-bordered toga
premō, –ere, pressī, pressus, press, press hard
pretium, –tī, *n.,* price
prīmō, *adv.,* at first
prīmum, *adv.,* for the first time
prīmus, –a, –um, first
prīnceps, –cipis, *m.,* leader
prō, *prep. w. abl.,* for, in behalf of, in front of, before
probō, –āre, –āvī, –ātus, test, prove, approve
prōcēdō, –ere, –cessī, –cessūrus, go forward, advance
prōdūcō, –ere, –dūxī, –ductus, lead out, prolong
proelium, –lī, *n.,* battle
prohibeō, –ēre, –hibuī, –hibitus, prevent, keep from
prope, *prep. w. acc.,* near
properō, –āre, –āvī, –ātūrus, hasten
prōpōnō, –ere, –posuī, –positus, put forward, offer, present
proprius, –a, –um, (one's) own
prōvideō, –ēre, –vīdī, –vīsus, foresee

prōvincia, –ae, *f.,* province
proximus, –a, –um, nearest, very near, next
pūblicē, *adv.,* publicly
pūblicus, –a, –um, public
Pūblius, –lī, *m.,* Pub´lius
puella, –ae, *f.,* girl
puer, puerī, *m.,* boy
pugna, –ae, *f.,* battle, fight
pugnō, –āre, –āvī, –ātus, fight
pulcher, –chra, –chrum, beautiful
Pūnicus, –a, –um, Punic, Carthaginian
pūpa, –ae, *f.,* doll, little girl
putō, –āre, –āvī, –ātus, think
Pyrrhus, –ī, *m.,* Pyr´rhus, *king of Epirus*

Q

quam, *conj.,* than, as
quartus, –a, –um, fourth
quattuor, four
–que *(joined to second word),* and
quī, quae, quod, *relat. pron.,* who, which, what, that; *interrog. adj.,* what
quīndecim, fifteen
quīnque, five
quīntus, –a, –um, fifth
quis, quid, *interrog, pron.,* who, what
quō modō, how *(in what manner)*
quod, *conj.,* because, since
quondam, *adv.,* once (upon a time)

R

raeda, –ae, *f.,* carriage, omnibus
rāmus, –ī, *m.,* branch
rapiō, –ere, rapuī, raptus, carry off, steal
ratiō, –ōnis, *f.,* account, reason
recipiō, –ere, recēpī, receptus, take back, recover, receive
reddō, –ere, reddidī, redditus, give back
redigō, –ere, redēgī, redactus, drive back, reduce
redūcō, –ere, redūxī, reductus, lead back, bring back
rēgia, –ae, *f.,* palace
rēgīna, –ae, *f.,* queen
regiō, –ōnis, *f.,* region
rēgnum, –ī, *n.,* kingdom, royal power
regō, –ere, rēxī, rēctus, rule, reign, guide
relinquō, –ere, relīquī, relictus, leave behind, abandon
reliquus, –a, –um, remaining, rest (of)
remaneō, –ēre, remānsī, remānsūrus, stay behind, remain
remedium, –dī, *n.,* remedy
remittō, –ere, remīsī, remissus, relax, send back
removeō, –ēre, remōvī, remōtus, remove
repellō, –ere, reppulī, repulsus, drive back, repulse
rēs, reī, *f.,* thing, matter, affair; **rēs pūblica,** public affairs, government
respondeō, –ēre, respondī, respōnsus, answer
restō, –āre, restitī, —, remain
retineō, –ēre, retinuī, retentus, hold back, keep
reverentia, –ae, *f.,* respect
revertō, –ere, revertī, reversūrus, return
rēx, rēgis, *m.,* king
Rhēnus, –ī, *m.,* the Rhine river
rīdeō, –ēre, rīsī, rīsus, laugh (at)
rogō, –āre, –āvī, –ātus, ask, ask for
Rōma, –ae, *f.,* Rome
Rōmānus, –a, –um, Roman; *as noun,* a Roman
ruīna, –ae, *f.,* downfall, collapse; *pl.,* ruins

S

saccus, –ī, *m.,* sack, bag
sacer, –cra, –crum, sacred
sacerdōs, –ōtis, *m. & f.,* priest, priestess
sacrificō, –āre, –āvī, –ātus, sacrifice *(+ dat.)*
saepe, *adv.,* often
salūs, salūtis, *f.,* health, safety
salūtō, –āre, –āvī, –ātus, greet
salvē, salvēte, *pl.,* hello
sānus, –a, –um, sound, sane
sapientia, –ae, *f.,* wisdom
Sāturnus, –ī, *m.,* Saturn, *a god*
saucius, –a, –um, wounded, hurt
saxum, –ī, *n.,* rock
scēptrum, –ī, *n.,* scepter
schola, –ae, *f.,* school
scientia, –ae, *f.,* knowledge, science
sciō, –īre, scīvī, scītus, know

Scīpiō, –ōnis, *m.,* Scipio (Sip´io)
scrībō, –ere, scrīpsī, scrīptus, write
sēcum = cum sē
secundus, –a, –um, second
sed, *conj.,* but
sedeō, –ēre, sēdī, sessūrus, sit
semper, *adv.,* always
senātor, –ōris, *m.,* senator
senātus, –ūs, *m.,* senate
sententia, –ae, *f.,* motto, feeling, opinion, saying
sentiō, –īre, sensī, sensus, feel, realize
sēparō, –āre, –āvī, –ātus, separate
septem, seven
sepulchrum, –ī, *n.,* tomb
sermō, –ōnis, *m.,* talk, conversation
servō, –āre, –āvī, –ātus, save, guard, preserve
servus, –ī, *m.;* **serva, –ae,** *f.,* slave, servant
sex, six
sī, *conj.,* if
sīc, yes
Sicilia, –ae, *f.,* Sicily (Sis´ily)
signum, –ī, *n.,* sign, standard, signal
silva, –ae, *f.,* forest, woods
similis, –e, like, similar
sine, *prep. w. abl.,* without
singulī, –ae, –a, *always pl.,* one at a time
socius, –cī, *m.,* ally, comrade
sōl, sōlis, *m.,* sun
sōlus, –a, –um, only, alone
solvō, –ere, solvī, solūtus, loosen, pay
somnus, –ī, *m.,* sleep
sordidus, –a, –um, dirty
soror, –ōris, *f.,* sister
spatium, –tī, *n.,* space, time, lap (*in a race*)
speciēs, speciēī, *f.,* appearance
spectō, –āre, –āvī, –ātus, look (at), watch
spērō, –āre, –āvī, –ātus, hope (for)
spēs, speī, *f.,* hope
spīrō, –āre, –āvī, –ātus, breathe
spondeō, –ēre, spopondī, spōnsus, promise, engage
sportula, –ae, *f.* small gift-basket
statua, –ae, *f.,* statue
statuō, –ere, statuī, statūtus, establish, determine, arrange
stō, stāre, stetī, stātūrus, stand, stand up
stomachus, –ī *m.,* stomach
studiōsus, –a, –um, eager, studious
studium, –dī, *n.,* eagerness, interest; *pl.,* studies
sub, *prep.,* under, close to (*w. acc. with verbs of motion; w. abl. with verbs of rest or position*)
subigō, –ere, –ēgī, –āctus, subdue
submittō, –ere, –mīsī, –missus, let down, furnish
suī, *reflexive pron.,* of himself, herself, itself, themselves
sum, esse, fuī, futūrus, be
summus, –a, –um, highest, top of
sūmō, –ere, sūmpsī, sūmptus, take
super, *prep. w. acc.,* over, above
superbia, –ae, *f.,* arrogance, pride
superbus, –a, –um, haughty, proud, snobbish
superō, –āre, –āvī, –ātus, conquer, excel, overcome
supersum, –esse, –fuī, –futūrus, be left (over), survive
supplicium, –cī, *n.,* punishment
suscipiō, –ere, –cēpī, –ceptus, undertake
sustineō, –ēre, –tinuī, –tentus, hold up, maintain, endure, withstand
suus, –a, –um, *reflexive adj.,* his, her, its, their; his own, her own, its own, their own

T

taberna, –ae, *f.,* shop, tavern
tablīnum, –ī, *n.,* study, den
tamen, *adv.,* nevertheless
tandem, *adv.,* at last, finally
tangō, –ere, tetigī, tactus, touch
tardē, *adv.,* slowly
tardus, –a, –um, late, slow
Tarentīnī, –ōrum, *m. pl.,* the people of Tarentum
Tēlemachus, –ī, *m.,* Telĕm´achus
tēlum, –ī, *n.,* weapon
templum, –ī, *n.,* temple
tempus, –oris, *n.,* time
tendō, –ere, tetendī, tentus, stretch
teneō, –ēre, tenuī, tentus, hold, keep; **memoriā teneō,** remember
terminus, –ī, *m.,* end, boundary
terra, –ae, *f.,* earth, land

terreō, –ēre, terruī, territus, scare, frighten
tertius, –a, –um, third
texō, –ere, texuī, textus, weave
theātrum, –ī, *n.,* theater, amphitheater
Ti., *abbreviation for* **Tiberius**
Tiberis, –is, *m.,* the Tī´ber, *a river in Italy*
Tiberius, –rī, *m.,* Tībē´rius
timeō, –ēre, timuī, —, fear, be afraid
timidē, *adv.,* timidly
timidus, –a, –um, timid, shy
Tīrō, –ōnis, *m.,* Tī´rō
toga, –ae, *f.,* toga (*cloak*)
tōtus, –a, –um, whole, all
trādō, –ere, –didī, –ditus, give *or* hand over, surrender, relate
trādūcō, –ere, dūxī, –ductus, lead across
trahō, –ere, trāxī, tractus, draw, drag
trānō, –āre, –āvī, –ātus, swim across
trāns, *prep. w. acc.,* across
trānsportō, –āre, –āvī, –ātus, transport
trēs, tria, three
tribūnus, –ī, *m.,* tribune, *a Roman official*
tribuō, –ere, tribuī, tribūtus, grant
trīgintā, thirty
triumphō, –āre, –āvī, –ātus, triumph
triumphus, –ī, *m.,* triumph
Troia, –ae, *f.,* Troy
Troiānus, –a, –um, Trojan; *as noun,* a Trojan
tū, tuī, you *(sing.)*
tum, *adv.,* then
tuus, –a, –um, your, yours (*referring to one person*)

U

ubi, *adv.,* where; when
Ulixēs, –is, *m.,* Ūlys´sēs
ūllus, –a, –um, any
ulterior, ulterius, farther
ultimus, –a, –um, last, farthest
unda, –ae, *f.,* wave
ūnus, –a, –um, one
urbs, urbis, *f.,* city
ūro, –ere, ussī, ustus, burn
uter, –a, –um, which *(of two)*
ūtilis, –e, useful
uxor, –ōris, *f.,* wife

V

valē, valēte, *pl.,* good-bye
valeō, –ēre, valuī, valitūrus, be strong, be well; *imper.* **valē,** farewell
vāllum, –ī, *n.,* wall
variē, *adv.,* variously
varius, –a, –um, changing, varying, various
veniō, –īre, vēnī, ventūrus, come
ventus, –ī, *m.,* wind
Venus, –eris, *f.,* Vēnus, *goddess of love and beauty*
vēr, vēris, *n.,* spring
verberō, –āre, –āvī, –ātus, beat
verbōsus, –a, –um, wordy
verbum, –ī, *n.,* word; **verba faciō,** make a speech
Vergilius, –lī, *m.,* Virgil
vertō, –ere, vertī, versus, turn
vērus, –a, –um, true
Vestālis, –e, Vestal, of Vesta
vester, –tra, –trum, your, yours (*referring to two or more persons*)
vestis, –is, *f.,* garment, clothes
via, –ae, *f.,* road, way, street
victor, –ōris, *m.,* conqueror, victor
victōria, –ae, *f.,* victory
videō, –ēre, vīdī, vīsus, see; *passive,* seem
vīgintī, twenty
vīlla, –ae, *f.,* country home
vincō, –ere, vīcī, victus, conquer
vīnum, –ī, *n.,* wine
vir, virī, *m.,* man
virgō, –ginis, *f.,* virgin, maiden
virīlis, –e, of a man
virtūs, –tūtis, *f.,* manliness, courage
vīs, —, *f.,* force, violence; *pl.,* **vīrēs, –ium,** strength
vīta, –ae, *f.,* life
vīvō, –ere, vīxī, vīctus, be alive, live
vīvus, –a, –um, alive, living
vix, *adv.,* scarcely
vocō, –āre, –āvī, –ātus, call, invite
volō, –āre, –āvī, –ātus, fly
vōs, vestrum, you (*pl. of* **tū**)
vōx, vōcis, *f.,* voice, remark
Vulcānus, –ī, *m.,* Vulcan, *god of fire*
vulnerō, –āre, –āvī, –ātus, wound
vulnus, vulneris, *n.,* wound

English–Latin

A

able (be), possum, posse, potuī, —
about, dē, *w. abl.*
absent (be), absum, abesse, āfuī, āfutūrus
across, trāns, *w. acc.*
advice, cōnsilium, –lī, *n.*
affair, rēs, reī, *f.*
affect, afflict with, afficiō, –ere, affēcī, affectus
afraid (be), timeō, –ēre, timuī, —
after, *use abl. abs.;* post (*prep. w. acc.*); postquam (*conj.*)
aid, auxilium, –lī, *n.*
all, omnis, –e
ally, socius, –cī, *m.*
alone, sōlus, –a, –um
always, semper
and, et, –que, atque
another, alius, –a, –um
answer, respondeō, –ēre, respondī, respōnsus
appearance, speciēs, speciēī, *f.*
approach, accēdō, –ere, accessī, accessūrus (*w.* ad)
approve, probō, –āre, –āvī, –ātus
arms *(weapons),* arma, –ōrum, *n. pl.*
arouse, incitō, –āre, –āvī, –ātus
arrive, perveniō, –īre, –vēnī, –ventūrus
as, quam *or use abl. abs.*
ask (for), rogō, –āre, –āvī, –ātus
await, exspectō, –āre, –āvī, –ātus
away (be), absum, –esse, āfuī, āfutūrus

B

bad, malus, –a, –um
battle, pugna, –ae *f.;* proelium, –lī, *n.*
be, sum, esse, fuī, futūrus
beautiful, pulcher, –chra, –chrum
because, quod; *use particip. or abl. abs.*
begin, incipiō, –ere, –cēpī, –ceptus
between, inter, *w. acc.*
bind, ligō, –āre, –āvī, –ātus
body, corpus, corporis, *n.*
book, liber, librī, *m.*
boy, puer, puerī, *m.*
brave, fortis, –e; **bravely,** fortiter
breathe, spīrō, –āre, –āvī, –ātus
brother, frāter, frātris, *m.*
but, sed
by, ā, ab, *w. abl.*

C

call, vocō, –āre, –āvī, –ātus; appellō, –āre, –āvī, –ātus; **call out,** ēvocō; **call together,** convocō
camp, castra, –ōrum, *n. pl.*
can, possum, posse, potuī, —
cannot, nōn possum
capture (by assault), expugnō, –āre, –āvī, –ātus
care, cūra, –ae, *f.*
carefully, cum cūrā
carry, portō, –āre, –āvī, –ātus; **carry on,** gerō, –ere, gessī, gestus
catch sight of, cōnspiciō, –ere, –spexī, –spectus
cause, causa, –ae, *f.*
certainly, certē
chance, cāsus, –ūs, *m.*
charge of, (put in) praeficiō, –ere, –fēcī, –fectus
children, līberī, –ōrum, *m.*
citizen, cīvis, cīvis, *m. & f.*
citizenship, cīvitās, –tātis, *f.*
city, urbs, urbis, *f.*
clearly, clārē
climb, ascendō, –ere, ascendī, ascēnsus
close, claudō, –ere, clausī, clausus
colonist, colōnus, –ī, *m.*
come, veniō, –īre, vēnī, ventūrus; **come together,** conveniō, –īre, –vēnī, –ventūrus
compel, cōgō, –ere, coēgī, coactus
complete, cōnficiō, –ere, –fēcī, –fectus
comrade, socius, –cī, *m.*
constant, perpetuus, –a, –um
contain, contineō, –ēre, –uī, –tentus
convenient, commodus, –a, –um
country, patria, –ae, *f.*
courage, animus, –ī, *m.*
cry out, clāmō, –āre, –āvī, –ātus

D

danger, perīculum, –ī, *n.*
daughter, fīlia, –ae, *f.*

day, diēs, diēī, *m.*
death, mors, mortis, *f.*
deceive, fallō, –ere, fefellī, falsus
deep, altus, –a, –u; **(deeply) move,** permoveō, –ēre, –mōvī, –mōtus
defend, dēfendō, –ere, dēfendī, dēfēnsus
depart, excēdō, –ere, excessī, excessūrus
desert, dēserō, –ere, dēseruī, dēsertus
deserve, mereō, –ēre, meruī, meritus
desire, cupiō, –ere, cupīvī, cupītus
determine, statuō, –ere, statuī, statūtus
dinner, cēna, –ae, *f.*
discipline, disciplīna, –ae, *f.*
dismiss, dīmittō, –ere, dīmīsī, dīmissus
divide, dīvidō, –ere, dīvīsī, dīvīsus
do, faciō, –ere, fēcī, factus; **do harm to,** noceō, –ēre, nocuī, nocitūrus (*w. dat.*)
drag, trahō, –ere, trāxī, tractus
draw, trahō, –ere, trāxī, tractus
drive, agō, –ere, ēgī, āctus
duty, officium, –cī, *n.*

E

eagerness, studium, –dī, *n.*
easy, facilis, –e; **easily,** facile
end, fīnis, fīnis, *m.;* terminus, –ī, *m.*
endure, sustineō, –ēre, –tinuī, –tentus
enemy, inimīcus, –ī, *m.* (*personal*); hostis, –is, *m.* *(usually pl.)* (*national*)
entrust, mandō, –āre, –āvī, –ātus; committō, –ere, –mīsī, –missus; crēdō, –ere, –didī –ditus
equal, pār, *gen.* paris
establish, cōnfirmō, –āre, –āvī, –ātus
every, omnis, –e
example, exemplum, –i, *n.*
excel, superō, –āre, –āvī, –ātus
excellent, ēgregius, –a, –um
explore, explōrō, –āre, –āvī, –ātus

F

fall, cadō, –ere, cecidī, cāsūrus
fame, fāma, –ae, *f.*
familiar, nōtus, –a, –um
family, familia, –ae, *f.*
famous, clārus, –a, –um
farmer, agricola, –ae, *m.*
father, pater, patris, *m.*
fear, timeō, –ēre, timuī, —
feel grateful, grātiam habeō
few, paucī, –ae, –a
field, ager, agrī, *m.*
fifth, quīntus, –a, –um
fight, pugnō, –āre, –āvī, –ātus
find, inveniō, –īre, invēnī, inventus
first, prīmus, –a, –um
fit, aptus, –a, –um
flee, fugiō, –ere, fūgī, fugitūrus
fold, plicō, –āre, –āvī, –ātus
food, cibus, –ī, *m.*
foot, pēs, pedis, *m.;* **on foot,** pedibus
for, (*conj.*), nam; (*prep.*), prō, *w. abl.;* ob, *w. acc.*
foreigner, barbarus, –ī, *m.*
foresee, prōvideō, –ēre, –vīdī, –vīsus
forest, silva, –ae, *f.*
fortify, mūniō, –īre, –īvī, –ītus
four, quattuor
free (*adj.*), līber, –era, –erum; (*v.*), līberō, –āre, –āvī, –ātus; expediō, –īre, –īvī, –ītus
freedom, lībertās, –tātis, *f.*
fresh, integer, –gra, –grum
friend, amīcus, –ī, *m.*
friendly, amīcus, –a, –um
friendship, amīcitia, –ae, *f.*
from, out from, ē, ex, *w. abl.;* **(away) from,** ā, ab, *w. abl.*
furnish, submittō, –ere, –mīsī, –missus

G

gate *(of a city or a camp),* porta, –ae, *f.*
Gaul, Gallia, –ae, *f.;* **a Gaul,** Gallus, –ī, *m.*
general, dux, ducis, *m.*
get, get ready, parō, –āre, –āvī, –ātus
girl, puella, –ae, *f.*
give, dōnō, –āre, –āvī, –ātus; dō, dare, dedī, datus
go away, discēdō, –ere, –cessī, –cessūrus
god, deus, –ī, *m.*
good, bonus, –a, –um
grain, frūmentum, –ī, *n.*
grateful, (**be** *or* **feel**) grātiam habeō

great, magnus, –a, –um
guard, praesidium, –dī, *n.*

H

hand, manus, –ūs, *f.*
harm, do harm to, noceō, –ēre, nocuī, nocitūrus (*w. dat.*)
harmony, concordia, –ae, *f.*
harsh, dūrus, –a, –um; **harshly,** *adv.*, dūrē
hasten, mātūrō, –āre, –āvī, –ātus; properō, –āre, –āvī, –ātūrus
have, habeō, –ēre, habuī, habitus
he, is; hic; ille; *often not expressed*
head, caput, capitis, *n.*
health, salūs, salūtis, *f.*
hear, audiō, –īre, –īvī, –ītus
heavy, gravis, –e
her (*poss.*), eius; (*refl.*), suus, –a, –um
hesitate, dubitō, –āre, –āvī, –ātus
high, altus, –a, –um
himself, (*intens.*), ipse; (*reflex.*), suī
hinder, impediō, –īre, –īvī, –ītus
his (*poss.*), eius; (*reflex.*) suus, –a, –um
hold, teneō, –ēre, tenuī, tentus
hope (for) (*v.*), spērō, –āre, –āvī, –ātus; (*noun*), spēs, speī, *f.*
horse, equus, –ī, *m.*
hour, hōra, –ae, *f.*
house, casa, –ae, *f.*; domus, –ūs, *f.*
how (in what manner), quō modō

I

I, ego, meī; *often not expressed*
if, sī *or use abl. abs.*
in, in, *w. abl.*
increase, augeō, –ēre, auxī, auctus
influence, addūcō, –ere, addūxī, adductus; (*noun*), grātia, –ae, *f.*; auctōritās, –tātis, *f.*
injustice, iniūria, –ae, *f.*
instruction, disciplīna, –ae, *f.*
interest, studium, –dī, *n.*
into, in, *w. acc.*
island, īnsula, –ae, *f.*
it, id; hoc; illud; *this is often not expressed*

J

journey, iter, itineris, *n.*
just, aequus, –a, –um; iūstus, –a, –um

K

kill, interficiō, –ere, –fēcī, –fectus
king, rēx, rēgis, *m.*
kingdom, regnum, –ī, *n.*
know, *perfect tense of* nōscō, –ere, nōvī, nōtus, *or of* cognōscō, –ere, –nōvī, –nitus; sciō, –īre, scīvī, scītus

L

land, terra, –ae, *f.*; **native land,** patria, –ae, *f.*
large, magnus, –a, –um
late, tardus, –a, –um
lead, dūcō, –ere, dūxī, ductus; **lead across,** trādūcō; **lead a life,** vītam agō; **lead back,** redūcō; **lead out,** ēdūcō, prōdūcō
leader, dux, ducis, *m.*; prīnceps, –cipis, *m.*
learn, nōscō, –ere, nōvī, nōtus; cognōscō, –ere, –nōvī, –nitus
leisure, ōtium, otī *n.*
letter (*of alphabet*), littera, –ae, *f.*; (*epistle*), litterae, –ārum, *f.*
level, plānus, –a, –um
life, vīta, –ae, *f.*
like, amō, –āre, –āvī, –ātus
little, parvus, –a, –um
live a life, vītam agō; **dwell,** habitō, –āre, –āvī, –ātus
long, longus, –a, –um; **no longer,** nōn iam
look (at), spectō, –āre, –āvī, –ātus
loot, praeda, –ae, *f.*
lose, āmittō, –ere, āmīsī, āmissus
love, amō, –āre, –āvī, –ātus
lower, īnferior, īnferius

M

maintain, sustineō, –ēre, –tinuī, –tentus
make, faciō, –ere, fēcī, factus
man, vir, virī, *m.*; homō, hominis, *m.*
manner, modus, –ī, *m.*
many, multī, –ae, –a
master, dominus, –ī, *m.*

messenger, nūntius, –tī, *m.*
middle (of), medius, –a, –um
money, pecūnia, –ae, *f.*
month, mēnsis, –is, *m.*
most, plūrimī, –ae, –a
mother, māter, mātris, *f.*
motto, sententia, –ae, *f.*
mountain, mōns, montis, *m.*
move, moveō, –ēre, mōvī, mōtus; migrō, –āre, –āvī, –ātūrus; cēdō, –ere, cessī, cessūrus
much, multus, –a, –um
my, meus, –a, –um

N

name, nōmen, nōminis, *n.*
nation, gēns, gentis, *f.*
native land, patria, –ae, *f.*
nature, nātūra, –ae, *f.*
neighboring, fīnitimus, –a, –um
neither (of two) (*adj.*), neuter, –tra, –trum
neither . . . nor (*conj.*), neque . . . neque
never, numquam
nevertheless, tamen
new, novus, –a, –um
next, proximus, –a, –um
no longer (*adv.*), nōn iam
no one (*noun*), nēmo, *dat.* nēminī, *m.*
noble, nōbilis, –e
nor, neque
not, nōn
nothing, nihil, *indecl. n.*
now, nunc
number, numerus, –ī, *m.*

O

obtain, obtineō, –ēre, obtinuī, obtentus
on, in, *w. abl.;* **on account of**, ob, *w. acc.*
one at a time, singulī, –ae, –a; **one . . . the other**, alter . . . alter
opinion, sententia, –ae, *f.*
order, iubeō, –ēre, iussī, iussus
other, alius, –a, –ud; **the other (of two)**, alter, –era, –erum
ought, dēbeō, –ēre, dēbuī, dēbitus
our, noster, –tra, –trum
ourselves (*intens.*), ipsī; (*reflex.*), nōs
out of, ē, ex, *w. abl.*
owe, dēbeō, –ēre, dēbuī, dēbitus

P

part, pars, partis, *f.*
peace, pāx, pācis, *f.*
people, populus, –ī, *m.*
pitch camp, castra pōnō
place, locus, –ī, *m.; pl.* loca, –ōrum, *n.*
plan, cōnsilium, –lī, *n.*
pleasing, grātus, –a, –um
poor, miser, –era, –erum
praise, laudō, –āre, –āvī, –ātus
prepare, parō, –āre, –āvī, –ātus
present (be), adsum, esse, adfuī, adfutūrus
present, dōnō, –āre, –āvī, –ātus; prōpōnō, –ere, –posuī, –positus
preserve, servō, –āre, –āvī, –ātus; cōnservō
price, pretium, –tī, *n.*
prisoner, captīvus, –ī, *m.*
prove, probō, –āre, –āvī, –ātus
province, prōvincia, –ae, *f.*
public, pūblicus, –a, –um
punishment, poena, –ae; *f.;* supplicium, –cī, *n.*
put, pōnō, –ere, posuī, positus; **put in charge of**, praeficiō, –ere, –fēcī, –fectus

Q

queen, rēgīna, –ae, *f.*
quickly, celeriter

R

rank, ōrdō, ōrdinis, *m.*
rather, *expressed by comparative*
read, legō, –ere, lēgī, lēctus
ready, parātus, –a, –um; **get ready**, parō, –āre, –āvī, –ātus
receive, accipiō, –ere, accēpī, acceptus
region, regiō, –ōnis, *f.*
reinforcements, auxilia, –ōrum, *n.*
remain, maneō, –ēre, mānsī, mānsūrus; remaneō
remember, memoriā teneō
remove, removeō, –ēre, remōvī, remōtus
report, nūntiō, –āre, –āvī, –ātus

rest (of), reliquus, –a, –um
reward, praemium, –ī, *n.*
right, iūs, iūris, *n.*
river, flūmen, flūminis, *n.*
road, via, –ae, *f.;* iter, itineris, *n.*
rule, regō, –ere, rēxī, rēctus
run, currō, –ere, cucurrī, cursūrus

S

sacred, sacer, –cra, –crum
safety, salūs, salūtis, *f.*
sail, nāvigō, –āre, –āvī, –ātus
sailor, nauta, –ae, *m.*
same, īdem, eadem, idem
save, servō, –āre, –āvī, –ātus; cōnservō
say, dīcō, –ere, dīxī, dictus
scare, terreō, –ēre, terruī, territus
sea, mare, maris, *n.*
see, videō, –ēre, vīdī, vīsus
seek, petō, –ere, petīvī, petītus
seize, occupō, –āre, –āvī, –ātus
send, mittō, –ere, mīsī, missus; **send away,** dīmittō; **send back**, remittō
settler, colōnus, –ī, *m.*
severe, gravis, –e
shape, fōrma, –ae, *f.*
sharply, ācriter
she, ea; haec; illa; *often not expressed*
ship, nāvis, nāvis, *f.*
shout, clāmō, –āre, –āvī, –ātus
show, mōnstrō, –āre, –āvī, –ātus; dēmōnstrō
sight of, (catch) cōnspiciō, –ere, –spexī, –spectus
signal, signum, –ī, *n.*
since, *use abl. abs.;* quod (*conj.*)
sister, soror, sorōris, *f.*
sit, sedeō, –ēre, sēdī, sessūrus
slave, servus, –ī, *m.*
small, parvus, –a, –um
soldier, mīles, mīlitis, *m.*
some . . . others, aliī . . . aliī
son, fīlius, –lī, *m.*
speech, ōrātiō, –ōnis, *f.;* **make a speech**, verba faciō
spend *(time)*, agō, –ere, ēgī, āctus
stand, stō, stāre, stetī, stātūrus
standard, signum, –ī, *n.*
state, cīvitās, –tātis, *f.*
strange, novus, –a, –um
street, via, –ae, *f.*
stretch, tendō, –ere, tetendī, tentus
studies, studia, –ōrum, *n.*
suitable, commodus, –a, –um
summer, aestās, –tātis, *f.*
supply, cōpia, –ae, *f.*
swift, celer, celeris, celere
swiftly, celeriter
swiftness, celeritās, –tātis, *f.*

T

take, capiō, –ere, cēpī, captus
teach, doceō, –ēre, docuī, doctus
teacher, magister, –trī, *m.;* magistra, –2e, *f.*
terms, condiciō, –ōnis, *f.*
than, quam *(conj.)*
thank, grātiās agō (*w. dat.*)
that (*demonst.*), ille, illa, illud; is, ea, id; (*relat.*) quī, quae, quod
their, eōrum, eārum, eōrum
themselves (*intens.*), ipsī, –ae, –a; (*reflex.*), suī
then, tum
there, ibi
they, eī, eae, ea; illī, illae, illa; *often not expressed*
thing, rēs, reī, *f.; often not expressed*
think, putō, –āre, –āvī, –ātus
third, tertius, –a, –um
this (*demonst.*), hic, haec, hoc; is, ea, id
three, trēs, tria
through, per, *w. acc.*
till, colō, –ere, coluī, cultus
timber, māteria, –ae, *f.*
time, tempus, –oris, *n.;* **one at a time**, singulī, –ae, –a
to, ad, *w. acc.; dat. of indir. obj.*
too, *expressed by comparative*
touch, tangō, –ere, tetigī, tactus
town, oppidum, –ī, *n.*
train, exerceō, –ēre, exerecuī, exercitus
transport, trānsportō, –āre, –āvī, –ātus
two, duo, duae, duo

U

under, sub, *w. acc. or abl.*
understand, intellegō, –ere, –lēxī, –lēctus
undertake, suscipiō, –ere, –cēpī, –ceptus
unfold, explicō, –āre, –āvī, –ātus
unhappy, miser, –era, –erum
upon, in, *w. abl.*
urge on, incitō, –āre, –āvī, –ātus
useful, ūtilis, –e

V

varying, varius, –a, –um
very, *expressed by superlative;* **very carefully,** magnā cūrā
victory, victōria, –ae, *f.*

W

wagon, carrus, –ī, *m.*
wait, exspectō, –āre, –āvī, –ātus
war, bellum, –ī, *n.*
warn, moneō, –ēre, –uī, –itus
watch, spectō, –āre, –āvī, –ātus
water, aqua, –ae, *f.*
we, nōs; *often not expressed*
well, bene *(adv.)*
what (*pron.*), quis, quid; (*adj.*), quī, quae, quod
which, quī, quae, quod
who (*rel. pron.*), quī, quae, quod; (*interrog. pron.*), quis, quid
whole, tōtus, –a, –um
why, cūr
wide, lātus –a, –um
winter, hiems, hiemis, *f.*
with, cum, *w. abl.; sometimes abl. alone*
without, sine, *w. abl.*
woods, silva, –ae, *f.*
word, verbum, –ī, *n.*
work (*verb*), labōrō, –āre, –āvī, –ātus; (*noun*), opus, operis, *n.*
worse, peior, peius; **worst,** pessimus, –a, –um
wound, vulnus, vulneris, *n.*
write, scrībō, –ere, scrīpsī, scrīptus

Y

year, annus, –ī, *m.*
you, tū (*sing.*); vōs (*pl.*); *often not expressed*
your, tuus, –a, –um; vester, –tra, –trum; **yourselves** (*reflex.*), vōs

Subject Index

A

Achilles, 97
Acta Dicturna, 122
advertising, Roman, 141
Aeneas, 162, 170, 172, *185,* 186, *187,* 192, 197, 202, 207, 249, 255, 276, 337
Aeneid, 162, *163,* 185, 249
Aeolus, 172
agriculture, Roman, 344
Agrippina, 378
Alcinous, 261
Alexander, 97
alphabet, 4-6
 Greek, 6
 Latin, 6, 140
 Semitic, 6
alphabetic writing, 5
America, 3
amphitheater,
 Arles, France, *279*
 Nîmes, France, *47*
Amphitrite, house of, *111*
Anchises, 197
Angles, 254, 260
animism, 310
Antioch, Turkey, *344*
Aphrodite, 311
Apollo, 286, 292
Appian Way, 30, 34, 70
apprenticeship, Roman, 78
aqueducts, Roman, 70
Arcadians, 202
Arch of Diocletian, *296*
Arch of Titus, *xii*
arches, Roman, 1, *237*
Ares, 311
Aristotle, 97, *99*
arithmetic, Roman, 213
Arles, France, *279*
army, Roman, *see* **soldiers, Roman**
art, Roman, *106*
artisans, Roman, 345
Asia Minor, 162
Atrium Vestae, 293
atrium, *111, 125, 126*
Atticus, 323
augures, 312
Augustulus, Romulus, 380
Augustus, Emperor, 34, 68, 70, 105, *132*, 152, 226, 278, 331, 345, 378
Aurelian, Emperor, 70, 378
Aurelius, Marcus, 378
Aventine Hill, 69, 279

B

Baalbek, Lebanon, *221*
Bacchus, 286, 301, *302,* 304
banking, Roman, 50
barbarians, 178
baths, Roman, *79,* 337
Baucis, 357, *358, 360*
Braccata, 58
bread, Roman, 264
bridges, Roman, 307
Britain, 13
 Roman invasion of, 81, 105, 254, 260
Bronze Age, 353
Brundisium, 34

C

Caelian, Hill, 69
Caesar, Julius, 2, 7, 47, 81, 236, 250, 254, 285, 307, 311, 319, 331, 378, *379*
calendar, Roman, 331
Caligula, 378
Campania, 34, 253
Campo Vaccino, 68
Campus Martius, 69
Canova, *363*
capital letters, 6
Capitoline Hill, 68, *182*

Capitolium, 68
Capua, 34
Carthage, *185*, 186, 192, 296, 299
Catholic Church, 70
Ceres, 148, 286, 292, 311
Charybdis, 265
Chinese *(people)*, 5
Christianity, 35, 260, 311
Cicero, 2, 3, 7, 105, 318, 323, 326
Cincinnati, Ohio, 332
Cincinnatus, 328, 330, 344
Circe, 255, *256, 258,* 261, 265
Circus Maximus, 69, 279
circus, Roman, 279
City of the Seven Hills, 68
Claudius, Appius, 34, 69-70
Claudius, Emperor, 105, 378
clothing, Roman, 178-179
Cocles, 306
colleges, Roman, 213
Colosseum, Roman, *119, 219,* 225, *226,* 279
Comata, 58
Constantine, Emperor, 311, 379
Constantinople, 379
Consualia, 312
Consus, 312
Coriolanus, 339
Cornelia, 62
Cumae, *93,* 200
Cyclopes, 167

D

Daedalus, 362, *363*
Danube River, 307
Dardanelles, 162
Demeter, 311
dental practices, Roman, 302
Diana, 231, 286, 292
Dido, Queen, *185,* 186, *187,* 192
Diocletian, 379
Diogenes, *93,* 140
dolls, Roman, 52
Doric temple, *175*
Dougga, Tunisia, *298*

E

Edict of Caracalla, 379
education, Roman, 78
Egypt, 85
Egyptians, 5
Elysium, 197
Emperor Justinian, *2*
Empire, Roman, 2, *12,* 70, 309
  decline of, 378-380
  glory of, 378
  map of, 102-103
engineers, Roman, 307
English *(language)*, 3
Epirus, 367
Esquiline Hill, 69
Eternal City, 70
Etruria, 280
Etruscans, 6, 311, 312
Europe, 46
Eurylochus, 255
Evander, 202
exclamations, Roman, 165

F

Fabricius, 372
family, Roman, 20
farming, Roman, 344
Fates, 207
Faunus, 134
festivals, Roman, 52, 134, 312
fibula, 179
fire protection, Roman, 70
flowers, Roman, 360
food, Roman, 43, 242-243
footwear, Roman, 179, 234
Forum Baths, 140
Forum of Julius Caesar, *128*
Forum, Roman, 68, 69, 128, *285,* 366
furniture, Roman, 127

G

Gaius, Emperor, 378
games, Roman, 278
Gaul, *47,* 58, 236

Genius, 310, *310*
Georgics, 210
gladiatorial contests, 226, 279
gladiators, Roman, 119, 141, 226
Glaucus, 265
gold, Roman, 302
Golden Age, 352, *353*
graffitti, Roman, 140-141, *141*
Greek *(language),* 2, 3, 7
Greeks, 6, 91
Gregory, Pope, 260
Guerin, *185*
guests, Roman, 326
guilds, Roman, 345

H

Hadrian, 105
hairstyles, Roman, 179
hats, Roman, 179
Helen of Troy, 172, 337
herbs, Roman, 259
Herculaneum, 111, 140-141, *244*
holidays/celebrations, Roman, 151, 312
Homer, 97, *99,* 162, 249
Horatius, 306, 309, 333
hosts, Roman, 326
House of Telephus, 140
house, Roman, *125, 126*
Huns, 380

I

Icarus, 362, *363, 365*
ideographic writing, 5
Iliad, 162
Incitatus, 378
industry, Roman, 345
Iron Age, 353
Isis, 311
Italy, 13
  map of, *57*
Ithaca, 255, 261, 267, 276
  King of, 249

J

jewelry, Roman, 179, 223
Julian
  Calendar, 331
  Emperor, 378
Juno, 68, 172, 292, 311, 337
Jupiter, 286, *286,* 290, 292, 311, 357, *358*
  Temple of, 68, *298*
Justinian, 2
  Code, 2
  Emperor, *2*

K

Kitty Hawk, NC, 365
knights, Roman, 377

L

lararium, *111*
Lares Familiarēs, *111,* 162, *165*, 310, *310, 311*
Latin
  America, 3
  influence upon English, 254, 260
  language, 1-3, 76, *passim*
  people, 3
Latium, 1, 34, 253
Latona, 231
Lavinia, 207
libraries, Roman, 158
Lincoln Memorial, *175*
liquamen, 242
Livia, 345
logographic writing, 5
Lotus-eaters, 167, 255
ludi, 152
  circenses, 152
  scaenici, 152
lūdus litterārum, 212

M

Macedonia, 97
Magna Charta, *45*

mail, Roman, 237
Mantegna, *379*
marriage customs, Roman, 29, 271
Mars, 286, 292, 311
Martial, 223, 278
materials, Roman clothing, 178
meals, Roman, 243
meat consumption, Roman, 139
medical, Roman
personnel, 319
treatments, 94
Menelaus, 337
Mercury, 286, 292, 357
metals, Roman, 355
mērum, 242
Midas, King, 301, *302,* 304
Middle Ages, 7, 69
Milan, 379
milliarium aurem, 34
Minerva, *263,* 286, 292, 311, 337
Minucius, 328
Mithraism, 311
monotheism, 311
mortgaged land, Roman, 299
mosaic, *81, 330*
Mt. Vesuvius, 111, 140, 253
munera gladiatoria, 151
Muscosus, Pompeius, 280
Muses, *163*

N

Naples, 140
Narcissus, 105
Native Americans, 5
Nausicaa, 261, *263*
Neptune, 172, *173,* 286, 292
Nero, 378
newspapers, Roman, 122
Nîmes, France, *47*
Niobe, 231
North Africa, 85
Numa, King, 112

O

Octavian, Emperor, 378
Odoacer, 380
Odyssey, 212, 249
Orbilius, 153
Ostia, 85, 95, 294
Ovid, *353, 360*

P

paedagōgī, 212
Palatine, 68
Hill, 68, 279
Pales, 68, 312
Palilia, 312
palla, 178
Pallanteum, 202
Pantheon, 69
Paris, 337
patrons, Roman, 124
pax Romana, 378
Penates, 310
Penelope, 249, 267, *273*
Philemon, 357, *358, 360*
Philip, 97
Phoenicians, 6
pictographic writing, 5
Plautus, 280
plebian class, Roman, 342
Pluto, 148
Polyphemus, 167, *169*
polytheistic, 311
Pompeii, 79, *106, 125,* 140-141, *243-244, 310*
Pomponia, 323, 326
Pons Aemilius, *307*
Pons Sublicius, 307
Pontifex Maximus, 293, 311
Pope Gregory, 260
population, Roman, 70
Porsena, 306
Portus, 85
Poseidon, house of, *111*
Poussin, Nicolas, *302*
Priam, 337

Primigenia, Fabia, *93*
professions, Roman, 345
Prometheus, *353*
pronunciation, 7-9, 13
Proserpina, 148
publishing, Roman book, 195
Publius, 236
Punic Wars, 155, 299
Pyrrhic victory, 370
Pyrrhus, 367, 372

Q

Quintus, 87, 153, 323, 326
Quirinal Hill, 69

R

Ravenna, 379
Regia, 293
religion, Roman, 310-312
Rembrandt, *99*
Remus, 283
Renaissance, 3
Rhine River, 307
River Pactolus, *302*
roads, Roman, 34-35
Roberts, David, *285*
Roman Empire, *see* **Empire, Roman**
Romance languages, 2, 67, 76
Rome, 1, 13, 40
  decay of, 295
  founding of, 68, 312
Romulus, 112, 283
rostra, 68

S

Saint-Remy, France, *237*
sandals, Roman, 179, 234
sarcina, 116
Saturn, 290
Saxons, 254, 260
school, Roman, 212-213
  of rhetoric, 199
  subjects, 155
Scylla, 265
Semites, 6
senate, Roman, 288
Servian Wall, 70
Sheitla, *296*
ships, Roman, 274
shops, Roman, 345
shrine, household, *310*
Sibyl, 197, 200
Sicily, 19, 85
  map of, 164
Silenus, 301
Silver Age, 353
Sirens, 261, *262*
slaves/slavery, Roman, 32, 92, 98, 104-105
soldiers, Roman, 34, 116, 169, 176, 206
Spartacus, 105, 118, *119*
spices, Roman, 259
spirits, Roman, 310
sports, Roman, 213, 279
Statius, 323, 326
Statue of Liberty, 275
stilus, 212
stola, 178
Stradano, 249
streets, Roman, 64, 69
Suetonius, 378
syllabic writing, 5

T

Tarentum, 367
Tarquins, 306
taxes, Roman, 345
Telemachus, 267, *273*
Temple of
  Jupiter, 68, *298*
  Venus, *119*
  Venus Genetrix, *128*
  Vesta, 293
temples, Roman, 220, *221, 237*
Terence, 280
theater, Roman, *227,* 279
Tibaldi, *169*
Tiber River, 1, 68, 69, 307
Tiro, 105, 318
toga, 178

Togata, 58
toys, Roman, 278
traffic, Roman, 64
Trajan, Emperor, 307
travel, Roman, 34-35
Trieste, *227*
Trojan War, 162, 170, 172, *187,* 249, 255, 337
Trojans, 202, 207
Troy, 162, 185, *187,* 255, 337
Tullus, King, 112
tunic, Roman, 178
Turkey, 6, 162
Turnus, 207
Twelve Tables of the Law, 212, 366

U

Ulysses, 167, *169,* 170, *249,* 255, *256, 258,* 261, *262, 263,* 265, 267, 272, *273,* 276, 337
United States, 3, 7
Uranus, 290

V

vase, red-figured, *168, 269*
Vatican Museum, *195*
Venus Genetrix, Temple of, *128*
Venus, 162, 286, 292, 311, 337
  Temple of, *119*
Vergil, 2, 140, 157, 162, *163,* 185, 210, 249
Vesta, 129, 292, 310
  Temple of, 293
Vestal Virgins, 129, 293
Via Lata, 64
Via Sacra, 50
victory celebrations, Roman, 367
Viminal Hill, 69
Volsci, 339
Vulcan, 207, *208,* 286, 292

W

wheat, Roman, 85
wine jars, Roman, *88*
wines, Roman, 253
women's duties, Roman, 190
Wright brothers' memorial, 365
writing, 5
  tools, Roman, 212

Z

Zeus, 311

Grammar/Vocabulary Index

A

ablative
  absolute, 256-257, 281
  case, 16-17, 47-48, 72
  of accompaniment, 114, 143, 193, 222
  of agent, 188, 215
  of manner, 226-227, 246
  of means, 59, 72, 115, 188
  of *place from which,* 93, 107
  of *place where,* 42, 59, 72
  of respect, 239, 246
  of *time when,* 227, 246
  of *time within which,* 228, 246
accusative
  case, 16, 21, 47-48, 54, 72, 137
  of extent of space, 228, 246
  of *time how long,* 228, 246
active infinitive
  future, 334, 347
  perfect, 329, 347
  present, 26
active voice, 173-175
adjectives, 20, 31, 36, 98
  as substantives, 59-60, 72
  comparison of, 353-354, 363, 368-369, 381-382
  dative with, 364, 382
  first declension, 82, 263-264, 282
    irregular, 263-264, 282
  interrogative, 232, 246
  order of, 137
  possessive, 203, 204, 215
  second declension, 98, 108, 263-264, 282
    irregular, 263-264, 282
    neuter, 82
  third declension, 273-274, 282
  third person reflexive, 320, 346
  superlative in *-limus,* 364, 381
adverbs, 33
  comparison of, 358, 363-364, 382
  formation of, 134-135, 144
apposition, 121
assimilation, 101
attributes, 14

B

be, to, 98-99, 108, 112-113
borrowed words, 18, 29

C

cases, 14, 15, 16
commands, *see* **imperative**
common translation, 27
comparison of
  adjectives, 353-354, 363, 368-369, 381-382
  adverbs, 358, 363-364, 382
conjugation
  first
    future tense, 46-47, 72, 149
    present
      imperative, 64, 72
      present, 26-27
  second
    future tense, 76-77, 108, 149
    present
      imperative, 77
      tense, 76-77, 108
  third, 124-125, 130, 143, 149, 154
    future, 149, 154, 180
  fourth, 130, 143, 154
    future, 149, 154, 181
    imperative, 130
    perfect tense, 130
conjunctions, 33, 120

D

dative
case, 16, 53-54, 72, 137
with adjectives, 364, 382
declension, 16
first
adjectives, 82, 263-264, 282
irregular, 263-264, 282
nouns, 17, 31
second
adjectives, 98, 108, 263-264, 282
irregular, 263-264, 282
neuter, 82
nouns, 30, 31, 63, 71, 82, 107
neuter, 82, 107
third
adjectives, 273-274, 282
nouns
feminine, 168, 180
ī–stem, 268, 282
masculine, 168, 180
neuter, 237-238, 245
fourth
nouns, 287, 313
fifth
nouns, 319-320, 346
demonstrative
hic, 290-292, 313
īdem, 303, 313
ille, 290-292, 313
is, 296-297, 313
derivatives, English, 56, 294
direct
object, 113
statements, 335, 347

E

emphatic translation, 27

F

fifth declension of nouns, 319-320, 346
first
conjugation
future tense, 46-47, 72, 149
present
imperative, 64, 72
tense, 26-27
declension
adjectives, 82, 263-264, 282
irregular, 263-264, 282
nouns, 17, 31
fourth
conjugation, 130, 143, 154
future, 149, 154, 181
imperative, 130
perfect tense, 130
declension
nouns, 287, 313
future
active
infinitive, 334, 347
participle, 325, 347
perfect, 197-198, 215
tense
first conjugation, 46-47, 72, 149
second conjugation, 76-77, 108, 149
third conjugation, 149, 154, 180
fourth conjugation, 149, 154, 181

G

gender, 14
genitive case, 16, 40-42, 71, 137

H

hic, 290-292, 313

I

īdem, 303, 313
idiomatic expressions, 130-131
ille, 290-292, 313
imperative
fourth conjugation, 130
present
first conjugation, 64, 72
second conjugation, 77
imperfect tense, 157-159, 181
indicative mood, 64, 340-341, 347-348
indirect
object, 53-54, 137
statements, 335, 347
infinitive, 26, 64, 340-341, 347-348
future active, 334, 347
object with certain verbs, 204, 214-215
perfect
active, 329, 347
passive, 334, 347
use of, 113-114, 143
inflection, 14
intensive adjective/pronoun *ipse,* 307-308, 313-314
interrogative
adjectives, 232, 246
pronouns, 232, 245
intransitive verbs, 187-188, 214
ipse, 307-308, 313-314
is, 296-297, 313

L

Latin phrases used in English, 45, 128, 152, 171, 191, 235, 266, 289, 305, 309, 322, 327, 366, 371
linking verb, 16

M

mille
declension of, 297, 314
use of, 297, 314

N

neuter
adjectives, second declension, 82
nouns
second declension, 82, 107
third declension, 237-238, 245
nominative case, 15, 16, 137
nouns, 14-17, 36
first declension,17, 31
second declension, 30, 31, 63, 71, 82, 107
neuter, 82, 107
third declension, 168, 180, 237-238, 245
of ī–stem, 268, 282
fourth declension, 287, 313
fifth declension, 319-320, 346
number (singular/plural), 14, 15
numbers, declension of, 136, 144
numerals, Roman, 23

O

object
direct, 113
indirect, 53-54, 137

P

participle
future active, 325, 347
perfect passive, 250-251
present, 324, 338, 346-347
passive
perfect
infinitive, 334, 347
participle, 250-251
tense, 207-209, 215
voice, 173-175, 181
perfect
active infinitive, 329, 347
passive
infinitive, 334, 347
participle, 241, 250-251, 252
as an adjective, 163, 181
used as a clause, 250-251, 281
tenses, 207-209, 215
tense, 87-88, 108, 130

person (first, second, third), 25
personal pronouns, 25-26, 193, 215
pluperfect tense, 197-198, 215
possessive adjectives, 203, 204, 215
***possum*, conjugation of,** 262, 282
predicate nominative, 16, 114
prefixes, 51, 96, 101, 117, 133, 156, 201, 211, 230, 241, 361
prepositions, 47-48, 51, 72, 224
present
- participle, 324, 338, 346-347
- passive infinitive, 188-189, 214
- tense
  - first conjugation, 26-27
  - second conjugation, 76-77, 108

progressive translation, 27
pronouns
- interrogative, 232, 245
- personal, 25-26, 193, 215
- reflexive, 372-373, 382
- relative, 221-222, 245

Q

questions, asking, 118-119, 144

R

reflexive
- pronouns, 372-373, 382
- third person adjective, 320, 346

relative pronouns, 221-222, 245
root, Latin, 51, 96, 177

S

second
- conjugation
  - future tense, 76-77, 108, 149
  - present
    - imperative, 77
    - tense, 76-77, 108
- declension
  - adjectives, 98, 108, 263-264, 282
    - irregular, 263-264, 282
    - neuter, 82
  - nouns, 30, 31, 63, 71, 82, 107
    - neuter, 82, 107

sentence analysis, 82-84, 108
stem vowel, 27
subject, 16, 114
suffixes, 206, 289, 332, 343, 377
sum
- future tense, 112, 143
- imperfect tense, 159
- perfect tense, 112-113, 143
- present tense, 98-99, 108

superlative of adjectives in *-limus*, 364, 381

T

third
- conjugation
  - future, 149, 154, 180
  - verbs, 124-125, 130, 143, 149, 154
- declension
  - adjectives, 273-274, 282
  - nouns
    - feminine, 168, 180
    - ī–stem, 268, 282
    - masculine, 168, 180
    - neuter, 237-238, 245
- person reflexive adjective, 320, 346

transitive verbs, 187-188, 214
translation techniques, 13-14

V

verbs, 25-26, 36
- first conjugation
  - future tense, 46-47, 72, 149
  - present
    - imperative, 64, 72
    - present, 26-27
- second conjugation
  - future tense, 76-77, 108, 149
  - present
    - imperative, 77
    - tense, 76-77, 108
- third conjugation, 124-125, 130, 143, 149, 154
- fourth conjugation, 130, 143, 154
- present stem, 26
- principal parts, 28
- three ways to translate, 27

vocative case, 92-93, 108
voice
active, 173-175
passive, 173-175, 181

W

word
order, 14, 16, 21, 137
sense, 130-131
words often confused, 308, 374

Credits

The publisher wishes to acknowledge the following sources for the "Latin for American Students" sections in *Latin for Americans, First Book*.

Grant, Michael, *A Social History of Greece and Rome*. Charles Scribner's Sons, 1992.

Johnston, Mary, *Roman Life*. Scott, Foresman and Company, 1957.

Tannahill, Reay, *Food in History.* Crown Publishers, Inc., 1988.

Warsley, Albert, E., *501 Tidbits of Roman Antiquity.* Auxilium Latinum Press, 1978.

Cartography: Mapping Specialists Limited, p. 57, pp. 102-103, p. 164.